Italian Ethnics: Their Languages, Literature and Lives

Proceedings of the 20th Annual
Conference of the American
Italian Historical Association

Chicago, Illinois
November 11-13, 1987

Dominic Candeloro

Fred L. Gardaphe

Paolo A. Giordano

Editors

Volume XX in the series of Annual Proceedings of the American Italian Historical Association.

ISBN: 0-934-675-21-X--hard cover
ISBN: 0-934-675-22-8--soft cover
ISSN: 0743-474X
Library of Congress Catalog Card Number: (90-083301)

Published in the United States of America by
The American Italian Historical Association
209 Flagg Place
Staten Island, New York, 10304-1148

DEDICATION

This volume is dedicated to the memory of a great scholar and friend of the AIHA: Professor Robert Harney 1939-1989.

Table of Contents

Lives

Memoirs

Introduction

The 1987 American Italian Historical Association's conference was held in Chicago November 9-11, and had as its theme "Italian Ethnics: Their Languages, Literatures and Lives." The choice of the theme was made with an eye toward broadening the scope of the organization and realizing the interdisciplinary mission of AIHA. The result was a program with a wide variety of topics, methodologies and disciplines that mixed the scholarly, the folkloric and the literary interests of the two hundred and fifty registrants from the United States, Italy and Canada.

From the one hundred conference papers we have chosen thirty-two for publication in the proceedings, and have organized them in four categories: "Languages," "Literature," "Lives," and "Memoirs." The generous selection represents the depth and breadth of the scholarship in the field of Italian American studies.

Some of the essays are finished products resulting from long years of research. Some are first-hand accounts of experiences of Italian Americans—the raw material of history. And still others are preliminary studies that may ultimately emerge as book-length studies. The articles in the Italian language reflect a healthy trend as Italian and American scholars of immigration and literatures build closer relations through the Association.

These proceedings begin with the brilliant keynote address presented by Poet Joseph Tusiani, Professor Emeritus at the Herbert Lehman College. In "Two Languages, Two Lands, Perhaps Two Souls," Tusiani explores the many dualities encountered by the American immigrant. His profoundly learned discourse electrified the conferees and elicited an eloquent response from Giose Rimanelli of SUNY-Albany.

The confusion created when Italians, Italian Americans and Americans interact in a political effort to promote the Italian language in a California school is the subject of Paola Sensi-Isolani's contribution which opens the "Languages" section. Salvatore La Gumina compares the unsuccessful political efforts of Italian Americans in Port Washington, New York, to get the Italian language taught in their schools in the 1930s with the successful effort in the 1970s. Lina Unali and Franco Mulas explore the linguistic habits of the Sardinian immigrants they have interviewed. The nuances of the Canadian-Italian languages is the subject of the paper by Jana Vizmuller-Zocco. The concluding paper of this section is by Mary Pecoraro Cawthon who introduces us to the history and language of the Albanian-speaking Italians in Sicily and Madison, Wisconsin.

The "Literature" section with four papers is the smallest, but represents a growing segment of the AIHA community. Robert Viscusi's essay was originally a banquet speech at the 1987 conference. His remarks open our section on literature. His thesis, that the notion of Italian American is no longer a social but a cultural condition, is relevant to all the essays in this volume. Sebastiano Martelli's thorough account of the themes of emigration and America in the literature of southern Italy examines a long ignored facet of Italian American studies and places that literature in the context of Italian literary history. Lucinda La Bella Mays presents a loving sketch of Arturo Giovannitti's involvement in the Lawrence Strike, enhanced with excerpts from Giovannitti's own writing. Using Sister Blandina Segale's diaries as her major source, Diane Raptosh analyzes Segale's life from a feminist perspective, comparing her experiences to whose of a wide variety of nineteenth century women. Joseph Velikonja's essay is based on his 1987 AIHA Luncheon Address. It is both a survey and a critique of the Association's research and scholarship since its founding in 1967.

The "Lives" section opens up with Italian Consul General of Chicago, Leonardo Baroncelli's summary of a century of official Italian presence in Chicago. Lucia Chiavola Birnbaum's challenging essay on Italian and Italian American feminism is a strong example of the sophisticated perspectives that scholars of Italian Americana can gain from an intimate knowledge of the current Italian scene.

Ernest Rossi describes NSC1, the report that initiated an integrated U.S. policy toward Italy. He also describes George Kennan's recommendation that the Italian Communist Party be outlawed in early 1948, even at the risk of civil war in Italy.

Jerome Krase uses original research of New York city's Italian American neighborhoods to examine the phenomenon of stereotyping Italian Americans. Krase's interdisciplinary approach documents historical changes in Little Italies and previews what may be in store for the future of these ethnic enclaves.

Judith DeSena's report on the impact of paid work on Italian women in the Williamsburg section of Brooklyn supports the idea that such work leads to more education and to greater participation in voluntary associations.

Frank Cavaioli critiques Richard Alba's thesis of the twilight of ethnicity by suggesting that as Italian Americans become more successful and more "like" other Americans, they have become more capable of developing organizations to preserve their ethnicity.

Andrew Sanchirico explores the world of small business and its often overlooked importance in the lives of Italian Americans. Angela Danzi's study of the midwife in the immigrant community presents new material on such themes as women's history, professionalization and generational differences.

Frank Femminella's contribution is the result of research on both sides of the ocean. His argument suggests that the experience of the Molisani-Americans of Cortland, New York is best understood through the notion of cultural pluralism.

John Andreozzi examines the roles played by the Catholic and Protestant churches in centering the lives of Italians in Milwaukee and argues that the Milwaukee experience is a microcosm of the religious acculturation of Italian Americans.

Gianna Sommi Panofsky's article on Italian anarchists in Spring Valley and Chicago, with its heavily researched sources reminds us that the nature of American immigration was not a conflict free story of "socially respectable" mobility into middle class over three generations. The study and the sources she introduces are a healthy reminder of the important role that radicalism plays in the Italian American experience.

Conrad Woodall's narrative details the 1895 lynching of Italians in Walsenburg, Colorado and offers an alternative analysis to that of John Higham's *Stranger in the Land.*

Ferdinando Fasce's preview of a larger work of social history is an example of the sophisticated and purposeful use of oral history as he seeks to elicit a feeling for immigrant life in the Scoville Brass Company by analyzing the experiences of four oral history informants.

Luigi Di Comite and Michele Di Candia are Italian demographers who present preliminary findings based on Italian sources and on the newly available ship manifests in the National Immigration Archives of the Balch Institute of Philadelphia.

Giuseppe DeBartolo's examination of the statistical reports of Calabrian immigration provides a glimpse into the important demographic characteristics of emigration from this southern Italian region and provides insight into the effects the emigrations had on the region of Calabria.

"Memoirs," our final section, could well have been included in the "Lives" section. However, we decided to create a separate section that would emphasize the close connection between scholarly work and personal history. Drawing on a wide variety of contemporary sources, Michael LaSorte presents a philosophical essay on oral history and its application to Italian American studies and sets up a context for the following essays.

Adria Bernardi's "The Burden of a Name" is a chapter from her recently published *Houses with Names* (University of Illinois, 1989). Her elegant essay on names as the cornerstones or burdens of ethnic identity will strike a familiar note to scholars of all ethnic phenomenon.

Richard Juliani's contribution is the result of his first visit to Molise, the region of his father's birth. Juliani weaves scholarly research with personal recollection to create an interesting split-level document that reminds us that what we study can be very close to what we are.

Theresa Cerasuola shares information gleaned from her father's diaries which provides a personal account of the immigrant experience.

Edoardo Lebano presents the highlights of a fascinating research project based on hundreds of citizenship documents and oral histories of Italians in Vermillion County, Indiana.

Al Montesi presents in prose, then poetry, an impressionistic rendering of his family's history from Ancona to Memphis. It is at once a primary source from a second generation Italian American and a secondary documentation of the first generation's experience.

Anthony Fornelli reports on the multiple influences of creating new traditions in Chicago's "Festa Italiana." Widely emulated in many American cities, "Festa Italiana" has enhanced Italian political power, raised funds to support cultural and civic institutions and has solidified community support of cultural retention.

This publication is made possible through generous grants and support from the Italian Consulate General of Chicago, Amerital Unico Club of Chicago (Festa Italiana), the Italian Cultural Institute of Chicago, *Fra Noi,* Governors State University, Columbia College, the Italian Cultural Center and the Joint Civic Committee of Italian-Americans.

We acknowledge especially the personal support of Consul General Leonardo Baroncelli, the Reverend Father Lawrence Cozzi, C.S., Virginio Piucci, Vice-President of Governors State University, Lya Dym Rosenblum, Vice President for Academic Affairs of Columbia College, Professor Philip Klukoff, English Department Chairperson of Columbia College., and Professor Anthony Julian Tamburri of Purdue University.

Though in its shortcomings this publications cannot match his robust excellence, it is dedicated with love and respect to the memory of Bob Harney (1939-1989).

Keynote Address
Two Languages, Two Lands, Perhaps Two Souls

Joseph Tusiani
Herbert Lehman College

Some of you may recall that I was fortunate to know Arturo Giovannitti well, and even intimately. He called me his "Mercoledì." Indeed, I was to him, in the last years of his life, what "Friday" was to Robinson Crusoe. I was tempted, therefore, to share with you some of my recollections of one of our greatest Italian Americans; but I resisted the strong temptation after Professor Giose Rimanelli invited me to speak of Arturo in his Molise, in their Molise, this past June. I was aware, on that occasion, of my unique distinction: I was the only one, there, who had known Giovannitti, the only one who—thanks to Giose Rimanelli—could reveal to the entire Molise the great poetry of Giovannitti the man.

So here I am, today, confronted with a topic not of my choice—a topic suggested by our irresistibly impetuous Dr. Candeloro, aware, so I believe, of the line from *Gente Mia and Other Poems* that seems to him to interpret the spirit of our Convention. I hasten to add that the line he chose is immediately followed by a question:

Am I a man or two strange halves of one?

Let me attempt to give an answer, then, by begging you, first, to remember that I speak as an interpreter of inner life rather than history, and, as such, cannot but ask *you* to ask yourselves in what manner can a personal experience understand and prolong the history of a whole ethnic group. Or maybe I should not strive for an answer at all, but only recapture in tranquility—as Wordsworth would say—the feeling that prompted the line in question.

"Two languages"—but what did I mean by that? To give you an idea of what I did *not* mean, I will run the risk of sounding facetious.

Who is the author of the following lines?
"Buona notte! Buona notte!" Come mai
La notte sarà buona senza te?
Non dirmi buona notte, che tu sai,
La notte sa star buona da per sè.
It is Shelley.
And who wrote the following quatrain?
I twine, far distant from my Tuscan grove,
The lily chaste, the rose that breathes of love,
The myrtle leaf and Laura's hollow's bay,
The deathless flowers that bloom o'r Sappho's clay.
The author is Ugo Foscolo.
And who is the author of the following?
Ridonsi donne e giovani amorosi
M'acconstandosi attorno, e perchè scrivi,
Perché tu scrivi in lingua ignota e strana
Verseggiando d'amor, e come osi?...
Canzon, dirotti, e tu per me rispondi—
Dice mia Donna, e il suo dire e il mio cuore—
Questa è lingua di cui si vanta Amore.

It is Milton, as many of you have already guessed. I could go on for hours quoting Italian lines by Longfellow, Rossetti, Rainer Maria Rilke, and even Jacobus Revius, and French lines, of course, by D'Annunzio, Marinetti and Ungaretti.

By "two languages," then, I do not mean a linguistic exercise, admirable in itself, but nonetheless confined to the strictures of novelty or to the transitoriness of a poetic whimsicality. I mean, instead, a new type of emigration, apparently the most rewarding but substantially the most tragic one—the emigration from one language to another.

The reality of deracination brings with it several problems or traumas—first of all, that of a new language. At this point, utterly unconcerned with the theories of bilingual education and its ever debatable advantages or disadvantages, I would like to place myself at the very center of the issue so as to convey the notion that, much more than a sociological problem, a spiritual dilemma is here involved.

Do I regret my origin by speaking

this language I acquired? Do I renounce,
by talking now in terms of only dreams,
the "sogni" of my childhood?

A poet, in other words, sees the phenomenon of bilingualism not as a conquest of a "conditio sine qua non" for the immigrant's process of Americanization, but rather as a betrayal or denial of his original world—indeed, of his very origin, his very self. This vision could seem paradoxical if something else did not come into the picture. Bilingualism becomes suddenly synonymous with disintegration of family unity—an altogether unpremeditated adverse effect of the immigrant's deracination. A mother, that is, no longer understands her own son:

Mother, I even wonder if I am
the child I was, the little child you knew,
for you did not expect your little son
to grow apart from all that was your world—
the world that he saw first with your own eyes—
simple and untranslatable and pure...
Yet of a sudden he was taught to say
"Mother" for mamma, and for cielo "sky."
That very day, we lost each other.

What sounds like an irrelevant, ephemeral question of sheer semantics—the difference between "mother" and "mamma," "cielo" and "sky"— is suddenly charged with a responsibility that baffles the linguist. Of course, the poet's anguished observation must be analyzed within the strict confines of its lyric vitality; it is never the less valid as a new, if not wholly unsuspected, facet of one of the most complex problems of emigration.

In what way does a mother lose her son, and a son his mother, as soon as "sogno" becomes "dream," and "mamma" is translated into "mother"? Words being articulate sounds that symbolize and communicate an idea, the term "mamma," unlike the newly acquired one of "mother," symbolized and communicated a whole world of feelings and traditions which no alien expression can comprehend and respect. To abolish it means to reject the existence of a childhood intimately linked to all the great and little episodes, to all the important and unimportant emotions attached to and inspired by that very word. What's in a name? Yes, that which we call a rose by any other name smells, indeed, as sweet; but would a rose recognize itself if called a chrysanthemum?

Two languages, two lands, perhaps two souls...
Am I a man or two strange halves of one?

These two pentameters seem to deny assimilation and, consequently, Americanization. They stress, instead, ambivalence—an ambivalence of thought and feelings, of doubt and truth, of dream and reality. By posing a question they also deprive one of the satisfaction of an immediate, positive answer. Formulated in different terms, the question is: To what extent can the Italian-American immigrant assimilate a new language and a new civilization, and in what way can he forget and even renounce himself in the midst of compelling exigencies? A poet's reply, naturally, is wholly his own. He tells us that no such thing as total absorption will ever be possible, that the new land's traditions will never be totally—that is, spiritually—accepted, and that the difference between "Silent Night" and "Tu scendi dalle stelle" is exactly the line of demarcation between Manhattan and Italy.

But now my new-found land is
the western world, this new,
mysterious Atlantis
where men like me and you,

called immigrants, are silent
when Silent Night is sung
on this Manhattan Island
by people old and young,

by all save those, like me
and you, uprooted friend,
who think of Italy,—
our lost "presepe" land.

Without disturbing DeSaussure, I invite you at this point to determine the results of these two languages. If it is true that from the *langue* we derive our *parole*, that from the language already at our disposal the very moment we are born we take the vocabulary that most singularly befits our cultural capacities and emotional temperament, can we say, then, that the *word* we create out of two languages has a dual scintillation, a twofold resonance? I can only say that, if a poet were a philosopher (which he is not, though he may have and follow his own philosophy of life), he would possibly agree with Etienne Bonnot de Condillac's concept of language as a "methode analytique"; but this is the question: If "les langues nous fournissent les moyens d'analyser nos pensees," do we not own and use a double set of tools for the analysis of our own tragedy and triumph?

How logical is now the step to the second component of the triad—"two lands!" Do I mean *two countries*? If you think right now of G.K. Chesterton's "My country, right or wrong," is like saying "My mother, drunk or sober," then the answer is No. By "two lands" I meant, and mean, obviously, America and Italy. But is this the right order? Or should I have said Italy and America? The concept of country you have inherited from your parents or grandparents was shaped or preconditioned by the concept of *their* country. It is far more than the blissful recollection or ecstatic imagining of panoramic beauty with which to compare or contrast familiar vistas. It is even more than the Stentorean boast of the "land of Dante, Leonardo, Michelangelo, Verdi, etc."—a very dangerous rhetorical boast if we recall Dante's "Sanz'esso fora la vergogna meno—." It is the land of our parents' and grandparents' proverbs and traditions that honeycomb our minds and enrich our lives—the precious, inexhaustible lore that transmutes an adage into a moral law, and a simple action into a solemn ritual. Are you aware, then, of the wealth of your inner resources? Think of it, in Dante's words, as two daylights in one.

> E di subito apparve giorno a giorno
> essere aggiunto, come quei che puote
> avesse il ciel d'un altro sole adorno.

Of course you can picture two suns in the sky but can you withstand their might? Grasses would wither, the entire fauna would be fatally scalded, the whole earth would crumble in ashes. Yet these two daylights in one miraculously save and double our energies, rekindle our vision, and brighten our path.

And so we come to the third component of our triad—"two

souls," preceded by "perhaps" which needs clarification as a premise to the invisible and intangible.

I am sure that, without my realizing it in the fervor of the creative moment, the expression "two souls" was prompted by my recollection of a Latin antecedent. In his *Noctes Atticae* Aulus Gellius informs us that Quintus Ennius, the father of Latin poetry, used to say that he had three hearts because he knew Greek, Oscan, and Latin ("tria corda habere sese dicebat quod loqui graece et osce et latine sciret"). But, as I said, it is that "perhaps" that must be explained. Not Ennius but Horace prompted, I believe, my sorrowful intervention. I do not know how many of you remember Horace's magnificent hexameter "Caelum non animum mutant qui trans mare currunt" (those who cross the sea, change the sky, not the soul). The line, as you see, has to do with emigration. But what did Horace know of the laborer's emigration? He, who often traveled from Venosa to Rome, had crossed the sea only once, for a most inglorious parenthesis of military service, not in search of bread. With my "perhaps," then, I accept and, at the same time, reject the Horatian dictum. It is true, no change of sky or climate can make us forget who we are. Crossing the sea, we carry far more than our scanty belongings—we carry our remembrances, our griefs, our joys, our past, our very soul. But, once we land with no certainty of ever crossing the same sea gain, does our soul remain untouched by the new sky and the new shore? In a recent Latin poem of mine, dedicated to Giose Rimanelli, the author of *Molise, Molise*, I took Horace to task.

Caelum non animum mutant qui trans mare cur-
    runt?...
Ah, verum non est: res fit amara animus,
fit feritas eadem caelique marisque novorum,
fit sine sole dies, et dolor et lacrimae.
Mons venerande, vale! Cuspes iucunda, valeto!
Longe me expectat pars tenebrosa mei.
Pars ego sum terrae quam passus sum procul a te,
pars hominum quibus es nomen inane vetus.

(Does he who crosses the sea change but the sky, and
    not his soul?

It is not true! His soul becomes a bitter thing,
becomes the very bitterness of the new sky and the
    new sea,
becomes a day-less sun, disconsolate weeping.
Farewell, my sacred mountain! O joyous peak,
    farewell!
Far away I must encounter the dark part of my self,
for I am part of the land I must bear far away from
    thee,
part of a throng to whom thy ancient fame is nought.)
    Perhaps two souls, then; and two souls, you must admit, are
better than one. When one does not function, the other will.
With our two souls, therefore, let us sing America, the America we, too, have built. Incidentally, you are already forgiven
if you forget the Horatian line I have mentioned; but, for
God's sake, jot down and never forget a more majestic one, a
glorious hexameter by none other than Vergil about our emigration, a memorable line that all Italian Americans should
memorize and flaunt, and that may even be the theme of our
next Convention:
    Quae regio in terris nostri non plena laboris?
    (Is there a land our labor has not filled?)
    Yes, it is Vergil (*Aeneid* I, 450).
    With our two souls, then, let us start anew, every day
afresh. Surely you recall Don Giuseppe Vella's soliloquy in
Leonardo Sciascia's *Consiglio d'Egitto*: "Se ogni foglia
scrivesse la sua storia, se quest'albero scrivesse la sua allora
diremmo: eh si, la storia.... Vostro nonno ha scritto la sua storia? E vostro padre? E il mio? E i nostri avoli e trisavoli?... C'è
ancora l'albero, si, ci siamo noi come foglie nuove.... E ce ne
andremo anche noi..." Yes, like leaves, we too, shall leave, but
not before writing our story, the story of the sap that has
nourished us.
    At the very conclusion of his "Song of the Bicentennial," the
poet of *Gente Mia* intones his American paean (American,
mind you, not Italian-American) for all to hear and re-echo.
With the same vehemence and civic pride with which Paul of
Tarsus announced his Roman citizenship in a moment of
doubt and danger, he reminds all Italian-Americans of the in-
controvertible proof of their equality. To add solemnity to his

statement, he even uses the language of Rome:
    Civis Americanus sum. I swore
    allegiance to the Flag of Fifty Stars:
    long live America for ever more!
    Now I belong where countless wounds and scars
    create a morning and an epic song
    that neither time nor silence ever mars.
    Now, only now for every suffered wrong
    do I discover who I am at last—
    the multitudinous Italian throng.
    I am the present for I am the past
    of those who for their future came to stay—
    humble and innocent and yet outcast.
    I am the dream of their eternal day—
    the dream they dreamed in mines bereft of light—
    I am their darkness and their only ray,
    their silence and their voice: I speak and write
    because they dreamed that I would write and speak
    about their unrecorded death and night.
    O glory! I'm the bread they came to seek,
    the vine they planted to outvanquish doom,
    their most majestic and enduring peak.
    For this my life their death made ample room.

A Mesmeric Sculpture: Tusiani, the Humanist

Giose Rimanelli
SUNY—Albany

How respond to sapience if not with none too sapient observations? I recall Horace, familiar to Joseph Tusiani: "Maxima pars vatum, pater et iuvenes patri digni, decipimur specie recti." Most of us poets, old and young, are deceived by the appearance of correctness. But in your case, Joseph—and allow me to address you directly—I forget Horace. You have that character, and you are that poet: better, a surviving Humanist, in the old great tradition. It is about this major aspect of your personality that I would like to spend the ten minutes graciously granted to me by the president of this conference, Dr. Dominic Candeloro.

Instead of improvising, the good writer writes. And remembers: as I do remember today a brief article that I wrote about you so many years ago, when *La parola del popolo,* a journal printed in Chicago, wanted to honor you. It is indeed appropriate that that honor is today repeated in Chicago, and for me to further elaborate on that article.

You were to me an articulated sculpture at that time, Joseph, and thus you have remained: a human monument that inspires and teaches. This is what I said at that time, and it is valid now. Your magic, my dear friend, becomes flesh and blood through your sculptural observation: of things, of men, of the landscape. Solid as an ancient stump, you find the hours that other do not find. You bend over the text, you observe it, you smell it, you read it, you re-read it, you get soiled with it. The text of your attention becomes object and instrument directed by your will to possess. The love that you discover in yourself for the object of your preference inebriates itself with carnality. I noted this in your translations, excellent as the originals. In fact, to become conscious of love through the text, through your almost carnal violence of the text, finally metamorphoses in the rendition of two presences: Michelangelo-Tusiani. Tasso-Tusiani. Alfieri-Tusiani. You become, Joseph, translator and author without, however, ever taking away anything from the other, without ever taking away anything from yourself.

You are a mesmeric sculpture, Joseph. You are of today and you are of yesterday. Time has come to a halt in your eyes; and that which your eyes observe—things, men, words, landscape—assume a lustre and a vibration while preserving the film-patina of their originary structure. Your magic, Joseph, is human angelism.

It is always with modesty that I approach your statue, Joseph. You live on Tomlinson Avenue, in the Bronx. Nevertheless when I see you elsewhere, as of yesterday in Molise and as of today in Chicago, or I open one of your books, it seems to me that you are breathing on me. I hear your breath and your voice: perhaps it is that of Socrates, perhaps that of Caesar. Often the soul of the pilgrim, the emigrant, the notebook of thanks whines through it. But there is always a Gregorian organ that plays in you, and I imagine the vastness of the meadows, the sunken ships, the cathedral spires, the perpendicular atonal sonority of one who observes the scene around and within him on a wall. You say:

Civilization is/ what we in it destroy—
the man that razes towns/ to make playgrounds for
the boy.

You are a man of fate, Joseph. You are one who seeks himself and others, somewhat like Tagore, knowing implicitly that by so doing you are participating in your own realization, your epiphany. But to seek to understand as you do, Joseph, with things and me, the words, the landscape signifies naught else save to arrange all in an ordinary manner. And this need for order is born in you by the awareness that man explores in continuity seeking laws and forms, hence creating exactly that order which already exists in him.

You, Joseph, are statue but also the metaphor of this your statue. And to create—as you do with *Gente mia*—(a likeness in your effort to discover and to remember) is an act of faith. It is this act, this movement that finally concretizes itself in image. To realize, in the final analysis, means naught else

save to persist, to make oneself statue, sculpture.
   What would my life be now
   if I were still with my familiar trees?
   Thus do you exclaim.
Now let me tell you something: Heraclitus, whom you know very well, declared that every cosmology begins with self-consciousness, with self-knowledge. His is the notion that the elements are disposed in a continuous flow, and hence, in a state of constant transformation. This is man. The *anima hominis* projects itself in *anima mundi*. From oneself to others, because the flux is internal and external; from autobiography to cosmology. And the whole is enclosed in a symbolic act: that of writing, which helps to understand and to interpret, to articulate and to organize, to synthesize and to universalize human experience.

Your experience, Joseph, that co-involves the whole process of your creativity, accordingly translated itself into theory. That is how I interpret it. And this theory becomes form, volume. And form, which is the language of scholastic philosophy, is in close relationship with the *anima*. Form is not necessarily in the order of facts, but it is necessarily in the order of the creative process: this is an activity that is continuously exercised toward the outer from the center. And you, Joseph, know this center, that is this sculpture, that is this metaphor.

I often go walking through the Bronx where Joseph Tusiani lives and where, for a time, also lived my fellow-regionalist Arturo Giovannitti, with Tusiani's words on my lips:
   Call me, whoever you are, and tell me
   whatever you please. Speak even
   of wind and heaven to
   a wounded eagle in the grass, of bread
   and fire
   to a famished beggar in the snow.
   Be cruel and be rude
   but talk to me and let me know
   that I am not alone
   in this my human solitude.
Even this human solitude of Joseph Tusiani is a metaphor. It's your metaphor, Joseph, which almost all of us have learned to love.

Languages

Italian Language and Culture Promotion: The Pitfall of Cross-Cultural Misunderstanding

Paola Sensi-Isolani
St. Mary's College of California

Introducing a new language in a public school system already strapped for money is no easy task. When the language is Italian, and the state is California, where it is said that Spanish speakers will outnumber English speakers by the year 2000, the task becomes even harder. Yet this is what was attempted in the public school district of a California University town when American school officials and parents, Italian professors and representatives of the Italian government, as well as Italian-Americans were involved in establishing Italian language instruction at the elementary school level.

This paper will look at the interaction between these groups; an interaction which was fraught with misunderstanding and antagonism as people from two different cultures tried to work toward the common goal of Italian instruction in a public school system.[1]

Both Italians and Americans came to the program with the assumption that there would be no cultural differences between them. Yet the Italians' emphasis on familism, personalism, individualism and particularly their concern with status were not values shared or even understood by the Americans. Neither did the Italians share or understand the Americans' emphasis on team work, grass roots organization, egalitarianism and voluntarism. Both groups were moreover, virtually ignorant of the workings of each other's culture. While the Italians, who had lived in the United States for some time, could speak English, the Americans did not know a word of Italian. By virtue of their Italian birth and education the Italian-Americans involved in the program were able to straddle both cultures. They thus became cultural brokers, mediating between the two groups, but in the process having to face the dilemma of their own cultural identity and loyalty. The Italian language program was visualized as a cooperative effort. The public school district was to oversee its implementation; the Italian department of the nearby University was to be responsible for organizing and supervising its academic aspects; local Italian government officials were to furnish the books and pay the instructors for the first year. The one parent who had originally proposed the program and who was described by the Superintendent of Schools as "a community advocate for public education," was to coordinate the entire effort.

The role of this one parent volunteer was a major issue for the Italian representatives who were not used to the concept of volunteer work, and had been raised in a school system where parental input had until very recently, been minimal. Because this one parent had been instrumental in establishing the Italian program in the public schools the Italians found that they were forced to work with her. While they recognized that the program would not have existed without her, they considered her lack of an official title or affiliation as an indication of her low status. From their cultural perspective she was a woman who wasn't paid for her work, someone who had no officially recognized expertise.

Within the American cultural context this woman was accepted as someone who knew something about teaching children. She had an elementary school credential, had seen five of her children through the public school system, and had been involved in PTA activities for more than 20 years. But while she organized teachers, published a newsletter, lobbied successfully on behalf of the program with the School Board, and made contact with school district parents, she was viewed, and in fact referred to by a high Italian official, as "solo una madre," who had no business involving herself with the program.

Concern with official titles and respect for the social hierarchy which these titles reflect is very much a part of the Italian cultural system. The Americans in the program were for their part, unconcerned with titles and resisted using them even when they had them. They were unable to comprehend how Italians ranked themselves in terms of titles and the status they denoted. They further noticed that this concern prevented open communication because the Italians always deferred to their perceived Italian superiors, even when they disagreed with them.

The Italians, for their part, had little grasp of the workings of an American school system. They come from a culture where decisions at the local level are directly influenced by political maneuvering at higher levels of government. In such a culture having patrons in places of influence can ensure favorable decisions. This is often the case even in the United States, but it is not the case in the California Public School System, which is controlled by locally elected School Boards. Thus when the School Board had to approve whether Italian instruction would be introduced in the Junior High School, an important Italian official believed that he had guaranteed a successful outcome because he had spoken with a foreign language consultant in the State's Department of Education. This man he believed, would behave as a patron and bring his influence to bear on the School Board.

By assuming that anyone, least of all a consultant employed by the state could influence a local decision, this Italian was working solely within the parameters of Italian culture when The School Board approved Italian instruction in the Junior High School. He could not recognize that the grass roots effort of one parent, (lobbying the School Board, getting parents to attend the meeting etc.) rather than pressure from an official in Sacramento had been responsible for the favorable vote.

Just as the Italians saw the need for patronage in order to exert influence, they also could not escape from using the power of their position to ensure familistic goals. Italy is still to some extent a familistic society where allegiance to family and the furtherance of the interests of some of its members often take precedence over civic duty or objective criteria. Operating from the cultural principle of "familismo", one of the Italians involved in the program encouraged a close relative to assume more and more control. By virtue of his position he urged the other Italians in the program to accept this person as the future director. The fact that this person was known to be a bad teacher who lacked both experience teaching children and university affiliation was overridden by the fact that she was a close relative of one of the influential Italians. When it looked as if his relative might not be officially employed by the program, the Italian threatened to abandon his institution's support for it.

The Americans were, for their part, both naive and idealistic when it came to "familismo." They could not believe that someone could so openly try to obtain an advantage by virtue of his/her relationship to someone in power. They could not, furthermore understand that people might abandon support for the program if it did not promise gainful employment for their relative. As a result they did little in the way of political maneuvering to ensure that the position would be filled by a more competent person.

While the Americans saw those involved in the program as people who were to cooperate with each other, they quickly noticed that each Italian was reluctant to consult with others, each wanting to run the program as his own show. The Italians were perceived as not wanting to work as a team. They were, moreover, operating from the cultural dictate that said that those in high position knew best. Given this fact they saw no need to consult with those who were in their eyes less qualified. The Americans, instead, expected a democratic approach, where equal weight would be given to an individual, whether that person's expertise was academic or practical.

The individualism of the Italians extended even further and they were perceived by the Americans as wanting to gain recognition and glory from the program for themselves as individuals. Each Italian felt that the program's success was due to his individual work, and each tried to gain advantage for himself by projecting this image. The Americans, instead, saw the success of the program as bringing credit to the group as a whole and constantly criticized the Italians for not being what they termed "team players."

In their attempt to understand those they were meant to work with, the Americans involved in the program turned to Italians who had lived in the States for some time. These Italian-Americans with close ties to Italy attempted to interpret Italian values for the Americans. They at the same time mediated with the Italian representatives in the hope that they might better understand their American counterparts. They acted in essence, as cultural brokers between the two groups.

Because like all brokers "Janus like, they faced in two directions at once,"[2] these Americans of Italian birth were faced with a cultural dilemma. Love for their country of birth pushed them to try to mediate between the two groups in order to preserve the Italian language program. On the other hand, their inability to justify the behavior of Italian officials pushed them to encourage the Americans to abandon the project.

They realized to their dismay that in their attempt to interpret Italian culture and behavior to the Americans, they were teaching them to distrust most Italians, their motives and their values. They were in fact, describing an Italian world view which was very similar to Foster's "Image of Limited Good,"[3] which he found prevalent in peasant societies:

Peasants are individualistic... each minimal unit (often the nuclear family...) sees itself in perpetual, unrelenting struggle with its fellows for possession of or control over what it considers to be its share of scarce values. This is a position that calls for extreme caution and reserve, a reluctance to reveal true strength or position. It encourages suspicion and mutual distrust, since things will not necessarily be what they seem to be, and it also encourages a male self-image as a valiant person, one who commands respect...

While a feeling of solidarity was created between these Italian-Americans, it was a solidarity based on a very grim set of shared beliefs. The conviction that the behavior of Italian officials was representative of the behavior of most people in official positions in Italy, and the realization that in spite of the Americans' naivete, they could more easily identify with their moral principles than with those of the Italians.

Because of the problems that had occurred, by the end of the school year the continuation of the program was in doubt. In spite of these uncertainties it was decided to continue with plans for an Italian program in the district's Summer School.

By this time the Americans had learned that they would have to modify their behavior. They became more circumspect when dealing with Italian officials, and decided that since

Italians did not make good "team players," it would be better to keep them off the team.

The Summer Program was a great success and received extensive coverage in the area's newspapers and television. There is no doubt that this success can in part be attributed to the fact that cross-cultural misunderstanding was avoided because Italian representatives were not involved. Moreover, the Summer program was seen by students, parents, and the community, as a serious academic enrichment program without ethnic overtones. This is largely because the Italian-Americans who helped with the program kept a low profile and those parents who were instrumental in establishing it and working on it were not Italian. [4]

There is no doubt that American students should be exposed to one of the world's richest languages and cultures. Unfortunately, languages already established in the schools, and competing languages that seem more useful make this project quite difficult. What however renders the introduction of Italian even more difficult is the attitude of Italians themselves. For Italian officials to succeed in their efforts they must appoint people who can both understand and adapt to the values of American culture. Furthermore, while they should involve Italian-Americans, they must concentrate on recruiting non Italian-Americans to their cause.

Italian will only have credibility as a subject in the U.S. when educated people will not automatically assume that it is only Americans of Italian descent who are interested in studying the Italian language. In short, every effort must be made to move the instruction of Italian language and culture out of the Italian-American ghetto.

Lastly we Italian-Americans who were born and educated in Italy have a special role to play. Because we have a foot in both cultures, we must attempt to mediate between Italians, second and third generation Italian-Americans, and Americans. Our role as cultural brokers should ensure that lines of communication between these groups remain open.

---

[1] This paper does not attempt to look at the infighting that took place between those American Public School administrators who fa-

vored the program, and those who opposed it.

[2] Wolf, Eric. "Aspects of Group Relations in a Complex Society," in *Peasants and Peasant Societies*, T. Shanin ed., Penguin, 1971; pp.50-66.

[3] Foster, George, "Peasant Society and the Image of Limited Good," *American Anthropologist*, vol. 67, no.2; April 1965.

[4] More recently those members of the School Board who have supported the Italian program have been deprecatorily named the "Europeanists" by their opponents in the district. These opponents are trying to rally parent support for a program in a non-European language and culture.

Language Retention and Ethnic Politics: A Case Study of an Italian-American Community in the 1930s

Salvatore J. LaGumina
Nassau Community College

The issue of bi-lingualism in contemporary society evokes heated responses. On the one hand opponents argue that public money should not be spent to foster perpetuation of ethnicity because it is inherently isolative and therefore an obstacle to desirable assimilation, while on the other hand proponents maintain that a healthier and fairer approach to education on behalf of those whose native language is not English requires support for foreign language study in order to comprehend lessons, which if taught exclusively in English, would leave them at a disadvantage. Advocates of one school of bi-lingualism assert that the study of native languages is designed as a temporary measure until the student learns to function in English. A second group, although a minority, strenuously maintains that study of native languages constitutes an ongoing process designed not only to understand various academic subjects, but also to offer young people a sense of pride in their ethnic heritage.[1] Without getting into the merits of the argument, it can be said that immigration history offers ample evidence that ethnic groups have utilized their collective strengths to promote the teaching of their native languages.

From 1880 to 1917, there were German-English bi-lingual schools in Cincinnati, Indianapolis, Baltimore and in an unknown number of rural places. In many a non-public school (chiefly parochial) German flourished even before 1880. There were also French schools in New England and Scandinavian and Dutch schools in the mid-west. In other words offerings in languages other than English were part of the American educational landscape wherever demand was powerful enough. While the mobilization of the Italian element was not a major feature of bi-lingualism, it did, on occasion, serve as a rallying point for the ethnic community. Study of the dynamics of nationality organizations attempting to wring concessions from the ruling educational establishment with respect to offering Italian language classes in a town with a substantial Italian-American population could serve therefore, as an enlightening lesson concerning the juxtaposition of political/ethnic power and Italian language education. Such in fact is the intention of this article as it explores the forces and factors operative in the Italian-American enclave of Port Washington, New York in the 1930s as the group sought to promote teaching of Italian in the local public schools.

Port Washington was by the turn of the century, one of several Italian enclaves which had emerged in the suburban climes of Long Island, New York. Drawn by the flourishing sand mine industry which saw the generous soil of Port Washington yield a mineral which was extensively mined for transformation into building materials to satisfy the voracious needs of a burgeoning New York City, Italian immigrants from the Avellino area began to arrive at the site by the mid-1880s. Subsequently they were joined by immigrants from Sardinia and together formed the largest element of sand pit workers locally. Accordingly, this enclave became the nucleus of a major and vibrant ethnic community replete with its panoply of ethnic institutions. So extensive was the proliferation of Italian nationality organizations that in 1937 local Italians found it necessary to form a central committee as a kind of umbrella group designed to promote cooperation among societies when planning individual organizational functions as well as to encourage joint sponsorship of events, thereby overcoming contention and rivalry which had previously plagued the community. The coming together of these Italian organizations facilitated a number of civic causes of importance to the ethnic community such as applying pressure to establish a county district court in Port Washington. The most remarkable cooperation, however, revolved around efforts to foster local education and accordingly offers a revealing example of the high priority this community accorded to this commodity.

The small but growing number of the ethnic group who were being graduated from Port Washington schools integrated themselves into collective efforts to introduce the study of Italian into the school system. In March 1935, 125 Italian-American residents signed a petition calling upon the Port Washington School Board to present Italian among the foreign language options in the district. John Jenkins, spokesman for the Italian community, went before the board stating "...it would please the Italian families in the community very much if teaching the Italian language could be included in the regular curriculum." He maintained that in view of the vast sums being expended for things of lasting value it would be desirable to improve the education of the young by offering Italian, emphasizing the point that the language was already being taught in many city and state colleges. "The Italian people are willing to stand the necessary increase in the budget for the purpose," he further informed the board.[2]

Despite unanimity within the Italian community over this issue and the validity of the cause, the Italians were to be denied by the school board. In covering this episode, the Port Washington *News* printed the remarks of an opponent of Italian language study who apparently made an impression on the board but whose views are revealing about the bias with which the Italian population had to contend. "If these people adopt this country they should be taught our language, and if they desire another language, it should be learned at their own expense," asserted this individual who simultaneously possessed a convenient blind spot in his thinking since in fact the school district did offer foreign language studies in French and Spanish. In rendering its negative decision the school board cited prohibitive additional costs of $500 for new personnel, voting unanimously to reject the request to include Italian stating it "...was not essential at this time."[3]

Understandably rankled by the decision, the Italian community did not, however, seem to be able to marshall its forces in a drive to alter it. For example, Italian-Americans failed to coalesce for the election of Italian-Americans or others sympathetic to their cause to the school board where they could have a voice in policy-making decisions. Italian-

Americans were conspicuous by their absence on the board throughout the entire era. Aside from a Dr. Calvelli, who was appointed to the board for a term in 1931, one can find no other Italian name on the board throughout the rest of the decade. Dr. Anthony Ressa did run but lost a race for a board position in 1935. In 1942 Dr. Calvelli ran and lost, coming in third in a race for two board seats.[4]

The significance of the school board as a key center of influence cannot be overestimated. In the absence of genuine home rule because Port Washington had not received incorporation as a village or a town, the school district came closer to physically defining the community than any other governmental entity such as sewer or fire districts. As a student of the subject put it:

> In many respects the school board is viewed as the governing body of Port Washington directly affecting the lives of the residents more than any other local unit, with almost every meeting and statement of the board front page news in the local weeklies.[5]

The absence, therefore, of Italian-Americans on the local school board or even as candidates in sufficient number during this period indicates lack of political clout. A perusal of the Port Washington *News* in the 1940s, 1950s, and 1960s reflects a continuing dearth of Italian-American candidates for the posts; apparently only one of that nationality was a candidate in that stretch of years. In the 1970s the situation changed as Italian names became more prominent as candidates with a number of them gaining election and serving as board members: J. Marro, Carl Salerno, J. Raimo and Loretta DiBenedetta are cases in point. One of the most active Italian Americans in school board matters was Charles Demeo who headed a taxpayers organization which opposed larger budgets in the 1970s. Significantly in 1974 the school board belatedly approved a petition to offer courses in Italian in the district explaining that it was convinced that there was a "... solid cultural reason for offering it here."[6] That action elicited favorable editorial comment in the community newspaper which was certain to warm the heart of the Italian element even at such a late date:

> The beauty of the Italian language and the wealth of

literature written in Italian make it an important
language for young people to be able to learn. And it is
more important here, in a community where so many
are of Italian descent, to make as much as possible of
the rich culture available.[7]
Failure to obtain school board approval for Italian in 1935
did not prevent the Italian community from implementing its
own programs for encouraging Italian culture in the area. The
entire ethnic group was behind efforts to promote Italian
culture among the second and third generation. In August
1935 the John Marino Sons of Italy Lodge and the Italian Mutual Aid Society sponsored a dinner for 18 Italian-American
graduates of Port Washington High School. One of the speakers was the same John Jenkins of the class of 1926 who argued the case of the Italian language before the school board,
and whose speech at the dinner rang with chauvinistic pride
which caught the attention of the press.

To all you people here this evening, let me say that
the Italian people are in the process of a new era. We
have been given a flaming torch by our ancestors and
fathers, so let us carry on and feed this torch with the
spirit which will always stamp us the premier Americans of the United States.[8]
Charles Hyde, publisher of the Port Washington *News*, and
"...a friend of every Italian in Port Washington," also addressed the graduates as did Albert DeMeo, who in 1916 had
become the first Italian-American graduate of the local high
school. DeMeo, who now held a position as an assistant district attorney, enjoyed a reputation as a gracious toastmaster.
"His sharp wit and ready sallies indicated why he has enjoyed
so great a success in the courtroom...." Finally, a Prof. Medici
spoke to the audience in such forcible Italian that his oration
impressed even the staid reporter who, not possessing knowledge of Italian, nevertheless observed. "His audience was held
spellbound by the silvery and smooth oratory that flowed
easily from his lips."[9]
If the Italian community could not obtain cooperation for
the study of Italian from the public school authorities, it could
and did make the language available for study in Port Washington on a private basis, at least for a period of time in the

1930s. During the hey-day of the course offerings, students rendered public the fruits of their learning, winning acclaim of the community. On one occasion in 1937, these Evening Class students gave such an outstanding performance that it merited favorable comment of the local press for the excellence of the poems that were recited, the lusty rendition of familiar Italian melodies, and talented portrayal of a one-act comedy. Similarly in 1938 the Italian Evening Class continued to provide cultural programs for the community.[10]

One may speculate that the explanation for the board's rejection of the petition to offer Italian in 1935 lay in the awareness of the political inhospitality of the period, that is that Italy's aggression in invading Ethiopia and the dictatorial posturing of its premier, Benito Mussolini, placed Italy and Italians outside the realm of respectability. These forces may indeed have been operative, and to be sure leaders within the enclave were profuse in their support for Italy's adventurism into Africa, although local newspaper coverage does not substantiate a climate of overt reaction against the ethnic group in connection with Italy's international standing.[11] On the contrary the community's Italian-Americans enjoyed a prominent profile in Port Washington in the second half of the 1930s as detected in the growth of ethnic organizations and activities. Furthermore, the ethnic group achieved in Port Washington what they were unable to achieve in virtually any other locale--high media visibility. Alone among local ethnic groups and in an extraordinary departure from their overlooked status in other communities, a local English-language weekly regularly featured lengthy columns devoted to Italian ethnic affairs. Not of the mere public relations releases type, these were rather columns which allowed George Zuccala, a local community leader, to express opinion and to exhort. Notwithstanding such visibility, school district policymakers were not amenable to inclusion of Italian.[12]

What then accounted for failure to obtain an Italian language program in the 1930s whereas it came to fruition in the 1970s? One cause was probably a latent, unconscious but effective prejudice on the part of the native-born population who were in control of the school establishment. A second factor may be attributed to Italy's declining prestige and respectability--even if this is hard to document locally. Another reason undoubtedly relates to the prevailing view among educators that the study of Italian was regarded academically as an inferior option when compared to the study of French, Spanish, and German. Fourth, one has to acknowledge the relative powerlessness of Port Washington's Italian-Americans in school matters largely due to under-representation in school policy positions and as influential faculty members--despite their otherwise high profiles in other civic and educational activities.

By contrast the climate of the 1970s was more conducive to accepting Italian as a language offering. The period of international tension which had relegated Italy an outcast was past, Italian-Americans enjoyed more respectability as faculty members and perhaps most of all, ethnic group members were very visible in school board matters and thus in a position to affect policy. The last point seems to argue the case that a minority group must first organize itself effectively if it is to achieve and maintain a political presence, for without it the group commences from a position of relative weakness rather than strength.

One final point. Attainment of the inclusion of Italian in the foreign language program within the community of Port Washington constitutes only a partial victory in that unlike French or Spanish which are offered on the junior high school level, students can commence a study of Italian only on the high school level, that is, only in the Ninth Grade. Thus Italian must rely on two types of students: those who pass up language offerings in the junior his school or those who take another foreign language and also take the Italian option in the Ninth Grade and thereby become the consumers of two foreign languages--an option decided upon by a distinct minority. It is to be noted that those enrolled in Port Washington's Italian classes are primarily of Italian background--one estimate placed them at 80 percent of the enrollment.[13]

Interestingly, in almost a replay of the Port Washington language interest of a half a century ago, local Italian-Americans--specifically members of the John Marino Lodge of the Sons of Italy, recently have introduced private study of Italian youngsters in the 8-10 group on Saturdays. At this writing there also seems to be available an Italian language class for adults sponsored by the same organizations. As admirable as are these volunteer efforts, they are not substitutes for formal programs of the public schools which can marshall the resources of the school district to carry out its enterprise. Thus, although Italian-Americans have formed a significant enclave in Port Washington for a century, and notwithstanding the fact that they presently represent 25 percent of the population, they have achieved only partial success in promoting Italian languages offerings in the school district. The effort to advance the cause of Italian language study requires perseverance and constancy on the part of Italian-American organizations. It also requires the exercise of political clout.

---

1 For further discussion on this topic see: United States Commission on Civil Rights, A Better Chance To Learn: Bi-Lingual Bi-Cultural Education, Publication 51, 1975; Theodore Anderson and Mildred Boyer, Bilingual Schooling in the United States.

Vol. I, 1970; Tome Bethel, "Against Bi-lingual Education," *Harpers'*, February 1979, pp. 30-33; Francesco Cordasco, *Bi-Lingual Schooling in the United States*, A Sourcebook For Educational Personnel, 1975.

2 Port Washington *News*, March 15, 1935.

3 Port Washington *News*, April 12, 1935. Interviews corroborate non availability of Italian courses and the absence of Italian-American faculty. Helen Dejanna *Interview*, June 20, 1983.

4 Port Washington *Post*, May 3, 10, 1935. Port Washington *News*, April 24, 1942.

5 Samuel Kaplan, *The Dream Deferred, People, Planning and Politics in Suburbia*, 1977.

6 For examples of Italian-Americans running for the school board see: Port Washington *News*, May 5, 1972 and May 7, 1981.

7 Port Washington *News*, June 20, 1974.

8 Port Washington *News*, June 20, 1974.

9 Port Washington *News*, June 25, 1937.

10 Port Washington *News*, May 5, 1939.

11 Port Washington *Times*, August 23, 1935.

[12] Port Washington *News*, May 5, 19, and June 7, 1939.

[13] Telephone *Interview*, Nancy Zarv, Port Washington Italian language teacher, November 18, 1986.

Linguistic Attitudes of the Sardinian Immigrants in the United States, 1900-1930

Lina Unali
Franco Mulas

This paper is based on a linguistic analysis (leading toward a cultural interpretation) of the interviews we made in the past four years with the generation of Sardinians who immigrated to America in the first three decades of the twentieth century. Previous reports of this have been presented in papers read at the various meetings of the American Italian Historical Association in the years 1983-1986 and at the last Conference of the European Association of American Studies, Budapest, 1986.

A basic observation must be made concerning the phenomenon which can be termed 'Sardinian trilinguism'. We might even modify the phrase into 'conscious Sardinian trilinguism' since there was a constant awareness on the part of people speaking Sardinian that their language was not simply a kind of "deformed Italian"; that Italian was the national language and as such it had to be spoken with scholastic clarity and precision, fluency in Italian being somehow the natural outcome of obedience and of a sense of duty to the Nation; and finally that English was the language of the host country, an additional difficulty in an already difficult environment, a barrier, but at times a cause of surprise and even of amusement.

An interesting question is which of the three languages came each time first, which was, so to say, exhibited, protended, for how long, while the other two were kept in memory waiting, in which occasion did the shift from one to the other occur and how. From a linguistic point of view the starting position of the first Sardinian generation of immigrants can be thus described:

Sardinian was spoken within the family and the circle

of relatives and friends.

Italian was a substitute for Sardinian in certain more formal occasions. It could also be used at intervals, as for example, during a conversation mainly conducted in Sardinian.

American English was mainly connected with the immigrants' working activity and the place where it occurred.

This classification is adequately supported by what an old immigrant, Roberto Lai from Cagliari, who lived in The United States in the twenties, recalled during the interview: After work we used to meet in a square near Greenwich village, where I lived, I do not remember the name of the square, but I remember that there was an Italian church. We spoke of Italy and also of Sardinia. We spoke Sardinian, but if there was someone who did not understand Sardinian, we spoke Italian, and if there was someone who understood neither Sardinian nor Italian, we spoke American, of course, what we could manage to say.

There were other languages that the Sardinian immigrant practiced or understood, more fragmentarily than Italian and Sardinian. Giuseppe Fresu from Oschiri said during the interview that there was no problem in understanding the Mass because it was in Latin. To the question "comente faghizzis a cumprendere sa missa?" ("How could you understand the Mass ?"), he answered "Sa missa daghi fidi in latinu bi fiada pagu differenzia da innoghe." ("Since the Mass was in Latin there was little difference from here.") At the time the Mass was always celebrated in Latin.

Spanish may also be considered as a language mostly understood by the Sardinian immigrants. The affinities between Sardinian and Spanish is due both to their common Spanish origin and to the historical reason that Sardinia was under Spanish domination for about three centuries. An immigrant said that a Spaniard working not very far from his factory once mockingly addressed himself and his friends with the words: "Mira sos tontos comente trabaglianta," and the reply followed with no delay as if formulated in the same language "tontos e toi" ("Who are those fools working over there?" "You are fools!" He reported the Spanish words in Sardinian as though they had been pronounced in this language.[1]

The frequency in the use of the three main languages Sardinian, Italian and American English cannot be seen as fixed or permanent. The amount of words and phrases taken from each of the three varied from immigrant to immigrant and with the passing of time. In a way, immigration meant immigration into a language. The quicker the single immigrant was able to master the new language the more fruitful the experience in the American continent would prove. An immigrant, Dettori by name, said during the interview, with an unhappy face: "Those who could speak English there did it in a twisted form, and it was the same for me. Then I began to learn grammar and so we went along as well as we could." As the marginality of the immigrant in the new society decreased, his grammar improved, his English became more fluent.

From the point of view of learning how to read and write in the new language, the immigrants can be perhaps divided into two categories: those who went to night school and those who did not. The first generally speak with enthusiasm about their teachers, wonderful connecting links between themselves and the host country. Giovanni Garau from Gonnosfanadiga made the enthusiastic comment : "The master was a female!" He added that he had gone to school "because Americans did not understand Italian." One often draws the conclusion that on the part of the Sardinian immigrant there was the idea that after all "all languages were created equal." Spanedda from Cargeghe said, "When the Americans spoke, we did not understand anything; when we spoke Sardinian, it was their turn not to understand anything."

Those who went to night school were the smartest and often their expertise in English became with the passing of time so remarkable that they were able to help the other immigrants acting as interpreters. Tilocca from Burgos said during the interview: "Once they arrested two Sardinians, one of them was from Bottida. I spoke English and I was able to save them, they did not know the language." There is generally a direct relationship between the immigrants' knowledge of English and their actual success within American society. One determined the other. Perhaps the immigrant we appreciated the most from the point of view of his syntactic precision in the spoken language, was Rombi, from Carloforte, who died not very long ago, aged 94. He had become instructor in the Merchant Navy, had been the founder of the Fraterna Carolina, the powerful society of Carlofortines in New York, and had been a successful man in the New Continent.

The always interesting problem is how the new language interplayed with the native speech. The comprehension and use of toponyms which were the first words the Sardinian immigrant were generally remembered during the recollection of his American experience. "West Penn" was the first word in English pronounced by Giovanni Garau from Gonnosfanadiga during the interview. West Pennsylvania was the place where the coal mines were. The second was something like "Royl Ram," Royn Ram, Royal Ram, not understandable to the interviewer but for him unforgettable. Diego Tanda from Nughedu San Nicolo', born in 1894, immigrated in 1913, after transforming in his recollections the New York Battery into a "batteria" according to the unwritten rules of transformation of English words into Italian, insistently mentioned a phantomatic "Hodzam" which although sounding like the sequence of two Chinese monosyllables, after a time we understood to stand for "Hudson." Be it said tangentally, at Hodsam or Hudson, Diego Tanda said "there was a team of Spaniards with whom we talked with ease."

As the Battery was transformed into a Batteria so a firm near Niagara Falls, first called Welandia Ship Canal by Agostino Pirastru from Ozieri, born in 1897, immigrated in 1923, was in the course of the interview sardized into "Su Canale." While the first word was the typical Italian rendering of an American term, "Su Canale" characterized by the Sardinian masculine article creates no doubt in the listener as to its origin. This opens the subject of linguistic hybridization. The process of transformation of English into Italian was partly similar to that of other Italian immigrants, partly different. What they had in common was that the English words were generally made pronounceable through the transformation of closed into open syllables.

The words we heard during the interviews are the usual:

fattoria for firm; carri for cars; ruffi for roofs; ticchetta for ticket; saida for cider; bombi for buns; abbassamento for basement; unioni for trade unions.

The well known Broccoli, meaning Brooklyn, Buffalo' with a strange final "o"; Bristole, Connectichette, Massacisa o Massa for Massachusetts, Detroito, Noiorca and also Nuova Jorca, Nuova Jolca; strette o stretta for street; both new forms resembling the original latin form for street, namely strata, strata jugera; cocco, meaning coke, not coconut; straica or straico, meaning strike; a bordo (meaning room and board and not on board as in Italian); Bucco, book and in particular the English grammar, often the only book present in the house.

There was a certain number of past participles such as: quitato, meaning abandoned; stoppato, stopped; collettato, meaning collected (which may remind us of the new Italian words used in computer language such as the ugly new coinage formattare, formattato); liccare, to like, while in Sardinian liccare means to lick; vassinare, to wash; startare, to start.

Some words which may be considered more closely connected than others to the Sardinian origin of the immigrants, such as: bollo di suppa to mean bowl of soup. Some words which are perhaps the result of 'independent coinage', on the part of individual immigrants, may be in conjunction with people speaking Italian dialects such as Neapolitan: jabbarella, little job, dicerello, little ditch, storicello, little store. In the conversation of the old Sardinian immigrants we interviewed these Italian American words acquire an additional interest because they seem to fluctuate in utter isolation in their minds as pieces scattered after a shipwreck in a sea of words belonging to different linguistic systems. They have not been submitted to further evolution.

Among the first words the immigrants recollected there were, besides toponyms, those related to the specific work in which they were engaged and to the type of contract. Giovanni Garau did what he called 'piece work' which can be probably translated into Italian as "lavoro a cottimo." In practical terms, it meant that he was given a dollar for each wagon he filled with coal. The already mentioned Agostino Pirastru from Ozieri, instead "lavorava a shift". The Carlofortines pronounced the word "longshoremen" their most common occupation in the New York Harbour, in a perfect way.

Place and type of contract were extremely important and as such memorized, ("The American language was bread at that period," said Pirastru from Ozieri), but for quite different psychological reasons. Also curses of various kinds enjoyed a right of precedence in memorization. It must be said that the curse is natural in the mouth of Sardinian peasants. In the Northern parts of the island it is called 'irrocu' and one can produce very easily interesting 'irroccos', in close succession, without feeling inhibited in the least. To the question addressed to Luciano Ledda of Esporlattu "To whom did you say son of a bitch?" The answer was sincere and prompt: "To everybody." The man added he had never been willing to learn the language because he had always been among Sardinians and Italians. So only the curse was expressed in English. It was certainly much less poetic and full of evocative power than in Sardinia where it often recalls old sacrificial rites, such as the deprivation of the eyes during the 'ordalia' in old Phoenician and Mediterranean cults, but its utterance was equally satisfactory and therefore memorable.

Sometimes the most common American curse has even been used back in the native village to invent nicknames in order to better identify the character of an immigrant. At Anela there lived a man who immigrated to the United States in 1907, called Ziu Gaddemma, a nickname which clearly derived from the constant use he made of the angry trisyllabic expression, very often heard in America.

But this must not lead us to believe that the Sardinians had non-puritanical speech habits. Actually they were puritanical in the extreme, if the word can be safely used outside the domain of English and American history and culture. The curse was the occasion for minor violations of their very strict codes of behaviour: it expressed a very familiar attitude of irritation towards other men and themselves. Giovanni Vargiu, although remembering only "parolacce e bestemmie," "dirty words and curses"—no other word could be found in his memory of the American language—was unwilling to use them in front of his children during the interview held in his house in Sardinia, so to say, out of their natural context.

Of course the shift from one linguistic system to the other can also be seen from an almost carnevalesque point of view, as an upturning of the natural order of things. A Sardinian asking for rice with a Sardinian-Italian pronunciation was instead given raisin, papassa, and the immigrant Giovanni Vargiu from Siligo was amused by the recollection. The list of misunderstandings, qui-pro quo is endless. The contamination of forms,the upsetting of the normal appearance of linguistic reality, may be called the "Babel effect" in immigration. The word "world" lost its character of fixity typical of a secluded, ancient rural society and presented itself with completely new sounds and meanings. The laughable stories still told within the family group and with friends number in the hundreds. Upon reaching California, an immigrant from Anela had written a letter to his father requesting him to send from Sardinia, notoriously very rich in salt marshes, as much salt as he could because on the perimeter of various estates there was written "FOR SALE". Everybody knew that 'for' meant 'per', in Sardinian "pro Sale" of course meant salt. There could be no doubt about it. It was written in the same way. Another immigrant who had gone to a shop to buy cheese, being unable to make himself understood,pronounced the not very Sardinian curse "fosse ucciso"—"Would that he was killed." The result was immediate. Cheese was brought to him. These occurrences may not have an interest in themselves but they may help to reconstruct the atmosphere of playfulness which in the happiest moments surrounded the life of the immigrant and his memory of it. Some stories may have even been invented in order to amuse other immigrants in the few hours which were not devoted to the unavoidable fatigue of working for survival.

The radical differences between the two worlds, the Sardinian and the American, originated the strangeness of the new experience in which things that had never occurred had a chance to do so. Some of them had almost magical contours. If we defined the linguistic confusion "the Babel effect," this can be rightly called as it was done in another occasion, "The Arabian Nights effect."[2] The American reality was seen as full of marvels and wonders, described as magic, exotic, as an almost mysterious entity of which the immigrant understood very

little but which struck him greatly. Many years after his return to Sardinia the immigrant can still describe as typical of
New York reality: "Unu trenu chi caminaiat in aria, unu
trenu chi caminaiat sutta terra." ("A train which ran in the
air, and a train which ran under the earth."). Luciano Ledda
said that "if you go to Broadway on New Year's Day they kiss
you." Almost all the immigrants we interviewed, especially
those who spent a long time in the New York area, spoke
about skyscrapers touching the sky, so tall that in order to follow them in the air "it was necessary to lean against the
walls." The immigrant Giovanni Casula said of New York
"that it was beautiful because there were the things they had
never seen here, as the machines moving underground which
were called buei "buei" and the cars went "from one side to the
other of the sea." The mines themselves could produce a special kind of wonder. Tilocca, from Burgos, remembered with
these words the mine where he worked at Tams, West Virginia: "The mine did not go down into the earth, it was on the
surface, it was a mine just the same, actually it was a mountain and we went through it as we go from here to Bolotana."
Bolotana is the name of a Sardinian village, in the centre of
Sardinia, about 7 miles from Burgos.

The technological development of the last fifty years has
somehow left the returned immigrant, of the generation here
considered, untouched. The real surprise at the miracles of
technology had occurred several years ago and after that
nothing can invoke surprise anymore.

We have tried to describe certain aspects of the linguistic
reality of what we like to call "the American continent in the
mind", a continent explored under particular circumstances, a
continent remembered. We wish only to add a few words
about the non-verbal communication which was equally practiced by the Sardinian immigrants in the United States. It
was not only the language of gestures poetically described by
an immigrant and already referred to in one of our papers,
but also that of dance.[3] Giovanni Casella, who immigrated to
the United States in 1910 and returned in 1920, gave the account of a kind of 'happening' which had occurred to his group
of Sardinians in Utica, New York. One day, during the inter-
val of a church service, they had stood up and sung all to-

gether the rustic, "bo bo bo bo bo," the resounding echo of pastoral and primitive Sardinia, in such a way that the listeners, moved by a sense of utter pleasure, invited them to repeat the performance on the following Sunday. The same immigrant reported that a group of Sardinians once improvised a dance on the main street and that the passers-by stopped to watch the performance full of surprise and admiration. It was the reaction of the Americans to the most rhythmical and ancient surviving Sardinian language.

---

1 The immigrant Cherchi from Anela said: "Parlavo anche lo spagnolo un poco. Una volta eravamo in un lavoro e mi hanno mandato a portare un secchio d'acqua e vedo questo in alto che chiamava e non sapevo se chiamava a me, ha tirato fuori un fazzoletto e faceva segno un'altra volta che chiamava. Io credevo che era uno di quegli spagnoli del lavoro, invece era un dottore. Quando sono andato,ci ho detto "Che vuoi?"e lui mi ha detto "Sei spagnolo?"."No non sono spagnolo ma qualche cosa so parlare". "Vieni con me", mi ha preso a braccetto e mi ha portato dentro la baracca e c'era uno spagnolo che era venuto cinque o sei giorni prima poveretto, era malato e ho fatto da interprete. Gli ho detto , portatelo all'ospedale e l'ho aiutato a metterlo in macchina e non ho saputo piu' niente ne' del dottore ne' del malato. Questo e' successo a Bristole, nel Connectichette".

2 Cp. Lina Unali, Relazioni Interculturali e Letterarie tra l'Inghilterra e l'India, *Annali dell'Universita' di Cagliari*, Cagliari, 1983.

3 Cp. in Lina Unali, Franco Mulas, "Modelli di assimilazione e crisi nell'emigrazione dalla Sardegna alle Americhe negli anni '30"(published in *Americhe Amare*, by the Dipartimento di Studi Americani, Universita' La Sapienza, Roma, 1987) the reference to the interview to the immigrant Francesco Virdis from Bultei.

Politeness and Languages in Contact: Italians in Toronto

Jana Vizmuller-Zocco
York University

The interaction of Italian immigrants and the Anglophone Toronto population has been described in numerous publications. Nearly half a million people of Italian origin live in and around Toronto. It is small wonder, then, that such a consistent group has created a unique cultural atmosphere accompanied by its own version of Italo-Canadian or "italiese," as its language is variously labeled.

Since many first generation immigrants cling to their traditional life styles, dialect is alive and in many instances thriving, because second generations certainly understand if not speak it. Since the exposure to Italian is limited, and knowledge of English sometimes nil, italiese may be classified as a kind of koine, used by people from different dialect backgrounds. Its basis is formed by the various dialects, stripped of their phonetic, grammatical and lexical peculiarities, injected with a good dose of English and put on a skeleton of Italian grammar.

Some linguistic aspects of italiese have received intense scrutiny on the part of two scholars. G. P. Clivio has dealt with lexical borrowings from English to italiese. He offers at least two reasons why Italo-Canadians, when speaking italiese, use such English borrowings as /fárma/ (Engl. "farm," It. "fattoria") or /ósa/ (Engl. "hose," It. "tubo," "pompa). The former lexeme is taken from English because in the experience of Italians, a "fattoria" indicates a place quite unlike a "farm." In the latter case, the borrowed lexeme fills a gap in the vocabulary for those items which were unknown or not used by the Italian immigrant before settling in Canada (Clivio 1976, 1985, 1986).

M. Danesi, on the other hand, has described the phonetic process underlying the Italo-Canadian's pronunciation of bor-

rowed items. For example, all the words ending in a consonant in English have to undergo paradigmatic adjustments
consisting of a rule which adds a final vowel to nouns, to conform to the canonical form of Italian nouns, for example, Engl.
"truck," italiese /trókko/ (It. "camion," "autocarro") (Danesi
1985).

These studies have certainly contributed to our understanding of certain phenomena in italiese.

In asking the question "What happens when two culturally,
linguistically and socially different groups such as immigrants
and the host country population meet and interact?" one ex-
pects a multitude of answers. Psychologists tend to measure
the retention of ethnic identity of the immigrant group, its
psychosocial adjustment or ethnolinguistic vitality (for Italo-
Canadians, see Bourhis and Sachdev 1984). Sociologists study
the social acceptance and roles of both groups; historians
trace the origins of immigration, its reasons and results
(Harney 1978). Linguists concentrate on the *reciprocal* influences that languages exhibit when in contact.

However, there is an area which seems to have been relegated to the background by those interested in the consequences of the interaction of two cultures. This area deals
with pragmatics, which is generally defined, in a broad sense,
as the study of actions which have a goal, or in linguistic
terms, verbal communication which has a specific aim.
Austin's and Searle's works are classic examples of studies
which attempt to classify speech acts and their concomitant
intentions (Austin 1975, Searle 1979).

The following examples illustrate specific goals and their
verbal expressions in italiese. They were gathered in informal
situations; italiese was the commonly used language of interaction, although code-switching to English was not avoided.

Example 1: Greetings
"Ciao, Signora!"

This sentence is ungrammatical in Italian, where the expression depends on social factors, such as the age, social status and number of interlocutors. Thus, with "signora," one
could have "Buon giorno," "Buona sera," etc.

This greeting is not a calque from the English, since the last name is usually called for: "Hello, Mrs. Smith." It is likely however, that a type of simplification has occurred, resulting in a certain levelling of social roles, perhaps on the model of the English pronomial and verbal morphology. Moreover, the example demonstrates a scarce familiarity with the grammar of Italian. Especially where the use of pronouns is concerned, italiese is frequently inconsistent, mixing forms of address, especially where the polite forms are called for, for example: "Signora, quando lei sa la misura, mi telefona, ed ci dico il prezzo" ("lei"-"ci" alternation is ungrammatical in Italian, where "Lei"-"Le" is required; "ci" is a frequently used form of indirect object pronoun in Italian dialects and in "italiano popolare.")

Example 2: Asking permission to enter the house of a friend.
"Permesso!"
This word exists in Italian, but it is not used in circumstances which indicate familiarity. A student may use "Permesso!" when entering a professor's office, for example. Standard Italian has various versions, among which are "Si puo?" or "Ci fate entrare?" Of course, also in English there are a number of expressions that can be used such as "May we come in?"

The above are only anecdotal examples which show the pragmalinguistic dimension of verbal interaction. In both cases the goal or intended aim has been achieved, and it was through verbal expressions which belong neither to Italian nor to English, and yet both languages were utilized to create the intended goal. In the first example, a simplification of the complex Italian sociolinguistic rules has occurred. In the second example, the use of one particular rule of Italian was extended to cover other circumstances.

My research involves the general area of politeness and the speech act of apology in particular. There are, unfortunately, no clear cut answers as to what constitutes polite behavior in the eyes of a Canadian Anglophone living in Toronto and in the eyes of an Italian, living for example in Palermo. Evidently, some observable differences exist in classifying behavior as polite. It can be said that Anglophones are less likely to judge impolite the behavior of the individual since their rules of conduct allow for great variation (an obvious example is the manner in which individuals dress, which is not given great importance). The Italians tend to demonstrate even if indirectly social ostracism or disapproval. However, these are atheoretical or pretheoretical considerations which would need further research. Some psychologists, and Argyle and his collaborators in particular (Argyle et.al. 1986), suggest that rules (i.e. behavior that most people think or believe should or should not be performed) differ between England and Italy. For example, the expression of emotion is an integral part of behavior in some circumstances, however, it is more so for Italians than for the English (1986:296). Where would the Italo-Canadian fit? It would perhaps have been too simplistic and yet not entirely untrue to state that the Italo-Canadian's behavior is closer in this respect to the Italian's taking as example the extraordinary manifestation of joy by tens of thousands of Italo-Canadians in the streets of Toronto on learning that Italy had won the World Cup in 1982.

One aspect of polite linguistic behavior is the expression of apology. According to Austin (1975:152), apology belongs to the set of speech acts he calls "behabitives;" in Searle's terminology, apology is an "expressive" (Searle 1979:15). The speech act of apology occurs when at least seven conditions are met:

1) it involves a dialogue, mostly oral
2) it presupposes a situation (mostly extralinguistic) the details of which are known both to the speaker and the hearer (for example, the knowledge that harm has been done for which an apology is in order)
3) the speaker verbalizes his/her intentions (that is, genuinely wishes to express an apology)
4) apology is in many cases the socially expected form of communicating the speaker's psychological attitude
5) the hearer accepts and acknowledges the apology expressed
6) the hearer understands the force and intended meaning of the speech act
7) the speech act obeys common, unwritten but specifiable rules, although there are variations as to the possible man-

ner of individual expression (for example, some speakers know how to apologize profusely).

To apologize is then to have recognized one's fault and to mend it, using verbal expressions such as "I apologize," "I'm sorry," "Mi scuso," "Scusami," etc., and perhaps offer an amend or explanation. Goffman (1971:143) offers a ritualistic explanation of apology and he suggests that: "An apology is a gesture through which an individual splits himself into two parts, the part that is guilty of an offence and the part that dissociates itself from the dialect and affirms a belief in the offended rule."

The three steps (i.e. recognition, apology, amend) may be universal. Societies will differ as to the kinds and number of instances in which these steps are executed and in the verbal expression used.

Although no thorough treatment of this speech act exists for either Italian or English (but see Owen 1983), it is transparent that the two languages treat the steps equally. And yet, the circumstances in which they are applied are not identical (some examples of this difference can be found in Vizmuller-Zocco 1984). For example, for the English, apology is in order when one touches another person involuntarily; this situation does not have such a rigid rule for the Italian.

Without a well-balanced and theoretically sound description of the functioning of apology in both languages it is difficult to make comparisons. The problem is multiplied when we turn to the Italo-Canadians. Where do they fit in this picture? Which subset of rules do they follow? The questions as they are put are new for the immigrant contact situation. Pragmatics as seen through the speech act of apology has been investigated in depth in the language learning situation at a number of Hebrew classes in Israel. Through an experimental procedure, subjects were asked to respond to situations calling for an apology. These subjects were English and Russian speaking students learning Hebrew. The researchers found out that:

> Speakers of English can be described to be more intense users of direct expressions of apology...when compared with speakers of Hebrew, while speakers of Russian can be said to have an overall higher ten-

dency toward acknowledgement of responsibility. Such tendencies, when they differ from the target features, might be transferred by the learner into the new language across all situations. (Olshtain 1983:246).

The speakers of italiese, however, cannot be termed language learners nor is italiese a target language. However, the English no doubt influences a number of linguistic phenomena and I would like to add here also the pragmatic aspects of communication. Rather than preparing an experiment, I chose to observe one Italian immigrant for the period of two and one-half years and record her expressions of apology and the situations in which these appeared. Let's call the subject Connie; she is fifty-eight years old and has been living in Toronto for thirty years. At home she speaks "modicano," the dialect of her native town, to her husband, who also comes from Modica. To her twenty-eight-year-old son, she tends to answer in English. She works in a shirt-making factory with workers of various ethnic backgrounds. Her English proficiency must be separated into comprehension, which is excellent, and expression, which is heavily accented to the point of incomprehensibility on the part of a non-Italian speaker.

Connie was found to apologize in a number of situations which require an apology in English but not in Italian. No descriptions of the rules of apology exist for Sicilian, so the point of comparison is Italian. The following table illustrates some of the apologies:

Situation	italiese	English	Italian
1. touching another person inadvertently	skúsa	Sorry!	Scusa...
2. asking for permission to let her pass	sórri	Excuse me/ Sorry!	Permesso
3. interrupting someone speaking	skúsa	Sorry	Scusa...
4. not understanding someone else's utterance	skúsa	Sorry?	Scusa...

5. sneezing   skjúzmí   Excuse
me!

Connie engaged in numerous repairs such as "Non sapevo
che..." (I didn't know that...); "Non volevo..." (I didn't want
to...). In comparison to her husband, whose rules of apology
seem to be unlike the English and more like the Italian, she
overapologized. It is evident that she has learned the sociocultural rules of English and uses them in italiese.

It is impossible to make generalized conclusions about this
micro-study. Italiese has a protean form, but it can be said
that its existence is intricately interwoven with that of
English, be it on the lexical or pragmatic side. Apology, too,
presents a number of forms given its situations; variational,
individual ability and willingness to detect one's faults and to
take responsibility for them. In our case, it was the woman
who appropriated herself of the sociocultural rules of apology
in English and was able to use and sometimes overuse them
much more so than the man. But to confirm the validity of
this difference and attribute it to sex would be a mistake.
Firstly, more studies are needed, and secondly, Connie works
in an English speaking environment whereas her husband
works with Italians, although English is spoken on occasion to
clients. There is no doubt that the environment in which
English is learned plays an important role for the final competence one has of the rules of the language. The pragmalinguistic rules in italiese tend to follow those of English, as far as
apology is concerned. This is true not only for the verbal out-
put observed for Connie, but for a number of other speakers of
italiese. Our preliminary conclusions seem to suggest, therefore, that speakers of italiese appropriated themselves of the
situations which require an apology in English rather then
those in Italian and therefore deem it necessary to apologize
when speaking in italiese. English, therefore, has a much
more pervasive role and its influence covers not only the lexical but also the pragmatic aspects of italiese.

Works Cited

Austi, J.L. *How To Do Things With Words*. Oxford: Clarendon Press.
1975.

Bourhis, R.Y. and Sachdev, I. "Vitality Perceptions and Language Attitudes: Some Canadian Data" in *Journal of Language and Social Psychology* 3, pp. 97-126. 1984.

Clivio, G.P. "The Assimilation of English Loanwords in Italo-Canadian" in *The Second Lacus Forum*. Columbia: Hornbeam, pp. 584-589. 1976.

---. "Su alcune caratteristiche dell'italiese di Toronto" in *Il Veltro* 29, pp. 73-86. 1985.

---. "Competing Loanwords and Loanshifts in Toronto's italiese" in C. Bettoni, ed. *Altro Polo: Italian Abroad*. Sydney: Frederick May Foundation, pp.129-146. 1986.

Danesi, M. *Loanwords and Phonological Methodology*. Ottawa: Didier. 1985.

Goffman, E. *Relations in Public*. New York: Basic Books. 1971.

Harney, R.F. *Italians in Canada*. Toronto. 1978.

Olshtain, E. "Sociocultural Competence and Language Transfer: The Case of Apology" in S. Gass and L. Selinker, eds. *Language Transfer in Language Learning*, Rowley Mass: Newbury. pp. 232-249. 1983.

Owen, M. *Apologies and Remedial Interchanges*. Mouton: The Hague. 1983.

Searle, J.R. *Expression and Meaning: Studies in the Theory of Speech Acts*. Cambridge: Cambridge U Press. 1979.

Vizmuller-Zocco, J. " 'Chiedere scusa' in inglese ed in italiano" in *Le lingue del mondo* 49, pp. 433-437. 1984.

Ethnic Identity And Language: The Case of the Italo-Albanians

Mary Pecoraro Cawthon

When I am asked about my ethnic background, if the person really seems to care, I say that I have an Italian name and that my parents were both from Sicily, but that we always spoke Albanian and think of ourselves as Arbëresh or Italo-Albanians. In September I attended a picnic in Sacramento, California billed as the annual Arbëresh picnic. The people there, about 200 of them,were old friends from my Madison, Wisconsin neighborhood; from Sacramento, San Jose, a group from Fresno whose parents had emigrated from Maschito in Lucania in Southern Italy to California;and some Calabrese. There were also some immigrants from Albania as well as children or grandchildren of those immigrants. What we had in common was the language we spoke—Albanian or Arbëresh, which is an old dialect of Albania and which I had learned as my first language.

The Albanians of Italy are the largest linguistic minority in that country. It is estimated that between 92,000 and 100,000 people speak that language as their first language. Of the original villages that were established about 40 communities survive in Calabria, Basilicata, and Puglia and three villages in Sicily, where there were 10 colonies originally. Of all the surviving villages Piana degli Albanesi in Sicily is the one that most fiercely guards its ethnic identity in language, religion, and culture. It is called "Hora e Arbëreshvet"—the home ('patria') of the Arbëresh. This is the town from which my father emigrated in 1912 to Madison, Wisconsin. He went back in 1921 after serving in the American army in World War I to choose a bride, my mother. I was born a year later. The language we spoke at home and my first language was Albanian.

Piana degli Albanesi, originally called Piana dei Greci was founded in 1488. It celebrated its 500th year in 1988. The people of the colony were from southern Albania called Toskeria or Epiro and were Greek Orthodox, hence the name Greci.

(It was changed to Albanesi in 1939 by Mussolini when he invaded Albania.) The original settlers were fleeing the Turkish invasion of their country. They were given refuge by Ferdinand I, King of Naples and Sicily. The Archbishop of Palermo, Barone, assigned to them a large plain that lies about 3,000 feet above Palermo and is surrounded by high mountains.

The family names of the refugees are still important names in Piana: Cuccia, Matranga, Schiro, Stassi, Barbato, and others that have become Italian names. These names were also the names of the families in Madison.

There are 8 churches in Piana, 7 of them with the Byzantine rite. Their priests wear the black dress and toque of the Greek church and they are allowed to marry and have families. Albanian is still the first language of the home in Piana although Italian is the official language of the schools and the government, as it is for 2 other Sicilian communities, Contessa Entellina and Santa Cristina Gela. The language has been lost in the settlements of Palazzo Adriano, Mezzojuso, Biancavilla,(originally Albavilla) San Michele di Ganzeria, and S. Angelo di Muxaro (Agrigento).

The migration of Albanians to Italy took place between the years 1448 and 1543. When Alphonse I of Spain was King of Naples he appealed for help from the Albanian leader Scanderbeg to put down an uprising near Crotone in Southern Italy. Scanderbeg sent Demetrio Reres and his two sons with an army. After suppressing the revolt the Albanians asked to stay because of the troubles with the Turks in Albania. They settled in 12 villages and later went to Sicily where they founded 4 villages.

Scanderbeg, as George Kastriota was known, is Albania's national hero. Every Albanian (Arbëresh) town has as its main street the name of Giorgio Kastriota. It was under his leadership that the Albanians battled against the Turks when the Turks were conquering the whole Balkan Peninsula. Scanderbeg's father, John, who was ruler of Albania, had been forced to send his four sons to Istanbul, where they were trained in the Corps of the Janissaries. George alone survived and became one of the Sultan's favorite generals. He was given the title "Bey'and since he was called Iskander in Turkey be became "Scanderbeg." It was his friendship with the King of Naples that led to the migrations to Italy. Later, when Ferdinand of Aragon became King of Naples and Sicily, he also received aid from Albanian troops to put down revolts in Italy and Sicily. He also permitted settlements by Albanian refugees.

Another reason for granting lands to Albanians was that constant war had depopulated whole regions. Plague and disease had also decimated the peasant population and workers were needed to till the land of the vast holdings. Contessa Entellina in Sicily bears the name of the person who asked and received peasants to occupy her estate.

Scanderbeg died in 1468 and more Albanians fled to Italy and Sicily, some to join those already there and others to settle in new colonies. Scanderbeg's last words were faithfully recorded:

> My faithful warriors, the Turk will conquer our country and you will become his slaves..Bring my son, that beautiful son of mine so that I may warn him.... Abandoned flower, flower of my love, take your mother and prepare three galleys, the best ones you have, lest the Turk know about it and come and take possession of you...Go to the beach. There you will find a shady, sad cypress: Tie my horse to it and on my horse unfurl to the winds my flag and on my flag hang my sword. Turkish blood lies on its cutting edge, there death sleeps. The arms of the frightful warrior will stop mute under the tree. When the bora (snow) will blow, the horse will neigh, the flag will turn here and there and the sword will jingle. The Turk will hear and sad and trembling will turn back.

The Turk did not turn back but conquered Albania and made it a Muslim state. History says that the toughest group, among the last to leave, went to Sicily from Himara and Chamaria in 1485. They landed at Solunto but were refused refuge because of fear of retaliation from the Turks. They found their way to northwest Sicily and the Monreale Diocese where they were given permission to settle on the plain now called Piana degli Albanesi.

These are the Arbëresh of Hora who still struggle for cultural survival. Awareness of their heritage is growing stronger. At Easter time and April 23, St. George's Day. special celebrations take place. The old rich costumes of Albania are worn by the young women who take part in the processions. Classes are held after regular school so that children can learn to read and write their native language. Young writers publish a monthly magazine "Mondo Albanese" written mostly in Albanian. In Calabria there is a publication "Katundi Yne" (Paese Nostro). There have been cultural exchanges with Albania. There are Albanian studies in the departments of Literature at the Universities of Rome, Palermo, Padova, Napoli, and Bari with the largest group of students at the University of Palermo.

The Sicilians consider these people "difficult and contentious." They have had to defend themselves against the surrounding communities with cunning and force. From being mercenaries in the 15th and 16th century, they became revolutionaries in the 19th century during Italy's struggle against the kings of Naples and Sicily.

In the years after settling in Sicily the local landlords and the Catholic Church whittled away at the privileges which they had originally given the Albanian settlers. After the abolition of feudalism their land grants were taken from them. They were reduced to abject poverty. The fact that they maintained their own Byzantine religion and ethnic cohesion aggravated matters. Latin-rite bishops replaced Byzantine-rite priests with Latin-rite priests upon the death of an Albanian priest. While the papacy paid lip service to the notion of equality between the rites, the hierarchy remained hostile to the Albanians.

When the struggle for unification began in Italy the Arbëresh were ready to fight. Trevelyan, an English historian of Italy described Piana as "the hearth of freedom in Western Sicily." Arbëresh revolutionaries had already been in touch with Garibaldi before he arrived in Sicily. Francesco Crispi, an Arbëresh leader went to Genova to confer with Garibaldi. When Garibaldi landed in western Sicily at Marsala the fighting had already begun. In April an uprising against the Bourbon king had already broken out in Palermo. The Arbëresh of Hora were the hard core of the forces and they had begun guerilla actions against the army in the countryside.

Two Italian revolutionaries from Garibaldi's group went to Sicily to meet with the revolutionary committee from Hora. One of them, Corrao has described this visit, "Then we headed towards Hora which had become one of the most active centres of the revolution. The Bourbon police surrounded Hora in an attempt to capture us, but the Arbëreshi protected us and organized our escape. The police arrested the Arbëresh women, Katerina Musakia, the wife of the chairman of the committee, Peta, Gioachina Kosara, Concetta Benicci, and others. The Arbëresh girl Giovanna Peta from Hora of the Arbëreshi brought the Italian national flag to Palermo hidden in her clothes."

Garibaldi himself stopped to rest in Hora on his way to Palermo: there he was received with cheers. The Arbëresh from other villages had joined in the struggle and alone with four thousand Sicilian volunteers defeated the Bourbon forces in hand at Calatafini. In his memoirs Garibaldi wrote: "We spent the rest of the day in Hora in order to march more freely towards Palermo." About his march to Palermo: "In no part of the world, other than Sicily, would a march like that from Hora to Marino, from Marino to Misimeri have been possible."

From Albania, a woman writer of the day, Dora D'Istria wrote, "The small town of Hora, the biggest center inhabited by the Arbëresh of Sicily occupied an important place in the uprising "

The unification of Italy did not remedy any of the ills of the latifundi system there. By the 1890s the population of Hora was composed mainly of landless laborers and poverty-stricken tenants. In 1890 sharecroppers and day laborers joined together in the FASCIO movement of Italy. This was a movement to teach the poor how to organize to get control of their own lives and acquire land for their own livelihood. Locally politics was dominated by the middle class so the Fascio group organized to fight for control of the municipality.

The Fasci movement was brought to Hora by a native son, a medical man in his 30s, Dr. Nicola Barbato In April of 1893 he recruited virtually all of the adult population—men and women—except for the wealthy Fasci movement. The police estimated the membership at 2,300, more than twice as many as that of any Fascio outside of Palermo. The women of Hora were particularly active in the movement and entered the Fascio with great enthusiasm.

The movement taught them the hard-headed politics of organization and elections. Several Socialist candidates won municipal office in Hora. The whole local council and the deputy to the parliament became socialist before World War I and communist subsequently. The present mayor Andrea Cuccia is a communist. Party headquarters are in the piazza in Hora next to Shen Maria, the Byzantine church of the Madonna of Odgiditria whose icon was brought to Hora from Albania.

Ever since the Fasci, the Arbëresh of Hora have retained their triple loyalty—to communism, to the Albanians of the homeland, and to Greek Christianity. Since May 1893, every May Day, the Arbëresh of Hora have gone to a remote mountain pass, the "Fortella della Ginestra" to hold the May Day meeting. The speeches are delivered from Dr. Barbato's stone, a rock slab where he had stood to address them. May 1, 1947 the Mafia hired the bandit Giuliano to shoot down participants. Fourteen people were killed causing a national political scandal. The surviving members of his band were finally convicted in 1956 for the massacre, he having been assassinated in turn by the Mafia. In Hora, the Mafiosi have been less powerful than elsewhere in the province since the Fascio movement of the 1890s.

Because of geography (steep mountain terrain), religion, culture, and politics, the Arbëresh of Hora were isolated. Their xenophobia isolated them from their Sicilian neighbors who always looked upon them with suspicion. Sicilians were called "Liti," the expression being contemptuous. They did business with them—fish peddlers, produce peddlers, those selling household goods went to Hora from Palermo, 16 miles away. Intermarriage withSicilians was discouraged. In Hora there was a saying "Vajza jime, gjegjem ti, mirr Arbëresh e jo Liti, se te chan Shpi edhe kusi." (My dear daughter, listen to me, marry Arbëresh and not "Liti", because he will break [bring down] your house and your pots.)

This sense of "we" against "them" persisted in the Sicilian

neighborhood in Madison where I grew up. Actually, we were an Arbëresh community within the larger Sicilian community. There were about 65 Arbëresh families in Madison in the 1920s, '30s, and early '40s when I lived there. The first Arbëresh went to Madison in 1905 from Piana. Many of the rest who followed from there were related to the first of the families. These were the Maisano, Cuccia, Parisi, Paratore, Barbato, and Licali families. The first ones worked for the railroad, the Lorillard Tobacco Company, or started a business. Later the arrivals worked mostly in construction, almost all of them for John Icke, a former city engineer turned private construction owner. When I was a child I thought this man's name was all one word—"Joniki."

In 1912, the year my father arrived from Piana to live with his cousins, the Paratores, the Arbëresh formed a mutual aid society "I Lavatori d'Italia di Mutuo Soccorso e Beneficenza," always referred to as "la società" by all of us. They built a club house for meetings and for social things such as playing cards, boccie, but mostly for talking politics. In the tradition of their home, Hora, most of the members were socialists and anticlerical, meaning the Catholic Church. Until 1948 the meetings were conducted in Albanian and one of the by-laws that lasted until the end of World War II was that membership was limited to Arbëresh, their offspring, or someone married to an Arbëresh woman.

Of the 65 families in Madison only 15 or 16 families attended the Catholic Church, St. Joseph's, which had an Italian speaking priest. When I say family, I mean the women and children went, the men only for weddings, baptisms, funerals, maybe. The rest of the Arbëresh did not attend any church. They went to the Italian Methodist Mission Church or sent their children there. A few families in the early years had their children baptized at Grace Episcopal Church, but never attended services there.

When my father was a bachelor, he and some friends went to Sunday School and English classes at the Italian Methodist Mission. The classes were all taught by young American women and there were also picnics and parties at the church. After he married my mother he did not go to church. My mother and all the children in our family went to St. Joseph's.

I was baptized when I was ten days old. When my next two siblings were born, two girls, my father did not want them baptized because he said he wanted to see if they would turn out better or worse without baptism. My mother finally walked them over to the church one working day when my sisters were 3 and 4 years old. They were baptized by special arrangement and the first Papa knew about it was when he arrived home from work and found the godparents at our house for dinner. The next two children were baptized as infants despite his objections.

We went to church and catechism, but on Sundays we had to listen to Papa's sermon as well as the priest's. I went one year to the parochial school, St. Joseph's, but only in the first grade. My father did not permit me to attend because a "Liti" threw a tin can at me one day and wounded me over the eye. He called the "Liti" animals or worse. When my youngest sister, Nina was 5 she went to school at St.Joseph's and stayed through the 5th grade. She was the only Arbëresh pupil at the school.

I also remember that once when one of the members of "la società" died and was buried as a Catholic (because of his wife's wishes) the men accompanied the body on foot just to the door of the church and then waited outside and smoked until the Mass was over.

This distrust for the clergy and for "real Sicilians" seems to have been true only in Madison. Arbëresh in other communities were Roman Catholic and socialized with other Italians in their communities. When I asked my mother why so many of the families in Madison went to the Methodist Mission and the men did not go to church at all, she said it was "because the men were all socialists and sat around talking politics all the time." An older cousin of mine had a different idea. She thought it was because at the time "they were all 'morti di fame' and had become 'rice Christians.' " The Methodists gave away food and clothing during the depression and the young ones at Sunday School got candy and cookies.

There was little inter-marriage between the Arbëresh and Sicilians. We were not allowed to play with the young people and neither were my friends. We went to Draper School, they went to Longfellow. There were no social events at church that we could attend because we were not allowed to go to CYO dances. Some of the Arbëresh went to Central High where they became friendly with "Liti" students. One of my friends says that when her cousin married a "Liti", the girl's mother said she could never hold her head up among the Arbëresh because this had taken place. But then she couldn't refuse because the young man's father was influential in the Sicilian community and the mother was a widow. He was the local "capo" for the Mafia. Although the Arbëresh kept themselves apart from the Sicilians when it came to non-Italians it was a different story. I was allowed to have American friends and to go to their homes. The young men went to dances in nearby small towns where there were German and Scandinavian communities. Many of them married girls from these towns. Arbëresh girls were not allowed to date but when we finally left home most of us married non-Italians. Nick Stassi of Madison who is the unofficial historian for the Italian community says he has kept track of most of us and that 95 percent of the Arbëresh married non-Italians.

Several Arbëresh women were the first to go to the University of Wisconsin in Madison and two to teachers' colleges in the 1930s. Before that Arbëresh women worked as housekeepers in hospitals, in restaurants. Several had worked at the tobacco warehouse when it was in existence. They were more independent and had more spirit than the Sicilian women. True, the university was only 5 blocks away from home which was an incentive, but it was also close by for the Sicilians. I think the Arbëresh pushed education more, even for girls. Both my father and mother urged us to be educated and take advantage of every opportunity to better ourselves.

The Arbëresh because of their political background in Hora took to American ideas and ideals more easily than the Sicilians of the community. They also seemed to learn good, accent-free English. Many of the phonetic sounds occur in both English and Albanian.

The alphabet of the Albanian language is made up of 36 phonetic sounds. Some of the equivalent English and Albanian sounds are the following:

h—always aspirated as in the English *h*and, *h*am, unlike the silent *h* in Italian.

dh—pronounced *th* as in *the* and *they.*
th—pronounced *th* as in *th*row and too*th.*
ç—pronounced *ch* as in *ch*urch
sh—pronounced *sh* as in *sh*oe and wa*sh*
g—invariably hard *g* as in *g*o, *g*et and *g*i
ë—pronounced e as in her and term
j—pronounced like the *y* as in *y*es and *y*ear
y—pronounced like the *u* in French d*u.*
c—is pronounced *ts*

What is this Albanian language? On a chart showing the
Indo-European family of languages, Albanian stands alone on
its branch So does Armenian with which it is often con-
fused..Most linguists agree that Albanian is the direct descendant of ancient Illyrian. The Illyrian people occupied the
whole of what now is the Balkan Peninsula between the
Danube River and the Aegean Sea. The remnants of the old
Illyrians were found in Albania and can be traced by similar
words occurring in Illyrian and Albanian, *mal* is mountain,
shegë is pomegranate, *bisht-* tail. Illyrian "bile" became "bië",
"barka" became "barku." The name of a Illyrian tribe was
"Delmat" from the word for sheep, "dele." (I have a cousin in
Hora who is becoming a priest who changed his Italian name
from Giovanni Pecoraro (shepherd) to Jan Delmeri, the Albanian equivalent).

The language was learned at home from the mother. Children of mixed marriages did not learn Albanian if the mother
did not speak it. Consequently, the language among American
Arbëresh is dying out. But those with Arbëresh backgrounds
seem to know that they are not like other Italians. We always
seek each other out and are always thrilled to meet some one
of the same blood. We are always greeted with the cry that we
are "gjaku i shprishur," literally, blood that has been dispersed or scattered. This from Moslems from Albania, Roman
Catholics from Yugoslavia, or someone from the orthodox
community of Albanians from Worcester, Massachusetts.

The Albanians from Shqiperia (present day Albania) especially admire the Arbëresh for keeping alive for 500 years the
language of their homeland and especially the passion for independence for their old home even though they knew they
could never return. The Arbëresh admire the Albanians be-

cause in spite of 500 years of domination by the Turks they were able to emerge and soar like eagles, for which Shqiperia if named. Shqiperia means "land of the eagles."

BIBLIOGRAPHY

Drizari, Nelo. *Spoken and Written Albanian, A Practical Handbook.* Frederick Unger Publishing Co. New York, 1947.

Frasheri, Kristo. *The History of Albania, A Brief Survey.* Tirana, 1964.

Hobshaum, E.J. *Primitive Rebels, Studies in Archaic Forms of Social Movement In The 19th and 20th Century.* Manchester University Press, 1974. Chapter on Millenarianism.

Nasse, George N. *The Italo-Albanian Villages of Southern Italy.* National Academy of Sciences, National Research Council, Washington, D. C., 1964.

Petrotta, Salvatore. *Albanesi Di Sicilia*, Storia e Cultura. Edltori Stampatori Associati, Palermo, 1966.

Schiro, Giuseppe.*Gli Italo-Albanesi.* Discorso pronunciato dal Pronunciato il 26 agosto, 1961 a Biancavilla.

"Garibaldi and the Arbëresh Fighters." Article published April 1, 1986. *LIRIA*, an Albanian newspaper in Boston.

Literature

What is Italian-American Literature?

Robert Viscusi
Brooklyn College
City University of New York

You do not need to hear from me that the expression *Italian-American* is a complicated and troublesome one. Lately it has been the vogue to ask whether it means anything at all. Ethnicity is changing, the argument runs, and it has become just a matter of choice. This argument gains plausibility when a graduate student goes out with a tape recorder and asks people in northern California if they think they are ethnics, and if so, what kind. And the people say, well, you know, maybe, sometimes, and it all depends. So the graduate student concludes that ethnic identities have become Lifestyle Options. As I say, it sounds plausible enough. Indeed it carries a certain message of truth. But I have to begin by recalling, and I hope you will forgive me for asserting something so obvious, that market research is only one form of historiography. It has its limits. It is very good at tracking the salability of images and notions at any given split second of financial time. But when we consider the source of these images, when we assess the durability of these notions, and when we contemplate the long-term uses to which they have been and can be put, then market research must sit down in the audience and listen to what other kinds of history have to say.

There are many other kinds of history, and most of them are represented in the professional study of Italian America past and present. I can only speak for one of them--a kind of subset of literary history. Literary history, you may say, is my neighborhood, and I live currently in that part of it which is devoted to thinking about the relationships between language and money. From this point of view the term *Italian-American* is so rich with meanings that it is very difficult to know where to begin to tell you about them all. Some of them will be so familiar that all I need to do is mention them and you will be able to think of any number of examples of what I mean. Thus, for example, the term *Italian American* comes into use as a result of the large-scale reorganization of capital, both in Europe and in the Americas, at the end of the nineteenth century. In that connection, it is a term which treats a population as if it were a convertible currency--a currency that could be removed from its connection with real commodities, and, in a climax of fungibility, turned into anything else at all anywhere else upon the busy, lucrative planet. *Italian-American,* when used to mean an underclass of exportable labor, is an old expression, full of meaning for historians and still applicable to the lives and careers of thousands of persons who move with a steady regularity between Campania or Bari and Cambridge or Brooklyn.

Another familiar use of the term *Italian-American* employs it to categorize the clients of social service organizations. This is the famous Italian-American ethnic who is in the process of disappearing. This creature was for a hundred years a steady, large chunk of the workload of policemen, social workers, state psychologists, and industrial-strength guidance personnel. From the financial point of view, this person is like the index of the money supply, very useful in predicting interest rates and in deciding upon the prospects for long-term capital investment. As I say, this ethnic is a familiar character to us all. Now, both the convertible-currency Italian-American and the money-supply Italian-American have had important roles to play in the growth of Italian-American literature. Their lives, as we all know, were almost ceaselessly difficult, as neither human nature in general nor their cultural heritage in particular had prepared them to live the dramatic existences, full of spectacular rises and catastrophic falls, which make the careers of quotations on the bourse. But these were the lives they were forced to live, suffering the distant manipulations of persons and interests so far removed from themselves in social space as to make laughable any notion of mutual understanding or consideration. *Italian-American* was the name, in literature no less than in social work, of a tragic destiny, and you find this very fully reflected in the novels of Pietro Di Donato, Jerre Mangione, John Fante, Mari Tomasi, and the poems of Arturo Giovannitti and Giuseppe Zappulla.

Now it is no news that this era of our history has passed its zenith. Our very presence here, celebrating the twentieth anniversary of this extraordinary association, is as good a piece of evidence as one needs in order to assert that our social position has altered and to infer that our literary identity must alter with it. Some of us, indeed, are now wealthy. Others, a very large number of others, have entered that vast American great plains of resource where one is neither rich nor poor but has acquired at least a modicum of personal and family capital. This capital comes in three kinds: financial, social, and cultural. Financially, we have positions, entitlements, pensions, houses, cars, vacations, disposable years in which to aim our lives and the destinies of our children. Socially, we have rank, networks, and all those little calling cards that have written on the back of them, in invisible letters two inches high, the word *Initiative*. We are in a position to do as we like, or at least to plan doing so. Culturally, we have educations, we have travel, we have inherited understandings of our history and our prospects. This cultural capital is the prime requisite of a thriving literature, and I am here to tell you that our literature has begun to thrive. From Helen Barolini to Diane DiPrima, from John Ciardi to Joseph Tusiani to Gilbert Sorrentino and Gregory Corso--but I should not name names lest I ignore twenty for every one I include. Not names, but an identity is what I want to specify before I sit down.

In the cultural economy I have been suggesting, the term *Italian-American* is no longer the name of an exchange factor, but instead it is the name of a capital accumulation. This is why we no longer need to call ourselves ethnics. We are in possession. We have moved from the margins, where existence is too lively to be borne, and in the direction of the campus and the country club, where it is possible to sit and discuss the desirability of buying a little house in Tuscany or of taking a second master's degree. We have passed now, not only through Ellis Island and the River Rouge plant of Henry Ford, but also through the anterooms of a thousand funeral parlors, where we have watched our migrant grandparents and our ethnic uncles and aunts in the process of becoming solid blocks of marble and granite, no longer the chips and pawns of others but the gods and goddesses to whom our children will, in the fullness of time, want to proclaim their affinity. This great transformation is the beginning of a new kind of literature and of a very different set of referents for the term *Italian-American*.

It now means, to choose only the most important among its new connotations, that we have arrived at a point where we finally are ready to confront the full cultural implications of our historical identity. *Italian-American*, at this level, is the name of a deep and resounding contradiction. Without the strength of our newly accumulated substance, we could never have faced the fullness of this contradiction. As provisional and fungible ethnic Americans, we could not confront Italian culture without being struck in the face with the same contempt we had escaped from eighty or a hundred years ago. Our best writers have always understood this. They have approached Italy in a gingerly fashion, knowing that *Italian* in literature means academies, barons, bishops, ceremonies, heroes, the great catalogue of verb inflections as precise, as delicate, as detailed and as bristling with shibboleth as the genealogy of a Ridolfi or a Rucellai. How connect this, in any event, with *American*, which in literature means open prairies, Baptist preachers, lynch mobs, runaway slaves, the unpunctuated ramblings of Faulkner's idiots and the surreptitious tug at the zipper of Allen Ginsberg's index finger? Italians are skeptical and pessimistic and they know so much they have already forgotten everything. Americans are gullible, optimistic, and they view history with the cheerful ignorance of Huckleberry Finn graduating from Stanford with a degree in sex therapy. When these two words meet in the expression *Italian-American*, the social anthropologists may rejoice, but the cultural historians may simply be covering their ears.

Our literary destiny, nonetheless, is to confront this formidable contradiction. Earlier, I think, we were scarcely able to do so. For every heroic bricklayer like DiDonato, who went to work with the *Divine Comedy* in his pocket, there were many thousands of others, who, like Mario Puzo's mother, simply wanted to forget it all and get on with buying the house in Long Island. Now, however, we are ready in a large way. Our children are at Harvard and Northwestern. Our association is stocking its archives and beginning to put into circulation its peculiar questions about the meanings of our history. And our writers have begun to speak with considerable authority of the mutual pollution which must occur if the Italian and the American traditions are finally and fruitfully to mingle and flourish. Novels of intermarriage like those of Gilbert Sorrentino and Carole Maso are perhaps the clearest index of the current agenda of our writers and our literary historians. *Italian-American* is giving up its career as a statistician's pigeonhole at the same time and at the same speed that it is becoming a cultural identity, an historical passport into a new space where the great visible indices are not bandannas and caps, not stigmata still bleeding along the lines of other people's whips, but instead they are signs of high clear purpose, little television screens that say: "Flight 501, New York-Milano, departing 9 p.m."

I have never liked being an ethnic. The attentions of police and social workers have never seemed pleasant to me. But that does not mean that I, or you, or any of us, need to think that we are no longer going to be Italian-Americans. It simply indicates that the word is in the process of meaning something new, something deeply rooting in the American gardens of intertwining columbine and honeysuckle. We are ready to discover what it means to be Italian from an American point of view and American from an Italian point of view. Our history as price fluctuations in the labor market is largely over, no doubt. Our history, however, as capital, like our history as philosophers and poets, is just beginning.

Emigrazione e America nella letteratura del Sud d'Italia

Sebastiano Martelli
Università di Salerno

La relazione rientra in una ricerca,.che ho in corso da alcuni anni. avente ad oggetto il tema "letteratura ed emigrazione", e piu specificamente la presenza del fenomeno emigrazionistico nella letteratura italiana otto-novecentesca—ricerca di cui ho gia pubblicato alcuni risultati negli ultimi tempi—attraverso una verifica di tipo comparatistico, che, affidata ad una forte contaminazione pluridisciplinare—storia, antropologia, sociologia oltre ad una comparazione di forme e modelli letterari—possa indicare freenze, scarti, differenze ed omologazioni di una produzione letteraria segnata da un fenomeno storico di proporzioni e riflessi vastissimi.

Se è vero che alla grande emigrazione italiana otto-novecentesca "è mancato un Verga, è mancato cioè il grande romanzo o anche solamente un filone narrativo che fosse il corrispettivo adeguato del fenomeno", e pur vero che significanti incursioni, sia pure quantitativamente limitate, possono rintracciarsi tra i maggiori protagonisti della letteratura coeva: De Amicis, Pascoli, Pirandello, testimonianze letterarie, che, come ho avuto occasione di dimostrare in altra sede, sono collegate fra loro da interessanti fili letterari e culturali.

L'autore di *Cuore* si imbarca nel marzo del 1884 per un viaggio in Sud America su una nave che trasporta 1600 emigranti; l'obiettivo iniziale e quello di ricavare dal viaggio un libro su "I nostri contadini in America", ma presto il progetto si modifica e la scrittura si concentra sul viaggio, sulla nave con il suo carico umano di emigranti, i luoghi dello sbarco e delle terre visitate. Questo materiale confluirà nell'opera sull'*Oceano* pubblicata nel 1889; da quel viaggio nasceranno anche altre tre brevi prose che De Amicis raccoglie sotto il titolo *In America* e che l'editore romano

Voghera pubblica nel 1897 in una raffinata plaquette con disegni ed incisioni.

Ma soprattutto va sottolineato che il viaggio, le esperienze di quella traversata serviranno a preparare i materiali per quella che è stata definita "la piu straordinaria *short novel* ottocentesca sull'emigrazione" e cioè Dagli Apennini alle Ande, il pezzo forte di quel libro *Cuore* che, tra molte incredulità, ha continuato a circolare in tutto il mondo per molte generazioni.

Pur veicolate da una ideologia emigrazionistica—che non è solo prodotto di tensione sentimentale ma si aggancia all'intenso dibattito storico-politico, che tiene banco in Italia per alcuni decenni fino al periodo giolittiano incluso e con forme e motivazioni diverse anche nel ventenio successivo—nonostante questo, dicevo, le prose deamicisiane sopra ricordate sono anche cariche di toni "desolati e funebri", di "un'atmosfera lugubre e mortuaria" nelle raffigurazioni degli emigranti, della e del viaggio, raffigurazioni che non sono solo frutto dello "stile dominante delle raffigurazioni dell'epoca, sia letterarie sia iconografiche (si veda l'illustrazione topica, il momento dell'imbarco) che predilige i connotati stereotipatamente necroforici" (Berton)—che vanno collegati anche al d fuso "culto dei morti" nella letteratura e nel'arte tra Otto e Novecento agli altri di malattia, disgrazia (sifilide, tubercolosi, alcolismo, ecc.).

Ed ancora, il tema della morte non domesticata come nel racconto deamicisiano raccolto nella plaquette *In America*: un contadino lombardo che chiede di imbarcarsi sulla stessa nave che sta riportando lo scrittore in Italia dall'Argentina; il contadino avverte la morte vicina e chiede in maniera accorata e disperata di poter andare a morire in patria tra i suoi familiari.

Ma un più ampio spettro di materiali e valenze letterarie e linguistisi ritrovano certamente in *Italy*, una delle liriche più significative dei *Poemetti* di Pascoli, il vertice della poesia sull'emigrazione, ma anche una delle composizioni piu significative della poesia pascoliana e di tutta la poesia italiana tra Otto e Novecento.

Sullo sfondo del paesaggio agreste romagnolo e di una civiltà contadina morente si genera il dialogo tra la bambina

Molly, figlia di emigrati—rientrata nel paese dei genitori a cercare la guarigione—e la nonna sull'onda delle modulazioni linguistiche alimentate da lingue diverse, la cui incomunicabilita sciolta via via come da flussi sotterranei proveti dalla campagna.

La campagna, la civiltà contadina delle radici, sono il luogo salvifila terra della guarigione dalla malattia contratta con l'emigrazione nei luoghi dell'altra civiltà, quella americana della città, delle macchine, del progresso.

Con originali soluzioni linguistiche ed egemoni referenti simbolici e mitologici in *Italy* si concentrano peculiari segmentazioni letterarie ed ideologiche: l'adozione non mimetico-realistica dello slang italo-americano che nella giustapposizione-confronto con l'italiano a doppio registro, quello alto letterario e quello popolare, cioè costruito sulle cadenze e strutture profonde del parlato dialettale, popolare, veicola simbolicamente il confronto tra due civiltà, l'una che muore, l'altra del futuro; il tema decadente città-campagna, civiltà urbano-industriale e civiltà della campagna; la città, la civiltà americana, l'emigrazione come malattia, la campagna e la civiltà contadina come luogo salvifico, di guarigione.

Fra i testi piu interessanti della letteratura del Sud d'Italia sull'emigrazione certamente si pone la novella "L'altro figlio", un testo tra i meno conosciuti di Pirandello, prima che i Fratelli Taviani la utilizzassero due anni fa nel loro film pirandelliano *Kaos*. E la storia triste di Marograzia, una donna che vive in un paesino siciliano nei primi anni del Novecento, un paesino svuotato di giorno in giorno dall'emigrazione che ha segnato profondamente anche la vita di Marograzia: da quattorrazia si consuma nel pianto per i due figli partiti per l'America e di cui non ha piu notizie; disperatamente cerca di affidare ai paesani che partono un messaggio per i figli che non potra mai arrivare a destinazione.

Il testo—come ho dimostrato in una relazione presentata al convegno pirandelliano dell'Universita di Stony Brook lo scorso anno—è un interessante concentrato di materiali storico-antropologici della cultura positivistica di fine Ottocento. Ma i toni e codici decisamente prevalenti nella novella sono quelli del lutto, della morte, in una gamma

convergente funebri: disgrazia, malattia, follia, tutti strettamente collegati ad una sorta di causa fondante,
l'emigrazione.

L'ideologia pascoliana della campagna, come luogo salvifico
e totalmente ribaltata: la campagna in questo testo
pirandelliano e tutta attraversata dalla morte; l'emigrazione è
come una grande ombra silenziosa che svuota le case, i vicoli,
desertifica il paesaggio, lascia segni indelebili di malattia,
disgrazia, follia.

Dovranno trascorrere oltre venti anni—anni che tra l'altro
sono segnati da un esodo migratorio di proporzioni di massa,
quasi biblico—perchè possa rintracciarsi una nuova opera
letteraria di qualche consistenza: si tratta del romanzo
Emigranti, dello scrittore di origine calabrese Francesco Perri,
pubblicato da Mondadori nel 1928.

Si tratta di un romanzo che è una sorta di concentrato di
molti reperti diffusi nella letteratura e nella pubblicistica
sull'emigrazione tra Otto e Novecento; estraneo a qualsiasi
apertura al romanzo europeo "della crisi", questo romanzo di
Perri è un reperto, rozzo ma polimorfo, in cui confluiscono
diversi modelli di romanzo: da quello regionale e verista a
quello di consumo (da Varona, Zuccoli, Brocchi), al romanzo
sociale (Bersezio, Cena, Valera), ma anche D'Annunzio,
Oriani, il romanzo popolare, lacerti carducciani e pascoliani,
gli stampi del romanticismo naturalistico, il tutto su una base
storico-antropologica che entra in commistione con i diversi
modelli di romanzo, una commistione funzionale ad un
pubblico di lettori nuovo e più vasto che in quegli anni venti si
andava formando; insomma la risposta ad un "orizzonte di
attesa" di un pubblico popolare che in forme, luoghi e tempi
diversi si sarebbe avvicinato alla "storia delle vittime"
dell'emigrazione di un villaggio contadino del Sud.

Abbiamo già detto che il topos dell'emigrazione come lutto è
già *presentura* e nell'iconografia otto-novecentesca, ed è facile,
così come è stato fatto per Pirandello e per Perri, rinviare *sic
et simplici* al naturalismo, al regionalismo; ma si tratta di
conclusioni prevedibili e liquidatorie che lasciano fuori la
verifica più importante come questa sull'emigrazione e cioè
una verifica sui livelli e dislivelli dei materiali utilizzati dallo
scrittore, sull'assemiverse tipologie di questi materiali, da

quelli storici e cronachistici a quelli della tradizione orale; da quelli antropologici a quelli letterari, l'incrociarsi dell'immaginario sociale e di quello letterario; il confronto-scontro fra l'identità storico-antropologica delle rasistenziale individuale alimentata da differenziati flussi.

Nella letteratura meridionale otto-novecentesca i *topoi* ricorrenti di disgrazia, lutto, morte non sono solo materiali cronachistici e realistici, in realtà a me pare essi vadano a confluire in una macrostruttura genetica antropologica che e quella dell'emigrazione come contenitore di disgrazie, malattie, lutti, morte.

Il grande antropologo ed etnologo Ernesto De Martino, nella sua opera *Morte e pianto rituale*—una eccezionale escursione sul lamento funebre e sui rituali della morte—nota come ancora negli anni dell'ultimo dopoguerre dell'Italia del Sud l'emigrazione venisse vissuta come "equivalente critico della morte".

Già in occasione della partenza si ripetono gli stessi rituali del corso "accompagnamento" degli emigranti che partono richiama il corteo funebre.

Nella dimensione antropologica, dunque, l'emigrazione e anche "un'espe un'esperienza di morte che si esprime in primo luogo nella descrissione di legami costitutivi dalle personalità del migrante. Partire e anche far morire gli altri, per lo meno simbolicamente e, al tempo stesso, esporsi al pericolo della perdita di sé" (Lombardi Satriani).

Con l'emigrazione si consuma un distacco traumatico dalla comunità familiare del villaggio, cesura e strappo nel flusso degli affetti e dei referenti culturali. Il viaggio è verso l'ignoto, verso una terra senza dove, senza confini, vissuto come "perdita della Heimat", della "sicura esistenziale", crocevia di lacerazioni destorificanti e, quindi, luttuose; un viaggio senza ritorno, avvertito tale anche dai membri della comunità rimasti in paese.

Nell'universo folklorico delle culture mediterranee la morte domesticata attraverso l'elaborazione del lutto costituisce uno snodo centrale nella vicomunitaria: l'elaborazione del lutto, i riti funebri, il pianto sul cadavere ed altri eventi rituali consentono al morto di attraversare il "ponte" che unisce i due mondi, un canale di comunicazione simboli morti e consentono ai vivi il "superamento della crisi della presenza" (De Martino), quindi una domesticazione della morte stessa.

Il "ponte" è un referente simbolico assai diffuso nella cultura folklorica della morte, in particolare nel Meridione d'Italia; e di pochi anni fa un corposo e suggestivo studio su questo tema degli antropologi Lombardi Satriani e Meligrana, *Il ponte di San Giacomo. L'ideologia della morte nella cultura del Sud.*

Solo l'orizzonte religioso rimane come unico ma parziale sostituto di quelaborazione del lutto per chi muore lontano dal villaggio edai familiari. Le lacerazioni dell'emigrazione creano uno stato di angoscia, di fissiti nel dolore poichè esse fanno saltare tutti gli argini difensivi/individuali e comunitari; insomma se l'emigrazione "è equivalente critico della una morte non domesticata, violenta; il viaggio degli emigranti è un viaggio verso l'ignoto, quindi il nulla."

Niente di più lacerante del terrore di una morte non domesticata, deprivata degli eventi rituali e simbolici propri della cultura della comunita di appartenenza.

Questa fissità struggente si somma ai dati strutturali che l'emigrazione porta con se a cominciare dallo "schock culturale" originato negli emigrano-scontro con un'altra società, con un'altro mondo di valori, di comportamenti e di norme, dove le relazioni interpersonali e i codici nonscritti, il significato dei simboli e la lingua, i ritmi del lavoro, la dimensione del tempo e il modo di vederlo, la percezione dello spazio antropologico e sociale sono diversi; la cultura originaria dell'emigrato subisce un assalto, una ferita profonda.

La lingua diviene il macrosegno della impossibilità della comunicazione, della rottura dell'unità etnico-linguistica, dello strappo dall'orizzonte conosciuto e proprio della comunità ed insieme del precipitare in un conte piu referenti, senza piu incertezze che creano angoscia simile a quella provocata da uno strappo familiare luttuoso.

Allora nella mente e nell'animo dell'emigrante si accampa un processo di ricostruzione e mitizzazione all'incontrario; il paese è ora opposto all'America travolgente, al tempo senza storia della civilta americana egli oppone il tempo ciclico, senza sviluppo, antropologicodella sua civiltà agro-pastorale delle origini; un tempo scandito dalle stato dai proverbi.

Tutto nella memoria dell'emigrante e recuperato in una luce diversa, la lontananza ne muta radicalmente i contorni.

Nel suo animo si accampa un "sentimento-struggimento" della patria, quella Heinweh che è nostalgia, "dolore della casa, della terra natale", del "focolare".

Nell'emigrato si approfondisce quotidianamente questo status di sospeso essere "a mezza parete" per usare la pregnante definizione di Frigessi Castelnuovo e Rizzo nel loro lavoro dal titolo omonimo pubblicato nel 1982 da Einaudi e frutto di indagini sociologiche ed antropologiche tra gli emigrati italiani degli anni Cinquanta e Sessanta nella Svizzera tedesca: presi in questa trappola continuano i due sociologi—come un alpinista in pericolo aggrappato alla parete nell'impossibilita di scendere e di salire. Il cambiamento interculturale si risolve in questa impotenza, in questa ambivalenza, in questo conflitto permanente.

E' un conflitto sentimentale ma anche antropologico, una crisi della presenza—per ripetere la definizione de-martiniana—"vuoto di appartenenza, di riferimento", "rischio di non poterci essere in nessun mondo culturale possibile".

Solo il ritorno può sciogliere il nodo di queste angosce, ed il ritorno è sempre lì sullo sfondo come ultimo risolutivo taglio; ma in gran parte del meridione l'emigrazione è vissuta come emigrazione senza ritorno.

Questa scissione provoca ulteriore angoscia, come si evince dalle lettere degli emigranti, a volte riproposte come topos modellistico in alcuni romanzi meridionali sull'emigrazione: e il caso di Perri in *Emigranti*, ma che si ritrova anche in altri romanzi europei ed italo-americani sull'emigrazione; c'è l'inserimento di modelli topici della epistolografia dell'emmigrante come quello della "lettera di saluto", studiati gia da Thomas e Znaniecki negli anni Venti nella loro monumentale opera, *The Polish Peasant in Europe and America (Il contadino polacco in Europa e in America)*, un modello "la cui forma deriva dalla funzione originaria dell'atto epistolare...denota lo scopo principale d'una comunicazione tesa a rinsaldare i vincoli di solidarieta familiare forzosamente spezzati dall'emigrazione" (Franzina).

Non manca in qualche racconto meridionale del secondo

dopoguerra la dimensione pavesiana dell'America, prima sognata, immaginata, mitizzata e che poi via via è spogliata di ogni traccia di mito, di idealizzazione: da paese della ricchezza e della felicità diviene il paese del provvisorio, senza identità, senza anima, e senza storia, regno del divenire frenetico e della superficialita che alimentano a dismisura lo sradicamento e la solitudine.

Alle figure femminili del "Nuovo mondo" segnate dai topoi positivistici che ne fanno apportatrici di malattia e disgrazia o pavesianamente disegnate con i loro tratti urbani di donne libere, senza complessi, indipendenti, instabili, superficiali, riluttanti ad ogni legame duraturo e definitivo, si oppongono le figure femminili del mondo delle madri, del paese.

La dicotomia America-paese, mito americano-mito della terra delle madri, diviene così un identema centrale dell'immaginario letterario, che, superate le manipolazioni e mistificazioni ideologiche e culturali degli anni tra le due guerre, si riproporra con i suoi tratti, piu letterari che antropologici, in una certa produzione narrativa del secondo dopoguerra.

Il ritorno al paese, alla terra delle Madri diviene percorso narrativo di un estremo tentativo di recupero delle memorie perdute, di riappropriazio salvifica della propria identita culturale, ricerca di una ardua mediazone e conciliazione tra due mondi diversi ed opposti per una impossibile uscita da quella condizione "a mezza parete," che da identema socio-antropologico dell'emigrato via via si costituisce come identema di una condizione più generale intellettuale ed esistenziale nel mondo moderno.

Arturo Giovannitti: Writings From Lawrence

Lucinda LaBella Mays

To understand the man, Arturo Giovannitti, one must understand the times and places in which he lived. In Italy, the promises of the Risorgimento—redistributed church lands and a less limited franchise—remained unfulfilled. To divert the Italian populace from labor unrest, bread riots, street fighting and higher taxes, Prime Minister Crispi attempted to recapture past glories with forays into African colonization which led to defeat in Ethiopia and international disgrace.

Giovannitti was born in 1884. The son of a liberal physician, he attended gymnasium and college as had his brothers before him. "It was not exactly hunger that drove me from my father's house," he told the Essex County jury in November, 1912. "I could now be a professional man down there."[1]

Yet, in 1900, at sixteen Giovannitti left the security of home, family and position and began a lifelong quest for the equality of opportunity and freedom missing in Italy which he hoped to find in the New World.[2]

Abandoning Roman Catholicism, he studied theology at McGill University, and worked on a Canadian railroad gang before venturing into the coal mines of Pennsylvania. He then attended Union Theological Seminary and served in several Presbyterian missions before solidarity and the brotherhood of man replaced institutionalized religion in his life.[3]

In his poem, "Credo," he best expresses this idealism and philosophy:[4]

> I believe that Evil-hate, jealousy, greed, cowardice and war—is not a part of the immutable destiny of man, but is a resultant of obscure forces that he can and will destroy when the sunshine of fraternity will clear his eyes and kiss and smooth his brow, the coffer of his invincible thought.

Physically about six feet tall, with patrician good looks, Byronic collar and flowing cravats, Giovannitti was impressive.

It was, however, his sympathetic understanding of the immigrant and his mastery of languages that thrust upon him the
role of spokesman for the downtrodden.

I believe in my Neighbor, my Brother and my Friend,
who however poor and humble and dishonored and
voiceless he may be, is always better than I, and to
him I reconsecrate each day my travail and my faith
so that we may march together towards the goal of the
great dream beyond the portals of the unknown.[5]

It was the closed portals of opportunity for the millworkers
of Lawrence, Massachusetts that brought national prominence to Arturo Giovannitti. The Massachusetts state legisla-
ture enacted a law to take effect January 1, 1912 which decreased the hours of women and children from fifty-six to
fifty-four hours a week. The millowners applied the law to the
men also.[6]

Suspicious millhands noted a speedup in the machines and
concluded the millowners were going to make up the two
hours without compensatory pay for them.[7]

The Italian workers held a meeting and decided to strike if
their envelopes were short. Counting their pay, finding it
lacking, they went on a rampage through the mill district,
protesting not only the short pay but the lint, dust and spu-
tum-filled air in the mills, windows nailed shut year round to
keep the air humid and hot so the threads would not break.[8]

The workers were reacting against the absence of guard
rails on the machines.and the vibrations that caused shuttles
and other parts of the machines to loosen, separate and fly
across the huge rooms injuring the workers. Not long before
the strike, a Polish girl caught her hair in the machines. The
part of her scalp torn away was placed in a paper bag and accompanied her to the hospital.[9]

Other complaints from workers ranged from hot drinking
water to sex with the overseers as a condition of employment.[10]

The millhands were retaliating for the years of sub-stan-
dard housing in over-priced wooden tenements.[11] Lawrence
was the most congested city in the nation with one of the
highest infant mortality rates of industrial urban areas.[12]

Witnesses told the House of Representatives committee

their children survived mainly on black bread spread with molasses or lard. The hearing revealed that the highest amount found on pay envelopes for women and children for a fifty-six hour week was $6.05. The lowest was $3.85.[13]

One worker shouted that first day of the strike, "We are going to fight them for more bread, we are going to get a pair of shoes for our barefoot children, we are going to get another set of underwear for them."[14] Another cried, "Better to starve fighting than to starve working.[15]

When Joe Ettor, the labor organizer for the Industrial Workers of the World, asked him to go to Lawrence, Giovannitti was secretary of the Italian Socialist Federation and editor of the radical journal *Il Proletario*.[16]

Lawrence, Massachusetts, a city of 86,000, had 74,000 inhabitants born abroad or to parents who were. Immigrants from fifty-one countries, spoke forty-five languages; most were inarticulate in English. The largest ethnic group was Italian.[17]

The mill owners were confident language barriers, Old World animosities, cultural and political differences would effectively prevent unified action by the mill workers.[18]

Joe Ettor, however, was fluent in English, Italian and Polish, and understood Hungarian and Yiddish. Arturo had mastered Latin, French, English and Italian.[19]

Between them, they rallied the workers, set up a strike committee with representatives from each ethnic group, opened soup kitchens and distribution points for food and funds from sympathizers all over the United States.[20]

It was the first strike of its kind. Unskilled, uneducated, unorganized workers marched in bitter cold and snow singing "The Internationale," "The Marseillaise," "Few of Them are Scabbing It," "In the Good Old Picket Line" and other labor songs. The famous rallying cry of the women, "We want bread and roses, too" was later set to music by James Oppenheim.[21]

Often the strikers gathered at the Lawrence Common to hear their leaders. It was there Arturo Giovannitti gave his "Sermon on the Common" which satirized the more famous one with its structure and message:[22]

And he, seeing the multitudes, opened his mouth, and taught them, saying,

> Blessed are the strong in freedom's spirit: for theirs is
> the kingdom of the earth.
> Blessed are they that mourn their martyred dead: for
> they shall avenge them upon their murderers and
> be comforted.
> Blessed are the rebels: for they shall reconquer the
> earth.
> Blessed are they which do hunger and thirst after
> equality: for they shall eat the fruit of their labor.

The main theme of Giovannitti's poetry is class war and labor exploitation, as evidenced in another passage of the same
poem:

> Therefore I say unto you, Banish fear from your
> hearts, dispel the mists of ignorance from your
> minds, arm your yearning with your strength, your
> vision with your will, and open your eyes and be-
> hold.
> Do not moan, do not submit, do not kneel, do not pray,
> do not wait.
> Think, dare, do, rebel, fight—ARISE![23]

The following Monday morning, a freezing January day, the
mill workers gathered at the mill gates to keep scabs from
working. There they were hit with icy blasts from the fire
hoses wielded by the militia.[24]

Giovannitti organized relief efforts for the strikers and continued writing and speaking. In the Syrian church on January
21st, he told those gathered, "No one cares for you, nobody is
interested in you...Nobody has any interest in your conditions...to raise you to the dignity of manhood and womanhood...you can hope in no one but yourselves. It is only by
your own power, your own determined will, your own solidarity, that you can rise to better things."

It was the solidarity of the workers, prohibited by city authorities from gathering in front of the mills, who devised the
moving picket line and became an endless chain of strikers
determined no one would work in the mills. Though maligned,
beaten, arrested and jailed, they rejoined their fellow workers
as soon as they were released.[25]

On January 29th, the police and militia clashed with the
strikers. Anna LoPezzi was killed. The police charged Joseph

Caruso with the slaying. Joe Ettor and Arturo Giovannitti
were arrested as accomplices and charged with inciting
Caruso. Neither had met Caruso until they shared the same
jail cell. All three were miles away from the scene of the murder, but the authorities wanted Ettor and Giovannitti removed, reasoning the strike would end without their leadership.[26]

In jail, Giovannitti indicted the goddess of the common weal
who had once had "planted her flags, Against the er-
mine...who now:

> When night with velvet-sandaled feet
> Stole in her chamber's solitude,
> Behold: she lay there naked, lewd,
> A drunken harlot of the street,
> With withered breasts and shaggy hair
> Soiled by each wanton, frothy kiss,
> Between a sergeant of police
> And a decrepit millionaire.[27]

Giovannitti and Ettor remained in jail without bail from
January 30th to September 30th. Their cells became study
halls where they read and discussed the contents of the warden's library. Sympathizers sent them volumes of Paine, Car-
lyle, Shelley, Byron and Kant. One Harvard student sent an
annotated edition of Shakespeare though other Harvard militia men rode their horses through the streets of Lawrence,
given leave and academic credit for "having a fling at those
people."[28]

While 20,000 marched continuously through the streets, Joe
Ettor celebrated his twenty-seventh birthday—in jail. Arturo's wishes were expressed in a poem written for the occasion:

> Well, Joe, my good friend, though we cannot pretend
> That we're happy we still can regale,
> We can laugh and be merry, though claret and sherry
> Are so scarce to us, even in jail...
> Let us drink a new toast to the dear Woolen trust,
> To the legions of "Country and God,"
> To the great Christian cause and the wise, noble laws,
> And to all who cry out for our blood;
> Let us drink to the health of the old Commonwealth,

To the Bible and code in one breath,
And let's so propitiate both the church and the state
That they'll grant us a cheerful, quick death...[29]
During the long months of incarceration without bail, under
a statute not invoked since the Civil War conscription riots,
Giovannitti translated Pouget's *Sabotage* from French to
English and wrote a thirty-six page introduction to the slim
volume in which he disagreed with Pouget's advocacy of de-
struction and violence during labor struggles, advocating instead non-violent means of sabotage to deal with labor troubles.[30]

For Giovannitti, an "eye for an eye" meant "an unfair day's
work for an unfair day's pay." He advocated reduction of out-
put, "a simple expedient of war... to be used only in time of actual warfare with sobriety and moderation, and to be laid
aside when truce intervened."[31]

During the long months of his imprisonment, the strike was
led by Bill Haywood, the flamboyant I.W.W. leader, along
with Elizabeth Gurley Flynn and Carlo Tresca. It was Haywood who asked Arturo to write about "16th century courts
trying to solve 20th century problems. "The Cage," Arturo's
war with history, an indictment of the evils which permeate
the social fabric, was the result.[32]

In the poem, "Ettor," Caruso and Giovannitti are symbolized in a green iron cage—the iron cage in which the three
were tethered during their trial—and surrounded in the
courtroom by moldering tomes, pre-sided over by an old hoary
man on the "fireless and god-less altar:

> For of naught they knew, but of what was written in
> the old, yellow books. And all the joys and the pains
> and the loves and hatreds and furies and labors
> and strifes of man, all the fierce and divine pas-
> sions that battle and rage in the heart of man,
> never entered into the great greenish room but to
> sit in the green iron cage. [33]

His most famous poem, "The Walker," in which he depicts
the long months of captivity on himself and the 200 other
prisoners, ensured for Giovannitti the title of the workers'
poet:

> I hear footsteps over my head all night...

> For infinite are the nine feet of a prison cell, and end-
> less is the march of him who walks between the yel-
> low brick wall and the red iron gate, thinking
> things that cannot be chained and cannot be locked,
> but that wander far away in the sunlit world, each
> in a wild pilgrimage goal...
> Who walks? I know not...
> One-two-three-four: four paces and the wall.
> One-two-three-four: four paces and the iron gate...
> The democracy of reason has leveled all the two hun-
> dred minds to the common surface of the same
> thought.
> I, who have never killed, think like the murderer;
> I, who have never stolen, reason like the thief;
> I think, reason, wish, hope, doubt, wait like the hired
> assassin, the embezzler, the forger, the counter-
> feiter, the incestuous, the raper, the drunkard, the
> prostitute, the pimp, I, I who used to think of love
> and life and flowers and song and beauty and the
> ideal...
> All my ideas, my thoughts, my dreams are congealed
> in a little key of shiny brass....
> Stop, rest, sleep, my brother, for the dawn is well nigh
> and it is not the key alone that can throw open the
> gate.[34]

When at last the trial neared its end, Giovannitti, in his address to the jury, spoke of the famed New England traditions which led to the American Revolution, the same traditions contradicted by the Salem witch trials, then went on to comment on the wage system and the "domination of one man by another before Lincoln's Emancipation Proclamation:

> ...But I say you cannot be half free and half slave and
> economically all the working class in the United
> States are as much slaves now as the negroes were
> forty and fifty years ago; because the man that owns
> the tools wherewith another man works, the man that
> owns the house where this man lives, the man that
> owns the factory where this man wants to go to work-
> controls the bread that that man eats and therefore
> owns and controls his mind, his body, his heart and

his soul...

Current Opinion reported in their January, 1913 issue, that Giovannitti's idealism and mastery of words held those in the courtroom spellbound, evident in this excerpt:

What about the better and nobler humanity where there shall be no more slaves, where no man will ever be obliged to go on strike in order to obtain fifty cents a week more, where children will not have to starve anymore, where women no more will have to go and prostitute themselves: where at least there will not be any more slavemasters but just one great family of friends and brothers. It may be, gentlemen of the jury that you do not believe that. It may be that we are dreamers; maybe that we are fanatics, Mr. District Attorney. We are fanatics. But yet, so was a fanatic Socrates, who instead of acknowledging the philosophy of the aristocrats of Athens, preferred to drink the poison. And so was a fanatic the Saviour Jesus Christ, who instead of acknowledging that Pilate or that Tiberius was emperor of Rome...preferred the cross between two thieves. And so were all the philosophers and all the dreamers and all the scholars of the Middle Ages who preferred to be burned alive...[35]

The jury deliberated six hours and returned a "Not Guilty" verdict for the three prisoners.

Settled in March, 1912, the Lawrence strike became a milestone in labor history. Twenty thousand unorganized, foreign-born, unskilled, uneducated immigrants (half of whom were women) led by radical labor activists—defeated the city and state governments, militia, police, Pinkertons, Burns men, newspapers and public opinion.[36]

Giovannitti, famed as the workers' poet, went on to become the editor of *Il Fusco*, contributing editor of *The Liberator*, wrote for *The Masses*, was secretary of the Italian Chamber of Labor, a dedicated anti-fascist and author of two volumes of poetry, *Arrows in the Gale* and *When the Cock Crows*.

The Lawrence poems were included in *Arrows in the Gale*. Florence Converse in the June 27, 1914 issue of *The Survey* wrote that the poems were meant, like arrows, "to sting and wound, to let blood; in all the lyrics we hear the Baptist's cry,

'Repent!' "
   Commenting on the unevenness of his poems, she added,
If he has failed to infuse into his English the subtle
Italian grace and passion of a Dante Gabriel Rossetti,
the blame must be laid upon the Pennsylvania coal
mines and the New York slums, our wells of English,
muddy and defiled, from which we have forced him to
drink.
   No doubt the railroad gang, the coal mines, the missons, the
schools of theology he attended had an influence on his poetry
and prose, but it was in Lawrence, Massachusetts that he
composed the words that encapsulate the philosophy of life
that is uniquely Arturo Giovannitti:
   And I believe in Thee also, Oh Lord, whoever Thou
   art, wherever Thou art, whatever Thy name, Oh Love,
   Oh Truth, Oh Father and Mother of all, not only because Thou seest above and beyond my mortal eyes,
   but because I also need in my pride and pain to bend
   and kneel before a Supreme Piety that will illumine,
   even if it does not explain to me, the terrible mystery
   of life.[37]

FOOTNOTES

1 Joyce L. Kornbluh, ed., *Rebel Voices: An IWW Anthology* (Ann Arbor, Mich., 1964), pp. 193-195.

2 *Dictionary of American Biography*, Supplement 6 (1956-1960) Charles Scribner's Sons, New York, 1980, pp. 238-9.

3 "A Poet of the I.W.W.'" *The Outlook*, pp. 504-6.

4 *Arrows in the Gale.* Frederick C. Bursch, 1914

5 *Ibid.*

6 Kornbluh, p. 159.

7 *Ibid.*, p. 159.

8 Donald B. Cole, *Immigrant City: Lawrence, Massachusetts. 1845-1921* (Chapel Hill, N. C., 1963), p. 75.

9 *Ibid.*, p. 75.

10 Philip. S. Foner, *Women and the American Labor Movement.* The

Free Press New York, 1979, p. 428.

[11] Kornbluh, p. 158.

[12] Foner, p. 428.

[13] U. S. Congress, House, Hearings on Strike in Lawrence, Mass., House Document no. 671, p. 382.

[14] Cole, p. 187.

[15] Foner, p. 429.

[16] *Ibid.*, p. 430.

[17] Cole, p. 95.

[18] *Ibid.* p. 11.

[19] Kornbluh, p. 159.

[20] *Ibid* p. 160

[21] Kornbluh, pp. 160, 173, 174, 180, 195.

[22] *Arrows*, p. 73.

[23] *Ibid.*, p. 77.

[24] Cole, p. 180.

[25] Foner, pp. 430-431.

[26] Kornbluh, p. 160.

[27] Giovannitti, "The Republic."

[28] Kornbluh, p. 159.

[29] "To Joseph J. Ettor, On his 27th Birthday," *Arrows* pp. 70-72.

[30] Emile Pouget, *Sabotage.*

[31] *Ibid.*, pp. 22-23.

[32] "A Poet of the I.W.W.," p. 504.

[33] *Arrows.* p. 88.

[34] *Ibid.*

[35] Address to the Jury, Salem, Mass.

[36] Foner, pp. 437-439.

[37] Giovannitti, "Credo."

BIBLIOGRAPHY

BOOKS

Cole, Donald, *Immigrant City: Lawrence, Massachusetts. 1845-1921* University of North Carolina Press, Chapel Hill, 1963.

Dictionary of American Biography, Supplement 6 (1956-1960). Charles Scribner's Sons, New York, 1980, pp. 238-9

Foner, Philip S., *Women and the American Labor Movement.* The Free Press, New York, 1979, pp. 426-458

Giovannitti, Arturo, *Arrows in the Gale.* Frederick C. Bursch, New York, 1914.

MAGAZINES

"A Poet of the I.W.W., *The Outlook,* pp. 504-6. Converse, Florence, Review, *The Survey.* June 27, 1914, pp. 346-7.

DOCUMENTS

U. S., Congress, House, *Hearings on Strike in Lawrence Mass.* House Document No. 671.

Italian/American Women on the Frontier: Sister Blandina Segale on the Santa Fe Trail

Diane Raptosh
College of Idaho

Most immigrant Italian women in mid-nineteenth-century America were neither expected nor allowed to work outside the home except when economic circumstances forced them to do so in order to contribute to the family income. Yet in the early 1860s, Rosa Maria Segale insisted on the right to choose her own vocational destination. "As soon as I am old enough," she announced as a pre-teen to her father, "I shall be a Sister of Charity." In 1866 at age 16, she entered the Sisters of Charity Motherhouse in Cincinnati, Ohio, and became "Sister Blandina" (Segale 3).

While she chose her own vocation, she had little choice in the matter of location. Nevertheless, when in 1872 she received word that she was being missioned to Trinidad, Sister Blandina was enthusiastic. She expresses her zeal in an early entry in her journal of correspondence, which late in her life was published in book form as *At the End of the Santa Fe Trail*. She addresses this as well as all of the subsequent entries to her sister in Cincinnati, also a Sister of Charity, known as Sister Justina. Sister Blandina makes it clear to her that

> ...I was delighted to make the sacrifice... Neither (my superior, Mother Josephine, nor I)... could find Trinidad on the map except on the island of Cuba. So we concluded that Cuba was my destination (12-13).

Upon hearing that her destination was not an island in the Caribbean but a small mining town in southwestern Colorado to which she would travel by rail, in winter, unaccompanied but for some cowboys possibly heading the same way, Sister Blandina was undaunted.

Perhaps more important for present introductory purposes

than Sister Blandina's exceptional characteristics are the patterns of migration and family in her early life, which mirror those of many first-generation Italian women in the U.S. In 1854, the Segale family gave up a life of "overseeing orchards" in Genoa, leaving politically volatile Italy for Cincinnati. Here the family of six, living in one room, hoped to eke out an existence on Ohio's land. Subsist they did, starting with a family-run corner fruit stand. In time the stand expanded to a confectionary store, a line of business known to include numerous Italians among its ranks (Weatherford 114).

Obviously we have no way to determine what Sister Blandina's life would have been like had she chosen or been recruited to stay at home and work in the family store. Had she done so, she no doubt would have been under the close supervision of her father, given the strictly patriarchal order of the typical Italian family. So supervised in her work for the immediate good of the family, Sister Blandina very likely would have had to sacrifice many of her autonomous needs and accomplishments: Hers may well have become a life of self-nullification, which Helen Barolini suggests is the end result of Italian/American women leading sacrificial lives (11). Her goals—and much of her *self*—submerged in this hypothetical scenario, Sister Blandina would have derived less spiritual and intellectual fulfillment and far less financial independence working at the family store than working for the church. Doing the former, she would not have been likely to receive even symbolic recognition as a jobholder. Similarly, had she decided to pursue alternative "homework"—to take in laundry or boarders, or to take up making artificial flowers, weaving, crocheting, or making shoes—as did many other Italian American women, she would have gained little acknowledgement relative to that she gained pursuing her chosen line of work. What wages she might have earned as a "homeworker" probably would have gone into the family account, while in her chosen vocation she remained more or less economically autonomous, enjoying cognitive and imaginative freedoms she might never have realized at home.

The relative freedom of mind Sister Blandina obtained in her work and travels resembles that of some nineteenth-century "mill girls" who left home to work in New England's textile mills. As Thomas Dublin has demonstrated in *Women at Work*, most young women who went to work in the mills at Lowell, Massachusetts, did so for reasons that pertain to, yet go beyond, sheer economic need. Dublin argues that while many of these women *did* have to contribute to the support of their families, "they were generally not sent to the mills to supplement low family incomes but went of their own accord for other reasons"(35). One such "other reason" is described by Sally Rice, who at age 17 left her home in Vermont to take a job "working out":

I have got so that by next summer if I could stay (at the mill) I could begin to lay up something... I am almost 19 years old. I must of course have something of my own before many more years have passed over my head. And where is that something to come from if I go home and earn nothing? (Dublin 37)

Despite the fact that work at the mills was arduous if not dehumanizing, young women like Rice often preferred it to what were sometimes tyrannical conditions working at home. Rice left home to earn "something of my own," which was obviously not possible in the family economy of her father's farm (Dublin 37). Like Rice, Sister Blandina was determined to earn something of *her* own, though with rather different ends in mind.

That Sister Blandina's mother, Giovanna, saw beyond purely familistic concerns can account largely for the fact that Sister Blandina ventured into domains less standard for the nineteenth-century Italian/American woman. Like many Italian mothers, Giovanna concerned herself almost singularly with the issue of her children's future—all of them in the new land daughters; the only son had stayed in Italy "to complete his studies" (Segale 2). Yet Giovanna's concern for her children's welfare differed in a significant way from that of most Italian mothers: She saw education as a necessary element of her daughters' lives. In spite of the Segale's early language difficulties and near destitution, Giovanna hired an English teacher for her daughters and somehow managed to pay for the lessons (Segale 2). Education was a gift few Italian women were given either in the "Old Country" or the U.S. in the nineteenth century. As one 59-year-old woman remembered, in

Italy "girls never went to school, but were made to work" (Weatherford 215). Not only did Sister Blandina receive language training, she attended Catholic grammar schools and later The Mount Saint Vincent Academy in Cincinnati. Choosing nuns as mentors and the convent as the sphere to supersede the home would not necessarily have marked Sister Blandina a defector from family expectation and tradition. Indeed, it was generally a source of family and community pride when a woman became a nun (Weatherford 226). But while Sister Blandina was adamant about her right to choose to do so, many other Italian women lacked that kind of tenacity. Some Italian families so feared independence in women that they frowned upon, even forbade, convent careers. As one Italian woman admits,

> I got married like everyone else. I did what was expected of me. The only other possibility I had considered as a young girl was to become a nun, but my parents were against this. Even my grandparents, who were very kind and loving, told me to pray for a husband. (Weatherford 227)

It hardly comes as a surprise to find that the Italians among Sister Blandina's family and friends were leery of her independence and aghast the day she told them of her assignment to travel alone to frontier Colorado. "Mother kept open house all day," Sister Blandina recalls, and

> [F]riends came in groups. Mr. Leverone and bride, his mother and the bride's mother, Mrs. Garibaldi, the Misses Gardelli and a host of others. Mrs. Garibaldi threatened to take off my habit. I said, 'Hands off!' Have you any right to detain Mary if John wishes to take her to California?'
>
> 'Oh, that is different[,]' [Mrs. Garibaldi said.] 'Yes, as different as heaven and earth. I have chosen my portion, Mary has chosen hers, each abides by her choice.' (15)

Sister Blandina did exactly that, only her mother refused to interfere with her decision. Giovanna's refusal to intervene coupled with Sister Blandina's ultimate defiance of her father's wishes constituted at least a significant challenge to the patriarchal Italian family: A good father and husband was meant to be both family head and adviser; wives and children, considered inferior, were expected to vow service and respect to that head (Yans-McLaughlin 223).

The narrative of Sister Blandina's last encounter with her father before she left for the train station suggests that for the first time her expected service and respect were on the wane:

[F]ather managed to see me alone. He took hold of me and asked, 'Have I ever denied you anything?'

I signified no.

'You have never disobeyed me in your life?' I assented.

'Now I command you—you must not go on this far away mission! Are you going?'

'Yes, father.' He let go the hold on my arm and walked toward the door. Not without my seeing his tears falling fast. He did not realize his hold on my arm gave me pain. (16)

The language here gives way to symbolic as well as physical removal. His psychological hold having proved ineffectual, his grip having given her a pain, her father approaches the door. Next sentence, next paragraph finds Sister Blandina in the railway station

at St. Louis between train time, [where] I got off to purchase a pair of arctics. I saw several Italian women selling fruit. One of them had a daughter standing near. (16)

No doubt that image gave Sister Blandina cause for reflection. Once back on the train, she pauses, attempting to articulate the effect of leaving home, family, even perhaps fruit stand and confectionary store:

That I succeeded in dignifiedly getting away from home is Thy Grace, oh, my God!

Forty-two persons accompanied me to the train, among them friends of old, but my purpose never faltered, not even in shadow... I see one trait strong in me, the straight service of God. Not the father whom I had never seen cry, nor the most patient, dearest mother whose heart is crushed at my being sent alone... (17)

That she escapes her paternalistic home, dignity intact, and disavows any responsibility to "serve" the family head or to sacrifice her aims in the name of benefitting the family unit is no small task. And it may be said that she merely forsakes one patriarchal order for another gravely masculinist, though otherworldly, regime. Yet neither feminist critic, ethnic historian, nor scholar of the frontier can deny she deserves critical attention. Few could argue with the fact she brought herself remarkably far geographically, spiritually, and intellectually, given that her nineteenth-century world was strictly circumscribed by ethnic, social, and gender-specific mores, as well as by bloodlines meant to keep men in authoritative positions and women submissive.

To an educated Italian woman coming of age in the mid-to-late 1860s, the convent must surely have seemed an attractive option. After all, where the nuns were so were the regions of learning. A product of this learning environment, Sister Blandina no doubt viewed these women as effectual agents in the world outside the home. As a youth she had observed them working among the sick and orphaned and had known that during the Civil War the nuns nursed soldiers on the battlefield (3). We are told by contemporary nuns and ex-nuns of the profundity of this impression of nuns which many Catholic-educated girls have shared. One ex-nun who grew up in the 1940s and attended Catholic schools throughout her youth explains that her perception of nuns as teachers seemingly larger than life was "typical of most students of that era... As a teacher myself, I now marvel at the amount of time the nuns spent with us in spite of their enormously crowded schedules" (Curb and Manahan 84). Echoing the words of Sister Blandina are those from one Virginia Apuzzo, who joined the order Sister Blandina joined (Sisters of Charity) precisely one century later, in 1966. Raised in an Italian family, and also a product of a Catholic education, Apuzzo recalls that in a time as near to ours as 1966, she believed a woman of her background had few alternatives. And, like Sister Blandina, Apuzzo *told* her father she was

> entering the convent[.] [H]e asked, 'What for?' Being the oldest daughter and grandchild in my Italian working-class family both pulled me toward and held me back from the convent. My mother had already

had a nervous breakdown. I knew I didn't want to get married, go insane, join the military, or go to jail....Where else could a woman in my day go to escape Con Edison and the A and P? (Curb and Manahan 285)

The fact that God emerges as the father figure and husband of sorts Sister Blandina finally opts for proves significant on even the most mundane level. *This* father, however omnipresent "spiritually," is forever absent physically. And as a quasi-husband figure he is conspicuously so, especially when Sister Blandina finds herself in the likes of the Colorado Territory or New Mexico—land intended, mythologically at any rate, not for women traveling alone but for men more rugged than most.

In spiritual terms, to be sure, Sister Blandina has God as father *in absentia*. But in her day-to-day life on the frontier she obviously had to take care of herself. Time and again she proves herself a willing pioneer, as, for example, when she receives a message that she and another Sister are to leave Trinidad for Santa Fe:

Both of us are ready to go when the conveyance comes to the Convent door. So this pioneer will still be in advance of the railroad... Protests from friends come in at every hour in effect to prevent our leaving. How useless!...(79)

Later in this passage we find priests, Italian citizens of Cincinnati, and various friends offering what promises to be a better course for Sister Blandina; yet she persists on her own. Thus proving herself an eager adventurer, Sister Blandina effectively dismantles one of the three most common stereotypes of the pioneering woman: the refined lady. The lady, who may be a missionary, a schoolteacher, or merely a woman with some civilized tastes, is usually perceived as being too genteel for the rough and tumble West. She is either uncomfortable, unhappy, or is driven literally crazy by the frontier. Usually the only way she can prove her gentility is to become a victim (Armitage and Jameson 12). The other two images that fail fully to accommodate Sister are those of the uncomplaining helpmate and the bad woman (Armitage and Jameson 12). Obviously Sister Blandina would have been hard-pressed to pull off the latter image. But it is useful to explore momentarily the figures of the lady and the helpmate. Doing so, however, we must keep in mind the unfortunate fact that there is at least a kernel of truth in each of these stereotypes, particularly in the images of the lady-as-reluctant-pioneer and the tireless helpmate. Both usually come west unwillingly and at a husband's insistence. In the process they leave behind, again, reluctantly, friends and family—a nexus of support groups (Armitage and Jameson 12).

Exemplifying the workworn but uncomplaining helpmate is one Amelia Stewart Knight. She traveled from Monroe County, Iowa, to the Oregon Territory with her husband and seven children in 1853, keeping a diary throughout most of the trip. What is never mentioned in her entries is that at the start of her journey she is already in the first trimester of another pregnancy. This unstated fact in mind, one is astonished all the more at an entry such as the following:

Friday, July 15th. Last night I helped get supper and went to bed too sick to eat any myself. Had fever all night and all day. It is sundown and the fever has left me. I am able to creep around and look at things and brighten up a little.... (Schlissel 209)

Addressing the fact of insufficient emotional supports to be had on the Overland crossing to California in 1862, one Jane Gould Tourtillott remarks on her stay in Humboldt City that

[I]t does not seem like a good place for women to stay, there are only four families here, the rest are single men. We came on six or eight miles and stopped.... (I am just as homesick as I can be.) I chanced to make this remark and Albert (my husband) has written it down.... (Schlissel 228)

Tourtillot made the journey with her husband and two small sons.

An almost unavoidable fact about the woman-as-helpmate is that usually her frontier experience came at the most inconvenient time in her life cycle. Thus married to men enthusiastic about bountiful lands lying west, these women were often pregnant or vulnerable to pregnancy in a period when contraceptives were at best unreliable and at worst unknown or thought immoral (Schlissel 4).

Sister Blandina proves to have been in the enviable position of being able to go west *willingly*—not as the disinclined wife keeping a stiff upper lip. What is more significant, though self-evident, is that being pregnant, giving birth, and raising as well as burying seemingly numberless children on the frontier were hardships Sister Blandina did not herself endure, as did so many other pioneering women. Nor did Sister Blandina come close to being driven delirious by the open spaces. Quite the contrary: Invigorated by her travels, fulfilled by her various religious and community duties, Sister Blandina appears to have lived among the best of the frontier worlds possible for women at that time.

To be sure, a single woman travelling alone on the frontier in turn-of-the-century America was rarity enough.[1] Lillian Schlissel, who collected diaries of women who travelled on the Overland Trail, found that of 96 diarists whom she considered in *Women's Diaries of the Westward Journey*, only two are by women travelling husbandless (99). One such woman left scant information about the trip. The other, Rebecca Ketcham, had substantial financial backing for the trip and was accompanied from Ithaca, New York, to Oregon by a party of people, among whom were men, many of them well-to-do (99). Little wonder, then, that Ketcham might be counted among that doubly rare breed of women who travelled and lived in the west without a husband and derived fulfillment doing so.

Clearly, Sister Blandina should figure prominently among such fulfilled pioneering female exemplars. Even without benefactors backing her, she was able to bring her visions to fruition. Indeed, she did everything that she as a child admired the nuns in her community doing: She cared for the sick and orphaned, taught numerous groups of people—Indians, Mexicans, Catholics and non-Catholics; the poor and the rich; the elderly and the very young. And, like the Sisters preceding her, she ended up nursing individuals on the battlefield. Sister Blandina's patients, though, were not victims of the Civil War but of scalpings or of gunshot wounds suffered in frontier violence.

The only other pioneering woman whose lifestyle and level

of fulfillment can compare to those of Sister Blandina is the late frontier figure, the single woman homesteader. She was no man's helpmate, and usually had behind her an education and cultural background which did not hinder her from "going it alone" and enjoying it (Armitage and Jameson 12). These homesteaders, more often than any other westering women, made claims to being happy, to having good neighbors, and to living as "one big family" (Armitage and Jameson 174). These single women often viewed homesteading as a personal adventure; an excerpt from one such homesteader's autograph album illustrates this point:

> We cannot be happier than we have been here... Can you not almost remember every day from the first, what has happened: Our laughing, singing, playing, working, our company, etc. (Armitage and Jameson 174)

Attracted to homesteading by the independence that proving up a claim offered, these women enjoyed the sense of com a lifestyle afforded as well (Armitage and Jameson 174).

Sister Blandina must also have enjoyed a similar feeling of independence in addition to what was very likely a pervasive sense of good will and community spirit among the Sisters with whom she worked—a sense twentieth-century feminists describe as *sisterhood*. In a September, 1879, entry, she attempts to express this sentiment to her sister:

> I want to tell you, dear Sister Justina, the genuine charity of this mission makes me forget the hardships attached to it.
>
> Since I arrived, January, 1877, I have not heard a murmur of complaint. Our urgent needs are many, but we are all cheerful and happy. (142)

No doubt Sister Blandina's mission entailed a good deal of sacrifice, hard work, and of course, religious commitment. Yet it also allowed her more freedom—psychic and physical—than her average Italian/American female counterpart, and than many other women in that era, for that matter. Hers, too, was a life of unexpected symmetries—one which balanced solitude with community, contemplation with action, quiescence with adventure. The following passage recounting the course of events on a January day in 1880 is typical:

> Six o'clock. As we were praying our beads in the
> Community room I saw a big blaze from the hospital
> chimney above the rooms where the last patients were
> brought in. I made a spring, saying at the same time,
> 'Mother of Mercy, help us!' I went to the convalescent
> ward and told all who were able to form in line to
> carry water for me to the second story. I sent one man
> for a bucket of salt, with instructions to bring the salt
> to me before the men handed me the water. I marvel
> how composedly I acted, because the thought upper-
> most in my mind was that the last patients will be
> cremated if the fire is not extinguished quickly. (148)

That she implored the Madonna to intervene in the midst of
this emergency did not prevent Sister Blandina from spring-
ing to action herself, as well as instructing others to do likewise.

In another episode in which Sister Blandina anticipates a
trip on the plains from Trinidad to Santa Fe, she proves herself to be very much like the "ranch men" whom she'd earlier
described as ever "ready for any emergency":

> We were told that 'Billy (the Kid)'s gang was dodging
> around, and we expect they will attack us tonight.' I
> proposed to Sister that we pray our beads out on the
> open plain... some distance from the house. Sister
> made no objection, but the Doctor did. However we
> said our beads and loitered around for some time.
> When retiring time drew near, both Doctor and Mr.
> Staab (our traveling partners) came to say they would
> remain at our door armed, 'So do not be alarmed if you
> hear firing; we shall protect you.'
>   'Very kind of you, gentlemen, but if you take my
> advice you will secure a good night's rest and be ready
> for an early start.' The Doctor looked disgusted at my
> want of perception. (97)

One is left with the impression that her male companions
"want" perception, that they would do well to look about for a
less bungled brand of gallantry.

Later, on this same journey, Mr. Staab and the Doctor spot
someone skimming over the plains. Composure intact, Sister
Blandina notices that,

by this time both gentlemen were feverishly excited. I
looked at the men and could not but admire the reso-
lute expression which meant 'to conquer or die!' I
broke the spell by saying:
'If the comer is a scout from the gang, our chance is
in remaining passive. I would suggest putting revolvers out of sight.' They looked to me as if to say
that a woman is incapable of realizing extreme danger....
'Please put your revolvers away,' I said in a voice
which was neither begging nor aggressive, but was
the outward expression of my conviction that we had
nothing to fear. Spontaneously the weapons went under cover... As the rider came from the rear of the vehicle, ... I shifted my big bonnet so that when he did
look he could see the Sisters. Our eyes met; he raised
his large-brimmed hat with a wave and a bow, ... and
then stopped to give us some of his wonderful antics
on broncho maneuvers. The rider was the famous
'Billy, the Kid!' (98)

The look in her eye calms; the tone of her voice is rich with
conviction yet never "aggressive." Indeed, her very *being* on
the frontier seems to palliate men too quick to the draw.

One is reminded here of another group of nineteenth-century American women who had a similar effect, often on men,
in the world of wage-earning work. Many times affiliated with
lay religious organizations, these women—usually protestant,
non-immigrant, and middle- to upper-class—ventured outside
the home also. They did so not in explicit religious garb, but
armed, rather, with what they were told were their inherent
"hallowed sympathies" and "Peaceful offices," which rendered
them—and all women—the moral and spiritual guardians of
humanity (Cott 67). With these gifts, which came to be known
as the canon of domesticity, these middle-class women took to
the road, as it were, with their nurturing potential. The canon
of domesticity promised, among other things, that all of the
redemptive, indeed paradisal, features of home could be had
away from home—so long as women followed certain rather
restricted paths out the front door. Among the most appealing
options, the canon of domesticity offered a rationale for

women to become teachers, missionaries, and writers. Since women had always taught children within the family and in small schools, that job remained compatible with subsequent marriage and promised to enhance a woman's moral sensibilities (Kessler-Harris 56).

We are left wondering why—in the abundant literature on women in the nineteenth century, more particularly in the works treating the canon of domesticity (or the cult of true womanhood, as the phenomenon is alternately referred to)[2]— is there no mention of Sister Blandina, or indeed, of Sisters like Sister Blandina? Where, likewise, in today's literature on *sisterhood* in the nineteenth century is there word of Sister Blandina? It seems that the notion of *sisterhood* for that era tends to include only the self-conscious and idealized concept of female friendship such as existed often in Protestant New England from the late eighteenth through the mid-nineteenth century (Cott 160). Of particular interest about these New England friends is that they infused their friendships with the spirit of Christianity, what with the eighteenth-century emphasis on religious affections having created new possibilities for women's personal relations as well as for their religious leadership (Cott 171). Yet what of the Catholic woman— or the nun—in this scheme of sisterhood? Is she not Christian? Is "Protestantism" taken to be tantamount to "Christianity" throughout the pages devoted to the topic? Indeed, the women referred to in these works treating sisterhood are almost always American-born Wasps, ranging from members of the middle class to the well-to-do. To be sure, feminist historians have combed the diaries and correspondence of such women. But the diaries of Sister Blandina have yet to be used to shed light on nineteenth-century women's issues like the cult of true womanhood and the notion of sisterhood, though it is clear that the possibilities abound: Sister Blandina is a nun among sisters, writing letters to her sister who is also a Sister.

And, of course, taking the discussions of sisterhood among New England Wasp women as cue, one is tempted to see Sister Blandina's epistolary relations with her sister as well as her bonds with the nuns as having enormous feminist potential. Indeed, one is hard-pressed *not* to see among Sister

Blandina and the various Sisters the beginnings of a feminist subculture—their alliances having provided all the women involved a rich source of strength and identity. Yet we must stop short of ascribing what we know as "feminist" motives to Sister Blandina, since such an "-ism" would have had little importance for her.

One also wonders whether the issue of gender has become rooted, as it should, in the works of ethnic historians— whether Sister Blandina and women like her have had their histories told. And last but not least, we must look to the historiography of the American frontier. Finally, the West is not merely a land of men among men; we can now read about women on that landscape, thanks to such works as Schlissel's *Women's Diaries of the Westward Journey*; *The Women's West*, edited by Susan Armitage and Elizabeth Jameson; and various works by Glenda Riley, among them *Women and Indians on the Frontier*. Indeed, even the imaginations of women have made it into the lore of the frontier, with Annette Kolodny's *The Land Before Her*. Yet in none of these works is there even passing mention of Sister Blandina.

We are fortunate, therefore, to have Sister Blandina's *At the End of the Santa Fe Trail* at our disposal. Feminist scholars, ethnic historians, and students of the American frontier would find the work of enormous interest. They may consider it the account of how one nineteenth-century Italian/American woman lived a remarkably autonomous life, making her presence felt in her immediate surroundings while inscribing her vision on the landscape. Or, if one is tempted to doubt the veracity of her account, as at least one scholar has,[3] her work is of interest for the ways in which it oh so gently chips away at masculinist frontier configurations. Doing so it sets forth new lore from a seldom-heard point of view: that of an immigrant Italian Catholic woman gone a'westering.

Footnotes

[1] It is important to keep in mind those women from other countries who were recruited to travel, usually alone, to the western frontier. For them, the journey had little to do with "adventuring" and everything to do with financial survival. Among these women, for example, were many European women recruited to be domestic servants on the Canadian prairies. See Milton's essay on these "Essential Servants" for a discussion of the frontier lives of these women.

[2] Barbara Welter named the "cult of true womanhood" in the article of that title, while another alternative phrase, "cult of domesticity" was introduced by Aileen Kraditor. Nancy Cott uses the term "canon of domesticity" to refer to the same set of social attitudes about womanhood in the nineteenth century. Mary Ryan's chapter entitled "Mothers of Civilization: The Common Woman, 1830-1860" discusses this same notion. Ryan's chapter is particularly useful for its treatment of women in the American West: She details the process whereby many female pioneers carried westward many of the new attitudes about domesticity and "feminine manners" which they had acquired in their eastern homes.

[3] Andrew Rolle quotes from the "good sister's" passage illustrating her meeting with Billy the Kid, noting that Ramon Adams, one of "the Kid's" biographers, casts doubt on the accuracy of the information and dating of Sister Blandina's meeting with the bandit.

Works Cited

Adams, Ramon. *A Fitting Death for Billy the Kid*. Norman, OK: University of Oklahoma Press, 1960.

Adams, Ramon. *Burs Under the Saddle*. Norman, OK: University of Oklahoma Press, 1964.

Apuzzo, Virginia. "Grace to Empower." *Lesbian Nuns Breaking the Silence*. Ed. Rosemary Curb and Nancy Manahan. New York: Warner, 1985. 285-287.

Armitage, Susan. "Through Women's Eyes: A New View of the West." *The Women's West*. Ed. Susan Armitage and Elizabeth Jameson. Norman, Okla.: University of Oklahoma Press, 1987. 9-18.

Barolini, Helen, ed. *The Dream Book: An Anthology of Writings by*

Italian American Women. New York: Schocken Books, 1985.

Cott, Nancy F. *The Bonds of Womanhood.* New Haven and London: Yale University Press, 1977.

Dublin, Thomas. *Women at Work.* New York: Columbia University Press, 1979.

Harris, Katherine. "Homesteading in Northeastern Colorado, 1873-1920: Sex Roles and Women's Experience." *The Women's West.* Ed. Susan Armitage and Elizabeth Jameson. Norman, Okla.: University of Oklahoma Press, 1987. 165-178.

Kessler-Harris, Alice. *Out to Work: A History of Wage-Earning Women in the United States.* New York: Oxford University Press, 1982.

Kolodny, Annette. *The Land Before Her: Fantasy and Experience of the American Frontiers, 1630-1860.* Chapel Hill and London: The University of North Carolina Press, 1984.

Kraditor, Aileen S. *Up from the Pedestal: Selected Writings in the History of American Feminism.* Chicago: Quadrangle Books, 1968.

Milton, Norma J. "Essential Servants: Immigrant Domestics on the Canadian Prairies, 1885-1930." *The Women's West.* Ed. Susan Armitage and Elizabeth Jameson. Norman, Okla.: University of Oklahoma Press, 1987. 207-217.

Quigley, Kate. "Certified Straight." *Lesbian Nuns Breaking the Silence.* Ed. Rosemary Curb and Nancy Manahan. New York: Warner, 1985. 83-91.

Riley, Glenda. *Women and Indians on the Frontier, 1825-1915.* Albuquerque: University of New Mexico Press, 1984.

Rolle, Andrew F. *The Immigrant Upraised: Italian Adventurers and Colonists in an Expanding America.* Norman, Okla.: University of Oklahoma Press, 1968.

Ryan, Mary P. *Womanhood in America: From Colonial Times to the Present.* New York: New Viewpoints, 1975.

Schlissel, Lillian. *Women's Diaries of the Westward Journey.* New York: Schocken Books, 1982.

Segale, Sr. Blandina. *At the End of the Santa Fe Trail.* Milwaukee:

The Bruce Publishing Company, 1948.

Weatherford, Doris. *Foreign and Female: Immigrant Women in America, 1840-1930*. New York: Schocken Books, 1986.

Welter, Barbara. "The Cult of True Womanhood." *American Quarterly* 18 (1966): 151-174.

Yans-McLaughlin, Virginia. *Family and Community: Italian Immigrants in Buffalo, 1880-1930*. Urbana: University of Illinois Press, 1982.

The Scholarship of the AIHA: Past Achievements and Future Perspectives*

Joseph Velikonja
University of Washington, Seattle

At this solemn occasion of the twentieth annual conference of the American Italian Historical Association, it may be worthwhile to look back—as the historians do—and to took forward—as scholars do—and assess the extent to which the Association achieved its intended goals of scholarship. Whatever has been done in the past may continue into the future; maybe not in the same direction, maybe not with the same intensity. But only we can change its course. Established scholars rarely do it. The redirection, if needed, requires new people, with new ideas and new goals.

My colleagues Frank Cavaioli[1] and Rudolph Vecoli[2] preceded me in reviewing both the history of the Association and the progress and achievement of the study of Italians in the United States. I intend to explore the specific role that the AIHA has played as an association and as an assembly of activists in the pursuit of scholarly recognition in American academia.

Frank Cavaioli has traced the roots of the Association and affirmed that the organization did not start as just another association of Italian Americans. The first discussions in the summer of 1965 led to the meeting at LaGuardia Memorial House on December 27, 1966, when the Association was formally constituted by 15 founding members. My professional colleagues felt that the Italian American experiences deserve the scholarly attention of researchers, not only of the Italian Americans. It was noticed that the presence and achieve-

* An abbreviated version of this report was presented at the luncheon meeting of the AIHA annual conference in Chicago, Nov. 14, 1987.

ments of Italian Americans often remain unrecognized among the numerous ethnic minorities, where the Italians are lumped together with other hyphenated white Americans of European descent. Studies of Italian American experiences were already appearing with increasing frequency and the names of Rudolph Vecoli, Silvan Tomasi Remigio Pane, Leonardo Covello, Antonio Pace, Salvatore LaGumina —to mention just a few—were recorded in the scholarly circles. But they worked in isolation.

The multicultural history of the United States came to the forefront in the aftermath of the Civil Rights Movement; the "Roots" and the bicentennial celebrations added new impulses. The slogans of pietisms slowly and reluctantly gave way to documentation and validation.

The American Italian Historical Association was and still is a minute speck in the cultural mosaic of American academia. The Association grew from fifteen founding members to over 100 in 1970, it reached 600 in the early 1980s and counts now almost 500 members. The external recognition of their achievements is slow to come. While the scholarly work is prominently displayed at the annual conferences of the Association and published in the Proceedings, it remains generally confined to the small circle of the initiated. The Association has not yet exhausted all the avenues for successful investigation or for an external recognition of its achievements.

Various publications have claimed to be the voice of the AIHA (*Italian-Americana*, lately *Fra Noi*). Members of the Association are prominent as editors and contributors to a number of books and periodicals that deal with ethnic and migration studies. With these activities they demonstrated the energy and vitality of their convictions and dedication to their scholarship. The Association can claim but a fraction of credit for these accomplishments.

A two-page *Newsletter* in the Spring of 1967 is the first AIHA publication. The first paragraph on the front page states eloquently the purpose of the organization:

> The serious study of the Italian experience in America has been a too long neglected chapter of American history. Aware of this situation a group of historians, sociologists, educators, and other interested persons

from various colleges and universities have met several times in the past few months to discuss the need for an organization which would, on a scholarly level, become an instrument for stimulating the study of the history of the Italians in the United States and Canada.[3] The aims and objectives of serious scholarly research remain to this day the primary focus of the Association.

The *Newsletter* already in its third issue in the Fall of 1967,[4] reports on the scholarly research of its members Frank Cordasco, Leonard Covello, Duane Koenig, and outlines plans for the first annual conference to be chaired by Salvatore LaGumina. Jean Scarpaci, a founding member, became the *Newsletter's* editor. Soon other names join the list: Leonard Moss, Silvano Tomasi, Lucian Iorizzo John Cammett, Andrew Rolle and Rudolph Vecoli, people who two decades later are still prominent among the scholars of the Italian experience.

Browsing through the collection of the *Newsletters* one encounters continuous reminders. Rudy Vecoli stated in his Presidential address on December 1, 1970, published in winter 1971 in the national *Newsletter*:

Through the AIHA we have come to know one another, not always face-to-face, scattered as we are throughout the continent, yet bound together by our common intellectual concern.[5]

He proceeded to outline the principal tasks of the Association:

1. the annual conferences, which constitute "significant contribution to knowledge, instructive and stimulating...";
2. development of joint programs on both sides of the Atlantic;
3. need for a journal of Italian-American Studies;
4. Newsletter as tool and informative source;
5. collection and preservation of the historical records of the Italians in America;
6. development of research tools, access to archival depositories;
7. educational programs, especially in-service courses for teachers in Italian American history.

This program was affirmed again and again by the presidents of the Association, more often as a call for assistance than a document of achievement. Peter Sammartino[6] and Giovanni Schiavo[7] presented additional views at the 1979 meetings at Rutgers University.

Let me say quite emphatically: I embraced these goals of the Association with enthusiasm when invited to join in 1967 and I am pursuing them to these days—as do many of my colleagues in the Association.

The national *Newsletter* is the primary link between members of the Association. Its prominence as an information source to the scholarly community is occasionally obscured by non-academic promotional advertisements and casual commentaries. It should be understood that for the members who for whatever reason do not and cannot attend the annual conferences, the *Newsletter* is the messenger that keeps them in touch with the Association. An expansion of it, by providing what Rudy Vecoli advocated almost twenty years ago,"current bibliography, review essays, and descriptions of research in progress" would bring it in line with similar professional newsletters that abound in the academic circles.

The second and more prominent document of the scholarly work is the set of conference proceedings. The volumes grew in size from 36 pages for the first and the second volume, to the impressive 300 page books in recent years. The 3100 pages contain contributions of 200 authors - the list reads like the Who's Who in American Italian studies: an indisputable document of achievement.[8] The special topics covered by the conferences and by the proceedings range from the assessments of the political life, novels, crime, power and class, radicalism, religion, to reviews of urban and rural life, family and communities, generations and professions, relations with Jews and the Irish, relations between the US and Italy and so on.

The organization and the scholarly work of the Association placed women in the position of deserved prominence before it became fashionable. One third of our regular members are women; fifty women authors are represented in the proceedings. The Italian immigrant woman in North America was the subject of the tenth annual conference in Toronto, evident in the volume of proceedings, edited by Betty Boyd Caroli, Robert Harnee and Lydio Tomasi.[9]

The scholarly activity is a product of individuals. It was not the active and generous financial support of the Italian American community that gave impetus to the research efforts: it was and remains to these days the dedication and enthusiasm of selected individuals that produced the results to which all of us could look with pride and satisfaction. The financial support, nevertheless, came from various organizations for the publication of the Proceedings. Their assistance is properly acknowledged— with gratitude—in the published volumes.

Shortly after the beginning of the Association, with the increased membership more research became associated with the organization. The polished research of earlier years nevertheless stands as an example of erudition side by side with the perceptive studies that appear in the expanded proceedings of more recent years. The attendance at the annual conferences grew from year to year; the increased number of participants, however, is accompanied by a loss of intimacy and personal relations that dominated the earlier gatherings.

The number of books authored by our members is impressive; it includes the names of Iorizzo and Mondello[10], La Sorte[11] and LaGumina[12], Scarpaci[13] and Gumina[14], Mormino[15] and Pozzetta[16], Nelli[17] and Rolle[18], Birnbaum[19] and Tricarico[20], the two Tomasi brothers[21], Marchione[22] and Cordasco[23], Schiavo[24] and Covello[25], Basile Green[26], Barolini[27], Harney[28], Mangione[29] and Martinelli[30], not to mention a rather long list of other authors who at one time or another were members of the Association.

The close relationship between the Association and the Center for Migration Studies enabled numerous professional activities that engaged scholars of Italian American experiences as a groups or as individuals. The promising conference in Florence in 1969[31], the edited volume on Italian Experience in the United States published in 1970[32], the symposia at the Casa Italiana in 1976[33] and at the Columbia University in 1983[34], totally or in part product of the Center's untiring energy, portray findings of numerous members of our Association.

The prospects:

Past achievements are a good indication of future perspectives. As an Association with an historical orientation we are bound to examine the past, including our own; the work ahead nevertheless needs some direction. It might be appropriate to consider various alternatives. As an Association, we cannot undo the past, as a group of scholars with ideas we can influence the future.

It should be evident that I speak from the angle of an external observer. Repeatedly—and sometimes annoyingly—I remind my colleagues about it. The first element of my "external view" is that I live and work in Seattle on the West Coast. Not in San Francisco, nor in Los Angeles, not in "Little Italy" or in an ethnic neighborhood. I am not surrounded by Italian immigrants, I do not move from one Italian heritage festival to another, nor do I fly to Italy on short notice. The Seattle perspective enables me to observe the scene with some detachment and permit me to avoid the immediacy of excitement, frustration or rewards. On the other hand, I lived on the East Coast and in the Midwest and I know Chicago as well or better than many Chicagoans.

The second external aspect is that I am not an Italian American though I am studying the Italians in America and elsewhere in the world. Not only the Italians, also other ethnics and nationalities. This permits me to view the Italian experience in a comparative light, and view the Italians in the United States in comparison with those in Argentina and West Germany, Canada and Australia. What frequently appears to be unique loses its uniqueness and becomes a more general trait in comparative analysis. The experience of an ethnic group viewed from the inside is most often presented as unique and nonrepetitive, hard to understand by anybody who did not experience it himself or herself. But when the Italians are placed side by side with the Ukrainians and the Poles, the Germans and the Croats, the Vietnamese and the Cubans, then the common pattern emerges. In this light, the ethnic research becomes even more important: the verification of common experiences, or the documentation of real uniqueness.

On top of all these, I am not an historian. Nevertheless, I

have a strong interest in the study of historical sequences.
The time has come for the Association to recapture the initial enthusiasm for scholarly research and for academic cooperation. From the start, the efforts of the AIHA engaged a great number of individuals, who soon found additional or alternative avenues for affirmation and activity. Numerous periodicals that now publish ethnic research findings were not even conceived at the time of the AIHA founding in 1966. Nevertheless, Rudy Vecoli's call for a periodical and my renewed effort a short while ago are only dreams so far, while series of periodicals of ethnicity exist and prosper.

Research that remains unknown has limited value. Inability to publish is the major deterrent to sustained scholarly efforts. Research, especially archival, is a lonely pursuit. Self stimulation cannot last forever. In realistic terms, the Association should consider:

(1) to expand the national *Newsletter*; and

(2) to speed up publishing of the *Proceedings*.

These two efforts can be carried out with the resources at hand, with a moderate increase of membership and with some reformulation of priorities.

The second goal is to make the work of the Association known to scholars of neighboring disciplines and interests.

The national organizations of historians, sociologists, archivists, librarians, geographers, psychologists, ethnic historians and modern language teachers all have associated membership for organizations, with rights and obligations. The Association should move from the realm of self-contained gatherings to the challenge of the professions. Research achievements of the AIHA members can well stand the scrutiny of larger assemblies for the quality of the work and for the persuasive nature of the findings. The Association has to affirm itself outside the restricted circles of the Association itself.

Joint research efforts with colleagues in Italy and elsewhere are only at their initial stages; the work of the Molise group and the persistent contributions of Professors. Mulas and Pietro Russo have demonstrated their usefulness. The Georgetown conference of 1976[35] was greatly enriched by the contributions of scholars from Italy. So is the present Chicago conference. We already see some results of the agreements between the AIHA and the universities in Italy. Projects with which we should be associated exist in various regions of Italy with the support of regional governments and of the Consiglio Nazionale delle Ricerche. International research projects are under way with the assistance of European foundations, including the Volkswagen Foundations with the recently approved and financed Labor Migration Project in Cleveland.

But fundamentally, by far the most lasting activity is the continuous research and publication of such research, be it in the AIHA publications or in alternative outlets. If the AIHA will not provide expanded possibilities, the active researchers will—as they do now—find other takers, with or without giving credit at least for the moral support that the AIHA has provided.

The experience of the Italians and Italian Americans in the United States and Canada has not been fully and totally documented. In my repeated regional surveys of coverage I pointed to major gaps in the historiography and do not intend to repeat here the statements made elsewhere.[36]

Let me indicate further some topical gaps - and hope that my review will stimulate younger researchers in particular, to tackle the problems. Young researchers are often like the Pirandello's *"Sei personaggi in cerca d'autore:"* enthusiastic potential scholars in search of a topic to be investigated.

For an historical association, history is the primary concern. The historical coverage of Italian experiences is far from being completed, either the two centuries of history of the republic, or the whole territory of the 50 states of the Union.

Why do we have to jump from Columbus to Mazzei and then almost to Antonini and LaGuardia, and forget the continuity of the Italian presence and activities? The local studies are often just minute segments of a larger picture, too often without the larger picture. The examples of excellent studies of Vecoli[37] for Minnesota, Cinel[38] and Gumina[39] for San Francisco, Nelli[40] for Chicago, Pozzetta and Mormino[41] for Ybor City, Tricarico[42] for New York, Juliani[43] for Philadelphia, Scarpaci[44] for New Orleans and Martinelli[45] for Scottsdale, Arizona, call for similar studies of Boston and the whole of New England, for Rochester and Milwaukee, Minneapolis and

Denver, Los Angeles and Spokane—and many others. I do not mention cities that have been studied decades ago, often without archival search, apologetic or accusative in nature and orientation.

The experiences of early Italian immigrants in the United States are presumably not the same as the experiences of Italians who came to the United States after World War II. Who is here to review the differences or to refute my speculation? Who is here to analyze for us the phenomenon of the Italians, who live temporarily in the United States, professionals, skilled workers and their families, who retain their firm commitments to Italy and cannot be placed side by side with the immigrants? These temporary residents hold Italian passports and receive most attention of the Italian representatives in the United States— and properly so. But they are only a fraction of the Italian presence in the country. Who will analyze their detachment from the Italian American communities or their reluctance to accept the"italianità"of other Italians in the United States, *'paesana'* for some, *'televisiva'* for others?

The language experts should take the spark from the research work of Joshua Fishman[46] - and maybe Mario Pei[47] - and explore the language transformation, not only the vocabulary but also the syntax structure, the symbolization (semiotics), the verbalization and the imagination that is associated with the verbal formulation. They should confirm or refute the 'deep structures' of Chomsky[48] and clarify for us the cost and benefits of bilingualism[49]. There is a need for an Italian equivalent to the German series on German speakers in various regions of the United States[50]. Remigio Pane is monitoring the appearance of noticeable Italian-Americans[51], maybe some of them will provide the answers to our questions.

As a geographer, I have often reprimanded my geography colleagues for not producing the most essential geographical aids to historical research: the maps and analyses of spatial distribution of the Italians, no matter how defined. Such maps are included in a recently published volume.[52] They portray the US distribution of people of Italian ancestry. But the maps for smaller areas, cities and metropolitan regions have not been produced. The information is available and waits to be exploited.

There is an urgent need to expand our comparative analyses: Italians and non-Italians, Italians here and Italians there, Italians now and Italians at some other time:

1. Comparative analysis of the Italian and non-Italian experiences. The Association has stimulated these comparative studies in the past, as evident in the volumes on the Italians and the Jews[53], and the Italians and the Irish.[54] I have not noticed yet much effort to compare the Italians and the Slavs (except for the work of Joseph Barton on Cleveland),[55] though the two ethnic groups share many communalities historically and territorially. I am aware of Thaddeus Gromada's and Eugene Kusielewicz's contribution to the meetings in 1971,[56] and Bogdan Raditsa's presentation at the Philadelphia conference in 1986.[57] The data exist and wait to be processed and analyzed.

2. Comparative analyses of the Italians in the United States and Canada with the Italian emigrants elsewhere are just at their beginnings. Samuel Baily[58] has studied New York and Buenos Aires. How about Chicago and Frankfurt, or Boston and Munich, or San Francisco and Cairo? Is the proximity to Italy really the major factor that makes the Italian migration to Western Europe temporary and migration to the United States and Canada permanent?

The Canadian Italian migration is reaching maturity. Robert Harney[59] deserves major credit for its study. When explored twenty years ago[60], the Italian immigration was in full swing, comparable to the pre-World War I period in the United States. How similar—or different—are the Canadian experiences from those in the United States? What are the variables that account for the differences? The Italians? The Canadians? TV? The stage of technology? The puzzle is here, who will solve it?

3. The Italians now and the Italians at some other time. The longitudinal studies of transformation of individual traits and the changes in aggregations are still rare among the Italian American studies; the assimilation and integration process of individuals and communities, especially in a multicultural context are difficult to grasp and to analyze in spite of

the publicity given to this social phenomena in educational curricula and in the information media. The bulk of past studies has been narrative and historically descriptive. While it remains important to tell and tell again the story, the research frontier ought to move toward analysis: an assessment of historical processes in light of contemporary analytical approaches. The structures and processes of the society, including their ethnic components, produce the results that we describe and review. This is a beginning and not the end of an investigation.

Scholarly work is not a forgotten art, it is at the core of our Association, it is the reason for existence of our Association. Scholarly work which brings us together—because of the topic of the investigation, namely the "Italians and Italian American Experiences in the United States and in Canada"—and not for the pietistic revivalism which is the purpose of numerous other organizations and institutions.

We have a long way ahead. On the tortuous route we occasionally lose the sense of direction and have to remind ourselves of our aims. Individually and collectively we can be proud of our achievements and can look forward with confidence to an even brighter future.

---

[1] Frank J. Cavaioli."The American Italian Historical Association: Twenty Years Later, 1966-1986,"Address presented at the 19th AIHA Conference in Philadelphia, November 15, 1987.

[2] Rudolph J. Vecoli."Los italianos en los Estados Unidos: una perspectiva comparada," *Estudios Migratorios Latinoamericanos*, 2/4 (Diciembre 1986): 403-429.

[3] *AIHA Newsletter* Number 1, Spring 1967.

[4] *AIHA Newsletter* Vol. 1, No.3, Fall 1967.

[5] *AIHA Newsletter* Vol. 4, No.2, Winter 1971, pp. 1-4.

[6] Peter Sammartino, "Ideas for Italian American Research," pp. 285-287 in Remigio U. Pane (ed.). *Italian Americans in the Professions*. Proceedings of the 12th Annual Conference of the AIHA, Rutgers University, October 26-27, 1979. Staten Island: AIHA, 1983.

[7] Giovanni Schiavo, "Research on the Italian Americans: Accomplishments and Work to Be Done," pp. 1-7 in Remigio U. Pane (ed.).

Italian Americans in the Professions.

8 Seventeen volumes of the Proceedings were published and three additional are in preparation; 195 authors contributed 251 articles and commentaries; 40 authors are represented by more than one item. The most frequent contributors were Richard Juliani (5 titles), Rudolph Vecoli (4), Salvatore LaGumina (4), and Jerry Krase (4).

9 Betty Boyd Caroli, Robert F. Harney, Lydio F. Tomasi (eds.). *The Italian Immigrant Woman in North America.* Proceedings of the Tenth Annual Conference of the AIHA. Toronto: The Multicultural History Society of Ontario, 1978. xvi, 386p.

10 Luciano J. Iorizzo and Salvatore Mondello. *The Italian Americans.* Rev. ed. Boston: Twayne, 1980. 348p.

11 Michael La Sorte. *La Merica: Images of Italian Greenhorn Experience.* Philadelphia: Temple University Press, 1985. xiv, 234p.

12 Salvatore LaGumina. *The Immigrants Speak: Italian Americans Tell Their Story.* New York: Center for Migration Studies, 1979. xvi, 209p.

13 Vincenza [Jean] Scarpaci. *A Portrait of the Italian Americans.* New York: Schribner's, 1983. xxxiii, 240p.

14 Deana Paoli Gumina. *The Italians in San Francisco, 1850-1930/ Gli Italiani di San Francisco, 1850-1930.* New York: Center for Migration Studies, 1978. xiii, 230p.

15 Gary Ross Mormino. *Immigrants on the Hill: Italian Americans in St. Louis, 1882-1982.* Champaign, IL: University of Illinois Press, 1986, 289p.

16 Gary Ross Mormino and George Pozzetta. *The Immigrant World of Ybor City: Italians and their Latin Neighbors in Tampa, 1885-1985.* Champaign, IL: University of Illinois Press, 1986, 430p.

17 Humbert S. Nelli. *From Immigrants to Ethnics: The Italian Americans.* New York: Oxford University Press, 1983. viii, 225p.

18 Andrew F.Rolle. *The Immigrant Uprised: Italian Adventurers and Colonists in an Expanding America.* Norman, OK: University of Oklahoma Press,1968. xvi, 391p. Andrew F. Rolle. *The American Italians: Their History and Culture,* Belmont, CA: Wadsworth, 1972. ix, 130p. Andrew Rolle. *The Italian Americans. Troubled Roots,* Norman, OK: University of Oklahoma Press, 1980. xviii, 222p.

19 Lucia C. Birnbaum. *Liberazione della Donna: Feminism in Italy*. Middletown, CT: Wesleyan University Press, 1986. 368p.

20 Donald Tricarico. *The Italians of Greenwich Village: The Social Structure and Transformation of an Ethnic Community*. New York: Center for Migration Studies, 1984. 184p.

21 Silvano M. Tomasi. *Piety and Power: The Role of Italian Parishes in the New York Metropolitan Area (1880-1930)*. New York: Center for Migration Studies, 1973. xi, 201p. Silvano and Lydio Tomasi edited a number of volumes on Italian migration, most of them published by the Center for Migration Studies, Staten Island.

22 Margherita Marchione (ed.). *Philip Mazzei: Selected Writings and Correspondence*. Prato, Italy: Cassa di Risparmi e Depositi di Prato, 1983. 3 volumes.

23 Francesco Cordasco edited numerous volumes on Italian Americans.

24 Giovanni E. Schiavo. *The Truth About the Mafia and Organized Crime in America*. New York: Vigo Press, 1962, 318p. [This is the last in the long list of books written or compiled by Schiavo].

25 Leonard Covello. *The Social Background of the Italo American School Child: A Study of the Southern Italian Mores and Their Effect on the School Situation in Italy and America*. Leiden: E. J. Brill, 1967. xxxii, 488p.

26 Rose Basile Greene. *The Italian American Novel: Document of the Interaction of Two Cultures*. Rutherford, NJ: Fairleigh Dickinson University Press, 1974. 416p.

27 Helen Barolini (ed.). *The Dream Book: An Anthology of Writings by Italian-American Women*. New York: Schocken Books, 1985. xiv, 397p.

28 Robert F. Harney (ed.). *Gathering Place: Peoples and Neighborhoods of Toronto*. Toronto: The Multicultural History Society of Ontario, 1985. 304p.

29 Jerre Mangione. *An Ethnic at Large*. New York: G. P. Putnam's Sons, 1978. 378p. [Paperbeck published by the University of Pennsylvania Press, 1983].

30 Philis C. Martinelli. *Ethnicity in the Sunbelt: Italian-American Migrants in Scottsdale, Arizona*. ASC, 1987.

[31]*Gli Italiani Negli Stati Uniti. L'emigrazione e l'opera degli italiani negli Stati Uniti d'America.* Atti del III Symposium di Studi Americani, Firenze, 27-29 Maggio 1969. Firenze: Istituto di Studi Americani, 1972. xviii, 585p.

[32] Silvano M. Tomasi and Madeline H. Engel (eds.). *The Italian Experience in the United States.* Staten Island: Center for Migration Studies, 1970. x, 239p.

[33] Silvano M. Tomasi (ed.). *Perspectives in Italian Immigration and Ethnicity.* New York: Center for Migration Studies, 1977. viii, 216p.

[34] Lydio F. Tomasi (ed.). Italian Americans. *New Perspectives in Italian Immigration and Ethnicity.* New York: Center for Migration Studies, 1985. viii, 486p.

[35] Humbert S. Nelli (ed.). *The United States and Italy: The First Two Hundred Years.* Proceedings of the 9th Annual Conference of the AIHA, Georgetown University, Washington, D.C., October 8-10, 1976. Staten Island: AIHA, 1977. x, 242p.

[36] Joseph Velikonja. "Italian Americans in the East and West: Regional Coverage in Italian American Studies, 1975-1983," in L. Tomasi (ed.). *Italian Americans. New Perspectives in Italian Immigration and Ethnicity.* New York: Center for Migration Studies, 1985. 142-172, 419-421.

Joseph Velikonja. "Places, Communities and Regions in the American Italian Studies—Territorial Coverage," in Jerome Krase and William Egelman (eds.). *The Melting Pot and Beyond: Italian Americans in the Year 2000.* Staten Island: AIHA, 1987, 37-60.

[37] Rudolph J. Vecoli. "The Italians", in June Holmquist (ed.). *They Chose Minnesota: A Survey of the State's Ethnic Groups.* St. Paul: Minnesota Historical Society, 1981, 449-471.

[38] Dino Cinel. *From Italy to San Francisco: The Immigrant Experience.* Stanford, CA: Stanford University Press, 1982, viii, 347p.

[39] Deana Paoli Gumina. *The Italians of San Francisco, 1850-1930.* Staten Island: Center for Migration Studies, 1978, 230p.

[40] Humbert Nelli. *Italians in Chicago, 1880-1930: A Study of Ethnic Mobility.* New York: Oxford University Press, 1970, xx, 300p.

[41] George Pozzetta and Garry Ross Mormino. *The Immigrant World of Ybor City.*

[42] Donald Tricarico. *The Italians of Greenwich Village.*

[43] Richard Juliani. *The Social Organization of Immigration: The Italians in Philadelphia.* New York: Arno Press, 1981, xxxi, 229p.

[44] Jean A. Scarpaci. *Italian Immigration in Louisiana's Sugar Parishes: Recruitment, Labor Conditions, and Community Relations, 1880-1910.* New York: Arno Press, 1980, vii, 333p.

[45] Philis C. Martinelli. *Ethnicity in the Sunbelt: Italian-American Migrants in Scottsdale, Arizona.*

[46] Joshua Fishman. *Language Loyalty in the United States.* The Hague: Mouton, 1966, 478p.

[47] Mario A. Pei. *Invitation to Linguistics; a Basic Introduction to the Science of Language.* Garden City, NY: Doubleday, 1965, xi, 266p. Mario A. Pei. *Language Today; a Survey of Current Linguistic Thought.* New York: Funk and Wagnalls, 1967, ix, 150p.

[48] Noam Chomsky. *Language and Mind.* New York: Harcourt, Brace & Jovanovich, 1972, xii, 194p. For a recent review of Chomsky's views, see Fred D'Agostino. *Chomsky's System of Ideas.* Oxford: Claredon Press, 1986, xii, 226p.

[49] Toussaint Hocevar. "Equilibria in Linguistic Minority Markets," *Kyklos*, 28/2 (1975), 337-357.

[50] Institut fuer Deutsche Sprache, Manheim. *Deutsche Sprache in Europa und Uebersee. Berichte und Forschungen.* Stuttgart: Franz Steiner Verlag. Band 4.: *Deutsch als Muttersprache in den Vereinigten Staaten.* Teil I. *Der Mittelwesten.* [1979]; Band 10.: Teil II. *Regionale und funktionale Aspekte* [1985]; Band 12.: Teil III. *German Americans. Die Sprachliche Assimilation der Deutschen in Wisconsin.* [1987]. Notice also: Glen G. Gilbert (ed.). *The German Language in America. A Symposium.* Austin, TX.: University of Texas Press, 1971, xiii, 217p.

[51] Remigio Pane."Italian American Experience through Literarure and the Arts," pp. 222-247 in Lydio F. Tomasi (ed.). *Italian Americans. New Perspectives in Italian Immigration and Ethnicity.* See also: Remigio U. Pane (ed.). *Italian Americans in the Professions.* Staten Island, AIHA, 1983, viii, 290; Remigio Ugo Pane,"Seventy Years of American University Studies on the Italian Americans: A Bibliography of 251 Doctoral Dissertations Accepted From 1980 to

1977,*"Italian Americana* 4/2 (Spring/Summer 1978), 244-273.

52 James P. Allen and Eugene James Turner. *We the People: An Atlas of America's Ethnic Diversity.* New York: Macmillian, 1988. ["Italian Ancestry" pp. 122-126.]

53 Jean A. Scarpaci (ed.). *The Interaction of Italians and Jews in America.* Proceedings of the 7th Annual Conference of the AIHA, Towson State College, Baltimore, November 14-15, 1974. Staten Island: AIHA, 1975. viii, 117p.

54 Francis X. Femminella (ed.). *Italians and Irish in America.* Proceedings of the 16th Annual Conference of the AIHA, Albany, N.Y., November 10-13, 1983. Staten Island: AIHA, 1985. ix, 308p.

55 Joseph Barton. *Peasants and Strangers: Italians, Rumanians, and Slovaks in An American City, 1890-1950.* Cambridge, MA: Harvard University Press, 1975. 217p.

56 Francis X. Femminella (ed.). *Power and Class. The Italian-American Experience Today.* Proceedings of the 4th Annual Conference, At Kosciuszko Foundation, New York, October 23, 1971. Staten Island: AIHA, 1973, pp. 44-51.

57 Bogdan Raditsa. "A Croat among the Italians", Paper presented at 19th annual conference of the AIHA in Philadelphia, 1986.

58 Samuel L. Baily. "The Adjustment of Italian Immigrants in Buenos Aires and New York, 1870-1914." *American Historical Review* 88/2 (April 1983): 281-305. Samuel L. Baily."Patrones de Residencia de los Italianos en Buenos Aires y Nueva York: 1880-1914" , *Estudios Migratorios Latinoamericanos* l(1985): 8-47.

59 Most recent work of Robert F. Harney, see footnote 28.

60 Joseph Velikonja. "Gli Italiani nelle città canadesi—Appunti geografici," *Atti, Congresso Geografico Italiano.* Como: Editrice Noseda, 1965, 271-288.

Lives

Introductory Remarks
One Hundred Years of the Italian Consulate in Chicago

Hon. Consul General Dottore Leonardo Baroncelli

The establishment of an Italian Consular agency in Chicago dates back to the first years of this city's development in 1863 and coincides with early Chicago history as well as illuminates the paths of Italian immigration. The opening of an Italian Consulate was decreed by proposal of the first Crispi government on April 3, 1887, within a major reform plan of the consular network. The Chicago Consulate was assigned the territorial jurisdiction of the Central States which included: Illinois, Indiana, Michigan, Wisconsin, Iowa, Minnesota and Missouri.

The Crispi reform preceded, by only a few years, a more general restructuring of the Ministry of Foreign Affairs carried out by the same government with the intentions of modernizing Italian diplomacy and promoting emigration policies aligned with current national interests.

The Crispi administration and emigration as factor of a power's politics, have been clearly analyzed by Fabio Grassi, Professor of History at the University of Lecce and former Italian diplomat. In his study, the historian asserts that on the emigration issue the first Crispi Government played an important role toward modernization and that it represented one of the few post-unification moments during which the liberal government tried to implement "una politica dell'emigrazione e non una polizia dell' emigrazione."

Along with the expansion of the consular network in the United States, the establishment of a consulate in Chicago took place; however, due to a lack of necessary staff, it was not possible to completely satisfy the urgent needs of a massive immigration. Notwithstanding lack of personnel, the volume of consular documents increased remarkably and in particular those documents concerning the protection of the rights of Italian nationals.

As far as organization and assistance were concerned, aid to Italian immigrants ended up to weigh mainly upon private citizens following liberal principles, according to which the State's intervention was deemed appropriate only when private citizens were not able to satisfy on their own the needs connected to their status in the new society. Although supportive of emigrant freedom, the Crispi government was convinced that the phenomenon required some direct intervention of the State and not be left entirely to the pressure of contingent reasons. Crispi thought that Italian emigration might have contributed somehow to the promotion of Italian foreign trade with America. To this end he requested that consuls abroad should point out names of *"italiani di successo"* of those Italians who *"si sono arricchiti onestamente"* in order to have them included in an early project designed to enhance the import of Italian products in the U.S. With few exceptions, the idea to utilize Italian communities abroad to disclose new markets to national agricultural and industrial production turned out to be, as a whole, not too realistic.

In his report, the Consul in Chicago observed in 1888, "I nostri emigrati ormai arricchitisi nell'industria locale richiedono ormar beni di lusso." The same Consul called the attention of Rome to the fact that consumption of local prominent Italian communities reflected the adaptation to a more American way of life and to preferences of the American upperclass in the search of refined and modern products.

All the consuls' reports gave interesting insights to Italian immigration which in their opinions fell short of intellectuals and managerial groups, and of the general conditions of Italy during the time which made Crispi's objectives appear too unrealistic to lean upon communities abroad in order to enhance national interests. The Italian attitude on assistance, associations and schools abroad continued to be based on liberal principles, and as underlined by Professor Grassi, they appeared to contradict the objectives of great power assigned to Italy.

Meanwhile, Italian immigrants often found themselves placed among the most unskilled groups of industrial labor and in competition with more skilled and better integrated ethnic groups or with American workers. As a result contractual and economic conditions of Italian workers remained in need of drastic improvement for a long time.

Crispi's government was however able to pass the first Italian immigration law, even if strictly inspired by liberal principles and relating only to the exclusive protection of emigrants' rights against possible abuse of transportation agents.

For a more pronounced state intervention, one had to wait until the Giolitti era and specifically the laws which were issued between 1910 and 1913. These laws included one which established a more comprehensive legal protection of the emigrants. Such a law for the very first time introduced in Italy a set of legislative provisions on the matter of protecting workers abroad, especially those continental emigrants.

The legislation underwent further changes and improvements and it was integrated within the years 1919 and 1922 by the various bilateral international treaties and through Italy's action in the International Organization of Labor. Thus, the consular office in Chicago was elevated in 1922 to Consulate General and staffed appropriately.

The Fascist regime first considered emigration to be a good means of disseminating its ideology. It pursued a plan of politicization of Italian governmental institutions operating out of the country, and placed special emphasis on the consuls' political role, which according to Rome, came before anything and was similar to the central function performed by "i prefetti"in Italy.

The Fascist government proceeded with a major expansion of the consular network and appointed one hundred and twenty politically oriented consuls. Its political action was also carried out by the party's parallel structure established abroad under the name of "i fasci italiani all'estero" which, besides the promotion of "italianità" and providing assistance to nationals, had as tasks, the political control of emigrants and discrete supervision of Italian diplomatic and consular missions.

During the Fascist period, reports from Chicago were often devoted to political orientations of emigrants and particular attention was given to the activities of anarchist and socialist groups. These reports best portray the idea of the political role assigned to the consulates by Rome. Such a role was performed by consuls with a varying degree of zeal, and in some instances the Embassy was called upon to intervene and moderate activity in order to avoid possible reactions of American public opinion of the way some consuls dealt with *"i gruppi sovversivi."*

In an interesting letter dated September 1929, the then Italian Ambassador recommended to the Consul General in Chicago to move with great caution regarding the case of the Garibaldi Institute, whose activity was not welcomed by the Chicago consul in light of the fact that it was run by a group of *"sovversivi"* financed by local protestants who were taking positions against the Italian government under the name of the hero of two worlds. In fact, the Ambassador called the Consul's attention to the American customs and laws governing freedom of association and on the possible negative repercussions for Italy's image that a press campaign developed on this issue might bring.

The Consul General played, however, an important role in later attending to the 1933 international exposition in Chicago with Balbo's transoceanic flight which highlighted Italy's participation in the same exposition. From all the reports of that time, a composite picture emerges and the Consul General's concern for immigrants' political orientations opposing the official ones became equal to their worry for defamation campaigns launched by the press on the subject of Italians and local organized crime.

Fascism not only virtually abolished, by way of several administrative provisions, freedom of emigration, but it also encouraged the return of emigrants. From the United States such homecomings were indeed favored by the great 1929 depression. Freedom granted by the liberal post-unification government and banned by the Fascist Government would be later reestablished with article 35 of the Constitution of the Italian Republic.

At this point a question might arise whether there has been in Italy an organic emigration policy before World War II. The answer can be hardly positive as a newly unified State like Italy had neither the interest nor the capacity to elaborate a global strategy. When such was done, the problem had been already faced either with nationalistic approaches of the Mussolini period.

To venture over the last forty years of Italian history appears to be much more complex as we are dealing with events still very close to our memory and which still await a more systematic analysis. In the years after the Second World War a great emigration took place in neighboring European countries as an effect of economic integration favored by the establishment of the European Community.

In the overseas countries such as the United States, where there are large communities of people of Italian ancestry, the Government's attention is mainly focused on the role of Italo-Americans in creating and in maintaining ties of friendship among the two countries and in promoting a better interaction of the Italian culture and language.

On a general perspective, from pure assistance, the State has gone to a more modern and effective vision of the phenomenon which has lately led to the elections of the "Comitati dell'Emigrazione Italiana" (Italian Emigration Committees) in various places of the globe as part of an effort to favor auto-decision and direct representation.

Meanwhile, Italy which until yesterday was an emigration country, has today become an immigration country, and we are now coping with problems related to a massive inflow of foreign workers from all continents. Such a development which took place in light of Italian economic growth, only a few years ago was for many just unpredictable.

One hundred years of Consular presence and commitments in Chicago have taught us something and past experiences may provide fruitful guidelines for the future.

la famiglia italiana e la famiglia statiunitense:
A comparative historical study

Lucia Chiavola Birnbaum

A comparative historical study of the family in Italian and in U.S. history helps to see both more clearly. There is a tendency to regard the patriarchal Italian family as fixed throughout the centuries, and to consider the typical U.S. family a progressive model of democracy. In reality, the Italian family has taken many forms in its long history, but always with women at the moral center; in 1948 Italian women placed women's equality in their new republican constitution and since 1968 they have woven what may be the strongest women's movement in the world. U.S. women have been in a condition of inequality since the founding of the nation; they have not, as of 1990, secured an Equal Rights Amendment to the constitution. And the economic condition of U.S. women is deteriorating. As in other European families, Italian daughters and wives were historically enjoined by church and state to subservience to fathers and husbands. In reality, Italian women exercised considerable family and community power. In their long peasant history memories of the prehistoric Mediterranean earth mother divinity were transmitted in the folklore. Italian women were the carriers of a moral tradition more millennial, more equalitarian, and more woman-centered than church doctrines of doctrinal catholicism[1] (and dramatically more woman-centered than doctrines of protestantism.)

In the 1890s Italian peasant women joined socialist fasci, and in the twentieth century they engaged in revolutionary struggles for land, bread, peace, and equality. Surmounting an impasse that has paralyzed U.S. women, Italian women since World War II have insisted on equality as well as women's difference from men—including the notable difference that women are mothers. Not locked in logic, nor into a

Lockean ethos, they have insisted on equality and protective legislation, and they have secured both. Since 1968 Italian women have loosed a political and cultural revolution, not only for genuine equality between the sexes, but for a democratic and socialist society that cherishes differences.

A comparative historical analysis of women in Italy and in the United States should be undertaken without U.S. ethnocentric myopia. An example of recent scholarship that replaces stereotypes about Italy with realistic appraisal is Joseph LaPalombara's, *Democracy Italian Style* (Yale University Press, 1987), a study that documents the salient fact that Italy today is one of the most democratic countries of the world.

A brief overview of the legal history of U.S. women begins with the omission of women from the Constitution of 1787, as well as from the Bill of Rights. In this bicentennial year it is appropriate to note that the U.S. charter of liberties legitimated slavery for black people and inequality for women. As feminist scholars have pointed out, U.S. founding documents were grounded on an "exclusively masculine system of justice based on English common law and eighteenth-century ideals of liberty and equality that did not apply to the vast majority of Americans. "[2]

After 1789 state legislation only slightly improved the legal status of women. States that passed Married Women's Property Acts interpreted the legislation narrowly. In the ferment for abolition of slavery and for democratic reform in the decades before the Civil War a U.S. women's movement emerged, but after the war the Supreme Court held that women were not full citizens. From 1872 to 1900 the high court denied women the right to vote and forbade them to practice law; holding that "person was male," male judges questioned whether women were "persons" under the law.

After 1900 U.S. women turned toward political action for protective legislation and for the vote. By 1908 nineteen states had passed laws setting maximum work hours for women and/or prohibiting night work for women. U.S. women, along with those of most European nations, obtained the right to vote after World War I. Not suffragettes during World War I (as were U.S. women) Italian women engaged in revolutionary activities demanding land, bread, peace, and worker control. Women and men occupied factories; at the end of the war, women holding their babies, led movements to occupy unused lands. Revolutionary aspirations were violently extinguished by the Italian fascist takeover in 1922.

From the 1900s to the 1970s the U.S. women's movement was divided between women who wanted equal rights and women who wanted protective legislation enabling them to work in outside jobs as well as in the home as mothers and wives. Up until the feminist movement of the '60s and '70s, U.S. women were defined legally in terms of their sex and their family roles as wives and mothers, not in terms of individual rights under the constitution.

With the Equal Pay Act of 1963 and the addition of the word "sex" to Title VII of the 1964 Civil Rights act, executive orders and Supreme Court decisions have brought U.S. women closer to equality under the law. In the Reagan administration, however, affirmative action for women and others has been checked. In the contemporary conservative backlash, women's equal rights are equated with danger to traditional patriarchal family values—or male privilege. Although abortion was declared constitutional in 1973, subsequent actions by federal and state agencies have put this option largely beyond the reach of most poor women.

In the view of most male U.S. historians, women have attained liberation in the U.S. because of the benefits of "the powerful democratic capitalism of the early nineteenth century" and the country's "powerful industrialization."[3] Donald Meyer in a recent comparative study, states that U.S. women have been liberated by "modernization" and Italian women have "endured their perpetuation of backwardness, not because of the patriarchy vested in Italian life, but because of the inability of Italian leaders to get a powerful Italian economic machine running."[4]

Meyer's study, published in 1987, is not only ethnocentric, it is factually inaccurate: Italy has gotten its economic machine running quite nicely: it is now the fourth industrialized nation of the world, overtaking Great Britain. Meyer, captivated by the stalinist proposition that women attained liberation insofar as they joined the industrial proletariat, assumes that "modernization" (with the U.S. as model) will bring women of the rest of the world up to the advanced status of U.S. women.

Women scholars in the U.S., less taken with national power than is Meyer, point out that the actual economic condition of U.S. women has deteriorated in the midst of the recent visible feminist movement, that narrow patriarchal/authoritarian values have made it impossible for women in the U.S. to secure child care, medical care, and other rights held by Italian and other European women. Far from being the vanguard of women's progress in the world, U.S. women have been pushed increasingly into poverty by a large wage gap between men and women, a wage gap that spells poverty for millions of women who head households. Women's poverty in the U.S. is deepened by the divorce rate[5] —twenty times higher in the protestant culture of the U.S. than it is in catholic Italy.[6] Fifty-six percent of the women who work in the U.S. live in poverty. If present trends continue, two-thirds of U.S. women will be working both at home and in outside jobs, and most will be living near poverty.

What makes the U.S. case of feminism more hopeless than hopeful is that the U.S. women's movement is not only thwarted by a hostile cultural environment, but because it has not been able to lift its gaze beyond women's concerns to equality for everyone (i.e., a democratic socialist society) it is vulnerable to the criticism of being self-centered. U.S. women are left with few allies in the war against them by anxious white protestant males in positions of eroding power.

Italian society and government, far from being as chaotic as superficial analysis suggests, has a core of franciscan values— deepened by marxist insights—that has been the ground for the creation, since the 1960s, of a successful welfare state democracy. Many forms of social insurance, from impressive worker rights to universal health care, supplement the stellar gains Italian women have made since 1968. Italy is a welfare state democracy that defies pejorative generalizations: only one Italian in four owns no real property; more Italians than Americans are homeowners.[7] Italian universities have opened their doors to everyone who has completed high school, thereby insuring genuine equality of opportunity.[8] The two major parties of Italy, the Christian Democrats and the Communists, are in agreement that all men—and all women—may not be created equal, but the state has a moral obligation to see to it that all men and all women are treated equally.[9]

My own study of Italian women[10] grounds contemporary achievements of Italian women on the preservation of an ancient woman-centered cosmology, a long Italian peasant past that transmitted women's values, and the ability of contemporary Italian women to finesse a genuinely pluralist political environment for progressive policies for women and others. Exploring the difference between the Italian and U.S. women's movements, I have suggested that differences in cultural values may determine the outcome of women's movements. In Italy an ancient woman-centered cosmology, and franciscan values, have nurtured women's concerns. This is in contrast to the male-centered cosmology and natural rights philosophy of the U.S. which have produced a hierarchical patriarchal system obscured by an overlay of liberalism.

Historical moment is also determinative. Italy is an ancient country that embarked after World War II on the creation of an equal society combining democracy and socialism. The U.S. began its democratic experiment two centuries ago— innovative, but flawed deeply from the outset by genocidal policies toward Native Americans, traffic in the slave trade, and a system of slavery so entrenched that a civil war was necessary to abolish it. Slavery was succeeded by an institutionalized racism that perpetuated the notion that some Americans are more privileged than others. In the twentieth century the notion of American "uniqueness" justified military expansion in the world in the name of extending democracy. The notion culminated in the 1960s with the U.S. invasion of Vietnam to prevent Asians from making their own political decisions.

With signs of the decline of the American empire in the 1980s, male executors of U.S. foreign and domestic policies have grown increasingly defensive/aggressive. The targets of their defensiveness/aggression are the poor and the vulnerable (of whom women and children are the majority)—in the U.S. and elsewhere, notably in Latin America.

The Italian peasant heritage was mentioned earlier as one

of the variables that has produced a strong Italian women's movement. A French feminist once said to me that she was astonished to discover that any Italian peasant woman had more self-assurance than the highly educated French feminists she knew. In *liberazione della donna*, I have suggested that it was this peasant self-assurance that enabled Italian feminists to put their hands on their hips in the '70s, and to declare, "L'utero è mio e me lo gestisco io," (it is my uterus and I will manage it) defying church and party. Feminist theoreticians can point to many contradictions in the very large and often anarchic Italian women's movement. More interested in reaching women's goals than in logical coherence, Italian feminists are likely to respond to this critique with: "Me ne frego!"

Trying to locate the difference between Italian and Italian American women, I would suggest that it is the loss of self-assurance in a U.S. environment where dominant protestants were intent on "americanizing" Italians (and others regarded as inferior) that helps to explain why women of Italy, are, in general, more self-assured in their feminism than are Italian American women.

There are other reasons a women's movement has been effective in Italy, and has been met with hostility in the United States. Italian women have benefited not only from a woman-centered culture, but from late nineteenth and twentieth century history. This history includes a socialist movement in which peasant women participated, revolutionary struggles during and after World War I, and the postwar experience of fascism which destroyed workers, women, and left organizations, but left unforgettable memories for Italian women. Under Mussolini, birth control and abortion were punishable by jail incarceration; women were forced out of jobs and women's role was limited to producing the twelve children that fascists considered the ideal fascist family. Living through fascism has given Italian women a clarity not available to women in liberal countries: fascists insisted on women's mental, moral, and spiritual inferiority. After 1968 Italian feminists would remember that fascists said that war is for men what motherhood is for women.[11]

During World War II, U.S. women went to work in factories, performing what had hitherto been regarded as men's work. Italian women went to war as partisans, helping to bring down nazis and fascists in a thousand ways, as soldiers, couriers, spies, mothers, wives—fighting, making soup for the hungry, hiding Jews. After the war U.S. women were subjected to highly effective propaganda to return to the kitchen and become consumers. In 1945 Italian women demanded and secured the vote; in 1948 they put equal rights into the Italian constitution, and between 1948 and 1968 put into place a series of protective laws for working mothers.

In the late '60s a large women's movement erupted in the U.S. and in Italy. Both were inspired by a new left spirit. In Italy this spirit was deepened by the ambience of left catholicism deriving from John XXIII. In the U.S., women made large demands, obtained a few concessions, but were largely countered with obfuscation and evasion. In Italy, women defying catholic church and communist party, demanded and secured—in the span of a decade and a half—divorce, subsidized nursery schools, equal family rights, women's health clinics, equal pay for equal work, legal abortion, and an advanced referendum against sexual violence. The Italian women's movement has successfully used women's political clout and tapped women's wisdom; it has been credited with the democratic "transformation" of the Italian communist party, with inspiring the wide nonviolence movement of the '80s, and with creating new democratic political forms, in parliament, in the parties, and at regional and local levels that point to the democratic/socialist transformation of Italy.

U.S. women have been checkmated by the illusions of two mirrored political parties. Italian women have benefited from the genuine pluralism of Italian politics—whose 10 to 15 political parties offer a variety of options, and enable women to play the large communist party off against the socialist, the radical, and other parties, and to insist on an unedited marxism.

Adopting an unedited interpretation of the judeo-christian gospel, Italian women and other left catholics have eroded the hegemony of Christian Democrats and traumatized papal catholicism by asserting rights of conscience for abortion and for all matters referring to life. Feminists and others have translated into liberation theologies John the XXIII's belief that the church is the people of God in history, offering an unprecedented challenge to the increasingly tense catholicism of John Paul II.

The family in Italy, as elsewhere, is in transition. To search for "family" we need to put aside the idea that the phenomenon is limited to the U.S. pattern of father-mother-children living in a nuclear household. In the long eons of Italian peasant history the family was extended, not nuclear: mother/father/children lived in an extended family culture of godparents, relatives, and community.

In contemporary Italy the family is characterized by a multiplicity of caring relationships. While the remaining beams of the authoritarian patriarchal family structure fall, the Italian landscape is characterized by pain, but also by caring. Natalia Ginzburg's novels depict nonfathers who nurture babies who are then wrenched from them by natural grandparents; natural fathers who reach beyond the artificial postures of parenthood (that sometimes make people insincere) to find their children; a homosexual couple takes in a young pregnant woman.[12] Italians have a keen sense of the change in the Italian family marked by the 1975 law that places family equality into the Italian canon and perhaps even more vividly suggested in the provision of the 1979 referendum against sexual violence that refers to marital rape. There is in Italy, as there is in the United States, a male malaise that Francesca Duranti delineates in her prize-winning book, *The House on Moon Lake.* Fabrizio considered himself "the unhappy incarnation of all the historic defeats of the twentieth century," including "rebellious women who questioned the rules of the game of love."[13]

This male malaise probably exists to a lesser degree in Italy, that highly politicized country where more than half of the electorate has a vision of a just and equal society, than in the United States where a potent cold war educational and intelligence system has destroyed vision and put radical options for change beyond the pale of discussion.

In Italy, feminists do not frighten most men; this is not unrelated to two cultural facts: Italian men are open in their love for their mothers; Maria—closer to the black madonna of third world peoples than to the blue and white madonna of the church—is the significant goddess of Italians. Italian feminists can ascend to peaks of Medea rage in denunciations of injustice, but they can also couch their feminism in nonthreatening language: in the '70s feminists said that their goal was to put the joys of private life into the social sphere.[14]

Because Italian feminists regard themselves as "other"— and they identify with the "others" of the earth—they have known, perhaps more deeply than their U.S. counterparts, that women's struggle comprises all people who suffer exploitation and discrimination. Italian feminists, although their posture is critical, are supported by the large Italian left—which includes not only marxists but left catholics. Aligning women with youth, children and old people[15] at home, they identify globally with the poor peoples of the third world.

Unlike the U.S. movement, Italian feminism has reached all the housewives; this is related to the unedited marxism of Italians since 1968 that has valued women's work of caring.[16] Italian feminists early adopted the strategy of demanding wages for the unpaid work of the housewife to legitimate women's demands.

In Italy, where one out of three people votes for the communist party—in contrast with the U.S. where citizens have a choice between two capitalist parties—there is a dynamic sense of participating in a "social transformation." a transformation in which women are playing a crucial role. Social transformation, in Italian feminist perspective, means eradicating patriarchy in the family as the first step to removing all hierarchy in society—all dominations of class, race, and sex.

From the spirit of left catholicism since Pope John XXIII, to the democratic "transformation" of Italian communism by Italian feminists, there has emerged a sense in Italy today that the goal is to work for a community where "tutti hanno dei diritti,"[17] (everybody has rights). With a comprehension of the economic change that has transformed Italy from a largely agricultural society to the front edge of twentieth century industrialization, Italian women speak of a "cultura dei servizi" (a culture of services) in a "cultura della liberazione per tutti" (culture of liberation of everyone).[18]

The culture of liberation in Italy emphasizes differences—the significance of women's differences (defined by women) from men. And differences (regional, ethnic, religious, experiential, etc.) among people as a cherished value in a genuinely democratic and equal society. This has brought an attitude (compatible with traditional Italian franciscan values) that there is no sharp line between the "normal" and the "deviant." A compassionate country tolerant of differences, Italy may be one of the least alienated societies on earth. Participation in elections is massive: 90 to 93 percent of the people vote (compare U.S. elections). Differences sort themselves out: northerners may run industry and finance, but southerners are the geniuses of twentieth century Italian political history; e.g., Antonio Gramsci, Enrico Berlinguer, Aldo Moro.[19]

In what I have elsewhere called "the world's most hopeful experiment in unedited marxism and an unedited interpretation of the judeo-christian gospel,"[20] Italians have created new democratic forms and practices—not only for women's concerns, but for workplace and neighborhood democracy, making frequent use of the referendum and other modes of direct democracy that were institutionalized in the U.S. in the early twentieth century.

Perhaps the sharpest difference between today's Italian family and that of tradition is that the birth rate in Italy is now one of the lowest in the world (slightly more than one child per couple)[21]. Yet the legalization of abortion in 1978 (overwhelmingly endorsed by every Italian region but one in the referendum of 1981), has brought a drop in the number of abortions. Historically Italian women aborted (illegally and dangerously) when it was necessary— times of peasant famine to the economic stresses of the twentieth century. Legalization of abortion in Italy after 1978 left the matter to a woman's conscience. In a society with fewer economic stresses than in the U.S., the number of abortions has dropped.[22]

The economic form that is growing most rapidly in Italy is the cooperative, exemplifying the shift toward more equal relationships in family and society. The aim is for the home to be immersed in a rich space of many cooperatives (work, transportation, recreation et al.) so that the family is not a nuclear shelter, but an integral part of a vast, very rich, social network.[23] Housing cooperatives combine the functions of shelter and service.[24] Contemporary statistics that indicate that more Italians than ever live together in single families miss the important fact that this new development embodies feminist thinking that women choose to live with their own, but want to work with others for a better society. Early on in the feminist campaigns of the '70s Italian women rejected stalinist notions of great communal kitchens and dining halls. Feminists emphasize the rights of the individual, including privacy, while working in a remarkable number of voluntary organizations, for a genuinely equal and just community in a world of nonviolence.

Heralded by the women's movement, a new culture is evolving in Italy. Instead of the traditional patriarchal assignment of women to the values of dedication, renunciation and sacrifice—with marriage as the norm—women are insisting on meaningful equal relationships. Today most requests for marital separation are initiated by women. There is also a contemporary Italian realization that connects a mother's happiness with the happiness of her children: "Una madre colta che conserva interessi e legami con il mondo esterno, che si realizza un lavoro soddisfacente, è certamente una madre migliore di quella costretta a impegnare ogni energia nei figli e a focalizzare su di loro tutte le proprie aspettative."[25] (a mother with interests and bonds in the outside world, who realizes herself in satisfying work, is certainly a better mother than the woman constricted to commit all her energies to her children and to focus conventional expectations on them).

The vast social change afoot in Italy involves change in personality, above all in the children. Montessori pedagogy is very popular in Italy: "Aiutami a fare da solo."[26] (help me to do it by myself). Italians believe that one reaches genuine democracy by starting with democracy in the family and in the schools.[27]

The changing Italian family was the theme of a conference held in Livorno 1986. The volume of conference proceedings includes Italian wedding photographs from 1920 to 1980. The 1920 photo depicts a traditional bride and groom and wedding party. A wartime wedding is shown of a soldier and his bride, in military dress. A postwar communist couple marry under a poster of Togliatti. A couple of the '50s iconoclastically are wed in swimsuits.

Concluding the series is a contemporary photo of an Italian couple. Although 1920 to 1980 has been a tumultous period in Italian history, the earlier and later marriage photos are similar: both are traditional and romantic weddings. The large change in the Italian family in the intervening sixty years is suggested in the book's title: *Dal dovere all'amore.*

What an Italian wife and mother may have done earlier with a sense of duty—she does, in Italy's very democratic environment today, with love.

---

[1] This essay follows Italian style in removing capital letters from any words referring to christianity or to communism.

[2] Joan Hoff-Wilson, "The Unfinished Revolution: Changing Legal Status of U.S. Women," *Signs. Journal of Women in Culture and Society*, Autumn 1987.

[3] See Donald Meyer, *Sex and Power. The Rise of Women in America, Russia, Sweden and Italy* (Wesleyan University Press, 1987).

[4] *Ibid.* See "Italy: An Epic of Pathos" and Part II, "The American Case." Also Part IV, The Genius of Individuals.

[5] Divorce was guaranteed early by the Protestant Reformation; it was not legalized in Italy until 1970.

[6] Sylvia Ann Hewlett, *A Lesser Life. The Myth of Women's Liberation in America* (William Morrow and Company, Inc., 1986).

[7] Joseph LaPalombara, *Democracy Italian Style* (Yale University Press, 1987), p 1.

[8] *Ibid.*, p 54.

[9] *Ibid.*, p 55.

[10] See Birnbaum, *liberazione della donna—feminism in Italy.* Wesleyan University Press, 1986; paperback edition 1988.

[11] *Ibid.*

[12] See my review of Natalia Ginzburg, *The City and the House* (Seaver Books, 1987) San Francisco *Chronicle Review*, May 3, 1987.

[13] *Ibid.*

[14] See Birnbaum, *liberazione.*

[15] Comune di Livorno. *Progetto Donna. Dal dovere all'amore. la donna nella famiglia che cambia.* (Belforte Editore Libraio, 1986). See Franca Bimbi, "Soggetti Politici del Quotidiano e Diritti di Cittadinanza."

[16] See *liberazione*; also Dal dovere, p. 3.

[17] *Dal dovere*, p. 5.

[18] *Ibid.*

[19] LaPalombara, *Democracy Italian Style*, p. 69.

[20] Birnbaum, "Profile: independent scholar sicilian style, "Independent Scholar, Fall 1987.

[21] *Dal dovere*, p. 39.

[22] *Ibid.*

[23] *Dal dovere*, p. 65.

[24] *Ibid.*, p. 66.

[25] *Dal dovere*, p. 96.

[26] *Ibid.*, p. 98.

[27] Of course the largest difference between Italy and the U.S. is that in Italy the sense of what is genuinely democratic is accompanied by the marxist belief that nobody has the right to exploit the labor of another.

NSC 1 And United States Foreign Policy Towards Italy

Ernest E. Rossi
Western Michigan University

Introduction

A seminal document of the Cold War regarding Italy is NSC 1, "The Position of the United States with Respect to Italy," dated November 14, 1947. This was the first staff paper produced for the newly established National Security Council, and it provided the rationale and recommended actions for the massive American intervention in Italian politics in that crucial period. The paper was based on a number of developments that had been occurring since Italy surrendered to the Allies in 1944 and it built logically on the pattern of analysis and decision making within the American government during 1947.

The document reveals that the United States had developed by this time a comprehensive foreign policy towards Italy, one that integrated economic, political and military aspects. A fully comprehensive policy was a new development because the United States lacked a historical policy towards Italy. Traditionally, the U.S. had no vital interests in the Mediterranean area and the late unification of Italy in 1861 did not conflict with American interests on the European continent. Until World War I, the only noteworthy incidents that affected American-Italian relations pertained to matters concerning Italian immigration and the treatment of Italians in the U.S.

The United States government applied the principle of non-involvement towards Italian colonialism in East Africa in the 1890s and in North Africa in 1911-12. At the conclusion of World War I, President Woodrow Wilson opposed Italy's claim under the secret Treaty of London that it be given frontiers based on clearly recognizable lines of nationality and strategic defense in Europe and the Mediterranean. He was unsuccessful, and in the 1920s American-Italian relations returned to matters relating to the establishment of immigration quotas. Fascist foreign policies were not considered to seriously affect American interests. The U.S. did little when Italy defaulted on its war debts, maintained a larger navy than it had agreed to, established a protectorate over Albania, or invaded Ethiopia in 1935. This policy of non-involvement was also applied towards the creation of the Rome-Berlin Axis, Fascist participation in the Spanish Civil War, the conquest of Albania, and Italy's anti-Comintern pact with Germany and Japan. After the outbreak of the war in Europe, President Franklin Roosevelt offered to help Italy achieve its "legitimate aspirations" in the Mediterranean, but this was rejected by Benito Mussolini. When Italy entered the war against France and Britain, the U.S. maintained its official neutrality, but this ended when Mussolini declared war on the U.S. four days after Pearl Harbor.[1]

American policy towards Italy during the war was conciliatory for it made a distinction between Italy on the one hand and Germany and Japan on the other. The United States pledged that Italians would be able to choose their own government after the war, and that Italy would not be burdened by a punitive peace treaty. Britain was given the authority to exercise major control in postwar Italy, but the American view of postwar Italy soon clashed with British intentions. Britain favored the restoration of the Italian monarchy, the reduction of Italian territory, and limitations on Italian rearmament; it also opposed the early economic rehabilitation of Italy. The U.S. favored economic assistance, a non-punitive treaty, the right of Italians to choose their form of government, and acceptance of Italy as a participant in the international community. [2]

The summer of 1944 marks the beginning of a new period of American-Italian relations, as the United States began to resist British pressures and pursue its own objectives. The principle of non-involvement and the secondary role of the U.S. in Italy were abandoned, and the American government dramatically increased its interventions in Italian economic and political life. Relief assistance was given, French troops were forced out of Italy, and Yugoslav troops out of Trieste. The American and British governments disagreed on the composition of the provisional Italian government and on the issue of whether the institutional question—monarchy or republicanism—should be decided by a popular referendum. In the peace treaty negotiations, the United States supported setting treaty limitations on Italian armed forces, freeing Fascist colonies, placing pre-Fascist colonies under a United Nations trusteeship, and foregoing reparations; and it took a pro-Italian position on the question of Venezia Giulia (i.e., the boundary with Yugoslavia). Generally, however, the American attempt to secure a non-punitive peace treaty with Italy was not successful, except that Italy retained its prewar boundary with Austria.

With the resumption of Italian sovereignty in 1946, the United States clearly became the dominant foreign power in Italy. The traditional policy of noninvolvement was abandoned, and American interests in Italy were now perceived to be primary ones. These interests argued for a dynamic policy of intervention into Italian economic and political life. Unrestricted by the lack of British, French or Soviet power in Italy, the United States used its economic resources and political influence to help reconstruct Italy along conservative Western democratic lines.

Postwar Italian Politics

From the fall of Mussolini's government in July 1943 to June 1944, the Italian government was headed by Marshall Pietro Badaglio. This government surrendered to the Allies, declared war on Germany and was accepted as a co-belligerent. A number of anti-Fascist political parties then emerged from the clandestine opposition to Mussolini. These included the Communist (PCI), Socialist (PSIUP, later PSI), Liberal (PLI), Christian Democratic (DC), the Action Party (Pd'A), the Labor Democratic Party, and the Republican Party (PRI). The relative strength of these parties with the Italian people was not determined until the first national election in 1946.

From June 1944 to December 1945, Italian politics was marked by party strife, for with the fall of Fascism, there was little that could hold the ideologically diverse groups together. Prime Ministers were taken (with the approval of Great Britain) from two parties which, as later elections showed, had little popular support, but provided moderate leadership: Ivanoe Bonomi of the Labor Democratic Party and Ferruccio Parri of the Action Party, a reformist who was made Prime Minister in 1945. When Parri's government fell in 1945, there was little likelihood that major social reforms could then be brought about by the democratic Left.

The coming into power of the Christian Democrat, Alcide De Gasperi, marks the beginning of a major period in postwar Italian politics. De Gasperi led seven consecutive cabinets, from December 1945 to June 1953. It was he who, with the help of the United States, defeated the radical Left and consolidated the position of conservative and moderate forces in postwar Italy. This did not happen quickly, however, for it was not until the elections of 1948 that it became clear that the radical Left could not take power by constitutional means.

In 1946, the United States became more politically active in Italy. It overrode the British veto against Count Carlo Sforza as the Italian Foreign Minister, joined with Britain to remove partisan occupation of factories, and supported De Gasperi's plan for local elections. But it also insisted on a coalition government that included the parties of the radical Left and the reformist Action party. The American government supported a plan to resolve the institutional question by a national referendum, and to limit the powers of the Constituent Assembly of 1946 to drafting a Constitution and ratifying the peace treaty, thus continuing the Italian government's power to rule by decree.[3]

The 1946 national election for the Constituent Assembly confirmed De Gasperi in office and removed the uncertainties of party strength. It showed that the reformist Action party was very weak, and that the three mass parties (Christian Democratic, Communist, Socialist) dominated the scene, accounting for 75 percent of the popular vote. A coalition government which included the three mass parties and the Republican Party was constructed, but conflict soon arose among these ideologically diverse groups, and within the Socialist Party.

In January 1947 De Gasperi traveled to the United States ostensibly to secure economic assistance, and to discuss the Italian political situation. After his return, Italy was granted a $100 million loan from the Export-Import Bank.[4] In May 1947 De Gasperi formed a new government without the Communists and Socialists. The Left claimed their exclusion from the government was the direct result of his January trip when he received orders in Washington to do so. De Gasperi's supporters deny this and stress his role in convincing the American government to view Italy as a friend and to grant it economic assistance.[5]

The splitting of the Socialist Party (PSIUP, later PSI) in January 1947 contributed to strengthening the Center in Italian politics. The Socialists were divided over whether to make a coalition with the Communists and continue a wartime unity of action policy. In January 1947 the anti-Communist wing of the party formally split and formed the Italian Workers Socialist Party (PSLI) under Giuseppe Saragat. The division necessitated a restructuring of the Italian cabinet. The new cabinet, under De Gasperi, included only the three mass parties; Count Sforza was brought in as Foreign Minister, replacing Pietro Nenni, the Socialist leader. This three-party government was a failure, for the parties could not work together because the Communist leader, Palmiro Togliatti, insisted on a Communist program as the price for cooperation. After two pre-Fascist Prime Ministers tried unsuccessfully to form a government, De Gasperi was recalled and formed a cabinet without the Communists and Socialists.[6]

The exclusion of the Left from the government in 1947 marks the beginning of two characteristic features of postwar Italian government and politics: anti-Communism and center party collaboration. As the 1948 elections approached, party realignments took place and De Gasperi took the opportunity to bring into the government the democratic Left and the Center-Right parties. This included the PSLI, the Liberal Party, and the Republican Party, with Count Sforza remaining as Foreign Minister. The Left opposition also coalesced into a Popular Front and offered a joint list of candidates in the 1948 elections. Thus the stage was set for the most important national election in postwar Italy—an election in which the Center and Right was pitted against the Left in the context of the broader Cold War that engulfed all of Europe.[7] The strategies and tactics of the war as it pertained to Italy were often decided in Washington, D.C.

Origins of NSC 1

In 1947, the Policy Planning Staff of the State Department was headed by George F. Kennan, the person who as Mr. X had written "The Sources of Soviet Conduct," in the July 1947 issue of *Foreign Affairs*. The article forms the intellectual basis for the adoption of the policy which came to be known as containment. Kennan wrote that the United States must adopt a "policy of firm containment designed to confront the Russians with unalterable counter-force at every point where they show signs of encroaching upon the interests of a peaceful and stable world."[8]

Earlier that year, on March 12, 1947, President Harry S. Truman spoke to Congress of the dangers to Greece and Turkey from Communist insurrections. He said that it "must be the policy of the United States to support free peoples who are resisting attempted subjugation by armed minorities or by outside pressures." Thus the Truman Doctrine was born. At this time the Doctrine applied only to Greece and Turkey, for Italy was not under threat of an insurrection. But its economy was on the verge of collapse and its government unable to act because of the inability of the coalition of Left, Center, and Right parties to agree.

The State Department documentary record of 1947 demonstrates that the primary emphasis of the great mass of embassy cables, diplomatic notes, memoranda of conversations, letters, reports and papers that passed between Rome and Washington was for the most part concerned with the poor condition of the Italian economy. The Italian ambassador to the United States, Alberto Tarchiani, and the Italian Prime Minister, Alcide De Gasperi, noted time and again that unless immediate and massive amounts of economic assistance were forthcoming, the economy would collapse, the Christian Democrats would lose control of the government, and there would be no way to resist a left-wing coup or insurrection.

Moreover, they argued, the Italian army was demoralized, poorly commanded, and ineffective; it too needed modern military equipment and a sign of support from the United States. The Italian leaders made demands for coal, grain, the extension of relief, the granting of credits from the Export-Import Bank, and other credits to help it meet its dollar shortage. Italy wanted a portion of the gold that was retaken from Germany after the war, scrap metal for its factories, gifts of Liberty ships, repayment of prisoner of war benefits, the transfer of surplus military equipment, and wrecked American ships lying in Italian territorial waters to be used for scrap metal, and other benefits.[9]

These requests were supported by a steady stream of cables from the American ambassador to Italy, James Clement Dunn, a career diplomat who was appointed to the Italian post in 1946. He supported the immediate granting of relief aid, the commitment to long-term reconstruction assistance, and any form of material or financial assistance that would help relieve the economic crisis.

By January 1947 when De Gasperi made his trip to Washington, Italy had already become an economic ward of the U.S. At this time the American emphasis was on preventing an economic collapse in Italy, and the larger political problem of Left-wing participation in the government and the threat of a revolution was not addressed in a direct manner.

On May 3, 1947, Dunn reported a deterioration in the Italian coalition of Christian Democrats, Communists and Socialists to the point that effective action by the Italian government to correct economic and financial conditions was impossible. "I am convinced," he cabled, "that no improvement in conditions here can take place under Govt as at present composed. Communists who are represented by second-string team are doing everything possible outside and within Govt to bring about inflation and chaotic economic conditions." He asked the new Secretary of State, George C. Marshall, to say to the press that the United States would lend its support to these democratic elements who preserved the freedom and liberty of the Italian people and who were opposed to totalitarian regimes of the extreme Right or the Left.[10]

Following a secret meeting with De Gasperi in which the

Italian Prime Minister predicted the collapse of his government unless immediate economic assistance was forthcoming,
Dunn analyzed the circumstances that plagued post-Fascist
governments. This analysis stressed the weakness of coali-
tions based on competitive philosophies, the token authority
given early Italian governments which led to parliamentary
and electoral jockeying, the party strife and ambitions that
resulted in unworkable ministerial organization, and the incompetence and inexperience of technical and political personnel in the Italian government. Dunn believed the problem
to be fundamentally a psychological one that could only be relieved by Draconian measures. These included strong political
leadership, political and economic reforms to thwart Communist attempts to create turmoil and build electoral support.
He further recommended that the United States continue to
supply wheat to Italy until a "competent strong government
emerged at which time the U.S. should give it material and
moral support." He listed a number of specific actions that the
Italian government ought to take and concluded that since the
Communists were opposed to these actions, it would be difficult for Communists to participate in a government that
would do so.[11]

On May 20, 1947, the State Department acted to make Italy
its political ward. After Tarchiani reported that De Gasperi
needed an immediate expression of support to stay in power,
Marshall authorized the following message to be sent to De
Gasperi: "You may count on the strong moral support of the
United States and that we will make a serious effort to assist
Italy in meeting her essential financial needs." On the same
day, Dunn was authorized by Marshall to pledge support to a
new non-Communist government of Italy the following items:
(1) consultations with Great Britain and France to join in
supporting possible treaty revisions; (2) new commercial, air
and trade agreements; (3) economic assistance from every
available source; (4) the transfer of surplus military equipment to Italian armed forces at lowest possible cost; and (5)
the taking of every opportunity to advertise to the Italian
people that the United States supported Italy and the U.S.
appreciated Italian progress. These pledges were relayed to
De Gasperi by Dunn on May 28, 1947 when the Italian Prime

Minister met with Dunn to confide that he was considering forming a single-party government.[12]

On June 5, 1947 Secretary of State Marshall gave the Harvard commencement address, in which he proposed American support for the economic recovery of Europe, a program that came to be known as the Marshall Plan. On the next day, Dunn was told in a cable from Marshall that a single-party government in Italy would suffer from too much opposition and that stability called for the inclusion of the PSLI, the right-wing socialists. Dunn was asked to "convey the impression of US hope that a way may yet be cleared for eventual PSLI participation in govt."[13] This could not be done immediately, Dunn reported several days later, but it was achieved within a few months.

These piecemeal reactions to the economic and political crisis in Italy constituted a unidirectional movement by the American government towards making Italy a virtual protectorate of the United States. Much of this activity related to the economic crisis and the political composition of the Italian government, which prevented the adoption of effective financial policies. The matter of Italian security was less often addressed, except insofar as the United States wished to improve the poor condition of the Italian army through the transfer of surplus American military equipment.

On June 2, 1947 the State Department requested from the Joint Chiefs of Staff an analysis of the military implications involved in the disposal of the Italian colonies, with particular reference to the British requirements for bases in Cyrenaica and perhaps in Italian Somaliland. The Joint Chiefs responded on July 3, 1947, with a model of cold war thinking as it applied to Italy. In a memorandum to the State-War-Navy Coordinating Committee (SWNCC),[14] a wartime policy coordinating group that was later to be replaced by the National Security Council, the Joint Chiefs said that it was in the interest of United States security to prevent any potentially hostile power from obtaining a firm hold in the Middle East and the Mediterranean areas. "Unfortunate and potentially catastrophic though it is, the USSR is our ideological enemy and our most probable enemy should war occur." The Soviet Union was engaged in improving its strategic position and increasing its military potential by controlling states over which it had no legitimate claim and to the great military disadvantage of the United States and its potential allies. Consequently, it was contrary to United States policy and military interests to accept any disposition of the Italian colonies which gave the USSR either unilateral or joint control of any colonies in question, even though this control were obtained under the guise of a United Nations trusteeship. Therefore, the Joint Chiefs concluded, it would be disadvantageous to the United States to allow Italy to resume control of any or all of her colonies "unless it had previously become clear that the future government of Italy will be non-communist and affiliated with the Western Democracies."

On September 24, 1947 the Policy Planning Staff of the State submitted a memorandum: "Possible Action by the U.S. to Assist the Italian Government in the Event of Communist Seizure of North Italy and the Establishment of an Italian Communist 'Government' in That Area."[15] The paper cited the increase in Communist strength in Italy, Communist reaction to their exclusion from the government by increasing propaganda, demonstrations, and strikes to bring a fall of the Italian government, and the threat to use force to bring about a change. It pointed out that under the peace treaty, the few remaining American and British forces in Italy had to be withdrawn from Italy within ninety days. Moreover, there was a treaty obligation to maintain the security and territorial integrity of the Free Territory of Trieste, and United States policy toward Italy was directed to support a friendly, democratic regime to safeguard American security aims in the Mediterranean.

The paper fully subscribed to the cold war theory as it applied to Italy. "There can be no question of the ultimate aim of the Italian Communist Party; this aim is the complete subjugation of Italy to Soviet Control." If the Communists could not succeed by constitutional means, the paper argued, they would try to disrupt economic life, undermine national and local governments, and set up "people's councils" in Communist areas.

The paper predicted that such a situation would evolve towards a civil war in which the Italian government would need to be assisted from the outside. Yugoslavia would enter the conflict and Italian Communists would seek aid from the Soviet Union; and Soviet control of the Italian peninsula would jeopardize American interests in Europe and the Mediterranean. Thus, to prepare for the eventuality of a Communist takeover of northern Italy, the Policy Planning Staff made a series of recommendations that looked toward Italian cooperation in supporting the retaining of American forces in Italy, the expansion of military facilities, and taking measures in the United Nations to thwart Yugoslavia.

In October and November 1947 a series of discussions, which came to be known as "The Pentagon Talks of 1947," took place in Washington between representatives of the United States and Great Britain.[16] Concentrating on the Middle East and the Eastern Mediterranean, the talks were based on the "conviction that the maintenance of security and tranquillity in the Middle East is a necessary condition of world peace."[17] Both sides presented papers that concluded that Italy was to be included along with Greece, Turkey and Iran as nations whose territorial integrity and political independence was important to the security of the U.S. and Britain.[18]

The thinking in the American intelligence agencies in the summer and early fall of 1947 reinforced the views that were emanating from the American embassy in Rome, the economists from the Treasury Department who were assigned to the Italian problem, the South Europe and Eastern Europe sections of the State Department, and the Joint Chiefs of Staff. On October 10, 1947 the Central Intelligence Agency (CIA) submitted a paper, "On the Current Situation in Italy,"[19] to the State-War-Navy Coordinating Committee. The study had been coordinated with the intelligence agencies of the departments of State, Army, Navy and Air Force. The paper pointed out the "vital strategic importance to prevent Italy from falling under Communist control," and it proceeded to analyze the economic, political, and military situation in Italy and in the Free Territory of Trieste. Concerning the economic situation, the paper concluded that the Italian need for foodstuffs and industrial raw materials had to be met to prevent an economic collapse, which would be politically explosive. The political situation was barely tolerable: the minority Christian Democratic government lacked working-class representation, and it needed to include the Saragat rightwing Socialists (PSLI) to improve its position.

The CIA report noted that U.S. and British forces would be withdrawn in December and that the Italian armed forces were incapable of major military operations. Italian forces would be able to maintain internal order, but they would be hard pressed if required also to defend the frontier and suppress internal insurrection. The report argued that the stability of the existing Italian government depended on its ability to obtain adequate economic support from the United States. Armed insurrection was a continuing Communist capability, but the most probable use of this force would be to create and exploit a revolutionary situation. Provided the threat of Yugoslav intervention was effectively neutralized, Italian armed forces could probably cope with a Communist insurrection that lacked general popular support. Regarding the Free Territory of Trieste, the study concluded that the underlying tensions remained and were being exploited by Yugoslavia, which was determined to acquire Trieste.

National Security Council and Italy

The National Security Council was created by the National Security Act of 1947 to give the President collective advice from officials of agencies involved in foreign affairs. The agency would advise the President with respect to the integration of domestic, foreign, and military policies relating to national security. The Council was authorized to form a staff headed by a civilian executive secretary; the first executive secretary was Sidney W. Souers, a formal naval officer. Souers organized the agency by creating three groups, staff members, secretariat, and consultants, the purpose being to maintain a link to operational officers, and recruit quality career personnel for the permanent staff. The consultants were the chief policy and operational planners for each department represented on the Council: State, Defense, Army, Navy, Air Force, National Security Resources Board, and the Central Intelligence Agency. George Kennan represented the Policy

Planning Staff of the State Department.[20]

The first NSC papers originated in the Policy Planning Staff (PPS) of the State Department. It is not unusual therefore that NSC 1, the first paper produced by the NSC staff, reflected the analysis of PPS thinking in the papers it had prepared for use in the Pentagon Talks of October 1947 and the September 24, 1947 paper on possible actions to assist the Italian government in case of a seizure of North Italy by Communist forces.

NSC 1, "The Position of the United States with Respect to Italy," underwent several revisions and updating in Winter of 1947-48. It drew in large measure on the two aforementioned PPS papers and was updated when circumstances in Italy warranted. NSC 1/1 was reported to the National Security Council on November 14, 1947.[21] The primary objective of the paper was to "assess and appraise the position of the United States with respect to Italy, taking into consideration the security interests of the United States in the Mediterranean and the Near East Area." The analysis of the problem made by the paper was essentially that of previous PPS papers. The conclusions were quite specific and called for full support for the Italian government and "equally satisfactory successive governments." The United States should ship wheat, give dollar credits, assist the Italian armed forces in the form of technical advice, give Italy sunken ships off the Italian coast as scrap material, and transfer certain non-combat equipment to the Italian armed forces. The report called for more economic aid, relaxation of onerous terms in the peace treaty, and for supporting Italy for membership in the United Nations. It asked for actions to combat Communist propaganda in Italy by an information program; and it sought to promote a more favorable attitude towards Italy by France and Great Britain and enlist their active support for U.S. aims. It argued for bringing violations of the peace treaty to the United Nations in the event Yugoslavia attempted to seize Italian territory, and for urgently adopting and effectively implementing a long-range program for the rehabilitation of Europe.

The report recommended that the United States "should not use armed force in a civil conflict of an internal nature in Italy." However, in the event that a Communist-dominated government was set up in Italy by civil war or illegal means, the U.S. should continue to recognize the legal government and assist it. A specific plan was then recommended that included the following measures:

(1) Notice by the Italian government to the four powers that it could not maintain authority throughout Italy and could not accept responsibility for the execution of the peace treaty.

(2) The U.S. should express alarm and notify Italy and the United Nations that in light of the new situation coming into effect so soon after the entry into effect of the peace treaty, that it must reconsider its position regarding the terms of the treaty.

(3) Following notice to the U.S. by Italy regarding its inability to enforce the treaty, the U.S. should request additional military facilities, including selected Italian naval and air bases.

(4) The United States should stop aid to Communist-dominated areas but continue it to areas under the control of the Italian government.

(5) If the Communists seize control of all or part of Italy prior to December 15, 1947 the U.S. should suspend withdrawal of its troops pending a reconsideration of the situation.[22]

The National Security Council considered NSC 1/1 and adopted its conclusions as an expression of the Council's advice to the President. NSC 1/1 was approved by the President on November 24, 1947.[23] On November 28, the Acting Director of the Office of European Affairs recommended to the Secretary of State that the measures set forth in NSC 1/1 be immediately communicated to all departments with the request that every effort be made to implement them without delay. It was also recommended that the military departments be advised that it may be shortly necessary to implement the military portions of NSC 1/1, that is, actions to be taken in case of a Communist insurrection.

The National Security Council decided that NSC 1/1 be revised within 45 days before the national elections in Italy.[24] NSC 1/2 submitted by the NSC on February 10, 1948 continued the same facts bearing on the situation and analysis put forth in the Pentagon Talks paper of 1947 and the September 24, 1947 PPS paper on possible actions to assist Italy in case of a communist takeover in North Italy.[25] It noted that Communist strength came primarily from the economic distress in Italy and secondarily from the creation of the Communist-Socialist coalition, which was presenting a joint list in the April 18, 1948 elections. The Communist campaign of strikes and agitation was the first phase of a major effort to take over the government either by winning elections, but, the paper argued, the party probably will not resort to a general strike or armed insurrection until the elections are over, and not until Congress acted on the European Recovery Program.

It is interesting to note that NSC 1/2 makes the Italian Communist Party an instrument of Soviet policy, rather than an independent party. For example:

> If the Communists fail to gain admission to the government and if the ERP is implemented, the Kremlin may then order armed insurrection in a final effort to prevent Italian recovery under a Western oriented regime.[26]

NSC 1/2 came to the same conclusions as NSC 1/1, but added a few more actions that the United States government might take in Italy, particularly in the event that a portion of Italy fell under Communist domination by virtue of armed insurrection or other illegal means. The U.S. ought to be prepared to deploy forces to government controlled sections of peninsular Italy and deploy forces to Sicily and Sardinia in strength sufficient to occupy those islands against indigenous Communist opposition. This would require first approval by the Joint Chiefs of Staff that it be militarily sound, and it would necessitate a partial mobilization. President Truman approved the conclusions of NSC 1/2 on March 15, 1948, one month before the Italian elections.

NSC 1/3 was given a different title: "Position of the United States with Respect to Italy in the Light of the Possibility of Communist Participation in the Government by Legal Means."[27] The new title reflects the increasing fear in the Policy Planning Staff of a Communist victory in the Italian elections. The analysis raises the stakes for the United States and for Italy, for the paper states that American "security interests in the Mediterranean are immediately and gravely threatened by the possibility that the Popular Front in Italy would win participation in the government, and that using a pattern made familiar in Eastern Europe, take over the control of the government and transform Italy into a totalitarian state subservient to Moscow."[28]

NSC 1/3 stated that if the elections were held that day the Popular Front would receive a plurality, but if unchecked, current trends indicated that a majority was not improbable. Six weeks remained for the United States to reverse this trend.

The conclusions of NSC 1/3 were less concerned with an insurrection, but with actions the United States needed to take if the Communists won the election. These actions were directed towards preventing Communist domination and promoting ways to facilitate continued opposition to the Communists. The list of recommended actions included: strengthening the United States military position in the Mediterranean; strengthening the potential of the U.S. military establishment; continuing economic aid to Italy only if it assisted in combating Communist control; providing military equipment and supplies only if they were received by anti-Communist elements; trying to detach the left-wing Socialists from the Communists; continuing to assist the Christian Democrats and other selected anti-Communist parties; stepping up propaganda; maintaining the U.S. position in Trieste; and reviewing aid to Greece and Turkey.

In the event the Communists obtained domination of Italy "by legal means," the paper recommended that the U.S. undertake a number of military and political actions. The United States should undertake limited military mobilization, promote combined staff planning with selected nations, and give aid to the Italian anti-Communist underground. In this case, the U.S. should oppose Italian membership in the United Nations.[29]

On March 15, 1948, the President approved the recommendation of the National Security Council in NSC 1/3 pertaining to the intervention in the elections and he approved the recommendations of NSC 1/2. This approval, however, was specifically given to only those recommendations to assist the

Italian government in the election campaign.

The role of George F. Kennan is significant in the evolution of the policy towards Italy, not only because of his authorship of the official containment theory of the Cold War, but because of his specific analysis of the Italian situation. The papers emanating from the Policy Planning Staff of the State Department and the papers prepared later by the National Security Council staff were written under his direction. It is very interesting to note, therefore, that his later disavowals of the militaristic interpretation of the containment policy seem to be refuted by the documentary record. Kennan has asserted that under his theory the Soviet Union had to be contained by political measures, not necessarily military ones, and that too often the vague words of the Mr. X article were misinterpreted.

In the hectic days of February and March 1948 when it appeared that the Popular Front might win a plurality or a majority in the Italian elections, Kennan was no less a cold warrior than John Foster Dulles. In the PPS and NSC papers the Italian Communist party was considered to be no more than an appendage of the Kremlin and ready to do its bidding even if called upon to stage an insurrection. Yugoslavia was also considered to be part of an international Communist conspiracy, for there was a real danger that Yugoslavia would assist Italian Communists. This view was expressed, even though Marshall Tito was having his falling out with Stalin at the time.

An example of Kennan's cold war thinking—in the militaristic sense—is evident in the documentation released 30 years later. In March 1948, Kennan was in Manila, where he had been forwarded the American embassy's cable traffic from Italy. At this time, Secretary of State Marshall wrote an urgent memorandum to Kennan and three other officials asking what effect a Communist election victory in Italy would have on the European recovery program. Kennan responded in a cable dated March 18, 1948. He argued that the Communist threat was directed from Moscow, and the Kremlin could feel itself overextended in East Europe and under extreme urgency, especially in light of the February coup d'etat in Czechoslovakia. The Kremlin leaders must try to break the unity of the West; the present situation in Italy therefore was very dangerous. Kennan went on:

> I am persuaded Communist[s] could not win without strong factor of intimidation on their side, and it would clearly be better that elections not take place at all than that Communists win in these circumstances.[30]

The concluding paragraph of his cable bears quotation in full:

> For these reasons I question whether it would not be preferable for Italian government to outlaw Communist Party and take strong action against it before elections. Communists would presumably reply with civil war, which would give us grounds for reoccupation of Foggia fields or any other facilities we might wish. This would admittedly result in much violence and probably a military division of Italy; but we are getting close to the deadline and I think it might well be preferable to a bloodless election victory, unopposed by ourselves which would give the Communists the entire peninsula at one coup and send waves of panic to all surrounding areas.[31]

John D. Hickerson, the Director of the Office of European Affairs in the State Department, a person with whom Kennan was often at odds, wrote on Kennan's cable:

> 1. Action to outlaw C.P. before election or to postpone election would be certain to cause civil war.
> 2. Non-communist parties have a good chance of winning election without any such drastic action.
> 3. Therefore action recommended by GFK seems unwise. Instead, U.S. Government should do everything it properly can to strengthen non-communist forces and parties. J.D.H.[32]

In the end, Hickerson's more diplomatic and political approach prevailed over the supposedly less militaristic views of Kennan.

Although Kennan's views on suspending the election were not adopted, every action proposed by NSC 1 that pertained to assisting the Italian government in the election campaign was carried out. The comprehensive campaign of intervention in the elections process included such actions as a general program of propaganda through the USIA and speeches by Ambassador Dunn favorable to the United States; statements that although American troops were being withdrawn from Italy in December 1947, the U.S. would continue its interest in the preservation of a free and democratic Italy; strengthening forces in the Mediterranean; sending military equipment to the Italian armed forces; re-proposing Italian membership in the United Nations; paying prisoners of war salaries; and returning monetary gold that Germany had looted from Italy in the war.

In addition to these actions a great deal of effort was directed towards the economic situation in Italy. Aid was increased and publicized, and Secretary Marshall stated that Italy would not receive European Recovery Program assistance if the Communists won the election. Ambassador Dunn made many public speeches and especially made it a point to appear at Italian ports when significant shiploads of American assistance arrived. Myron Taylor, President Truman's personal representative to the Vatican, was also dispatched to Italy and made a show of support for Church interests and its struggle against Communism.

Other actions were taken. The United States got Britain and France to agree that Trieste should be returned to Italy, a statement made in the middle of the election campaign that caused great jubilation among the government parties and which was condemned as a cynical act by the Soviet Union and the Popular Front parties. Funds were given to the government parties; and secret shipments of poster paper were sent to Italy for Christian Democratic posters. The American government also cooperated and promoted the intervention of private American groups, especially the Italian Americans in intervening in the election. [33]

The 1948 election was a watershed in Italian politics. It produced a massive victory for the Christian Democrats, who won 48.5 percent of the popular vote and a majority of seats in the assembly. The Popular Front coalition of the Left received only 31 percent of the vote. Since several significant factors were at work in the election, it is difficult to assess the impact of American intervention on the popular vote. But it is generally believed that without the American factor, the Center parties would have been hard pressed to construct a majority of seats.

Conclusions

NSC 1 pulled together for the first time a number of themes that had been gathering momentum in the State and Defense Departments. One can say that NSC 1 is the first comprehensive expression of American foreign policy towards Italy in the postwar period. Previous papers and policy actions were piecemeal and seemingly were responding to particular emergencies. Much of the earlier activity was concerned with the drastic economic situation in Italy. From administering wartime economic relief programs, the U.S. became more and more committed to rescue the Italian economy from collapse. The security question was first addressed regarding the Eastern Mediterranean. Given the strong views of the Joint Chiefs of Staff on the strategic importance of Italy and its former colonies, Italy was then included with Greece and Turkey in the Truman Doctrine. As particular events occurred, American security interests in Italy came to be considered foremost, especially after the Communist coup in Czechoslovakia in February 1948. The fear of a Communist victory in Italy by constitutional or illegal means was so intense in some quarters that it convinced George Kennan to call for a suspension of the Italian election. Fortunately this view did not prevail, but the massive intervention did prove that the United States was ready to do anything to keep Italy from falling under the control of the Left.

---

[1] Samuel Flagg Bemis, *A Diplomatic History of the American People*, 4th ed., (New York: Henry Holt, 1955), passim; H. Stuart Hughes, *The United States and Italy* (Cambridge: Harvard UP, 1953), passim.

[2] William Reitzel, *The Mediterranean* (New York: Harcourt, Brace, 1948), 26.

[3] Norman Kogan, *Italy and the Allies*, (Cambridge: Harvard UP, 1956), 123-25; Charles F. Delzell, *Mussolini's Enemies* (Princeton

UP, 1961), 563; Hughes, 151.

4 Igino Giordini, *Alcide De Gasperi* (Verona: Arnaldo Mondadori, 1955), 183.

5 Adstans [pseud.], *Alcide De Gasperi nella politica italiana*: 1944-53 (Verona: Arnaldo Mondadori, 1956), 92; Alberto Tarchiani, *America-Italia: Le dieci giornate de Gasperi negli Stati Uniti* (Milan: Rizzoli, 1947), 128.

6 Muriel Grindrod, *The Rebuilding of Italy* (London: Royal Institute of International Affairs, 1955), 40-50.

7 Grindrod, 49-50; Hughes, 156-57; U.S. Department of State, *Foreign Relations of the United States: 1948, Western Europe*, Vol. III (Washington: Government Printing Office, 1974), passim, hereafter cited as FRUS. Many documents cited in this paper were declassified in the mid-1970s; selected and edited versions of telegrams, letters, diplomatic notes, memoranda, reports and studies have been published in FRUS. Full texts and unpublished documents are in The National Archives, hereafter cited as NA.

8 X [George F. Kennan], "The Sources of Soviet Conduct," *Foreign Affairs*, 25 (July, 1947), 581.

9 *FRUS*: 1947, III, 835-1001, passim.

10 *Ibid.*, 891-92.

11 *Ibid.*, 896.

12 *Ibid.*, 909-11.

13 *Ibid.*, 919.

14 NA, State-War-Navy-Air Force Coordinating Committee, RG 353, Decimal File 091, Italy, Box 76, SWN 5436, July 3, 1947.

15 *FRUS*: 1947, III, 976-81.

16 *FRUS*: 1947, V.

17 *Ibid.*, 615.

18 *Ibid.*, 581.

19 NA, *General Records*, RG 59, State Department Decimal Files, 865.00/10-2247.

20 Sidney W. Souers, "Policy Formulation for National Security," *American Political Science Review*, 43 (June, 1949), 534-55.

21 For the full text, see, N.A., RG 341, NSC 1/1, O&D, 091, Italy, TS,

30 September 1947, sec. 1; for an edited text, see FRUS: 1948, III, 724-26.

22 *FRUS*: 1948, III, 726.

23 *Ibid.*

24 *Ibid.*, 765.

25 For the full text, see N.A. RG 319, NSC 1/2, P&O 091, Italy, TS, February 10, 1948, Case 3/8; for an edited text, see FRUS: 1948, III, 765-69.

26 *Ibid.*, 767.

27 For the full text, see, N.A., RG 319, NSC 1/3, P&O, 091, Italy, TS, March 8, 1948, Case 3/17.

28 *FRUS* : 1948, III, 775-76.

29 *Ibid.*, 779.

30 *Ibid.*, 848.

31 *Ibid.*, 849.

32 *Ibid.*

33 Ernest E. Rossi, *The United States and the 1948 Election in Italy*, Ph.D. dissertation (Pittsburgh: University of Pittsburgh, 1964), passim.

America's Little Italies: Past, Present and Future

Jerome Krase
Brooklyn College
City University of New York

I. The Ethnic Community: Symbols and Reality, When Fact is Fiction and *Vice Versa*

Almost everyone, writers, scientists and lay people, seem to be concerned with "stereotypes." Few people, however, actually understand what they are and the role they play in making social life possible in a complex world. Even fewer are able to explain how particular stereotypes come into being and are utilized by people to evaluate the world around them.

Most dictionaries provide two definitions of the word "stereotype." The first, relating to the printing process, is "a one-piece printing plate cast in type mold (matrix taken of a printing surface) as a page of set type." The second, used in social psychology, is "an unvarying form or pattern; specifically a fixed or conventional notion or conception of a person, group, idea, etc., held by a number of people, and allowing for no individuality, critical judgment, etc."

In the area of ethnic studies, including Italian American studies, it seems that many of those who are engaged in research and writing about any particular group attempt to destroy old negative stereotypes and create new positive ones. These "professional ethnics" are especially good at creating superhuman myths of their favorite groups. "Super Italians," for example, all claim to have descended from Leonardo Da Vinci and argue that the Mafia is merely a Hollywood creation.

Despite arguments against their use, stereotypes are inevitable. Some group stereotypes are more or less accurate. Some group stereotypes are more or less inaccurate. Generalizing about human beings creates stereotypes. The best explanation for the persistence of stereotypes is that they are useful. When people live in a complex social environment they find it necessary to categorize events, people and objects in order to deal effectively with the myriad of life occurrences that they experience. Without generalization the social world makes no sense.

Stereotypes, as all other social facts, have consequences and these consequences can be positive, neutral or negative both for those who employ the images and those who are their object. In this essay I will not be discussing traditional approaches to the study of ethnic stereotyping but will try to develop a different and perhaps more interesting way of investigating this common sense aspect of everyday modern social life.

Specifically, I will focus upon the Italian American neighborhood as a "stereotypical" phenomenon. Even more to the point, I am interested in discovering, describing and analyzing what there is of visual similarities in the neighborhood communities in which people who are of Italian extraction live. When people think of the Italian American community, a relatively common image comes to mind: The Urban Little Italy; colorful, lively, compact, as well as sensuous, sinister and hostile to outsiders. Is this image accurate? If so, why? What is the role of history and culture in creating this image and its reality? What are the implications of this image for the past, present and future of the community?

The origins of my research interests are both conventional and serendipitous. For almost twenty years I have been an activist social scientist who has simultaneously studied urban community life while involved in the search for solutions to practical community problems. My first modest contribution to the field was the demonstration of how the way people think of themselves (their self concept) affects the places in which they live; and conversely- how the way people define their neighborhoods has an effect on their own self conceptions. This, in turn, led to a second order problem of how people on the outside, especially those people with political and economic power, view particular people and neighborhoods. Along these lines the final question is: what are the impacts of these perceptions on people and their communities?

Practically speaking, on the negative side, when people think little of themselves, they devalue the places they inhabit and this can result in the neighborhood being destroyed from within. At the second level, when outsiders define the same people and their locales as negative, the community can be attacked from without. Throughout history Italian American communities have been highly valued by those who live within them but have been negatively viewed by those outside them.

For the most part, my earliest research focused upon inner city nonwhite minority neighborhoods. Communities which were treated with "benign neglect" during the 1960s and 1970s. It is obvious, however, that my theoretical apparatus could be easily adapted to the study of local communities anywhere, anytime and inhabited by anyone. There are many analogies that can be made between the fate of "Little Italies" and nonwhite ghettos in American society. The major differences can be traced to the relatively better ability of Italians to defend themselves both symbolically and territorially. One must note that Little Italies as long ago as the 1890s and as recently as the 1950s have been seen as "slums" and "criminal breeding grounds" by many social commentators.

The serendipitous side of my eleven-year study of Italian neighborhoods began as I attempted to collect photographs depicting Italian American community life in order to create a comprehensive archive of the "Italians of Brooklyn, Past and Present." As is still typical in Italian American Studies the project faced many financial and academic difficulties. Without institutional support for either my time or expenses, I asked students in an extra course I taught for no compensation, to provide photographic materials as part of their family histories. I also engaged several other students in Independent Study courses to go out and take pictures of "Italian Neighborhoods" in Brooklyn. Both projects awakened my interest in stereotypical phenomena: their origins, causes and effects.

As I surveyed dozens of family histories and related documents, I noticed striking similarities, not so much in the individual details of each story but in the general form of presentation. For example, each student's insistence and emphasis on the "uniqueness" of their heritage was generalizable. Stereotypically speaking, these Italian American students saw themselves as "different" from their cohorts. They also seemed to be responding to a general, negative stereotype of their counterparts. They seemed to be saying, "I am not like THEM." They tended to counterpose their own family history to that found in standard texts.

From a visual perspective, what they presented as a display of their families' lives were almost interchangeable. Pictures of family members and stages of development included some funeral cards with cameos of the deceased. It is not so much that they all looked alike, but that they saw life alike. i.e., as a series of family events: baptism, communion, confirmation, birthdays, graduations, weddings, deaths, holidays, festas, home and job and a great deal of candid eating around a table. The generational difference of their visions was most influenced by advances in camera technology; from early posed portraits to more spontaneous glimpses of everyday life. The questions then arise as to why ethnics see themselves and their lives in similar ways? How do others see them? How do these views agree, or disagree, with each other? How do these images affect lives and life chances?

The second chance awakening occurred as I began to mount exhibits of the students' and my own work. My Independent Studies documentary photographers especially surprised me in their choice of subject matter. I had instructed them to go out and take pictures of Italian neighborhoods in Brooklyn. They were students who were well aware of ethnic stereotyping and its negative consequences. They were in fact quite proud of their own Italian heritage and sensitive to anti-Italian bias. Several had on occasion complained of discrimination and the way that outsiders portrayed Italians in the media.

What they presented to me as the fruits of their labor in the field was a large collection of candid and a few "posed" photographs that could have easily been the result of an assignment to create a stereotypical view of Italian neighborhoods. Most of the same elements were there; pizza parlors, wash hanging out to dry, men sitting in social clubs or hanging on corners, weddings, food shopping, etc. What I assume had happened was that the students had interpreted the assignment "show me an Italian neighborhood," to mean "show me a neighborhood that *looks* Italian." They did not take an objective photographic survey. They focused on what in the neighborhood looked Italian and what someone looking at their photographs would recognize as Italian-like.

The third surprise happened as I was visiting an Italian American community organization store front office to talk about some city-funded social service programs. The group had recently mounted a photographic exhibition of the works of members. The framed prints were not of American locales but of places in Italy. Most of the pictures were more or less typical travel poster visions of Italy. One photo in particular fascinated me. It was of a triangular corner in a small Italian town. The image was quite ordinary in aspect but it intrigued me because my initial reaction to it was one of vague familiarity. I had seen it before, but where? I enquired as to the location of the scene and was told it was in a town in Apulia called Mola di Bari. I had at the time never been to Mola. I had travelled twice to Italy before the exhibit and once since. I had also surveyed many Italian and Italian America communities. Then it struck me that the scene repeated one that I had viewed in the Italian North End of Boston. The scale of the architecture was similar as were the stone streets, both a few centuries old.

I would not have been surprised by this observation if I had thought more deeply about it. There ought to be a connection between Italian Americans and Italy, and Italian American neighborhoods and neighborhoods in Italy. Discovering what the connections are, how they are expressed in visual appearances and analyzing their form and function became the goal of my subsequent research.

II. Questions and Explanations

If there are regularities in the structure and functioning of Italian communities and connections between communities in Italy and the United States we should ask what they are and why they exist. How does Italian culture influence the form and operation of the physical and social environments in

which people live? How does history create and modify the
Italian culture of community? What happens when this culture is transported to America? How does the experience of
Italians in American modify this culture? Can these questions
be posed and answered through the employment of visual
data such as photographs? I doubt that I will ever be able to
answer, or even address, all of these questions adequately in
this or any other form. I am however, brave or foolish enough,
to make an attempt.

There have been many studies of Italians and Italian
Americans. Books such as Joseph Lopreato's *Peasants No
More*, Carlo Levi's *Christ Stopped at Eboli*, Anne Cornelisen's
Torregrecca, and Edward Banfield's *The Moral Basis of a
Backward Society*. These are a few well known examples of
works which have focused on communities in various regions
of Italy and at different periods of history representing large
numbers of Italians who have migrated to the United States.
Studies of Italians in America are even more numerous and
cover almost all periods of history and locations here. Some
examples of this wide scope are the works of Humbert Nelli,
Italians in Chicago, 1880-1930, Herbert Gans, *Urban Villagers*, William Foote Whyte, *Street Corner Society*, Deanna
Paoli Gumina, *The Italians of San Francisco*, 1850-1930, Rudolph J. Vecoli, *Italian Immigrants in Rural and Small Town
America*. In all these studies the greatest emphasis has been
placed on the close relationship between Italian cultural values and local social organization. The anthropologists Conrad
Arensberg and Solon T. Kimball in their book *Culture and
Community*, have discussed the universal aspects of the cul-
ture-local community relationship. This influence, then, of
cultural values on the Italian community is not surprising.
My own works on ethnicity and local community life such as
Self and Community in the City, and those of others, have focused on the visible aspects of neighborhood spatial organization.

The shape of American ethnic communities is assumed to
be the resulting combination, through the processes of assimilation and acculturation, of immigrant and American cultural
values. Milton Gordon (1964), among others, has noted that
cultural assimilation (acculturation) takes place more rapidly

than structural assimilation (assimilation). That is, groups take on American culture at a faster rate than they blend into the new society. Part of structural assimilation is the random dispersal (for example geographic and occupational distributions) of the new group in the host society. There are many factors which work against this ultimate dispersal or homogenization.

It can be assumed that immigrants attempt more or less successfully to replicate their home environment in the new location. In the extreme, one might suggest that they also may choose to locate in environments which most closely resemble their native ones and which make possible the preservation of central cultural values. The process of creating an ethnic ghetto has elements of what Louis Wirth in his work *The Ghetto*, called "voluntary and involuntary segregation." Of course ethnic groups in the United States have relative degrees of power to select their own environments, to maintain them or to modify situations to suit cultural tastes. One must also take into account the degree of difference between the immigrant's society and the dominant American social and cultural systems.

Not only do immigrant communities have relative abilities to select, maintain and modify local environments to suit cultural tastes, they also differ in their ability and willingness to defend their neighborhood after it is established. The perseverance of urban Italian American communities is well documented. This local persistence is repeatedly demonstrated in Italy, for example the communities almost obliterated by earthquakes around Avellino in 1981 were rebuilt on the same sites despite warnings of potential repetition by national authorities. Incredibly, except for the Po River basins, there is almost no place in Italy not prone to seismic disturbance of disaster proportion.

Most Italian communities count their age in centuries rather than decades. During such long periods of continuous habitation, the attachment of culture to specific pieces of territory and spatial arrangements has ample time to develop. Fustel de Coulange in *The Ancient City*, referred to these attachments as "sacred," and used the ritual founding of Rome by Romulus and Remus as an example of the importance of the "home" territory to ancient and primitive tribes. For contemporary Italians the home continues to be sacred. One might suggest that the traditional Italian culture survives only to the extent that the local community survives and is maintained.

The Italian community in America is assumed to contain and display many elements of household, kinship and local association which they hold in common with their counterparts who remain in Italy. Much of the research on Italian Americans since the turn- of-the-century has focused on the processes of assimilation and acculturation whereby Italians become more American and less Italian in their ways. Almost all of the literature emphasizes the relatively slow rate of change among Italian Americans as opposed to other groups. This is especially characteristic of those Italian Americans found in urban, working class neighborhoods which have resisted change due to cultural habits, discrimination and voluntary segregation.

Despite the interest shown in the literature on the relationship between Italian American and Italian values,and the communities which represent and support those values, there has been little direct comparison of Italian communities in the United States and Italy. Carla Bianco's study of *The Two Rosettos* is a major exception to the rule. Her work is intriguing in that she notes not only common cultural elements but significant differences as well. For example she notes that because American Rosettans emigrated in an earlier period of Italian history and then were cut off from Italian influences, they have preserved some of the traditions lost in the town of origin. Although both Rosettos were built on the top of a hill, Bianca noted that American Rosettans did not employ Italian architectural styles when they built their houses. I would predict, however, that a trained, or even a merely sensitive eye would find ample evidence of spatial expressions of cultural connections in Rosetto, Pennsylvania. In a related vein Donna R. Gabaccia in *From Sicily to Elizabeth Street*, noted the similarity between the home environments of immigrants and the neighborhoods in which they settled on New York's Lower East Side between 1880 and 1930.

Of course most Italians did not have the opportunity, or interest as sojourners, to replicate topographically and architecturally their home towns. They came and stayed where economic opportunities presented themselves. For the most part these opportunities were in highly congested urban areas. Interestingly, dense environments were not unusual for Italian immigrants who left small, but highly populated villages and towns scattered throughout the countryside or who left behind congested neighborhood villages in large Italian cities. Italy remains today one of the most densely populated nations in the world, especially when one considers the ratio of population to residential spaces. This space, as well as arable land area, has always been limited on the Italian peninsula. Italy has a tradition of residential density.

We have every reason to expect that Italian and Italian American communities will be similar to one another and for these similarities to be expressed in spatial arrangements and uses of space. We can also expect that these similarities (and differences) can be seen and captured through photography. As noted by authors such as Edward T. Hall in *The Hidden Dimension*, and Mark LaGory and John Pipkin in *Urban Social Space*, there are significant differences in values toward territory and space evidenced in various cultures. American cultural life with its Anglo-Germanic traditions is significantly different from the Italian Mediterranean system. It is not hard to detect the visual differences between such cities as Oslo, Frankfurt, London, Milan, Rome and Palermo on the north-south European axis. It is also not hard to see that most American cities and "Old Stock" neighborhoods fit the Anglo-German and not the Southern European mold.

On a smaller scale some aspects of the differences among American ethnic groups have been noted by Gerald Suttles in his books; *The Social Construction of Communities*, and *The Social Order of the Slum*. Suttles went into considerable detail about the territorial notions of Italian Americans who shared a residential section of Chicago with Blacks and Hispanics in the 1950s. In his work on urban neighborhoods, Suttles coined the term "defended" neighborhood to describe the residential areas of working-class Italian Americans and similar groups. Because he was not a student of Italian culture he did not understand the degree to which "defensiveness" is part of the Italian culture of community.

Another social scientist who has written on the culture-environment connection is Amos Rapoport. He stated in his book, *Human Aspects of Urban Form*, that:

> The physical environment is then an expression of cultural cognitive categories such as wilderness, garden, city, public, private and so on which, if the environment is meaningful produce the appropriate cognitive schemata. More generally the built environment can be seen as the making visible of an 'ethnic domain,' a non-spatial concept linked to culture, values, symbols, status, lifestyle and the like. In many cases, therefore, cognitive categories and domains can be given direct environmental equivalents. (109-10)

There must be then, an Italian "ethnic domain." An extremely important, although often overlooked, aspect of neighborhood community life is visual. We should be able to "see" culture. For example, the tradition of sex segregation in some Islamic and Mediterranean groups results in a particular arrangement of residential structures whereby interior spaces are provided for their activities out of view of nonfamily members. The cultural value of modesty therefore has a physical result. Women are not generally seen in public places, unless there for specific purposes such as shopping and seldom alone. Whereas for men, casual lounging in public areas is common. Even more easily seen are values which reflect social structure, such as age, sex, occupation, class and caste are aesthetic values of color, design and form. Ideally, the local culture is an aesthetic expression of the local community. Most simply, the colors that people use to paint their houses are cultural expressions. With these ideas in mind, we should expect that Italian communities will have a certain "look" and that there should be some similarity in the appearance of Italian communities in Italy and the United States.

Based on hundreds of direct observations and thousands of photographs of Italian communities in Italy and the United States I can outline some of the elements of the "Italian Culture of Community." These elements express themselves in physical arrangement, uses and meanings of spaces and visual appearances. They are as follows:

1. The Italian community is small scale and based around the facilitation of family and personal relations.
2. The community has a high tolerance, if not a preference, for high human and physical density.
3. The community exhibits the supremacy of private over public values in regard to space and activities.
4. The culture emphasizes individuality rather than conformity.
5. Italian residential communities tolerate mixed commercial and industrial uses within their boundaries.
6. Age and sex segregation for spaces and activities is a general feature of Italian communities.
7. Italian communities show attachment to traditional architectural aesthetics as exhibited, where possible, in design and construction, as well as, colors and materials.
8. The Italian community places extreme value on the defense of individual and group territory.

The following section discusses one of the ways in which the Italian Culture of Community has impacted on the development of Italian urban neighborhoods in the United States. It also demonstrates how Italian community values have resulted in contemporary problems and makes predictions for the future of stereotypical "Little Italies."

III. Little Italies Never Die; They Gentrify

In Italy, two millennia of natural, economic and political disasters have found local communities to be virtually immovable. It therefore is not surprising that in the United States Italians have generally been the last to leave from changing inner city neighborhoods. This fierce attachment to the sacred soil, or pavement, has had many implications, both positive and negative.

In the 1950s, as in earlier government "slum clearance" programs during the Great Depression, many Italian American neighborhoods absorbed the blows of wrecking balls and bulldozers and then tried to find ways of living peaceably with low-income housing projects in their midst. Gerald Suttles notes this situation in his study of the Addams Area in Chicago (1968). Then came Federal Housing and Highway programs which lured the working and middle class to the suburbs while tearing apart viable communities to make it easier for cars and trucks to travel back and forth, and through the city. Expressways were added to housing projects as new neighbors and new dangers. Herbert Gans in *The Urban Villagers* documented the damage to Boston's West End Italian neighborhood by the extension of expressways into downtown Boston.

Between 1930 and 1960, Italian Americans, through default, in many instances became *The* inner city white ethnics, living side by side with minorities in deteriorating central cities. When the Federal and local governments finally recognized the problems of poor nonwhites in American cities, Italian Americans and other working class groups came to symbolize their oppressors. For example, busing for integration and neighborhood desegregation efforts at first focused on the few white communities left in large American cities. Residents of Italian American neighborhoods in the 1970s quickly became part of the increasingly vocal and socially conservative "Silent Majority." The dilemmas of working class Italian Americans and their hostility to Democratic party liberalism was painfully demonstrated by Jonathan Rieder's study of "Canarsie" in Brooklyn, New York. There local Italians and Jews reacted to the threat of Black invasion into their neighborhood

In the 1980s there are new threats to what is left of the traditional American Little Italies while at the same time that Italian American communities in the near suburbs and small towns come to realize that they are not immune to "progress" and change "American Style." Ironically, the greatest danger for urban Italian American neighborhoods comes in the form of Yuppies (Young Urban Professionals), co-ops and condos. The history and resulting local culture of the Italian community made it possible for them to survive in places no one else wanted for so long and yet this strength makes them most vulnerable in modern urban real estate markets. It could be concluded that urban Little Italies may exist only as "Ethnic Disneylands" in the future or perhaps as Pompeian-like ruins. Tour guides already speak in reverent tones of the Italian village-like life that once decorated the Little Italies, Sicilies and

Calabrias of Manhattan, Boston, Chicago and San Francisco. In recent years, there has been much talk, both informed and nonsensical, about a so-called *new* phenomenon in American cities-"Gentrification." Very simply, gentrification means the influx of higher status people into a particular area of a city. To some urban experts, particularly conservative economists, it is a blessing. To others, especially liberal social critics, it is a curse. Not long ago, the 1960's to be precise, the outflow of the gentry from the inner cities was seen as a major catastrophe by all except suburban developers. A leading civil rights proponent, Eleanor Holmes Norton, herself Black and, at the time Commissioner for Human Rights in New York City, openly expressed the fear that the city might become, in so many words- "too Black."

Today liberal social critics bemoan the movement of middle and upper-middle income people back to the central city be- cause it causes "displacement." Displacement is a term for the forcing out of less advantaged residents from a neighborhood as rents and housing prices rise to meet the demand of the invading gentry. These same observers had earlier complained about the movement out of the city of the middle class in the 1950s and 1960s as part of the "white flight" phenomenon. People then moved out of the city because they were racists and now they are moving back because they are racists, or so it seems. Undoubtably the perception of the middle class about the "livability" of the inner city has undergone significant change over three decades.

Throughout both these tidal movements of urban population some concentrations of white ethnic neighborhoods remained relatively unmoved. One of these anomalies was the Italian American neighborhood.

It is not that Italian Americans did not participate in the exodus of whites from the central cities, they did in large numbers move and create new neighborhoods in urban fringe or suburban areas. They also expanded older Italian American communities already outside the central cities. However, significant or peculiar remnants stayed behind. It is these vestiges of Little Italies which, after surviving urban renewal, housing projects and minority group expansion, became threatened by the new gentry invaders.

There is a simple theory to explain the rise and fall of our cities' cores and the Italian American anomaly. The United States is a young nation by old world standards and as an urban nation it is a comparative infant. American society is also probably the most anti-urban in the western world. One must note that our founding fathers especially feared the growth of cities and the rabble who would assemble there. Cities here have risen and fallen in single generations and some, already rising again. These cycles have taken place without the cut off of trade and communication by the Goths, Islamic Jihads, Mongol Hordes and/or bubonic plagues.

The key to understanding any city's history of stability and change has been the value of its center. This principle of urban ecology was first posited by Robert E. Park, Ernest W. Burgess and Roderick D. McKenzie in the 1920s as they studied the city of Chicago (1967). As the center increases in value, people and activities (such as business) move toward the core and compete for the space within. The most powerful are successful and occupy the prized positions. As the core decreases in value the process is reversed. In the 1920s they described five zones radiating out from the Loop to the Commuter Zone. Then the least desirable residential areas were in Zone II, or the "Zone of Transition." In that district one found "roomers," the "underworld," the "ghetto," Chinatown," "slums," and "Little Sicily." In 1987 the same zone is filled with upscale stores, high-rise office buildings and expensive apartments and restaurants.

In American society and culture the most important values are economic, or materialistic, and as in all societies our cities epitomize our civilization. In Italian society and culture the critical values are blood ties and the connection of family to a particular place. It is not that Italy and Italians are unmaterialistic, far from it, but in comparison to Americans they have always been far less successful at economics and politics than others. Although many like to think of Italy as Roman conquerors and Florentine sculptors, the "real" Italy for centuries has been millions of families struggling to survive in hostile environments ruled by materially and politically successful foreigners.

The defense of the Italian family has for ages been fought

from within the walls of its home- the house, village or neighborhood. The home is a fortress which can cut off the outside world with the closing of a gate, a door or a window. Italian neighborhoods have survived thousands of years perched on maintain tops, on the sides of sheer cliffs, tucked in by dangerous coves, crammed into exasperating cities, fighting against rising floods and tides, lava-spewing volcanoes and land-splitting earthquakes.

It is little wonder that Italians are the last to go from the constantly changing scene of American cities.

References

Conrad Arensberg and Solon T. Kimball. *Culture and Community*. New York: Harcourt, Brace and World, 1965.

Edward C. Banfield. *The Moral Basis of a Backward Society*. New York: The Free Press, 1958.

Carla Bianco. *The Two Rosettos*. Bloomington, Indiana: Indiana University Press, 1974.

Anne Cornelisen. *Torregrecca*. London: Granada Publishing Limited, 1971.

Fustel De Coulanges. *The Ancient City*. Garden City, New York: Doubleday and Company, 1967. Willard Small (trans.)

Donna Gabaccia. *From Sicily to Elizabeth Street*. Albany, New York: State University of New York Press, 1984.

Herbert Gans. *The Urban Villagers*. New York: The Free Press, 1962.

Milton Gordon. *Assimilation in American* Life. New York: Oxford University Press, 1964.

Deanna Paoli Gumina. *The Italians of San Francisco, 1850-1930*. Staten Island, New York: Center for Migration Studies, 1978.

Edward T. Hall. *The Hidden Dimension*. Garden City, New York: Doubleday-Anchor Press, 1969.

Jerome Krase. *Self and Community in the City*. Washington, D.C.: University Press of America, 1982.

Jerome Krase. "The Italian American Community: An Essay on Multiple Social Realities," in Richard N. Juliani (ed.), *The Family and Community Life of Italian Americans*. Staten Island, New

York: American Italian Historical Association, 1983; 95-108.

Mark La Gory and John Pipkin. *Urban Social Space.* Belmont, California: Wadsworth Press, 1981.

Joseph Lopreato. *Peasants No More.* Scranton, Pennsylvania: Chandler Publishing Company, 1967.

Carlo Levi. *Christ Stopped at Eboli.* New York: Farrar, Straus and Company, 1947.

Gary Ross Mormino. *Immigrants on the Hill.* Urbana, Illinois: Illinois University Press, 1986.

Humbert Nelji. *The Italians in Chicago,* 1880-1930. New York; Oxford University Press, 1970.

Robert E. Park, Ernest Burgess and Roderick D. McKenzie. *The City.* Chicago: University of Chicago Press, 1967.

Amos Rapoport. *Human Aspects of Urban Form.* New York: Pergamon Press, 1977.

Jonathan Rieder. *Canarsie.* Cambridge, Massachusetts; Harvard University Press, 1985.

Gerald D. Suttles. *The Social Order of the Slum.* Chicago: University of Chicago Press, 1968.

Rudolph J. Vecoli. *Italian Immigrants in Rural and Small Town America.* Staten Island, New York: American Italian Historical Association, 1987.

William Foote Whyte. *Street Corner Society.* Chicago: University of Chicago Press, 1943.

Louis Wirth. *The Ghetto.* Chicago: University of Chicago Press, 1928.

The Participation of Italian American Women in Community Organizations

Judith N. DeSena
St. John's University

Literature Review

Past research efforts have viewed working class women as primarily family oriented.[1] In addition, the working class in general, and working class women in particular have been viewed as living hard lives,[2] where they are powerless and ineffective to change their conditions.[3]

Voluntary participation has been viewed as part of the middle class character and therefore, not conceived as an activity for working class women. A study done in the late 1970s, however, finds that paid work is a prerequisite for community involvement and voluntary participation by working class women.[4] In fact, this study suggests that paid work for working class women serves to expand their social roles in the same way that education has for middle class women.

There is also evidence that working class women are moving from a "traditional" working class lifestyle to a "modern" working class lifestyle in that working class women belong to more groups outside the family than in the past.[5]

In addition, working class women are participating not only in organizations which provide human services, but also those which are social action oriented.[6] In these latter organizations, working class women organize around community issues and problems in an attempt to bring about change. For some women, involvement in organizations which focus on social action is their first experience in political organizations.

Italian Williamsburg

The Italian area in Williamsburg ranges from the Brooklyn-

Queens Expressway (Meeker Avenue) on the north to Grand Street on the south. It is bounded on the east by the Newtown Creek and on the west by Union Avenue.

In 1980, 28,061 people resided in this area.[7] Seventy-four percent of these persons were white, 7 percent were black, and the remaining 19 percent reported themselves as "other." The largest single ethnic group reported in 1980 was Italian. Residents over 16 in this area in 1980 were employed mostly in technical, sales, and administrative support positions (31 percent), and as operators, fabricators, and laborers (29 percent). The average median income for this area in 1979 was $11,898. In 1980, 41 percent of those 25 years and older had completed elementary school, while 47 percent had completed high school. Only 12 percent completed college.

This area of Williamsburg is made up mostly of smaller, multiple dwelling housing structures. In 1980, 20 percent of the area's housing had two dwelling units, 22 percent had three and four dwelling units, and 31 percent had five to nine dwelling units.

Based on these demographics, the area can be characterized as working class. The streets and homes are neatly kept and the flavor is clearly Italian. Pasta stores, pastry shops, pork stores, and Italian owned and operated fruit and vegetable stores create the commercial strip of Graham Avenue. The area is also made up of a number of community organizations and a settlement house. Some of these are social clubs where people gather for recreation, while others provide direct services, such as employment information and referral, counseling, etc. This area is sometimes referred to as "Italian" Williamsburg in order to differentiate it from the rest of Williamsburg.

Community Organizations: Women's Participation

People become involved in community organizations in a number of ways. For some, the organization draws interest. Others may be approached by members of an organization and asked to join.[8] In Italian Williamsburg, the number of community organizations increased with a grant under the Comprehensive Employment and Training Act more commonly called CETA. Around 1975, the federal government began considering not for profit organizations for CETA grants. A small group of community leaders in Brooklyn's Community Board 1, which is made up of two neighborhoods, Greenpoint and Williamsburg, developed a coalition in order to secure CETA funds. This group developed a proposal, and decided that fiscal responsibility for the contract would go to School Settlement Association since they had experience managing contracts. The proposal was submitted under their name with the support of other community organizations.

The School Settlement Association was awarded a $3 million contract to administer, and this included 295 jobs excluding administrative staff. In order to distribute these jobs through the Community Board, nearly twelve, new, not-for-profit organizations were formed in Greenpoint and Williamsburg. In many cases people were awarded jobs by a system of patronage in which individuals were rewarded for support and loyalty to community leaders or organizations. As a respondent described, it became a program of "jobs for a friend. The needs of the community were secondary." However, there were certain eligibility requirements which enabled unemployed and underemployed individuals to obtain CETA positions.

The location of these jobs along with eligibility requirements gave employment opportunities to Italian American women in Williamsburg. These CETA positions offered married women the opportunity to be reintegrated into the labor force, and in some cases, to develop a new skill. In addition, these jobs were close to home and allowed women the flexibility to pick up a child after school, to be home before their husbands and to carry out tasks to maintain the household.

For many Italian American women, CETA jobs served to prepare them for regular employment. Many went on to better jobs and to college. In fact, one of the organizations which emerged as a result of this contract was National Congress of Neighborhood Women. NCNW offered leadership training courses and instituted a two year college program (affiliated with a New York college) for local women. By 1981, when CETA funds were no longer available, and these jobs were terminated, many Italian American women were on their way to successful employment and/or higher education. In addition, many women remained active members of the community and participated in local organizations on a voluntary basis.

Implications for Theory

This study supports Schoenberg and Dabrowski's idea that paid work expands the social roles of working class women in the same way that education has served middle class women. In fact, in some cases, paid work may also be a pre-requisite to higher education for working class women. Moreover, the experience of paid work in one's own neighborhood adds to community involvement. This is the case in Williamsburg where Italian American women are tied to the community and involved in local issues.

Finally, this study points out the success of the CETA program for women in Italian Williamsburg. Many women were given the opportunity to develop marketable skills, and also the confidence necessary to become productive members of the work force.

---

[1] Lee Rainwater, et.al, *Workingman's Wife* (New York: Oceana Publications, 1959); Mirra Komarovsky, *Blue Collar Marriage* (New York: Vintage Books, 1967) .

[2] Lillian Rubin, *Worlds of Pain* (New York: Basic Books, 1976) Joseph Howell, *Hard Living on Clay Street* (New York: Anchor Books, 1973) .

[3] Ida Susser, *Norman Street* (New York: Oxford University Press, 1982) .

[4] Sandra Schoenberg and Irene Dabrowski, "Factors Which Enhance the Participation of Women in Neighborhood Social Life" paper presented at the annual meeting of the American Sociological Association, September 5-8, 1978, San Francisco .

[5] Kathleen McCourt, *Working Class Women and Grass Roots Politics*, (Bloomington: Indiana University Press, 1977).

[6] McCourt, *Working Class Women and Grass Roots Politics*; Marilyn Gittell and Teresa Shtob, "Changing Women's Roles in Political Vol-

unteerism and Reform of the City," *Signs: Journal of Women in Culture and Society*, 5 (Spring 1980): 64-75.

[7] Information on neighborhood demographics was obtained by examining tract data from the 1980 Census.

[8] Kathleen McCourt, *Working Class Women and Grass Roots Politics*.

A Sociodemographic Analysis of Italian Americans and the Twilight of Ethnicity

Frank J. Cavaioli
SUNY College of Technology, Farmingdale

It is the purpose of this paper to show that individuals organize along common grounds into interest groups or factions to strive in a democracy for the gains that will benefit their members. One of the strongest and most natural motivations for associational life is ethnicity. Using this premise we turn to the political emergence of Italian Americans by examining their increased socio-economic mobility since World War II. The descendants of more than 5,000,000 Italian immigrants since 1880 are presently into the third and fourth generations with the wealth, education, leadership and organizations to play a key role in public affairs.

American society is pluralistic and as Italians have become more assimilated, they have learned that through group activity they gain, maintain, and advance benefits society has to offer. Paradoxically, then, as the children, grandchildren, and great grandchildren take on the characteristics of the host society, the 12.2 million Italian Americans, as reported in the official 1980 census, are now more conscious and secure in their ethnicity. They are Italian American by choice rather than necessity, and they intend to use their newly acquired power to their advantage.

A sociodemographic analysis of the 1980 census points up the importance of Italian Americans as an ethnic group.[1] They are the sixth largest group, 12.2 million, constituting 5.4 percent of the U.S. population. Ninety-one percent live in urban areas; more than 50 percent live in the northeast. New York, New Jersey, Pennsylvania, and California contain the largest number of Italian Americans, or 53 percent of the total of this group. About 2.8 million live in New York State, or 23 percent. Altogether, ten states contain 80 percent of the

United States Italian American population: New York (2,811,911), New Jersey (1,315,632), Pennsylvania (1,205,823), California (1,144,102), Massachusetts (749,583), Illinois (604,304), Connecticut (561,542), Ohio (520,171), Florida (461,757), and Michigan (344,402).

The largest proportions of Italian Americans to their total populations were in Rhode Island (19.5%), Connecticut (18.1%), New Jersey (17.9%), and New York (16.0%). "For most states, in fact, the farther the state was from New York State, the smaller the proportions of Italians in the state." About 1,000,000 lived in New York City (14% of the city's total); 192,000 lived in Philadelphia (11% of the total); 139,000 lived in Chicago (5% of the total); 107,000 lived in Los Angeles (4%). Boston, Yonkers, and Buffalo each had over 50,000 Italian Americans. A total of 23 cities had over 25,000. These high concentrations make them very visible, allowing them to sustain their institutional life, and make them easier to organize.

Using ethnic data from the November, 1979, *Current Population Survey,* 68 percent of Italian Americans over 25 years old had high school diplomas, compared to 69 percent for the nation. Twelve percent graduated from college; one-third of Italian males had one year of college or more, a figure similar to non-Italian American males. In 1979, 5 percent of Italians born in Italy graduated from college, or half the 10 percent for the second generation. About one-third of the first generation were high school graduates, compared to 60 percent of the second generation Italian Americans.

In regard to family income, the 1979 CPS data showed Italian Americans doing very well as they earned $17,100 annual median income, as compared to $15,000 for the nation as a whole. Significantly, the second generation had a median income of $16,900 compared to $13,300 for the first generation. Only 15 percent of Italian American families earned less than $10,000, while 27 percent of U.S. families earned this amount. The 1979 figures also showed 37 percent of American families earning $20,000 or more, while 41 percent of Italian American families earned as much or more. In the critical states of New York, New Jersey, and Pennsylvania, Italian Americans had lower proportions of poverty compared to the rest of those states' populations. The rate in New York was 8 percent compared to 18 percent in the rest of the state. The rates were similar in New Jersey and Pennsylvania. Finally, the 1980 census data reveal the Italian American workforce heavily engaged in technical, sales, and administrative occupations. Thirty-six percent worked as salespersons, secretaries, stenographers, and typists. About 20 percent were in professional and managerial positions.[2]

These figures reveal Italian Americans to be in the mainstream of society. The statistical evidence demonstrate this large ethnic group as achieving a relatively high level of socioeconomic progress, though by no means the pinnacle of success. The evidence further indicates that they are poised for the future and should have a greater impact in society. Finally, it is clear that contrary to often-stated stereotypes, Italian Americans emerge as a group of fairly good occupational status and educational level, with high income levels to match and with very high mobility in all fields.[3]

In a provocative study on Italian Americans, Richard D. Alba has presented a challenging thesis to the concept of enduring ethnicity. In his book, *Italian Americans: Into the Twilight of Ethnicity* (Englewood Cliffs: Prentice Hall, 1985), Alba asserts that Italians and other European ethnic groups have become so structurally assimilated as to make them like the dominant white anglo saxon culture. He argued that the transition to third and fourth generations cast descendants beyond the Old World influences of grandparents and parents. Thus, from the third generation on, "adherence to ethnic culture is likely to be thinner, shallower than that of its predecessors."[4]

Alba employed general survey polls and data from which to base his theories. For example, younger Italian Americans exhibited attitudes similar to that of WASP's on abortion, capital punishment, divorce, homosexuality, premarital sex, women working. If there are any differences, they reflect the old generation's attitudes. Alba further asserts that ethnicity has declined because of macrosociological changes in the larger society, such as immigration restriction from 1921 to 1965, and social and economic advances made by Italian Americans since World War II. Central to his thesis is the employment of quantitative studies showing the high rate of intermarriage between Italians and non-Italians, thus leading to the decline of ethnicity. The intermarriage rate of third generation Italians, or later, was over 70 percent. The ethnicity that existed today was merely symbolic, nostalgic, and served as a leisure activity.[5] Alba emphatically stated his thesis in the following way:

> Italian Americans (and indeed other white ethnic groups) are rapidly converging with majority Americans. This means, first of all, that both are becoming alike in the important matters of social standing as well as those of culture. It also means that different ethnic origins no longer provide any very serious impediment to social relations, including those of the most intimate and enduring kind, as the rising tide of intermarriage will indicate. To be sure, ethnic differences have not altogether disappeared among those of European heritages in the United States, and it is unlikely that they will do so, at any rate for the near future. But they have become so mild as to constitute a barrier neither to achievement nor to extensive contact with individuals from diverse backgrounds.[6]

Despite the rising trend in interethnic marriage, and despite, or because of, educational and occupational mobility, there are other countervailing forces at work that actually have been reinforcing the sense of group consciousness among Italian Americans. As they become more assimilated into the host society, they have realized the pluralism and diversity of that society, becoming more aware of their distinctive heritage and seeking ways to protect their interests. The rampant individualism and apoliticism they brought with them have now been replaced by the American system of group competition and group activity. The very assimilative forces that are supposed to level and debilitate the distinctiveness of Italian American culture simultaneously reinforce and heighten that ethnicity through the protection and security of a democratic system: rising social status based on more education; increased wealth through economic success; greater numbers of persons with Italian names in public office; increased quality and effectiveness of their organizations; an awareness by officials that as Italian Americans rise on the socio-economic scale, they will escalate their input into the political system; the identification of an Italian American agenda and a sensitivity of that agenda by the public.

I wish to focus on the role of ethnic organizational life, a much neglected area of group activity. Italian Americans have created effective organizations to channel their individual power. They have adapted themselves to American associational life and created and used interest groups to achieve goals of mutual concern. It is true that most of the earlier organizations, motivated mainly by filiopietism, have been social in nature, fulfilling psychic needs, and were otherwise ineffective politically; today there are many influential organizations that have succeeded in attaining benefits in the political system. This is the obvious result of the high degree of socio-economic mobility.

Italian Americans have learned that in a democracy power flows from the people and the people can influence the government. They have learned that group action is more effective than individual action. Thus they organize along common values to influence government about their views. Italian Americans make demands of the political system, demands that are of great concern to them: work, fair treatment, family, respect for authority, ending criminal stereotypes. Emerging groups represent ongoing pressure, special ethnic appeals, public service, or particular expertise. The more important ones are: American Committee on Italian Migration; National Italian American Foundation; Commission for Social Justice of the Order of the Sons of Italy; and the American Italian Historical Association. Some of the other important recent organizations are: National Italian American Women's Organization; Italian American Congressional Delegation; Italian American Legislators in Albany, New York. There are many, many more, too numerous to mention. However, several of the most important ones will be discussed to demonstrate the maturation of Italian Americans and the effectiveness of their organizational life.[7]

The American Committee on Italian Migration, an affiliate of the National Catholic Resettlement Council, was formed in 1952 when Italy was in crisis after World War II. Its purpose was to liberalize the restrictive immigration laws and to assist Italian immigrants in making a smooth transition into American society. Nearly all nationality groups had well-organized committees on migration at that time. In addition to assisting Italian immigrants, ACIM used sophisticated lobbying tactics, provided expert testimony to congress, and conducted educational programs in fighting the discriminatory national origins system and getting the government to pass the 1965 Immigration Reform Law which placed all nations on an equal basis in the selection of immigrants to the United States.

When President Lyndon B. Johnson addressed the leaders of the American Committee on Italian Migration in the cabinet room of the White House on July 1, 1968, the occasion marked a milestone in the public affairs of Italian Americans. President Johnson said one of his proudest days as Chief Executive occurred on Liberty Island, New York Harbor, October 3, 1965, when he signed into law the Immigration Reform Bill, abolishing the unfair national origins quota system. "Today the golden door of immigration has never stood wider," he said. It took three years to end the old system and to commemorate the event. ACIM presented the President with three miniature caravels, replicas of Italian craftsmen of the type of vessels used by 11th century explorers. This meeting marked the triumph of a concentrated, organized, and sustained drive in the achievement of a specific goal of the Italian Americans who had long been regarded to be politically noninvolved in political affairs. ACIM demonstrated sophisticated and effective techniques in pressure politics unmatched in this group's experience. ACIM's triumph reflected the beginning of the political maturation of the Italian Americans as an influential interest group.[8]

The creation of the National Italian American Foundation in 1975 marked another milestone because it provided Americans of Italian descent with a visible presence in the nation's capital, served as a clearinghouse, and developed a national agenda. The recent history of NIAF chronicles the discipline, intelligence, and dedication of a group of successful Italian Americans who have been guided by a desire to preserve and extend ethnic benefits. NIAF is a non-profit, non-partisan organization, and therefore refrains from legislative lobbying as it maintains constructive relationships with both political parties in order to advance the interests of the Italian American community. NIAF has the power to have in attendance at its biennial dinners the highest public figures from President Gerald Ford, and candidates Jimmy Carter and Walter Mondale in 1976 to President Ronald Reagan, Vice President George Bush, and candidates Mondale and Geraldine Ferraro in 1984. NIAF has also intensified its work on government by forming a legislative network, helping to identify and work with Italian Americans in government service, and seeks to place in public jobs persons of Italian descent. NIAF operates actively in other areas: conducting national and regional conferences; honoring Italian Americans with the Fiorello LaGuardia Public Service Award; legislative internship program; a scholarship program; maintains ties with Italy; publishes a newsletter and other relevant literature; coordinates its work with other Italian American organizations; is planning a quincentennial celebration for the Columbus Year 1992; maintains an information referral program, a networking system, and youth activities.[9]

The problem of criminal stereotyping continues to plague this group. NIAF's Media Institute has addressed this issue by conducting several conferences on the subject; prominent members of the media participated. But it is the Commission for Social Justice, of the Order of the Sons of Italy of America, that has been in the forefront in combating ethnic stereotyping and bias. Modeled after the Anti-Defamation League of B'Nai B'Rith, the Commission was formed in 1980 to "insure equal treatment, concern, and respect for all Italian Americans and other ethnic groups." This organization is led by successful business and professional persons who monitor the media and gather hard evidence dealing with ethnic bias. It is not a censorship group, but seeks fair treatment for all.

The formation in 1966 of the American Italian Historical Association represented another achievement in the cycle of ethnic success in the United States. Americans of Italian descent became the last large ethnic group to organize a scholarly group, thereby making legitimate their past and giving to them a respectability so necessary in contemporary society. Its constitution states:

The Association is a non-profit organization devoted to the promotion of Italian American studies. Its objectives shall be the collection, preservation, development, and popularization of material having reference to the Italian-American experience in the United States and Canada.[10]

Though its members do not claim exclusivity in this area, they most assuredly are more motivated. The Association is not engaged in filiopietism or anti-defamation, or partisanship, or even engaged in Italian culture per se. There are numerous worthy organizations devoted to those causes. Through scientific and objective methodologies, the AIHA systematically studys and records the Italian experience in America. No other organization can make this claim.

The Association has actively conducted special programs in education. It has sponsored meetings, film, and book symposia, speakers bureau, and in-service courses. The proceedings presented at the annual conference are published by the AIHA and become part of the written record of Italian Americans. The AIHA provides vital expertise to other organizations.

Thus, it is not a question of whether Italian Americans exist at all. They certainly do as a macro-group, and the micro-ethnic organizations contend for the benefits available in society. There are hundreds, perhaps thousands, some more important than others in influencing public policy. It is no longer a question of whether they participate; they certainly do, individually and through group action. Professional pollsters are aware of this fact and ask the relevant questions in order to quantify the political behavior of Italian Americans. The Census Bureau tends to reinforce ethnic identification as it collects more ethnic data. This process tends to cancel out the assimilative effect in American culture. The residue of the Old World culture, though altered by the host society, provides very substantial purpose, as well as emotional value, to the hyphenate. Just as anglo saxon ethnicity will not disappear, so too Italian culture, or better still, Italian American culture, will not disappear. Thus, Italian Americans, who have achieved considerable social and economic success, operate through organizations from this premise of interest group politics, thereby providing important protections they would not normally gain through individual political activity.

[1] Nampeo R. McKenney, Michael J. Levin, and Alfred J. Tella, "A Sociodemographic Profile of Italian Americans," *Italian Americans, New Perspectives in Italian Immigration and Ethnicity* (edited by Lydio F. Tomasi) (Staten Island: Center for Migration Studies, 1985), pp. 4-31.

[2] N.R. McKenney, M.J. Levin, and A. Tella, pp. 4-31.

[3] *The Italian American: Who They Are, Where They Live, How Many They Are.* (Torino, Italy: Fondazione Giovanni Agnelli, 1980), p. 10.

[4] Richard D. Alba, *Italian Americans: Into the Twilight of Ethnicity* (Englewood Cliffs: Prentice Hall, 1985), p. 115.

[5] R.D. Alba, pp. 114-115, 134-150.

[6] R.D. Alba, p. viii.

[7] See, Andrew Brizzolara, compiler, *A Directory of Italian and Italian-American Organizations and Community Services* (Staten Island: Center for Migration Studies, 1976), pp. 1-108.

[8] Frank J. Cavaioli, "Italian Americans Slay the Immigration Dragon: The National Origins Quota System," *Italian Americana* 5 (Fall/Winter 1979), 71-100. Frank J. Cavaioli, "Chicago's Italian Americans Rally for Immigration Reform," *Italian Americana* 6 (Spring/Summer 1980), 142-156.

[9] Frank J. Cavaioli, "The National Italian American Foundation: 1975-1985," *Amadeo P. Giannini* (by Felice A. Bonadio) (Washington: DC: National Italian American Foundation, 1985), pp. 118-125.

[10] Frank J. Cavaioli, *The American Italian Historical Association: Twenty Years Later, 1966-1986*; paper presented at the 19th Annual American Italian Historical Association Conference, Philadelphia, November 13-15, 1986.

Small Business and Social Mobility Among Italian Americans

Andrew Sanchirico
State University of New York at Albany

The history of Italians in America is quite well known. The vast majority of Italian immigrants arrived between 1880 and 1920. Most were peasants from southern Italy and most settled in the industrial areas of the Northeast and Midwest. During the early settlement period Italian immigrants were extremely transient, moving from city to city in search of employment, oftentimes traveling back-and-forth between the United States and Italy. After imposition of immigration restrictions in 1924, however, the Italian American population became very stable. Not only did large-scale movement between Italy and the United States cease, but migration between American cities also decreased substantially. When immigration restrictions were eased in 1965, immigration from Italy increased once again; but it remains far below levels established early in the century and is far below levels from Asian and Latin American countries.[1] Italians are no longer the "new immigrants"—they are now part of the white European majority.

While this story is by now familiar, the changing historical circumstances of Italians has stimulated new scholarly issues and new interpretations of their experience in America. The socio-economic status of Italian Americans is one issue that has evolved over the years.

Throughout the early-twentieth century Italian Americans were generally considered a low status ethnic group. This common perception was supported by statistics which indicated Italians had below-average levels of educational achievement and occupational attainment. The primary issue during this period was why Italians were unable or unwilling to take full advantage of the social mobility opportunities available in America. The explanation most commonly presented, in various forms, was that Italians possessed a peasant-based working class culture that inhibited educational and occupational success (Gans 1962; Rosen 1959; Strodtbeck 1958; Whyte 1943).

In later years, however, Italian Americans exhibited substantial social mobility and have attained educational and occupational levels comparable to, or greater than, the larger white population. The socioeconomic success of Italians is documented in the 1980 United States census (U.S. Bureau of the Census 1983). For example, while 84 percent of Italians (aged 18 to 24) had completed high school, only 79 percent of the larger white population had done so. Italians have also caught up to the overall white population in occupational attainment. Among employed persons, 57 percent of Italians held white collar jobs, compared to 55 percent of white Americans. Given such statistics, the principal issue in recent years is why Italians have been able to raise their socioeconomic status so dramatically, especially considering the pessimistic predictions of earlier years.

This paper examines one factor that has greatly contributed to the social mobility of Italian Americans: their proportionately high involvement in small business ownership. My basic thesis is that, despite its historical image as a homogeneous working class group, the Italian American population has contained a substantial number of small business owners whose values and attitudes promoted the individual achievement and social mobility of future generations. I have chosen to focus on small business because its role in mobility is often ignored and is poorly understood. The paper utilizes previously published data and is largely speculative; but I hope it will provide the basis for further analysis of small business and social mobility among Italian Americans.

Since the nineteenth century, immigrants have had higher rates of small business ownership than native-born Americans (Light 1984; Waldinger 1986). All ethnic groups do not participate equally in small business, however. Some groups, most notably the Jews and Chinese, have historically displayed high rates of self-employment. Others, such as the Irish and French Canadians, have exhibited relatively low self-employment rates. Although Italians have not been as closely associated with small business as the Jews and Chinese, they have been more highly involved than most other ethnic groups. Italian immigrants and their descendants have been highly concentrated in grocery stores, fruit and vegetable stands, restaurants and taverns, truck farming, and contracting. They have also been highly represented among self-employed tailors, shoemakers, barbers, and masons. Indeed, Italian business participation has been so extensive that in the early-1900s Italian chambers of commerce were established in New York City, Chicago, and San Francisco (Foerster 1919, pp. 337-9).

Early evidence of Italian small business participation is derived from the census of 1900, which reveals that among European immigrant groups, Italians were second only to Russian Jews in percentage of self-employed retailers (Higgs 1976, p. 162). Italian involvement in small business is also demonstrated in community and case studies. In New Orleans at the turn-of-the-century, more than 50 percent of Italian household heads held white collar jobs, primarily as merchants, especially food retailers. The proportion of Italian grocers in the city was 19 percent in 1900, 49 percent in 1920, and 46 percent in 1940 (Margavio and Salomone 1981, pp. 355-6). Italians residing in Tampa, Florida, in the late-nineteenth and early-twentieth centuries were heavily concentrated in street trades, small shops, truck farming, and dairying. In 1909, for example, Italians received virtually all the licenses granted for street trades (Mormino and Pozzetta 1985, p. 349). Even in those highly industrialized areas that attracted unskilled laborers, Italians gravitated to the small business sector. In Pittsburgh in 1910 a six-block neighborhood contained six grocery stores and numerous other businesses (Bodnar, Simon, and Weber 1982, p. 81). In a survey conducted in Rhode Island in the 1960s, 21 percent of Italians were self-employed—lower than the Jewish self-employment rate, but higher than the rates of Portuguese, French Canadian, and Irish (Goldscheider and Kobrin 1980, p. 260).

My emphasis on Italian small business ownership is not intended to contradict the common portrayal of Italian immigrants as primarily unskilled laborers. Nor do I seek to dispute the conventional historical image of Italian Americans as predominantly working class. The Italians who came to this country during the great immigration wave did so for economic opportunities, and for most of these immigrants such opportunities were found in manual labor—in jobs that native Americans disdained. Their offspring found most of their employment opportunities in the burgeoning factory system. Statistically, a much larger percentage of Italians have been employed as laborers and factory operatives than have been self-employed as retailers and craftsmen (D'Alesandre 1974; Kessner 1977; Lieberson 1980). Nevertheless, I believe the literature exaggerates the impact of working class families and underestimates the influence of small business families on second and third generation Italian Americans. This notion is based on two considerations.

To begin with, a very large proportion of unskilled laborers were transient men—the proverbial "birds of passage"—who migrated to the United States (and other countries) for temporary employment rather than permanent residence. These sojourners remained in America until they accumulated sufficient funds or until slack economic periods reduced employment opportunities. Many returned to America again when employment prospects improved. As expressed by Robert Foerster in his classic study *The Italian Emigration of Our Times* (1919):

> Swelling in the plenteous seasons and years, shrinking with the approach of the leaner times, the armies of general laborers come and go; and more often than the case is with other classes, the same men appear twice, thrice or more times in a decade's immigration. The laborers, *par excellence*, are the true temporary immigrants. (344)

Because a large percentage of these sojourning men did not produce a second generation in America, the large contingent of unskilled workers had relatively less effect on future generations of Italian Americans than their large numbers might imply.

Secondly, unskilled labor was a temporary occupation for many Italian immigrants who eventually settled in the United States. That is to say, while low-paying unskilled jobs were adequate for youthful immigrants having little knowledge of the English language and American culture, such jobs were judged less satisfactory after acquisition of language and culture (and family). This is reflected in statistics compiled by Thomas Kessner (1981) from New York State census data, which reveal the proportion of Italians employed as laborers declined from 42 percent in 1905 to 27 percent in 1925 (p. 228). Kessner's study also reveals that employment in unskilled labor declined with length of time in America. In 1925, 22 percent of Italian household heads who had lived in this country less than seven years worked as unskilled laborers, compared to only 11 percent of those who had been here more than twenty-five years (p. 231). Most importantly for present purposes, a substantial number of those who left unskilled labor entered retail business. Quoting again from Foerster (1919, p. 338):

> We must remember that many general laborers, miners, and others are tempted to enter "bisinisse," and that they can do so by learning fifty words of English and buying a fruit stand. Sometimes the wife manages the shop or stand while the husband continues at his work. In New York many men have begun with a pushcart, then got the privilege of a stand, then a concession to sell garden produce in connection with a grocery store, and finally have set up a shop of their own.

The pattern of mobility out of unskilled labor and into small business ownership is demonstrated in Judith Smith's (1985) study of Italian and Jewish immigrants living in Providence, Rhode Island, in the early 1900s.[2] The study examined the occupational histories of Italian immigrant household heads, which was based on each immigrant's first recorded job, job held in 1915, and last recorded job. The distribution of first jobs closely mirrors the conventional image of Italian immigrants as predominantly unskilled workers.

Twenty-seven percent started their work careers as laborers (the highest percentage of any occupational category) and an additional 20 percent started out as factory operatives (the second highest percentage). Only 1 percent began as self-employed retailers (the smallest percentage) and an additional

17 percent began as self-employed craftsmen. Taken together, 47 percent of the sample began as unskilled workers and 18 percent as small business owners.

A different picture emerges, however, when last recorded jobs are examined. Laborers decreased to 19 percent and factory operatives decreased to 17 percent. On the other hand, self-employed retailers increased to 11.5 percent (the largest increase of any occupational category) and self-employed craftsmen increased to 19 percent. Consequently, by the time they reached the end of their work careers, nearly as many Italian household heads were self-employed (30.5 percent) as were employed as unskilled workers (36 percent) (Smith 1985, p. 37). The occupational patterns exhibited in New York State and Providence—movement out of unskilled labor and into small business—were typical of Italian American occupational patterns elsewhere in the United States. Variations existed, of course, depending upon the nature of the local economy, the relative position of Italians within that economy, and the size of the local Italian community. In some places mobility into the small business sector did not reach fruition until the second generation. But gradually, over the years, family businesses became a prominent part of Italian American communities across the nation.

Why did Italian Americans gravitate to small business ownership?

One reason Italians established small family businesses was to overcome discrimination and language and cultural barriers. The Italians who arrived in America during the main immigration wave were largely confined to the lowest ranks of manual labor and commonly received substandard wages. Most Italian immigrants eagerly accepted these jobs; they had come to America for work and took whatever was offered them.[3] Many others, however, were not content with low-paying unskilled work. For this latter group, employment opportunities in the more desirable occupations of the mainstream economy were severely limited—not only by the prejudices of the majority population, but also by their own language difficulties, lack of familiarity with the dominant culture, and lack of education and occupational skills. Small business ownership was the best alternative for those who possessed the necessary skills and had access to start-up capital. These businesses offered Italians means of avoiding the formal educational requirements and formalized hiring procedures that limited their employment opportunities. There was a much more positive, and possibly more important, reason why Italians gravitated to small business. Italians, like other immigrant groups, had special needs and preferences that were best served by co-ethnics (Light 1972, Waldinger 1986).

Ethnic food is commonly one of the special demands of immigrant groups. Among Italian immigrants, food was especially important. Regional food and traditional food customs, often tied to religious holidays and family gatherings, were deeply rooted in the culture of Italian immigrants. The diet and eating habits that Italians were accustomed to were far different from that found in America. So it was left up to the Italians themselves to produce, prepare, and distribute their traditional foods. In addition, as is the case with other immigrant groups, Italians generally preferred to do business with those who spoke their language and shared their culture. The needs and preferences of Italian immigrants supplied customers for the numerous food peddlers, grocery stores, bakeries, barbers, and shoemakers clustered in Italian neighborhoods. Gradually the most successful of these businesses began to serve the larger non-Italian population. Eventually, economic niches developed which sustained older Italian businesses and provided a growing market for newer enterprises. The proliferation of Italian restaurants over the past several decades epitomizes this trend (Levenstein 1985, pp.17-8).

Another factor that contributed to Italian small business ownership was the Italian family structure. The family was considered a social and economic unit in Italy and among Italian immigrants living in America. All members were deeply tied to and dependent upon the family, and all members (including young children) were expected to contribute to the household economy (Alba 1985; Covello 1967; Lopreato 1970). This emphasis on family obligation was widely condemned by commentators in America who viewed it as detrimental to individualism and individual achievement (Glazer and Moynihan 1979, pp. 97-8). However, the Italian family, which in an economic sense functioned as a work unit, was perfectly suited for the needs of small business enterprise. Family members were expected to contribute their labor to the family business, thereby maximizing operating hours and minimizing operating costs. In this way the family work unit helped to keep marginal businesses afloat and to make otherwise marginal businesses successful. Thus, although their family structure may have placed Italians at a disadvantage in the mainstream economy, it gave them a crucial advantage within the small business sector (Margavio and Salomone 1981; Smith 1985).

Thus far I have discussed Italian participation in small business ownership and identified some reasons why Italians gravitated to the small business sector. I turn now to the issue of small business and social mobility among Italian Americans. My contention is that small business families have a positive effect on offspring's achievement and that small business participation among first and second generation families helps explain the socioeconomic success of contemporary Italian Americans. The positive effect of small business families on offspring's achievement has received a great deal of attention lately, especially among those studying the success of ethnic groups highly concentrated in small business ownership (Bonacich and Modell 1980; Hirschman and M. Wong 1986; Nee and H. Wong 1985; Steinberg 1981). Precisely why small business families generate high achievement among their offspring is unclear, but the work of British sociologist Frank Bechhofer and colleagues is suggestive.

Small business ownership has traditionally been viewed as a means of social mobility in western capitalist societies. As such, small business represents a purposefully chosen route to upward mobility for the majority of proprietors. According to Bechhofer and colleagues, for most of these proprietors this purposeful action extends to the next generation. That is, small business ownership is perceived not only as a vehicle for personal mobility, but as a "springboard" for children's mobility as well (Bechhofer and Elliott 1978, p. 78). These families "want to give their children a 'better start,' to set them on the road to solidly middle class positions, and in this they will be conscious of the need for 'sacrifice,' and for the establishment of clear 'projects' " (Bechhofer et al. 1974, pp. 121-2). In order to see their goal of intergenerational mobility accomplished, small business families usually stress the importance of education and invest in their children's formal schooling, thereby providing them access to higher status occupations.

Small business ownership also attracts those individuals who seek occupational independence—who value "being one's own boss" and "making it on one's own." Bechhofer and colleagues suggest that, because proprietors place high value on independence, they view occupations that offer autonomy as well as mobility as particularly desirable positions for their children. The occupations that best satisfy these criteria are the independent professions. As they express it: "In terms of their aspirations for their children we might anticipate that small shopkeepers would view the traditional professions as especially desirable positions of higher status because they, more than most other occupations, retain the very highest levels of independence" (Bechhofer and Elliott 1968, p. 197).

Many of the above generalizations apply to Italian small business owners: They utilized the occupation as a means of upward mobility, they exhibited independence in acquiring and operating these businesses, and through their behavior they displayed a strong belief in making it on one's own. On the other hand, the parental attitudes described above are opposite those commonly attributed to first and second generation Italian parents, who, rather than being seen as supportive of their children's achievement, were typically portrayed as indifferent, or even antagonistic, to offspring's success. Thus, Glazer and Moynihan (1970, p. 197) claim that "accomplishment for the Italian son is felt by the parents to be meaningless unless it directly gratifies the family—for example, by maintaining the closeness of the family or advancing the family's interests through jobs and marriage."

Many Italian parents no doubt held the stereotypical views commonly attributed to them. But many others did not. Otherwise, the widespread intergenerational mobility that has been observed would have been virtually impossible. What many earlier studies failed to recognize adequately was the diversity that existed among first and second generation

Italian families. As emphasized, the Italian American population included a substantial number of small business families. It is my contention that, with regard to offspring's mobility, the attitudes of these families were closer to those described by Bechhofer than to those commonly attributed to Italian families. Furthermore, small business families supplied the major impetus underlying Italian American mobility. Supporting evidence is contained in Smith's (1985) previously discussed study of Italian and Jewish immigrants living in Providence at the turn-of-the-century.

Recall that Smith analyzed the occupational histories of Italian immigrants and uncovered large-scale mobility into the small business sector. She also examined the occupational attainment of their offspring.[4] The findings reveal that sons of self-employed retailers did exceptionally well in terms of intergenerational mobility. Twelve percent attained professional positions and 16 percent held city government appointments (the two highest white collar occupations listed in the study). Only sons of professionals (who made up less than 2 percent of the sample) did better, with 75 percent going into the two white collar occupations. Sons of self-employed craftsmen also did quite well, with 8 percent holding professional jobs and 2 percent city government positions. The positive influence of small business families on offspring's mobility is also reflected by the fact that, while 33 percent of all second generation men had fathers who owned businesses, 50 percent of all those who achieved professional and governmental positions came from small business households. By way of contrast, 37 percent of second generation men had fathers who were unskilled workers, but only 13 percent of those who entered professional and governmental positions came from such households (Smith 1985, p. 67).[5] Generalization from the Providence sample may, of course, be considered problematical. Italian Americans living in other neighborhoods and other cities experienced somewhat different patterns of intergenerational mobility, depending upon particular social and economic conditions. But there is no reason to believe, and no evidence to suggest, that small business families failed to play a significant role in other Italian American communities.

High participation in family business is not the only reason for Italian American upward mobility. But it made such mobility more extensive, and consequently, more dramatic. The socioeconomic success of contemporary Italian Americans cannot be fully comprehended without adequately appreciating the positive contribution of small business ownership.

Footnotes

[1] Early studies of Italians in America include those by Covello (1967), Foerster (1919), and Lord, Trenor and Barrows (1905). Recent works providing a general socio-historical overview of the Italian American Experience include those by Alba (1985), Lopreato (1970), and Nelli (1983). Historical examinations of Italians residing in different Amewrican communities include those by Barton (1975), Bodnar, Simon, and Weber (1982), Briggs (1978), Kessner (1977, and Smith (1985).

[2] The Italian sample consisted of all household heads residing in a six-block area of an Italian neighborhood as enumerated by the 1915 Rhode Island census. All members of these households were traced, through the Providence city directory, backwards from 1915 to the year in which they were first listed as Providence residents, and forward to 1940. The study pivots around 157 Italian male immigrant household heads. A parallel analysis was conducted around 70 Jewish male immigrant household heads.

[3] Many Italian immigrants intended to return to Italy as soon as they had earned enough money to purchase land there (Alba 1985, p. 47).

[4] Father's occupation is based on job held in 1940, or last job listed in Providence, or last occupation listed prior to death. Son's occupation is based on job held in 1940 or last job listed in Providence.

[5] The inclusion of Jews in Smith's study allows some comparative analysis. While many more Jews than Italians were self-employed retailers, Jewish mobility patterns were the same as for Italians. For example, 12 percent of retailer's sons attained professional positions, second only to sons of professionals. More dramatically, while 52 percent of second generation Jews came from small business families,

they held 78 percent of all professional positions.

Works Cited

Alba, Richard D. 1985. *Italian Americans: Into the Twilight of Eth-nicity.* Englewood Cliffs, NJ: Prentice-Hall.

Barton, Joseph S. 1975. *Peasants and Strangers: Ital-ians,Rumanians, and Slovaks in An American City.* Cambridge, MA:Harvard University.

Bechhofer, Frank and Brian Elliott. 1968. "An Approach to a Study of Small Shopkeepers and the Class Structure." *European Jour-nal of Sociology* 9:180-202.

___. 1978. "The Voice of Small Business and the Politics of Survival." *Sociological Review.* 26:57-88.

Bechhofer, Frank, Brian Elliott, Monica Rushforth and Richard Bland. 1974. "The Petits Bourgeois in the Class Structure: The Case of the Small Shopkeepers." Pp. 103-128 in *The Social Anal-ysis of Class Structure,* edited by Frank Parkin. London: Tavis-tock Publications Ltd.

Bodnar, John, Roger Simon and Michael P. Weber. 1982. *Lives of Their Own: Blacks, Italians, and Poles in Pittsburgh, 1900-1960.* Urbana: University of Illinois Press.

Bonacich, Edna and John Modell. 1980. *The Economic Basis of Eth-nic Solidarity: Small Business in the Japanese American Com-munity.* Berkeley: University of California Press.

Briggs, John. 1978. *An Italian Passage: Immigrants to Three Ameri-can Cities, 1890-1930.* New Haven: Yale University Press.

Covello, Leonard. 1967. *The Social Background of the Italo-American School Child: A Study of the Southern Italian Family Mores and Their Effect on the School Situation in Italy and America.* Lei-den: E.J. Brill.

D'Alesandre, John J. (1935) 1974. "Occupational Trends of Italians in New York City." Pp. 417-431 in *The Italians: Social Back-grounds of An American Group,* edited by Francesco Cordasco and Eugene Bucchinoni. Clifton, NJ: Augustus M Kelley.

Foerster, Robert F. 1919. *The Italian Emigration of Our Times.* New

York: Arno Press.

Gans, Herbert J. 1962. *The Urban Villagers: Group and Class in the Life of Italian Americans.* New York: Free Press.

Glazer, Nathan and Daniel P. Moynihan. 1970. *Beyond The Melting Pot.* Cambridge MA: The MIT Press.

Goldscheider, Calvin and Frances E. Kobrin. 1980. "Ethnic Continuity and the Process of Self-Employment." *Ethnicity.* 7:256-278.

Higgs, Robert. 1976. "Participation of Blacks and Immigrants in the American Merchant Class, 1890-1910: Some Demographic Relations." *Explorations in Economic History.* 13:153-164.

Hirschman, Charles and Morrison G. Wong. 1986. "The Extraordinary Educational Attainment of Asian-Americans: A Search for Historical Evidence and Explanations." *Social Forces.* 67:1-27.

Kessner, Thomas. 1977. *The Golden Door: Italian and Jewish Immigrant Mobility in New York City 1880-1915.* New York: Oxford University Press.

_____. 1981. "Jobs, Ghettoes, and the Urban Economy, 1880-1935." *American Jewish History.* 71:218-238.

Levenstein, Harvey. 1985. "The American Response to Italian Food." *Food and Foodways.* 1:1-24.

Lieberson, Stanley. 1980. *A Piece of the Pie: Black and White Immigrants Since 1880.* Berkeley: University of California Press.

Light, Ivan. 1972. *Ethnic Enterprise in America: Business and Welfare Among Chinese, Japanese, and Blacks.* Berkeley: University of California Press.

_____. 1984. "Immigrant and Ethnic Enterprise in North America." *Ethnic and Racial Studies.* 7:195-216.

Lopreato, Joseph. 1970. *Italian Americans.* New York: Random House.

Lord, Eliot, John J. D. Trenor and Samuel J. Barrow. 1905. *The Italian in America.* New York: B. F. Buck & Company.

Margavio, A. V. and Jerome Salomone. 1981. "The Passage, Settlement, and Occupational Characteristics of Louisiana's Immigrants." *Sociological Spectrum.* 1:345-359.

Mormino, Gary R. and George E. Pozzetta. 1985. "Concord and Dis-

cord: Italians and Ethnic Interactions in Tampa, Florida, 1886-
1930." Pp. 341-357 in *Italian Americans: New Perspectives in
Italian Immigration and Ethnicity*, edited by Lydio F. Tomasi.
New York: Center for Migration Studies.

Nee, Victor and Herbert Wong. 1985. "Asian American Socioeconomic Achievement: The Strength of the Family Bond." *Sociological Perspectives*. 28:281-306.

Nelli, Humbert S. 1983. *From Immigrants to Ethnics: The Italian
Americans*. New York: Oxford University Press.

Rosen, Bernard. 1959. "Race, Ethnicity, and the Achievement Syn-
drome." *American Sociological Review*. 24:47-60.

Smith, Judith E. 1985. *Family Connections: A History of Italian and
Jewish Immigrants Lives in Providence, Rhode Island 1900-
1940*. Albany, NY: State University of New York Press.

Steinberg, Stephen. 1974. *The Academic Melting Pot: Catholics and
Jews in American Higher Education*. New York: McGraw-Hill
Book Company.

Strodtbeck, Fred L. 1958. "Family Interaction, Values, and Achievement." Pp. 147-165 in The Jews: Social Patterns of An American
Group, edited by Marshall Sklare. New York: Free Press.

U.S. Bureau of the Census. 1983. *1980 Census of the Population*.
Volume I. Characteristics of the Population. Chapter C. General
Social and Economic Characteristics. Part I. U.S. Summary.
PC80-1-C1.

Waldinger, Roger. 1986. "Immigrant Enterprise: A Critique and Reformulation." *Theory and Society*. 15:249-285.

Whyte, William F. 1943. *Street Corner Society*. Chicago: University of
Chicago Press.

Old World Traits Obliterated: Immigrant Midwives and the Medicalization of Childbirth

Angela D. Danzi
SUNY College of Technology
at Farmingdale

In the first decades of this century the profession of medicine and the newly emerging specialty of obstetrics sought by various means to eliminate the competing practitioner, and to redefine childbirth from a natural occurence to a pathological event. The era of social childbirth, when women generally managed for themselves the events surrounding pregnancy and childbirth, was being supplanted by the era of medical childbirth, as birth came to be defined as an abnormal condition requiring special attention. The first casualty of this transition was the midwife.[1]

This transition took place within the context of the era of mass immigration to the United States. The so called "new immigration," masses of southern and eastern Europeans, presented innumerable challenges to health professionals, not the least of which centered around their preference for a female midwife. While other foreign born women showed some acceptance of the trained professional, Italian women maintained a strong aversion to a male birth attendant and to hospital births.[2] Yet, by 1940, the role of the Italian midwife had been largely supplanted by the male medical doctor who was affiliated with an expanding urban hospital. The widespread acceptance of the medical model has been attributed to doctor's access and control of knowledge and technology that promised to erase the pain and death associated with childbirth.[3] Much of the literature in this area has stressed the role of gender, and has characterized these changes in medical practice as a struggle between uneducated, unorganized, immigrant midwives, and elite, university-trained professional men.[4] It has generally been assumed that medical professionals were themselves either non-ethnic or anglo males.

This paper will discuss the role of the *levatrice*, the Italian midwife, in southern Italy and in the United States. Next, it will focus on the transition from midwife to doctor, from home birth to hospital birth, and propose a model of stages in this transition that can be applied to future research. Overall, the purpose of this model will be to briefly explore the role of both gender and ethnicity in this process.

The *levatrice* in Southern Italy and the United States

The midwife from antiquity was considered a person of some skill and respectability. In more recent times, she held the same stature in the local villages as a shopkeeper and purveyor of special services in the same way as a shoemaker, tobacconist, or tavern keeper. The traditional sign above the midwife's shop pictured a birthing chair used by women in labor, and a circle between two semi-circles, the Greek symbol of fertility. The work of the midwife was not limited to the immediate events around childbirth, but included the full range of questions and difficulties about pregnancy, infant and child care, and women's health and well being. The experience of pregnancy and parturition were the subject of many quasi-magical beliefs and traditions, and the midwife was also considered to be a specialist in applying these to cure disorders of all kinds, in the same way as the local barber or herbalist. When called to assist at birth, she would routinely care also for the infant and other children, prepare meals, and wash clothing. Midwives had also from the 14th century been given permission to baptize, but this practice, because it usually entailed costly gifts, was not always adhered to.[5]

During the nineteenth century many European countries, through standardized training and regulation, granted to the midwife a legitimate and permanent role in the delivery of care in childbirth. In Italy, midwives were required to undergo a formal two-year training period, a regulation that could be fully enforced only in the regions of the developed north.[6] The situation in the south, where rates of birth were higher, probably remained what it had been for generations: women learned how to deliver babies from their mothers or grandmothers, and from assisting at the deliveries of their own and their neighbor's children.[7] Undoubtedly, a small number of formally trained Italian midwives emigrated to the United States; a 1919 study comments on their capability, calling them "well-trained, scientific women" who were even more acceptable because they understood their subordination to physicians.[8] However, the vast majority of Italian born midwives in the United States were without formal education, and practiced exclusively in the immigrant enclaves of northeastern cities.[9] Midwifery was an occupation that unlike several others, was easily transferable to the United States, requiring neither an adjustment of technical or language skills, nor a capital investment.

By 1900 women born in the United States were moving away from the use of a midwife.[10] But for many immigrant women, and Italian women in particular, the midwife was the only acceptable birth attendant. In Chicago, for example, a 1908 analysis of over one thousand registered births found that midwives had attended 25 percent of Russian, 68 percent of German, but 86 percent of Italian births.[11] A 1905 New York study of 1,029 Italian births found that fully 93 percent were attended by midwives.[12] Additionally, an analysis of case records of the New York Midwifery Dispensary, which provided medical assistance in childbirth, found that between 1890 and 1913 virtually no Italian women registered for care. In contrast, significant numbers of German, Irish, and Russian Jewish women eagerly sought out their services.[13]

The reasons given for the immigrant woman's preference for a midwife have stressed cultural commonalities that would make women about to undergo a momentous experience prefer to be cared for by "her own kind," someone who spoke her own language and shared her tradition. Also significant was the issue of cost; midwives charged much less than physicians, and performed more services, acting as a nurse and housekeeper for several days after the birth.[14] But most importantly, the selection of a midwife related to the attempt to preserve deeply held family values. Italian men in particular were distrustful of any outside intrusion into the family, and

the professional male physician from their point of view inter-
fered in the most intimate area of family life, threatening female purity and chastity. For Italian women, birth although
frought with danger, was nevertheless a natural process, an
event they were likely to have witnessed first-hand; they
could not easily be persuaded that birth was an illness requiring medical attention.[15]

Pregnancy and childbirth dominated the lives of adult immigrant women. Foreign-born women had twice as many children as native-born, and a greater proportion of these were
Italians, Poles, Russians and other eastern Europeans. This
largely Catholic, formerly rural population retained old-world
notions about ideal family size, and viewed children as both a
blessing and a potential source of good fortune.[16]

Accompanying high rates of birth were high rates of infant
and maternal mortality. In New York City for the years 1905-
06, puerperal infection was a major cause of death for Italian
women, whose rate of mortality exceeded that of Italian
men.[17] In Buffalo's Italian quarter, infants died at a greater
rate than any other district in the city.[18] Compilation of
statistics in 1915 showed that nationwide the United States
had higher rates of infant and maternal mortality than many
other European industrial nations.[19] Culpability for this situation was attributed to the midwife, and the foreign midwife
came in for special criticism. Together with the rural southern
"granny" midwife, the immigrant midwife was the object of a
campaign that attacked her for her "careless, dirty and dangerous" ways. Most contemporary observers equated her lack
of formal training with incompetence, and the "midwife problem" sparked a controversy that pitted those who would le-
gitmate her role as a medical quasi-professional, against
those who would eliminate her presence entirely.[20]

A series of contemporary studies done around 1910 showed
however that the midwife had as good if not better record at
performing safe deliveries as the medical practitioner. This
was probably because many physicians at that time had less
training and experience than the midwife, and because in an
effort to hasten the birth process along, they often used dangerous or intrusive techniques.[21]

Many physicians expressed doubts that foreign midwives

could be educated, and that since such training programs "would only provide a little better care for the poor, ignorant foreigner," funds could better be spent in improving birth procedures for the middle class. Newly arrived immigrants were characterized thus:

> ...ignorant in every sense of the word, who do not speak English, who have but little money but are prolific breeders, and who come here with definite and fixed ideas in favor of the midwife rather than the doctor.[22]

Competition from foreign midwives was a real concern for medical professionals for two reasons. First, the only way for practitioners to learn about the birth process was through clinical experience, and foreign-born and poor women could more easily be used for this purpose. But their preference for midwives severely limited practitioners access to this population. Second, the status and prestige of the practitioner could not be raised as long as the unlettered, immigrant midwife continued to practice as effectively.[23] For many professionals, the solution to the midwife problem was to severely curtail immigration from southern and eastern Europe. Their voices were added to the chorus urging immigration restriction for these foreign groups.[24]

Midwives were also associated with abortion and the use of contraceptive techniques of varying effectiveness. These included the use of a variety of vaginal douches, a method common in Italy, the administering of drugs known to stimulate uterine contractions, as well as devices used to induce abortion.[25] For immigrant women, the Italian ideal of many children conflicted with the daily realities of frequent illness and unemployment and created terrible burdens. While many women simply accepted each new pregnancy with resignation, others would try any means to secure an abortion.[26] Medical professionals feared that if midwifery were to become legitimate, there could be no controlling the incidence of illegal abortion.[27]

The typical Italian midwife in the United States was a married woman, and the mother of several children. Midwifery was an acceptable way for her to supplement the family income. She was likely to have lived in the United States for several years, and be unable to read, write or speak English with any great facility. She more often than not practiced outside local regulation, caring primarily for friends and neighbors, and earning far less than the medical professional. While she could capably handle the routine birth, it was not uncommon for her to call in the local physician when there was a problem. Tending infants usually meant applying the *fasce*, cotton bindings believed to give support, and piercing the earlobes of infant girls for earings. She may also have treated ailments unrelated to childbirth. Because she was unlicensed, she was often unable to register births she had attended. She probably understood the importance of cleanliness in preventing maternal infection, and may have even employed forceps in difficult deliveries, or eye drops for the prevention of infant blindness. However her effectiveness rested not so much on a thorough and scientific knowledge of the birth process, but on a willingness to "watch and wait," to be a comforting friend and companion through the long hours of labor and childbirth. Italian women, given the choice, preferred a midwife with a reputation for cleanliness. Competent midwives were greatly admired and respected in their local communities, inspiring much trust and affection.[28]

The Demise of the Midwife

Some states attempted to regulate midwifery practice early in the century through examination and licensing procedures, but these were often confusing or contradictory, and largely unenforced. A 1910 survey of midwifery regulation found that while thirteen states had passed laws supervising midwives, only six had any real knowledge of the number of practicing midwives in their state, and only two maintained records of actual births. New York City and later New York State attempted a more comprehensive approach. After 1907, midwives were required to demonstrate literacy and competence, to work within stipulated guidelines, and undergo license review each year. In 1911, New York City also established what was to be the first and only municipal school for the training of foreign-born midwives at Bellevue Hospital, but the number of those completing instruction during its twenty years of existence remained quite small. It was not until 1930 that most states required midwives to be registered.[29]

More successful in controlling midwifery was the drive to professionalize medical practice, to formalize the content and context of medical education, to establish licensing and peer review procedures, and to monopolize access to health innovations and technology. These had the effect of eliminating competition from the non-medically trained practitioner, and limiting access to the profession largely to white male graduates of elite universities.[30] These developments were closely related to the transformation of the hospital, which during the nineteenth century cared for charity patients, but after 1910 focused more on providing care to private fee-paying patients. Medical practitioners had argued that the only safe place to provide health care was in the controlled environment of the hospital. Hospitals became extensions of the practices of local physicians, who acquired many benefits while retaining their autonomy.[31] By 1930, the majority of practicing midwives lived in the southern region of the United States. Among Italians in New York's Greenwich Village, for example, the few remaining midwives could not compete with the local general practitioner whose office overflowed with obstetrical patients.[32]

While the regulation of midwifery and the professionalization of medical education had varying impacts, the demise of the immigrant midwife has generally been attributed to larger social and cultural processes. The most important of these was the enactment of the Immigration Acts of 1921-1924, which in one stroke eliminated the supply of foreign midwives as well as the women who would demand her services. The remaining foreign born women were by 1920 rapidly moving out of their childbearing years, while second generation women were more likely to have smaller families, and to seek out the services of a medical professional.[33]

Explanations for the fairly widespread acceptance of the medical model among second generation women center on the process of "Americanization," an inevitable turning away from immigrant ways as they experienced increased economic success, and a new acceptance of the application of science and technology to everyday life. However, several questions re-

main. First, the long-standing cultural prohibition of male
birth attendants seems not to have existed to any degree in
second generation families. How did Italian men and women
overcome this extreme aversion? To say that
"Americanization" took place is merely to describe the outcome; while it may delineate the end result, it says very little
about the actual process. As Clifford Geertz has observed:

...what we are interested in is not the mere differences
between the past and the present but the way in
which the former grew into the latter, the social and
cultural processes which connect them... The problem
is to understand how, given such beginnings, we have
arrived, for the moment, at such endings.[34]

Explanations that focus on the acculturation of foreign-born
groups tend also to portray immigrant families as passively
accepting momentous changes, more acted upon than acting,
with no ability to make meaningful choices.

When we consider the medicalization of childbirth from the
point of view of the requirements of the developing profession,
other questions emerge.[35] In this regard, Eliot Freidson has
outlined the major problem of professionalization: how does
the professional move clients to obey? The central dilemma is
that the authority of the professional over clients cannot be
based on grounds of common education and experience. The
layperson lacks knowledge of occupational rules of evidence or
basic content of medical skill. The problem is compounded
when in addition to differential education, there exist also
differences in culture and socioeconomic status.

So long as such cultural differences exist, physicians
are unlikely to have much access to patients, for they
will not be consulted regularly and matter-of-factly.
And when he does come into contact with such patients, it is incumbent upon the physician who wishes
to work to in some way understand his patient's culture sufficiently to be able to teach them something of
his point of view and, where that is not possible, to
modify his own behavior to conform with the patients'
expectations rather than lose the patient.[36]

In some instances, the higher social status of the professional might command respect and obedience. But too much

social distance might make the client so uncomfortable and fearful that consultation is completely avoided. Italians as well as other immigrant groups, both educationally, culturally, and socially distant from the medical professional, presented special challenges.

The Transition to Medical Childbirth

Early in this century it was recognized that the cultural gulf between health professionals and immigrant women might successfully be bridged through the employment of women physicians and visiting nurses working out of neighborhood dispensaries or settlement houses. It was hoped that women health professionals could introduce foreign-born mothers first to pre and post natal care, and finally to the acceptance of medical care in childbirth.[37] In this same way ethnic physicians may have also been an important link between the two worlds, helping to minimize cultural and perhaps socioeconomic differences.[38]

The transition to medical childbirth was undoubtedly an uneven, multi-faceted process whereby contending forces and practices often coexisted. Nevertheless, it is possible to suggest a model of stages in the transition, which as ideal-typical constructs, can reflect the essential features of each. Sketched out in this way we can briefly explore important differences, and suggest avenues for future research. Given the special dilemmas presented by immigrant clients, this model assigns an important place to the gender and ethnicity of the professional.

In this model, childbirth is seen to vary along three dimensions: caregiver, site of care, and duration of care. The first major erosion of social childbirth occurred as male physicians began to attend births and to work alongside the midwife. By 1910, this was a fairly common occurance for births to immigrant women. Physicians were summoned by the family or in many instances, by the midwife.[39] Another important change occurred when physicians became the only birth attendant. While both of these changes gave physicians a substantially more important role, there were major disadvantages, since, because birth was still at home, there were severe limits placed on the ability of the physician to control all aspects of the situation. Physician control is fully realized in the medical model with the move to the hospital for delivery and afterbirth care, as well as the appropriation of the whole of childbirth including both pre and post natal supervision.[40]

	Social Childbirth		Medical Childbirth		
care giver/s	midwife or other woman attendant	midwife and ethnic/ female physician	health nurse; female/ ethnic physician	ethnic/ female physician	anglo/ male physician
site of care	home	home	health station; home	doctor's office; ethnic or religious hospital	doctor's office; hospital
duration of care	birth only	birth only	pre-natal birth	pre, birth and post-natal	pre, birth and post-natal

There were few professionals in the first wave of immigration from southern and eastern Europe,[41] and, with the important exception of Jews, numbers of physicians from these ethnic backgrounds until recently remained quite small.[42] After 1930 limited numbers of ethnic physicians were to be found in local enclaves.[43]

Like the ethnic physician, the ethnically or religiously affiliated hospital served specific populations within local communities, and provided a supportive environment where the immigrant patient could be cared for. While they usually lacked affiliation with medical schools, nursing programs, or internship and residency training, they were often the only institutions willing to accept non-elite physicians.[44] When Columbus Hospital was founded in 1892 in New York City to serve the Italian community, none of the twenty-one doctors on staff was Italian. By 1938 however, all of its 100 physicians and surgeons were of Italian descent, as were the staffs of at least two other New York hospitals. New York was reported to have at that time 1,150 physicians of Italian origin, or about one for every 1,000 Italian residents. At least a quarter of these physicians had received their training in Italy.[45]

The ethnic physician practicing in the immigrant enclave, like other local entrepreneurs, had the advantage of language and shared tradition in dealing with his clientele. He may have come from a local family, gaining patronage through informal kin or neighborhood networks. General practitioners had the long-time loyalty of families, treating ailments that literally spanned individuals lives from birth to death. The fear of hospitals displayed by so many Italians was certainly eased through the ethnic physician's affiliation with the local ethnically or religiously sponsored hospital. Italian American women, who had often experienced the suffering and death of childbirth through the loss of a mother or sibling, sought out the services of a sympathetic, trusted, and not too socially distant practitioner who could promise safer outcomes.[46] From their perspective, the selection of a medical professional may not have been a denial of tradition and family values, but a way to preserve those values by securing safe and painless outcomes.

Conclusion:

The professionalization of medicine and the Americanization of immigrant groups were parallel social movements whose leadership, goals and targeted populations often overlapped. The demise of the midwife and the ascendence of the medical professional were certainly outcomes of both movements; both were also opportunities for elites to gain new power. For immigrant women and their daughters, the social choices they made in selecting professional care had unintended consequences, the most profound of which was the loss of control over an important aspect of their lives.

This paper has suggested that for immigrant populations, the ethnicity as well as the gender of the physician may have been important in this process. Future research needs to deliniate more precisely what role ethnicity played in the transition, both on the supply side, i.e., the physician, and the demand side, i.e., the parturient immigrant woman. Also to be explored are differences in acceptance of the medical model between ethnic groups.

Footnotes

[1] Frances E. Kobrin, "The American Midwife Controversy: A Crisis in Professionalization," *Bulletin of the History of Medicine* 40 (1966): 350-363 ; Richard W. Wertz and Dorothy C. Wertz, *Lying-In: A History of Childbirth in America.* New York: The Free Press, 1977; Judy Barrett Litoff, *American Midwives; 1860 to Present.* Westport, Conn: Greenwood Press, 1978; John S. Haller, Jr., *American Medicine in Transition, 1840-1910.* Urbana: University of Illinois Press, 1981: 150-191; Nancy Strom Dye, "The Medicalization of Birth", in Pamela S. Eakins, (ed.) *The American Way of Birth.* Philadelphia: Temple University Press, 1986: 21-46.

[2] See for example, F. Elisabeth Crowell, "The Midwives of New York", *Survey* 17 (1906-07): 667-677; Grace Abbott, "The Midwife in Chicago," *American Journal of Sociology* (xx) 1915: 684-699; Rocco Brindisi, M.D. "The Italian and Public Health," in, Lydio F. Tomasi (ed.) *The Italian in America: The Progressive View, 1891-1914.* New York: Center for Migration Studies, 1972: 116; Michael M. Davis, Jr. *Immigrant Health and the Community* Vol. 5 of *Americanization Studies: The Acculturation of Immigrant Groups into American Society* Republished under the Editorship of William S. Bernard, Montclair, New Jersey: Patterson Smith, 1971: 198; Virginia Yans McLaughlin, *Family and Community: Italian Immigrants in Buffalo, 1880 -1930.* Ithaca: Cornell University Press, 1972: 106; Wertz and Wertz, *Lying-In,* p. 212.

[3] Dye, "The Medicalization of Birth," p. 42; Litoff, *American Midwives,* p. 139; Wertz and Wertz, *Lying-In,* p. 217.

[4] Barbara Ehrenreich and Diedre English, *Witches, Midwives and Nurses: A History of Women Healers.* Old Westbury, N.Y.: Feminist Press, 1973; G. J. Barker-Benfield, *The Horrors of the Half-Known Life: Male Attitudes Toward Women and Sexuality in Nineteenth-Century America.* New York: Harper and Row, 1976; Jean Donnison, *Midwives and Medical Men: A History of Inter-Professional Rivalries and Women's Rights.* New York: Schocken Books, 1977; Jane B. Donegan, *Women and Men Midwives: Medicine, Morality and Misogyny in Early America.* Westport, Conn.: Greenwood Press, 1978; Bar-

bara Katz Rothman, *In Labor: Women and Power in the Birthplace.* New York: Norton, 1982.

[5] Phyllis F. Williams, *South Italian Folkways in Europe and America.* New Haven: Yale University Press, 1938. See also, Donnison, *Midwives and Medical Men*, pp. 1-20.

[6] Raymond G. Devries, "Midwifery and the Problem of Licensure," in Julius A Roth, (ed.) *Research in the Sociology of Health Care.* Greenwich, Conn.: Jai Press Inc., Vol. 2, 1982: 84-85; Haller, *American Medicine in Transition, 1840-1910*, pp. 168-171.

[7] F. Roy Willis, *Italy Chooses Europe.* New York: Oxford University Press, 1971: 161.

[8] Davis, *Immigrant Health and the Community*, p. 211.

[9] Crowell, "The Midwives of New York," Abbott, "The Midwife in Chicago," Litoff, *American Midwives*, p. 136.

[10] For a study of childbirth among middle class women see, Judith Waltzer Leavitt, *Brought to Bed: Child-Bearing in America, 1750-1950.* New York: Oxford University Press, 1986; Abbott, "The Midwife in Chicago,"p. 685 ; Litoff, *American Midwives*, pp. 135-136.

[11] Abbott, "The Midwife in Chicago," p. 684.

[12] Crowell, "The Midwives of New York," p. 670; See also Davis, *Immigrant Health and the Community*, p. 198.

[13] Nancy Strom Dye, "Modern Obstetrics and Working Class Women: The New York Midwifery Dispensary, 1890-1920,".*Journal of Social History* Spring, 1987: 552.

[14] Wertz and Wertz, *Lying-In*, pp. 211-12; Litoff, "American Midwives," pp. 28-29; Haller, *American Medicine in Transition, 1840-1910*, pp. 176-77.

[15] Yans McLaughlin, *Family and Community*, p. 150; Elizabeth Ewen, *Immigrant Women in the Land of the Dollars: Life and Culture on the Lower East Side, 1890-1925.* New York: Monthly Review Press, 1985 p.131.

[16] Robert F. Foerster, *The Italian Emigration of Our Times. New York: Arno Press, 1969: 410; William I. Thomas and Florian Znaniecki, The Polish Peasant in Europe and America.* Urbana: University of Illinois Press, 1984: 243; Yans-McLaughlin, *Family and Community*, pp. 30, 107.

[17] Antonio Stella, "The Effects of Urban Congestion on Italian Women and Children," in Francesco Cordasco (ed.) *Italians in the City: Health and Related Social Needs.* New York: Arno Press, 1975. Dr. Stella reported that maternal mortality was second only to tuberculosis as a cause of death for adult Italian women.

[18] Yans-McLaughlin, *Family and Community*, p. 106.

[19] Wertz and Wertz, *Lying-In*, p. 203; Litoff, *American Midwives.*

[20] Crowell, "The Midwives of New York"; Kobrin,"The American Midwife Controversy"; Litoff, *American Midwives*, p. 73.

[21] Litoff, *American Midwives*, p. 77.

[22] Kobrin, "The American Midwife Controversy."

[23] Litoff, *American Midwives*, p. 77; Haller, *American Medicine in Transition*, p. 177.

[24] Haller, *American Midwives in Transition*, pp. 166-168; Wertz and Wertz, *Lying-In*, p. 214.

[25] Crowell, "The Midwives of New York," p. 673; Caroline F. Ware, *Greenwich Village, 1920-1930: A Comment on American Civilization in the Post War Years.* New York: Harper and Row: 179, 384; Rudolph M. Bell, *Fate and Honor, Family and Village: Demographic and Cultural Change in Rural Italy since 1800.* Chicago: University of Chicago Press: 54 ; Haller, *American Medicine in Transition*, p. 175.

[26] Ewen, *Immigrant Women in the Land of the Dollars*, p. 133.

[27] Crowell, "The Midwives of New York," p. 673; Haller, *American Medicine in Transition*, p. 175.

[28] Crowell, "The Midwives of New York"; Abbott,"The Midwife in Chicago"; Litoff, *American Midwives*, p. 41; Ewen, *Immigrant Women in the Land of the Dollars*, p. 132; see also, Angela D. Danzi,"Savaria the Midwife: Childbirth and Change in the Immigrant Community," in Judith DeSena (ed.) *Contemporary Readings in Sociology.* Dubuque, Iowa: Kendall-Hunt, forthcoming.

[29] Abbott, "The Midwife in Chicago," pp. 688, 694-697; Devries,"Midwifery and the Problem of Licensure,"pp.86-87; Litoff, *American Midwives*, pp. 56-57; Haller, *American Medicine in Transition*, p. 179.

[30] Randall Collins, *The Credential Society: An Historical Sociology of*

Education and Stratification New York: Academic Press, 1979: 138-146; Paul Starr, *The Social Transformation of American Medicine.* New York: Basic Books, 1982.

[31] Morris J. Vogel, *The Invention of the Modern Hospital: Boston, 1870-1930.* Chicago: University of Chicago Press, 1980; Collins, *The Credential Society,* p 145. Charles E. Rosenberg, *The Care of Strangers: The Rise of America's Hospital System.* New York: Basic Books, 1987; Litoff, *American Midwives,* p. 74.

[32] Litoff, *American Midwives,* p. 114; Ware, *Greenwich Village,* p. 384.

[33] Ware, *Greenwich Village,* p. 383; Litoff, *American Midwives,* p. 33; Dye, "The Medicalization of Birth," pp. 42-43.

[34] Clifford Geertz, *Islam Observed: Religious Development in Morocco and Indonesia.* New Haven: Yale University Press, 1968: 57.

[35] Eliot Freidson, *Professional Dominance: The Social Structure of Medical Care.* New York: Atherton Press, 1970.

[36] Freidson, *Professional Dominance,* p. 111.

[37] Abbott, "The Midwife in Chicago," p. 694; Nancy Dallett,"Creating the Healthy Neighborhood: Public Health at Greenwich House, 1900-1940."New York University: unpublished manuscript, 1988; Davis, *Immigrant Health and the Community,* p. 223-225. Pre and post natal care of the mother was urged to combat high rates of infant mortality. See, Virginia M. Walker, "How to Save the Babies of the Tenements." *Charities* Vol XIV (1905): 975. For a study of the rise of prenatal care see, Ann Oakley, *The Captured Womb: A History of the Medical Care of Pregnant Women.* New York: Basil Blackwell, Inc., 1984. For an analysis of discrimination against women in medicine during this era see, Gloria Moldow, *Women Doctors in Gilded-Age Washington: Race, Gender and Professionalization.* Urbana, University of Illinios Press,

[38] Davis, *Immigrant Health and the Community,* pp. 135-138.

[39] Dye, "Modern Obstetrics and Working-Class Women"; Litoff, *American Midwives,* p. 33; Haller, *American Medicine in Transition,* p. 160.

[40] Rothman, *In Labor.*; Wertz and Wertz, *Lying-In,* pp.132-177.

[41] Foerster, *The Italian Emigration of Our Time,* p. 329; Leonard

Covello, *The Social Background of the Italo American School Child.*
Edited and with an introduction by Francesco Cordasco. Totowa,
N.J.: Rowman and Littlefield, 1972: 277.

[42] Stanley Lieberson, Ethnic Groups and the Practice of Medicine.
American Sociological Review. 23 (October, 1958) pp. 542-29.

[43] Ware, *Greenwich Village,* p. 384 ; Yans McLaughlin also mentions
two Italian women physicians who practiced in Buffalo. See *Family
and Community,* p. 252.

[44] Vogel, *The Invention of the Modern Hospital*; David S. Solomon,
"Ethnic and Class Differences Among Hospitals as Contingencies in
Medical Careers." *American Journal of Sociology.* 66. (1961) No. 5:
463-71; Rosanne Martorella, "Italian Americans and Medical Education: An Exploratory Study." in Remigio U. Pane (ed.) *Italian Americans in the Professions.* Staten Island, N.Y.: American Italian Historical Association, 1983: 177-191; According to Davis, in 1921 most
physicians who practiced among the poor had no institutional affiliation. See Davis, *Immigrant Health and the Community,* p. 141.

[45] Antonio Mangano, "The Associated Life of the Italians in New
York City," *Charities,* XII (May, 1904) p. 478; Federal Writers Project, *The Italians of New York: A Survey* New York: Random House,
1938: 112-113; Davis, *Immigrant Health and the Community,* p.139.
Ratio of Italian physicians to residents based on New York City population of Italian foreign-born and native born of Italian parentage
for 1940. See Ira Rosenwaike, *Population History of New York City.*
Syracuse, N.Y.: Syracuse University Press, 1972: 204.

[46] Davis, *Immigrant Health and the Community,* p. 135.

Ferrazzanesi in Cortland, New York

Francis X. Femminella, Ph.D.
State University of New York at Albany

About 5 kilometers southeast of Campobasso, going all the way uphill from the base camp, one comes to what is described in the tour books as "a most pleasant sentinel"; a castle and fortification known as *Ferrazzano*. This remarkably well kept stone village, set high on the top of one of the Samnian Mountains, a chain within the Apennines, has, since Samnium times *watched over* Campobasso, the provincial and regional (Molise) capital. It is a tiny place, its population about 1600 people, occupying a total land area of about 18 square kilometers.[1] By comparison, Campobasso with a population of about 25,000 occupies about 50 square kilometers, and sets on a plain 200 meters below the mountain sentry.

Less than 2 kilometers further south and almost 300 meters below, lies the village of *Mirabello Sannitico*, even smaller than Ferrazzano, with a population of less than 1000, spread over about 25 kilometers of the steep mountainside. Over the centuries, it too has been *watched over* by this same Ferrazzano, not, however, in the sense of protecting and guarding, but rather in the sense of scrutinizing and keeping under surveillance. For the people of these villages occupied the same mountain and competed for the same essential, scarce resources, including food crops and water and, perhaps more important, even spouses.

The competition and the feuds were all part of the social history of these mountain people whose lives were hidden behind the stone walls surrounding their high perched villages and who, until this century, were among the most isolated of all the people of the Italian peninsula. These are the Molisani that Rimanelli and others have written about.[2] The "rough ridges of the Matese (Monti del Matesi)," of which Lalli[3] speaks, form the southwestern edge of the Sannio, while the

Samnian Mountains (Monti del Sannio) adjoin them, creating an equally formidable rocky range that makes up Central Molise, with the city of Campobasso its nucleus.

In these mountains, law and order was a function of moral imperative and that strange mixture of religious fervor that characterized peasant spirituality. The institutional organizations of government and religion were too often allied against the best interests of the peasants and so could not be trusted. The people had to make their own way, with honesty and integrity born of profound loyalty to their families, and to what they believed to be right.

In these remote and difficult places, what was to become of a family in which a son or daughter married an outsider, worse, not just any outsider but one from that particular village? The conflict between villages was brought directly into the kitchen, as it were. Imagine, if you will, the role upheaval between parents and children, the internal conflicts between husbands and wives and between them and their extended family, and the personal and communal alienation, to use social-psychological terms, that ensued. These Ferrazzanesi and Mirabellesi were said literally to have shot at each other if one was found taking a fig from the others' tree. To take a son or a daughter was at least equal to a fig, and surly merited an appropriate response.

Lalli describes the political and economic conditions that led up to the great emigration out of Molise around the turn of the century. Southern Italy in particular was a land characterized by poverty, the exploitation of the peasants, and largely devoid of hope. The villages of Ferrazzano and Mirabello fit in well with this characterization and, added to the malaise of oppression that afflicted the new nation, there was the particularistic conflict between the two villages with those deep festering sores created by the intermarriages. These continued to rankle even after the migration that ended in some new synthesis.

The purpose of this paper is to describe the life and progeny of one group of the Ferrazzanesi who came to the United States and reestablished to some extent, their social relationships here. In doing so, we hope to contribute to the literature on the Molisani in America. At the same time, these data are interpreted using the recently developed notion of *critical pluralism*.[4] In its simplest form, this refers to the recognition that Americans are people that have assimilated many aspects of the dominant culture, have retained some aspects of their social heritage, have made aspects of their culture part of America and have become fully integrated without being culturally homogenized. Only in this way can the final integration of Ferrazzanesi and Mirabellesi in America be understood.

The population for this study was found in Cortland, New York, a small city located in the south central part of New York state, about 30 miles south of Syracuse, New York. In 1925, there were in Cortland, 187 families who came from Ferrazzano and Mirabello. They referred to themselves and were known then and now as the *Campuasciani*, a dialect word for Campobasso. They made up about one third of the total Italian population of Cortland at that time; and they were the single largest Italian group there, the next being the 102 Siciliani families from Palermo and Messina who made up about 17% of the Italian population.[5]

In the course of this research, we have met and talked with a number of Ferrazzanesi and Mirabellesi both in America and Italy. We interviewed and had mail correspondence with 15% of the Campuasciani families in Cortland. From all of these contacts, two important phenomena were observed: *first*, the immigrants, and to a progressively lesser extent their progeny, engaged Americans in conflict, often hostile, violent conflict; and *second*, the offspring of the Molisani migrants think, act and feel as though they are Americans, and they claim to be Americans.[6] The connection between these observed phenomena is *critical pluralism*.

There was a wide range of feelings about their ethnic identity within the sample studied. The attitude of some may be summed up in the language of one who wrote, "Since I was born in Cortland, N.Y. in 1922, I have no knowledge of Molise, Italy. My parents both emigrated from Campobasso, Italy prior to 1914". Another asserted more strongly that, "My father's favorite expression was, 'If the old country had anything to offer besides poverty I would had (sic) stayed there.' That is all the knowledge I have of Italy." And still one more told us in answer to our queries about the Molisani, "...my people were born in Mirabello, Province of Campobasso. Therefore, I don't think we are Molinese (sic). If we are, it's news to me. My father and mother always referred to their town as being near Naples."

On one end of the continuum, there was lack of knowledge of one's origins and, more importantly, lack of interest in finding out about them. This was what American society and the American schools wanted for the children of immigrants. It was a social standard fostered by an ideology of conformity to the dominant society, and it was advocated in schools, in the press, and, ultimately, in law. On the other end, there was the alienation born of over identification and wishful thinking that so often resulted either in a breakdown—immigrant psychosis—or in the eventual return by the immigrants to the land of their origin.

The great American dream, and the hopes of the immigrants who stayed on, were perfectly congruent, and so they drove themselves, and many experienced competitive success. This achievement produced a wonderful story but it makes the accomplishment sound all too simple; it leaves out the pain and suffering that accompanied the triumph.

In Cortland, Charles Masterpaul, whose older brother changed their name from Mastropaolo, went through this. Charles remembers when his father came to Cortland from Campobasso and worked the whole night through at the Wickwire Corporation,[7] a factory that refused in the early days to hire Italians to work on the day shift. The "No Italian need apply" signs that appeared in the Wickwire Corporation hiring hall must be seen as the rejecting prejudice that it was. The internalized psychological violence it engendered in the Molisani there, must not be covered up nor must it be explained away. Wickwire did not hire Italians, because it preferred to hire people of its own kind. But economic necessity forced a change. The treatment of the Italians after they were hired is another story. The American workers treated the Italians as uninvited strangers. Clearly, there was conflict of interest. Clearly, there was territoriality operating. The owners, on the other hand, when they realized the contribution the Italians could make, invited them; then they exploited them.

The conflict between the immigrants and their host was similar to what Geertz observed in another context, it was "...neither dichotomous nor linear but dialectical."[8] The first Italians came to Cortland in 1892.[9] The respondents explained their or their parents' reason for migrating out of Ferrazzano and Mirabello in both economic and sociocultural terms. Farming was petering out; there were no jobs; they sought independence and freedom. Nick DiStefano came to Cortland in 1956, solely to assure that his children would have access to higher education. The immigrants belief that life could no longer be tolerated in Molise, was accompanied by the belief that Cortland was a place possessed of real possibilities. The Wickwire Corporation hired Italian labor contractors, *padroni,* to gather together and ship Italian workers to Cortland. One informant stated that in addition to hiring contractors, the Wickwires themselves went to the New York Port of Entry and recruited workers personally. In time the workers who came to Cortland and found employment sent for their wives and families and then also for their relatives who came to work either at Wickwire or on one of the two railroads that intersected the city: the Lehigh Valley Railroad or the Delaware, Lackawanna and Western Railroad.

There was no scarcity of employment in Cortland for anyone who was willing to work hard for low wages. Most American workers refused this kind of work and despised the Italian and Ukrainian and Polish immigrants who seemed to thrive on it. The Wickwire Corporation, which refused to hire Italians until they saw how well they worked, became the single largest employer of Italian male workers. In addition there were the railroads, the Wallpaper Company, Brockway Motors which made the famous Mack trucks, the Crescent Corset Company, the Cortland Corset Company and the Halsted Packing Company.

Italian immigrant life at the turn of the century was demographically and socially male dominated, but strong women, the hidden matriarchs, found ways to save the situations they found their families in. They opened their homes to boarders, mostly single men or some married men whose families were still in Molise to which they expected to return. They created homes away from home, giving meals, a place to sleep and for a few extra pennies, doing laundry.[10] They worked at what they knew, and when they needed to they brought the children into the act, cleaning, mending and taking care of the younger children. During World War I, the women began to work outside their homes. The corset factories utilized their sewing, crocheting and embroidering skills which they had been taught as children. When Jennie Consroe left the Crescent Co. in 1942 to raise her family, she was earning $14.00 for 40 hours work. Today the average wages are in the range of $10,000 to $12,000 a year. David Perfetti remembers his mother taking him to the Crescent Corset Co. at 6:00 a.m., where he would stack the pieces of garments his mother was working on, or do his homework, while he waited to walk across the schoolyard to go to classes at 8 a.m. At lunch time he would walk back to the factory where his mother would meet him; and they would eat their lunch together at the sewing machine, there being no lunch room or cafeteria provided. Back to school he would go, then return again to the factory to wait for his mother to take him home in the evening.

The Molisani from Ferrazzano and Mirabello were entering the life of the United States. There very presence evoked behaviors that alternately surprised, shocked and outraged them. As the host society began to reject them and engender in them feelings of being estranged intruders, they responded and that in turn called up rejoinders. The forms of *conflict* were many and they pervaded every aspect of life.

The stories we were told were tales of exploitation, of corruption, of discrimination, of industrial manslaughter, of neglect and denial, and of that subtle and insidious denigration that occurs with such finesse in the schools. There was conflict in the workplace, in residence, in politics and in church.[11]

In the factories, the hours were long, the pay was low, and the work strenuous. For the women, worry about their unsupervised children was an added burden since going out to work never relieved them of their domestic and child raising responsibility. The men loved their children but expected their wives to care for them. Except when the wives were sick. We heard a few times about the men taking over the household chores of cooking and cleaning (though usually it was more the cooking than the cleaning) in unusual situations. Working double shifts in order to earn extra money was not unusual, and respondents remember taking meals to parents so they could stay on. During the bean picking season, women and men worked in the fields, and the children accompanied them as much to be watched over as actually to work. After one respondent put in 25 years in a factory, his bosses let him train a young man for his job after which he was fired without pension or severance pay.[12]

Unionism in the early days in Cortland was ineffective. A local of the AFL-CIO Steel Workers of America was started, and one respondent became active, but it was too weak to achieve any real change. The work conditions were so bad that were the plant in Pittsburgh, it would have been closed. A worker, Molisano, who, because of lack of safety guards, fell into the molten steel, left a wife and 11 children and no compensation. After 60 years of hiring Italians, one who was active in the union was the first Italian promoted to foreman. When steel manufacturing became unprofitable, workers like one respondent with 42 years of service had his $29 per month pension cut off.

This was the conflict that these immigrants endured. That they were Italian means there was a nuance of difference as for example, in the treatment they received at St. Mary's church which was dominated by the Irish. But all immigrants suffered. That they were from Molise, means they did not want to associate with the Italians from Sicily, but preferred those from Abruzzi, Lazio and Campania. But neither, for that matter, did the other Italians want to associate with Sicilians. That they were from Ferrazzano and Mirabello meant perhaps that they knew how to ignore such family admonitions, so they married Sicilians and other Italians, and Irish, Polish, and Ukrainians as well.

Italian names to most ears are pleasant sounding but to the prejudiced they are strange and needed to be changed. Not only were names changed at ports of entry where immigration officials reconstituted peoples names as, for example, when my own father's name was changed from Audenzio to Lawrence, and in schools where, for example, Scordomiglia became Skordyne, but in Cortland most of the name changing took place at work. Liliana Torquati became Lillian Torcatti and later Lillian Kirk; Clementina Quattrochi became Clementine Smith; the Di Stefano's became Stevens; Valentino Pacelli became Charley Moore; Canistraro became Canestaro; Natale became Christmas; Palladino became Pauldine; Mastropaolo became Mastropolo or Masterpolo or Masterpaul; Ciarariello became Calario; Giovannina Musenga became Jennie, and later she changed it halfway back to Johanna.

At school there were many incidents of prejudice and conflict in Cortland as there were elsewhere. In the residential areas there was discrimination, and in the professions, where one was dealing with educated people, the conflict was no less. When one respondent wanted to buy a pharmacy where he had long been employed and which survived only because of his efforts, he was denied because the powerful Mr. Burgess "didn't want Italians on Main Street." And when his brother, a young lawyer, an activist for Italians in Cortland, was killed at the age of 39 by a drunk driver who happened to be a prominent lawyer in town, nothing was done about it.

After working and contributing to the city of Cortland for more than 50 years, there were, in the 1940s, no Italian firemen, no Italian policemen, no Italian politicians, no Italians employed in the better department stores. When Italians came to Cortland from Syracuse to visit *paesani*, they could sense the prejudice and feel it as they walked the streets. They had experienced the conflict also in Syracuse, but not to such an extent. Two questions kept coming to mind as we interviewed the people of Cortland: Why did they and/or their parents tolerate this treatment? And, perhaps more importantly, What did they do about it?

The road to Cortland from Albany, N.Y. (Route I 88) is a straight, limited access, toll free, superhighway, on which, were it not for the sheer beauty of the hills and the green fir trees at the higher elevations and the poetry inspiring fertile valleys below, were it not for this fine scenery, one might be tempted to exceed the posted speed limits. How different and how alike this countryside is to Molise, and to Ferrazzano in particular. The mountains of Molise are not round and rolling but high and peaked, and they are topped with *paesi* not trees; and the valleys are rugged, the wide ones are fertile, the others support only vines. The highways of Molise are also toll-free. But only natives and the suicidal speed on them. There are really only two superhighways in Molise; one travels along the Biferno, the other along the Trigno, the two major rivers of the Regione. But in both places there is a beauty and a feeling of being part of the terra firma, a feeling that is not found living in a coastal area. Cortland, like Campobasso, is a city surrounded by mountains and many of the Ferrazzanesi in Cortland who used to walk to Campobasso as children say there is a resemblance. They say that even the neighborhood life in Cortland at one time resembled a little, the life in the village.

In Cortland, the Italians began, upon their arrival, to establish themselves in residential patterns that put them into close proximity to their work at the Wickwire Corporation on South Main Street and the Crescent Corset factory also on South Main Street two blocks north. In time, the settlements exhibited clustering of family and *paesani* over three wards of the city, but the Italians from Molise were divided evenly in all three wards. This was the beginning of Italian ghettoization in Cortland.

The Italians of Cortland established a life for themselves, setting up institutions to meet their basic needs. To a large extent this typical chain migration was accompanied by a transmission of the values and life-styles of the former place of residence to the new. But, of course, an exact replication was neither desired nor possible. John Tucci attests to the fact that there was a singular tenacity to the old ways when it came to the table. People sought Italian vegetables, cheeses, olive oil, macaroni and spaghetti, fruits, sausage and salamis, and bread—but here he explains—everyone preferred the Sicilian style bread. Although there was some outmarriage there was a good deal of intermarriage between Italians from different regions. Molisani married Siciliani, Sgurgolani, Laziali, Napolitani and Baresi.

Similarly, with respect to religion, attending the Irish Catholic St.Mary's was supplemented by meetings in private homes to pray together in Italian. In 1905, they founded the Società Sant' Antonio which this year celebrated its 82nd anniversary. In 1917, they were given permission to establish a new church, named after St. Anthony, the patron of the church in Ferrazzano. The bells of this new church in Cortland were made in Agnone, Molise; and they were an important element in the religious life of Cortland Italians and the establishment of the Assemblia Christiana.

The Society provided a social and recreational opportunity to remember the families and life in Italy and to pass this on to the children. In Ferrazzano today, the *feste* are held in the *piazze*. Young and old listen and dance to the Rock music played by young musicians. In Cortland the major feast is celebrated for three days on the church grounds, where one finds: "Onions and peppers, sausages around, and roller coasters frantic in the air..." A magnificent parade, led by the "Old Timers Band" passes through the entire Italian neighborhood ending at the Church itself. At the feast day liturgy: "Children, brown-cowled as little Anthonys,/ before the statue in a double row/ advance as solemn as sweet imps can be, / most unaware of representing, each/ and all of them, their parents' grateful vows." [13]

As the Ferrazzanesi and Mirabellesi in Cortland had to learn to put aside ancient animosities in order to survive, so, on the wider scale, the Italians had to unite. In 1932, John Tucci, whose father came from Mirabello, helped to organize the Italians politically across party lines. Until very recently, when Cortland was part of his Senate District, Tarky Lombardy, whose grandmother was born in Ferrazzano, carried it with a 70% plurality each time he ran.

Of course, so much of the old culture is lost in Cortland. There are very few Italian Americans, and none of the grandchildren that we interviewed that knew the Italian folk fables. The American *school* system was effective in this respect. But it did teach the English language, and young Molisani used it to "move up" in American society. The mixed signals they received from their parents did not daunt them. On the one hand they heard how wonderful life in Molise was; on the other they heard the familiar "I'd rather be dead in the United States than alive in Campobasso." The immigrants became American citizens, and their children acquired American identities, shaped by the history of their parents and their own confrontation with the new land.

Off they went, young men and women, to business or to college. They were, in the large, highly successful. They became lawyers, pharmacists, dancers, models, teachers, principals, priests, plumbers, restaurateurs, realtors, salespersons, telecommunication specialists, et cetera.

As we ask the Molisani of Cortland why they took the "beating" that they did from the dominant power group, this is what is repeatedly pointed out to us. First, they felt there was nothing they could do about it. Second, they felt that there was hope for their children here. And third, they felt that there was security in the work. In Jennie Consroe's words, "They took it, they turned the other cheek, they worked hard and they sent their children to school."

During the depression years of the 1930s, Cortland was not hit as hard as many other places including the nation's large cities which were the major centers of immigration settlement; the plant cut back only one day a week. This created the comfortable situation in which the workers could at least depend on the regularity of their four day paycheck, which meant they could still pay off their mortgages. A return to the land of their fathers was completely out of the question for most of the Molisani in Cortland whose rate of return was exceedingly low if the memories of my respondents is accurate. We were told of returnees among the more recent migrants of the 1950s, but not among the earlier ones.

The people we have been describing are Americans of Italian parents or at least of Italian descent. Specifically, they are Molisani-American. Have they been assimilated into United States society? Or are they a distinctly separate community? From the point of view of Impact-Integration theory, a *critical pluralism* has evolved out of the dialectical relationships we have reported. What that means is that while on the one hand, there has been a good deal of "Americanization" of the Italians, on the other hand they were not homogenized into the society they entered. Moreover, that society, in its rejection and exploitation of the Italians, on the one hand, ultimately could not deny them, and on the other hand, did in fact itself become somewhat Italian representing a real structural and cultural change.

Critical pluralism implies something more, and it is evident in the lives of the people we interviewed, and especially the children and grandchildren of the immigrants. They think and feel that they are fully American. But they also think and feel that to be an American entitles one not to have to be a certain kind of American, not to have to be an Anglo-American, for example, but to be allowed to have a non-Anglo background. The anglo-conformity and melting pot ideologues would decry this kind of thought or feeling. The cultural pluralist would decry the assimilation that did take place. But for a theorist, critical pluralism explains how and why the residents of Cortland feel and think the way they do. What distinguishes one American from another are, in the words of Father Carlo Stirpe, the "nuances" that derive from ethnicity.[14]

The *Campuasciani* are today fully integrated into American society. They are an essential part of every aspect of it, they contribute to it and they profit from it. As for the immigrants, today we can say that they have achieved what they set out to do, namely, to free themselves or at least their children from the fetters of poverty and constraint which bound them in Italy, and to have a better life with more choice and opportunity. Whatever their individual experiences, as a group they were "fortunate pilgrims"; they succeeded. The Italian-Americans of today go on with their own struggles, still stereotyped, and in a more subtle way, still feeling the stings of prejudice, but better prepared and better organized to fight it.

---

[1] Figures are derived from the "Molise-Circoscrizione Comunali," Densita dalla popolazione (censim 1981). Assessorato al Turismo, Regione Molise.

[2] Giose Rimanelli, *Molise Molise.* (Isernia, Italy: Libreria Editrice Marinelli, 1979.)

[3] Renato Lalli, "Giovannitti e il Molise," in G. Rimanelli, S. Martelli and F.X. Femminella (eds.) in *Il sud e l'america: Molise ed emigrazione* (Molise, Forthcoming.)

[4] Gerard A. Postiglione, *Ethnicity and American Social Theory.* (New York: University Press of America, 1983.) pp. 203 ff.

5 Louis M. Venaria, "Settlement Patterns of Cortland Italians: The First Generation, 1892-1925," in L.M. Vanaria (ed.) *From Many Roots: Immigrants and Ethnic Groups in the History of Cortland County, New York.* (Cortland County Chronicles, Vol. 4, New York: Cortland County Historical Society, publication #18, 1986.)

6 I am indebted to Molisani in Cortland, especially: Tony Camillo, Frank Consroe, Jennie Consroe, Remo DeStefano, Tom Granato, Jr., Hon. Tarky Lombardi, Charles and Gilda Baranello Masterpaul, Ralph Passalugo, David Perfetti, Mary Stevens, Johnnie Stevens, Rev. Carlo Stirpe, John Tucci, and also the respondents to the mail questionnaire whose names are protected by a promise of anonymity.

7 See Diane Vecchio Wilson, "Assimilation and Ethnic Consolidation of Italians in Cortland, New York 1892-1930." in R.N. Juliani (ed.) *The Family and Community Life of Italian Americans.* (New York: The American Italian Historical Association, 1983.) p.183.

8 As quoted in Jonathan H. Gillette, "Italian Workers in New Haven: Mutuality and Solidarity at the Turn of the Century," in Joseph L. Tropea, James E. Miller and Cheryl Beattie-Repetti (eds.), *Support and Struggle: Italians and Italian Americans in a Comparative Perspective,* (New York: AIHA, 1986.) p.38.

9 Diane C. Vecchio, "The Influence of Family Values and Culture on the Occupational Choices of Italian Immigrant Women in Cortland, N,Y., 1890-1935, in L.M. Vanaria, (ed.) *From Many Roots.* p.37.

10 ibid, p.37 ff.

11 We have presented a number of these stories briefly in "The Integration of Southern Italians in American Society," Paper read at the international symposium "Southern Italy and America: Molise and Emigration," in Campobasso, Italy. June 26-28, 1987. (forthcoming.)

12 L.M. Vanaria, "St. Anthony's Day in Cortland: *La Festa* in Cortland, N.Y.," *New York Folklore,* vol. 6, Winter 1980, pp.161-170.

13 These and the line above are from: Joseph Tusiani, "Letter to San Gennaro," in *Gente Mia,* (Stone Park, IL: Italian Cultural Center, 1978) pp. 27-28.

14 Pastor of St. Anthony's Cortland, N.Y. Interview June 13, 1987.

Converting the Italians: Protestant and Catholic Proselytizers in Milwaukee

John Andreozzi

"While there are today probably 600,000 Italians living in the United States, there are not fifty Italian priests laboring among them," reported Milwaukee's *Catholic Citizen* in 1897.[1] With this article, editor Humphrey J. Desmond began a long series of editorials that drew national and international attention to what he referred to as the "Neglected Italians." The Italian question, he wrote, "concerns the religious welfare of an army of 50,000 Catholic Italian children in the great American cities—thousands of whom are going to school on the streets and thousands of whom (more fortunate) are enrolled in what we are pleased to call `the godless public schools.' "[2] If the Church could establish itself as the center of religious and social life in the Italian settlements, Desmond reasoned, the "Italian immigrants might then be a Legion of the Cross rather than material for the Mafia, rather than a jetsam and flotsam upon our shores to be gathered up into any belief or no belief."[3]

Responses from Catholic newspapers throughout the United States also focused on the scarcity of Italian priests and upon the "general backwardness of Italians arriving in this country in religious instruction."[4] Catholic newspaper editors felt Italians were in "a state little better than paganism" and were disturbed by Protestant proselytizing among the growing numbers of Italian immigrants.[5] And while Protestant and Catholics competed for the loyalty of Italians, both viewed the religious practices of the Latin immigrants as "problematic."

The Italian experience in Milwaukee is a microcosm of the religious acculturation of Italian Americans. All facets of the "Italian problem" and the struggle by Protestant and Catholic proselytizers to convert the immigrants and their children were present. Italian priests made an appearance after

Desmond's outcry, but tenuous clergy-parishioner relationships and sharp regional differences among the immigrants undercut the church as a central institution. Even after the creation of an Italian parish, five Protestant missions led by Italian ministers offered a dramatic challenge to the Catholic church between 1910 and 1930. Indeed, during these years Protestant and Catholic proselytizers were locked in battle for the souls of Italian immigrants and their children. Eventually the Catholics predominated, fulfilling Desmond's goal of making the Church the center of religious life in Little Italy. However it took many years and the religious education of the second generation to finally Americanize the religious expression of Milwaukee's Italians.

Individual Italians had been arriving in Milwaukee since the Civil War era and by the 1880s several colonies had appeared, the largest located in the Third Ward on the east side. In 1895, a brief article in the *Catholic Citizen* foreshadowed future developments:

> The proposition to open a church for Italians in this city or to assign a priest to them has been abandoned. It has been found that the Italian residents of the city speak a number of different dialects, most of them being Sicilians, and, on this account, it would be extremely difficult to find a priest who could preach to them.[6]

The nearest Catholic Church was St. John's Cathedral, an Irish parish located just north of the Third Ward colony. In September 1898 an Italian Mission was established that soon drew 100 Italian youngsters. During the first Sunday school classes the volunteer teachers had to content themselves with leading the children in patriotic songs, as the young Italians "had not learned any church hymns."[7] The continued success of the Italian Mission seemed assured when Rev. Rosario Nasca, a native of Sicily, arrived in May 1899. Under Nasca's leadership masses for the Italians were held every morning and evening at St. John's.[8] However, in June the Italian Mission at St. John's was closed. The *Catholic Citizen* observed: "The Italian people do not seem to have appreciated the efforts made in their behalf and the attendance was poor. The prospects for a permanent Italian Mission and school are not the brightest."[9]

The closing of the Italian Mission reflected the vast differences between Irish and southern Italian Catholics. At the end of the 19th Century, the U.S. Catholic Church was dominated by Irish Americans who had toiled for 50 years to gain respectability for the "immigrant Church." The Irish were "respectful and obedient toward the clergy," attended Mass regularly, participated in Confession and the Eucharist, and were generous in their financial support of the Church.[10] In Ireland religion mixed with politics as the Church was at the forefront of the anti-English, anti-Protestant movement. The Italian Catholic, however, has historically been ambivalent toward the Church. If he maintained any feelings of nationalism, he was aware that the Church had opposed the unification of Italy. In southern Italy, from which the majority of immigrants to the United States came, "the Catholic Church has traditionally either exploited the peasants or sided with the large landowner in his exploitation of them."[11] Church attendance and the sacraments were usually defined as the province of women and children and the men were often anticlerical. Italian religious expression was a "melding of ancient pagan beliefs, magical practices and Christian liturgy."[12] The multitude of southern Italian saints were not looked up to because of their moral example, but rather because of the magical, concrete powers each exerted upon the peasant's everyday life. The feast day, or *festa*, honoring a patron saint or the Madonna represented the highest expression of Italian religiosity.

Because of these differing religious beliefs, Italian immigrants in America felt alienated in the Irish churches. This alienation quickly brought to an end the first stage that, according to Silvano Tomasi, typified the growth of Italian parishes: the "attempt to incorporate Italian immigrants within the Irish parishes." In Milwaukee and other cities, there followed two other stages in this process of religious acculturation—the separation from the Irish and the building of the Italian churches, and finally, "a fusion of Italian and Irish, among others, into a new type of social group, the Catholic segment of the American population."[13]

* * *

Immediately after the St. John's Mission closed, the Third
Ward Italians, with the permission of Archbishop Katzner,
established a storefront mission. Rev. Nasca took up residence
on the second floor of Our Lady of Pompeii Mission, organized
night school courses, and dreamt of constructing an Italian
church and school. However, this goal proved quite difficult to
fulfill. Accustomed to government support of the Church, the
Italian immigrants could barely make Sunday contributions,
which totaled $5 per week in 1900, let alone finance the con-
struction of a church.[14] And many immigrants came to the
United States with the intention of remaining only a few
years, accumulating some savings, and then returning to
Italy. Finally, there was the poverty of the Italians, as Father
Nasca observed: "Most of my people are poor and the other
demands upon them are too great."[15]

The ailing Rev. Nasca was replaced by Rev. Bartolomeo Imburgia, who arrived from Sicily in 1900. An Italian Mission
Association of 12 prominent Italians was organized and, led
by Hasso Pestalozzi, had collected $1,000 from Italians
throughout Milwaukee by August 1901. Additional support
came from the Italian Mission Aid Society, composed of 11
distinguished non-Italians, including industrialist Thomas J.
Neacy and H. J. Desmond, editor of the *Catholic Citizen*.
These influential lay Catholics contributed money and organized a variety of impressive fund-raisers, such as a benefit at
the University Club at which Mayor Rose addressed 600 people.[16]

In January 1903, a lot was purchased and Rev. Imburgia,
who suffered from a bronchial infection, returned to Palermo.
He was succeeded by Rev. Joseph Angeletti, a native of Perugia.[17] This appointment infuriated the immigrants who
wanted a Sicilian pastor who spoke their own dialect. "Yes, it
is jealousy between Sicilians and northerners," said Salvatore
Palise. "Almost all of the people who go to church are Sicilians
and we want a priest of our own race."[18] Chancellor Schinner
promptly sent Angeletti to tend to the Italians in Kenosha
and appointed the son of Sicilian immigrants, Rev. Dominic
Leone, as his successor. Hasso Pestalozzi, a native of northern
Italy, angrily protested this move and resigned as president of
the Italian Mission Association. He claimed that the Sicilian

women had fostered this "tribal war" after Angeletti had attempted to clean out the "petticoat government" that reigned at the Mission previous to his arrival.[19]

In spite of this turbulence and a recession that left 40 percent of Italian laborers unemployed in the winter of 1903-04, Father Leone rallied the Italians around the building fund, and the Mission Aid Society and Catholic women's groups throughout the city sponsored various benefits.[20] Finally, in September 1904, work began on the church. The completed church of the Madonna di Pompeii was dedicated on May 15, 1905 amid the celebration of its 500 parishioners and other benefactors.[21]

The Third Ward Italians laid the cement sidewalk in front of the church, helped dig the foundation, and, despite seasonal unemployment, gave thousands of dollars to the land acquisition and building fund. Three religious societies and some of the more prosperous Italian families donated costly furnishings to their new church. However, without the active support of the Milwaukee Catholic community, the construction of Pompeii Church would have been a much more arduous and lengthy task. The wealthy and influential Irish and German Americans in the Mission Aid Society raised the bulk of the $28,000 for the plot of land, church and rectory.[22]

The Archbishop's office and the *Catholic Citizen's* H. J. Desmond had enthusiastically participated in these efforts as part of the national effort by the Catholic Church to keep the Italians within the faith. With the creation of the Italian nationality parish, Milwaukee's Catholic leaders could feel a sense of accomplishment in regard to the "Italian problem." Yet at the same time they were aware that other challenges were still to be met.

In 1892, St. Paul's Episcopal Church established a Mission House in the Third Ward and, while the Episcopalians did not attempt to proselytize among the Italians, they did offer social, recreational and educational programs that eventually attracted 100 Italians. However, few of these individuals became converts to the Episcopalian faith. The Mission House moved from the Italian colony in 1912, but by then other Protestant denominations had taken up active proselytizing among the southern Italians.[23]

Agostino Falzoni was hired in 1907 by the Evangelical Church to establish a storefront mission in the Third Ward. The following year, Katherine Eyerick, fresh from missionary training in Illinois, arrived to take over the Evangelical Mission.[24] She was bewildered by the strange customs of the Italians, especially their "incredible trust in the cult of the Virgin Mary." She saw her work in the Third Ward as "especially problematical because at least ninety percent are Sicilians—non-church-going, superstitious, largely illiterate, clinging tenaciously to foreign customs and foolish tradition— while their close segregation is a mighty bulwark to all advances from the American side." Eyerick persisted in her endeavor and managed to enroll 100 men in the mission night school.[25] In 1910 she traveled to Italy and there met Rev. Augusto Giuliani, an ex-priest who had converted to the Evangelical movement. He returned to Milwaukee with her and later became her husband. Giuliani's presence was a shot in the arm for the mission. In 1911 a new brick chapel was dedicated on Van Buren Street and an expanded program featured various classes, street meetings, and a daily Vacation Bible School for children. As Italians moved northward into the First Ward, a mission was established and a church was erected there in 1929. The strength of the Evangelical movement rested upon the respect the Italians were shown by the Protestant proselytizers and the efforts of Rev. Giuliani, who worked tirelessly to obtain food and clothing, act as interpreter, represent people in court, and offer assistance to those seeking naturalization papers. His leadership was the crucial factor in the conversion of many Sicilians to his church, which grew to 300 members by 1929, and represented the most successful Protestant activity among the Milwaukee Italians.[26] Giuliani and his proteges also established churches in Racine and Kenosha, and in 1922 organized the Italian Mission Council to coordinate activities in the three cities.[27]

Other Protestant churches also functioned among the Italians in Milwaukee. In 1915, Michael Cali, an Italian immigrant, organized a Seventh Day Adventist congregation that first met in private homes and later in a tent. Six years later, under the leadership of Rev. A. Catalano, the Italian Adventists constructed a small church in the First Ward that had 60 members.[28] In 1925, Joe Pirri and Joe DiOrio arrived in Milwaukee from Chicago, where both had been active in the Italian Christian Congregation. They too settled in the First Ward and began converting their Italian neighbors to the Pentecostal religion. Their services were held in homes and a storefront until, in 1927, a small brick church was constructed on Pearson Street. Pirri and DiOrio became the first pastors of the church which had about 75 members.[29]

An Italian Baptist church functioned for several years on the south side under the guidance of Rev. Dominic Raffone, who had organized similar congregations in nearby Racine and Kenosha.[30] Thus, by 1926, there were five Italian Protestant ministers and five Italian Protestant churches in Milwaukee, with a sixth in nearby West Allis. Some 500 Italian adults had become Protestants by 1929, and an estimated 500 Italian children were being instructed by Protestant teachers twice a week during this period. While the Protestants numbered only 8 percent of the approximately 12,400 Italians in Milwaukee, it must be remembered that many Italians ignored church or were very rarely involved in any religious expression other than the *feste*. Thus, the 1,000 Protestant converts represented a significant number, and this was taken very seriously by the Catholic Church.[31]

Catholic leaders were fearful of the Protestant proselytizing and their distress was further aggravated by the religious practices of the parishioners at Milwaukee's only Italian Catholic church. The southern Italians in the Third Ward had initiated yearly religious festivals, complete with street processions and amusements, that were well publicized in Milwaukee's secular newspapers. Even worse than these "pagan rituals" was the indifference of the southern Italians toward Catholic schooling for their children. Since 1899 H. J. Desmond had called for the establishment of an Italian parochial school, but few Italians were interested in supporting such a venture. In 1910, Our Lady of Pompeii was one of only six parishes, out of a total of 46 Catholic churches in Milwaukee, that did not maintain a parochial school. And Italians did not send their children to existing Catholic schools. The U.S. Immigration Commission found that 532 Italian youngsters in Milwaukee were enrolled in public schools and only 18 in parochial schools in 1910.[32]

To address the needs of "neglected" Catholic youth, a Milwaukee chapter of the Catholic Instruction League (CIL) was initiated in 1916 by the Jesuits. Its goal was to give "religious instruction to those of the Catholic Faith who could not (for any reason) or who did not receive instruction through the parish organizations...."[33] Italians were a focal point of concern, as was evident by the establishment of the first CIL Center at Pompeii Church and the third in Bay View among the 150 Piedmontese and Marchegiani families.[34]

The CIL enlisted a small army of lay people and Jesuits to teach "the more neglected children—Italians, Slavanians [sic] and others." [35]By 1922, the League had 20 centers, 300 teachers and 8,000 children enrolled. At the Pompeii Center alone, more than 600 children received weekly instruction from 60 teachers. As Italians moved out of the lower east side, Catholic missions, like those of the Protestant denominations, followed them. Pompeii Church set up St. Rita's Mission in the First Ward and the CIL established a center at this site. In 1927, there were 615 Italian children receiving religious instruction at Pompeii and 165 at St. Rita's. The CIL center at St. Matthew's parish included the children of Italian immigrants who had settled on the south side, and a number of Italian youth frequented the center at Bay View's Immaculate Conception Church.[36] The movement of about 25 Italian families to the vicinity of 90th and Adler in the northwest corner of West Allis was noted by Protestants and Catholics alike. Rev. Giuliani set up Calvary Church for the dozen Evangelical Italian families in 1918.[37] Rev. Peter Schroeder, who had served briefly as pastor of Pompeii Church, established The Little Flower Mission and School only three blocks away in 1926. "All Catholics of the Italian race and all other Catholics in the territory... are to belong to this parish," said the *Catholic Citizen.* Rev. Schroeder reported that "Proselytizing has been going on—was flourishing during Holy Week—and no time must be allowed to be wasted in combatting these influences and safeguarding the faith of the people, the children in particular...."[38] Rev. Joseph De Maria was brought in to keep the dozen Italian Catholic families within the faith— which he accomplished—and to reconvert the Italian Protestants—which he was not able to do. Both the Protestant Mission, later renamed Faith Church, and Little Flower Mission, now known as St. Therese's Church, quickly absorbed non-Italians and soon became multi-ethnic churches with English-language services, as Italians became a minority in each.[39]

In 1933 the CIL discontinued its activities and its work among the Italians was taken over by the Sisters of Charity of St. Joan Antida, who had just arrived from Italy. Earlier the Catholic Social Welfare Board sponsored a youth center in the Third Ward. The center, the National Catholic Community House, came into existence in 1919 and provided Italian youths with social and recreational activities. Approximately 70 boys frequented the center and some of them, who later emerged as civic-minded professionals in the 1930s, formed the Pompeii Athletic Club. When the community center closed in 1921, the club was taken under the wing of Father Fadanelli, who allowed the youths to use the basement of Pompeii Church for club activities.[40]

The activities of the Catholic Instruction League and, to a lesser extent, those of the National Catholic Community House were crucial in combating the Protestant proselytizers and imbuing Italian youth with American Catholic values. Other factors also served to neutralize Protestant inroads into Milwaukee's Italian communities. Baptist minister Dominic Raffone of Kenosha, who had commenced work in Milwaukee in 1922, died in 1926. Augusto Giuliani, the leader of the Italian Evangelical churches in Milwaukee, passed away in 1929, just as his new church was completed. His followers named the new edifice the Giuliani Memorial Church, but without the charismatic Giuliani, the Evangelical movement lost momentum. The tragic death of his successor, Rev. Re, in the early 1940s further hastened the demise of the Italian Evangelical church, and its remaining members, which included many non-Italians, merged into a nearby Methodist church in 1968.[41] The Italian Seventh Day Adventist congregation failed to attract new members and was disbanded in 1956. The Italian Christian Congregation continues to function and maintains a small east side edifice, but membership today has dwindled to 28 people.[42]

Interviews with the Italian Protestants reveal that the children of the immigrants often left the churches adopted by their parents. Protestant families were at times ostracized by Italian Catholics, and made to feel uncomfortable by non-Italian Protestants. Many of the young adults married within their Italian ethnic group prior to World War II, often to Catholics, and this usually resulted in their reconversion to the Catholic faith. Some Italian Protestants married Polish Catholics who were equally adamant about maintaining Catholicism as the family religion. As the immigrant families moved away from the east side, where all but one of the Italian Protestant missions were located, it became more difficult to regularly attend services. The children of the Italian Protestants frequently expressed displeasure with the Italian-language services, and some who did marry a Protestant spouse preferred to attend English-language churches, even if it meant joining a different denomination. Lastly, like Italian Catholics, the Italian Protestants often abandoned a particular church when the pastor's behavior offended them. There was a constant interchange of members between the Protestant missions serving Milwaukee's Italians, as individuals sought the most acceptable church and pastor. The Protestant proselytizing among Milwaukee's Italians reached its apex by 1929, but by World War II it was not a significant movement.[43] Several writers have noted that the "Protestant crusade to evangelize the Italians had failed," and this too was the case in Milwaukee. However, for twenty years proselytizers such as Augusto Giuliani had made impressive gains in the city. If nothing else, the competition of the Protestants for the souls of the Italians served to make Catholic leaders a little more tolerant of nationality parishes and immigrant customs such as the *festa*.[44]

While the threat of Protestant proselytizing subsided in the 1930s, the unique Catholicism of southern Italian immigrants continued to challenge church leaders. The most conspicuous difference between Italian Catholics and American Catholics was the manner in which Italians paid homage to their patron saints. Milwaukee's Italians had honored their patron saints with modest ceremonies beginning in the 1890s.[45] However, 1906, the year following the completion of Pompeii Church, marked the first religious festival that included a street procession, as "members of the Holy Cross society resplendent in badges and colors" led a parade of several hundred marchers. Thousands participated in the two-day festival along a gaily decorated Jackson Street that was "illuminated in the evening with row upon row of bright Japanese lanterns."[46] The 1907 Holy Cross festival featured arches of electric lights over Jackson Street, but the worried Bishop forbade dancing in the streets. About these *feste* the *Catholic Citizen* could only remark that the Italians celebrated "with a blithesomeness that comes odd to Catholics in this country."[47] While editor H. J. Desmond's articles focused on the need for a parochial school, the Italians were content to use their church to recreate the *feste* of their native villages. Following the lead of the Holy Cross Society, which was composed of natives from Santo Stefano di Camastra in Sicily, other Sicilians from Bagheria and Aspra initiated a summer street festival in 1910 to honor St. Joseph. Immigrants from Porticello, Sicily began to celebrate the Madonna del Lume *festa* in the same year. In the 1920s natives from the region of Puglia initiated the San Rocco festival and immigrants from Sant'Elia, Sicily, honored Addolorata.[48]

Each of the religious societies labored energetically to set up food booths, amusements, entertainment and fireworks at its *festa*, which usually began on Friday night and closed Sunday evening. On Sunday morning the members of the sponsoring society led the parishioners into Pompeii Church where High Mass was celebrated. Following the mass the men, usually in uniform, would carry the heavy statues through the streets of the "ward" and periodically stop as people pinned money on the image of the saint or madonna. Women of the auxiliary society would don colorful shawls and some would march in stocking feet behind the statue—as a gesture of thanks for prayers answered by their patron saint. The *feste* were the high point of the religious and social life in Little Italy, and for many immigrant men represented the rare occasions when they set foot in Pompeii Church.

Through the years the Third Ward became a mecca for Italians throughout the city as festivals were held from June through September. The celebrations grew longer and became more extravagant as the five societies tried to outdo each other in the grandeur of the festivals. Speeches by politicians heightened the status of a festival, as well as symbolizing the awakening political power of the Italians—Mayor Rose addressed the 1908 Holy Cross *festa*, Governor Blaine the 1924 Madonna del Lume festival, and Philip LaFollette the San Rocco celebration in 1930. As the years progressed, more and more "Americans" attended the yearly celebrations as the uniquely Italian events gained acceptance as social, if not religious, events. However, Catholic leaders were very concerned about these displays of Latin devotion. [49]

In addition to the *feste*, other Italian religious practices and attitudes were very different from those of American Catholicism. The problematic relations between priest and parishioner and the friction caused by the regionalism of both clerics and lay people continued well into the 1940s. In Italy the peasants often "felt little affection or reverence" for the priest and "the church as an institution."[50] Unlike the Polish or Irish Catholic, the southern Italian did not automatically respect the position of the pastor, but rather judged each cleric on his personal attributes. This traditional tension was aggravated by the fact that the American Catholic Church relied on its parishioners for its economic base. In one instance the priest at Pompeii Church demanded that every adult pay one dollar in dues each month. Many people refused to comply and others, about to marry, threatened to have a civil service if the priest attempted to collect back dues.[51]

In 1925, the new pastor at Pompeii, Rev. Bainotti, desired more money for living expenses than his predecessor had received. He also wanted to change the administrative structure of the church and to take out a second mortgage. He met with the men of the parish, who convinced him to retract his demands about the mortgage and administrative structure. However, the women were infuriated—they felt the men should have told Father Bainotti to leave his position as pastor. More than 70 women blocked the priest's entry to the church the next morning and two policemen were present the following day to ensure Father Bainotti's access to the building.[52] In 1927 Bainotti was involved in a confrontation that revolved around the annual religious festivals which utilized the church property and called for the priest to lead a street procession. The society sponsoring a festival usually gave the priest a sum of money as reimbursement for these services. Father Bainotti demanded that all profits from the festivals go to the church, refused to lead any processions, and would not allow the St. Joseph Society access to the church or the statue of its patron saint. In response the society had a facsimile of the statue made, erected a tent across from Pompeii Church, and persuaded a Syrian Catholic priest to bless the statue and lead the procession. A month later the Holy Cross Society repeated the same process. Southern Italians expected their priest to be a leader at the altar, but outside this arena his leadership was on precarious ground. The *feste* and their profits were the domain of the religious societies and their lay leaders.[53]

The strong regionalism among Italians also aggravated clergy-parishioner relations. Following Rev. Leone's departure in 1914 virtually all the priests serving Milwaukee Italians were of northern Italian ancestry. An unpopular decision by a priest, coupled with his northern background, was enough to discourage southern Italians from attending church, or cause for them to frequent a nearby non-Italian parish.[54] However, a common regional background did not necessarily prove to be an advantage in church attendance. Some of the northern Italian priests at Pompeii Church, such as Rev. Fadanelli, who was pastor from 1915 to 1924, had contacts and friends among the northern Italians in Bay View, but this seldom resulted in Bay-Viewites regularly attending the Third Ward church. The Third Ward was seen as southern Italian territory and immigrants from the two areas generally did not mix with each other. Rev. Fadanelli did set up a small Mission for the Bay View Italians in 1916 that functioned until about 1923.[55]

Events in the Italian settlement in West Allis further demonstrate the regionalism of Italians and conflicts between immigrants and Church leaders. Sicilian families from the Third Ward had been moving to the eastern part of the city since World War I and by 1930 more than 100 families had congregated in the area. A northern Italian priest traveled from Milwaukee's Third Ward to offer Mass and religious instruction in the basement of Holy Assumption parish, but the

Italians did not support this effort. Their leaders said they wanted their own church and started to raise funds, but the Archbishop said that the Italian community was not able to support a church because of its small size and high unemployment. So, in 1935, when Rev. Peter Enrietto was made pastor of St. Rita's parish in West Allis, he was instructed by the Archbishop to give "special attention to the Italo-Americans of West Allis."[56] Rev. Enrietto, a northern Italian, and Joseph LaBarbera, a leader in the Sicilian community, did not get along, with the result that most of the southern Italians did not attend St. Rita's. Instead, they continued to raise funds for an Italian church through their organization, the Our Lady of Mount Carmel Society. In 1938, the Italian men began constructing a small brick and stone church without the permission of the Archbishop. After a series of sometimes tense meetings and exchanges of letters, the Italians and Church authorities settled their differences, and Our Lady of Mount Carmel was dedicated as a chapel in 1939 and later became a church. To avoid further regional antagonism between Italian clergy and laymen, Rev. Leng, a non-Italian who spoke Italian, was made pastor. When Rev. Leng left in 1946, and was succeeded by two northern Italian priests, friction again developed between the clergy and lay leaders. The Archbishop then appointed Rev. Salvatore Tagliavia as pastor in 1948. Born in the Third Ward and the son of Sicilian immigrants, Rev. Tagliavia was related to many families in the congregation and was well received. In 1956, he was succeeded by Rev. Alfred Valentino, also the son of southern Italian immigrants. Like the Protestant and Catholic Italian churches in the northeast side of West Allis, Our Lady of Mount Carmel Church soon became a multi-ethnic parish.[57]

By the post war era regionalism among Italians had diminished considerably as the second generation matured and the third generation began to appear. Prior to their assignments at Mount Carmel Church, Rev. Tagliavia and Rev. Valentino, both sons of southern Italian immigrants, were accepted by the Piedmontese and Marchegiani in Bay View. Indeed, their presence as successive assistant pastors at Immaculate Conception Church, formerly an Irish bastion, helped to draw the attendance of northern Italians and the enrollment of their children in the parish school.[58]

The entry of second-generation Italians into religious orders symbolized the changing attitudes toward the Church and its clergy that became noticeable after 1930. The ordination of two men born in the Third Ward, Rev. Francis Balistreri in 1941 and Rev. Salvatore Tagliavia in 1945, served to bridge the gap between Italian cleric and layman. By 1954 three more men and 16 young women from Pompeii parish, and John Richetta from Immaculate Conception Church, had entered religious orders. In earlier years many young people were discouraged by their families from entering religious vocations.[59]

* * *

Prior to 1930 attendance at Pompeii Church was often poor and some of the parishioners who did attend seemed more interested in socializing than in the religious service. There were only a handful of Italian altar boys and the Holy Name Society disbanded in the 1920s. The *festa* seemed to represent the only religious activity that drew Italians in large numbers.[60] However, things began to change in the 1930s: attendance at Mass went up and the number of Pompeii parishioners increased by 10 percent. Perhaps the onset of the Great Depression caused people to turn more toward the Church for solace. Another factor in the increase in church membership was the opening of St. Rita's Mission in the First Ward, which was easily accessible for the many Italians who had moved northward during the 1920s. The arrival of the Scalabrinian Order marked an ongoing and larger assignment of Italian priests. Rev. Bainotti, who in 1925 became the first Scalabrinian pastor at Pompeii, had an assistant priest within four years who could help with the increased work demanded by the expanding church and its mission. The early 1930s saw the addition of new resources and projects that served to further draw the parishioners into the sphere of church activities. In 1930 at the Archbishop's request, and despite the misgivings of Rev. Bainotti, a conference of St. Vincent De Paul was organized by three Sicilians and two northern Italians.[61] In 1932 the Sisters of St. Joan Antida arrived from Italy and commenced a broad range of youth work at Pompeii Church and St. Rita's Mission. And, lastly, the southern Italian community, now interested in erecting its own parochial school, instituted a building fund by 1931.[62]

The arrival in 1935 of a new Scalabrinian pastor, Rev. Ugo Cavicchi, provided the parish with an energetic leader who led his congregation into a new era. To foster greater unity in the parish he met with presidents of the Italian associations and suggested that a memorial service be held for the Italian casualties in Ethiopia. The community leaders agreed and Cavicchi allowed several groups to wear their uniforms in Pompeii Church—something his predecessors would not have allowed.[63]

In response to crowded conditions at St. Rita's Mission, Cavicchi organized a committee of 36 immigrant and American-born men to assist in planning for a new building, a combination church and school. The committee went door-to-door collecting dimes and nickels from parishioners, many of whom were impoverished by the Depression. Enough money was raised to begin construction in September 1936, and another large amount was borrowed. Several Italian contractors provided free services. News of the parish and the construction program was spread throughout the congregation by means of *La Vita Parrocchiale*, a monthly newspaper founded by Father Cavicchi.[64]

In October the building committee led a large procession from Pompeii Church to the construction site, and the following April the completed basement was blessed by Archbishop Stritch, who addressed the 1,500 people present in Italian. Masses were henceforth conducted in the basement and a kindergarten and first-grade class were begun the following September. An article in *La Vita Parrocchiale* proclaimed:

The opening of a parish school marks the beginning of a new life for the parish. Children begin to know and love God above and before all things.... They start fulfilling their duties as good Catholics and as good citizens. It may surprise you to note that a good parochial school not only places the holy seed of our faith in the children but in many instances it awakens the dormant faith of the parents.[65]

The building program initiated by Rev. Cavicchi marked the development of Italian ethnic consciousness and the growing importance of religious activities among Milwaukee's Italians. In November 1937, when Rev. Cavicchi was transferred to a parish in New York City, the total membership of Pompeii Church and St. Rita's Mission had grown to 1,200 families.[66]" Not since the construction of Pompeii Church, more than 30 years earlier, had there been such a unified and active Italian parish.

The dedication of St. Rita's Church by Archbishop Stritch in July 1939 was highlighted by a parade of the Italian societies. The initial words of the souvenir program probably expressed what many of the parishioners were feeling: "The Dedication of St. Rita Church and Parochial School marks the successful culmination of one of the most important tasks ever undertaken by Milwaukee's Italo-Americans."[67] The construction of St. Rita's Church, unlike that of Pompeii, did not require outside help and the entire expense was borne by the Italians themselves.

As the student enrollment grew, St. Rita's parish constructed a school building adjacent to the church in 1944. The Sisters of St. Joan Antida staffed the school and also had a kindergarten and nursery at Our Lady of Mount Carmel Church in West Allis. The Sisters, with the support of the Italian community, opened St. Joan Antida High School, just three blocks from St. Rita's Church, in 1954.[68]

The events of the 1930s initiated a new stage in the development of Italian American religious values. The creation of a parochial school and a number of other parish organizations—such as the Christian Mothers Society, a credit union and the Catholic Youth Organization—reflected the increased importance of the church in the life of Milwaukee's Italians. The ethnic solidarity of the 1930s and the maturation of second-generation leaders found a focal point in the construction of St. Rita's Church and school. This unity and sense of *Italianità* witnessed the lessening of regionalism and the easing of priest-parishioner tensions. The many years of religious instruction, usually provided by non-Italians, had made an impression upon the American-born generation. The second-generation had begun to embrace American Catholicism and its emphasis on doctrine, rather than patron saints and *feste,* and its respect for the role of the priest, rather than anti-clericalism. While in Italy church attendance may have been seen as the province of the poor, in the United States it was viewed as a symbol of respectability that reinforced the newly achieved working-class and middle-class standing of many of Milwaukee's Italians. While still conscious of their minority status, the leaders of the Italian community were creating institutions and practices that more closely approximated the Irish American model of Catholicism. The *festa* continued to be important, but it was no longer the only important religious event. *Feste* were not held at St. Rita's, and its First Ward locale lacked the geographic stigma that many people, Italians and non-Italians alike, associated with the original Little Italy in the Third Ward.

* * *

At the turn of the century, east-side Italians broke away from the nearby Irish church and established Our Lady of Pompeii parish. Three decades later the construction of St. Rita's Church and school marked both the continued separation of the Italians from the Irish and their acceptance of some of the basic values of Irish American Catholicism. The adaptation of this parallel set of values in the 1930s led to the third stage in the religious acculturation of Italian Americans: the amalgamation of various ethnic groups into the larger American Catholic religious group. At the end of World War II Italians, no longer a minority group, shared in the improved U.S. economic climate and moved to neighborhoods throughout metropolitan Milwaukee, where they were usually content to attend the Catholic church in the vicinity. Some of the new suburbanites continued to regularly attend Pompeii or St. Rita's, but most were likely to limit their visits to the *feste* and other special events at Pompeii Church.

In the 1950s most of the old Third Ward was razed to make way for a freeway and Pompeii Church was finally torn down in 1967. The *feste* that had been resumed after World War II were discontinued, although they were revived on a smaller scale at St. Rita's in the 1970s. The yearly *Festa Italiana* celebration on the Milwaukee lakefront, begun in 1978 by the Italian Community Center, now represents a huge four-day version of the old *feste*. Attended by up to 200,000 people, the event features a mass and procession complete with statues of patron saints.

St. Rita's, the last Italian church in Milwaukee, now has parishioners of diverse backgrounds and many of the Italian members are elderly. Italian Americans still return to the east side parish for the celebration of St. Joseph's table in March and the small summer festival and street procession. However, the parish school now enrolls mostly Spanish and non-white students—in 1985 only 19 of the 145 attendees were Italian American.[69] St. Joan Antida High School also has developed a multi-ethnic student body. During the past two years, the Scalabrinian Order which had administered Pompeii and St. Rita's since 1925, gave custody of the parish to the Archdiocese. While many of Milwaukee's 21,000 Italian Americans partake in the *Festa Italiana* and special events at St. Rita's, it appears that ongoing religious expression typically occurs at a non-ethnic church.[70]

Today there are relatively few Italian Protestants in Milwaukee and only a handful of people are aware of the struggles between Catholic and Protestant proselytizers 60 years ago. The churches of Our Lady of Pompeii and St. Rita's served as nationality parishes that maintained Italian traditions while eventually, with the involvement of the Catholic Instruction League, Americanizing the younger generation. Contemporary Italian Catholics attend neighborhood parishes scattered throughout the city and suburbs and are probably comfortable with fellowship of other ethnic groups in their parishes. At least in outward behavior it appears that today's Italian Americans are well acculturated into Milwaukee's Catholic community, consistent with Tomasi's model.[71] The anti-clericalism, lack of religious instruction, regionalism and intense preoccupation with patron saints which characterized the immigrants are not traits shared by their children and grandchildren. Yet the Italian *festa* and the St. Joseph's table continue to be enacted as symbols of the unique religious and cultural traditions of southern Italy and the immigrants who journeyed to Milwaukee 90 years ago.

---

[1] *Catholic Citizen* (Milwaukee) 6 Nov. 1897: 4.

[2] *Ibid.*, 20 Nov. 1897: 4.

3 *Ibid.*, 13 Nov. 1897: 4. In 1900 Desmond published a pamphlet entitled, "The Neglected Italians," and distributed it among church officials in the U.S. and Italy.

4 *Ibid.*, 27 May 1899: 3.

5 *Ibid.*, 28 Oct. 1899: 1.

6 *Catholic Citizen*, 30 March 1895: 5.

7 *Ibid.*, 15 Oct. 1898: 4.

8 *Ibid.*, 19 Nov. 1898: 5; 27 May 1899: 3.

9 *Ibid.*, 3 June 1899: 5. Nasca had travelled to Milwaukee from Newark at the suggestion of an Italian priest in Chicago, perhaps in response to the plea for Italian priests voiced in Desmond's article.

10 Rudolph Vecoli, "Cult and Occult in Italian American Culture," *Immigrants and Religion in Urban America*, eds. Randall Miller and Thomas Marzik (Philadelphia: Temple University Press, 1977). 34. Milwaukee's huge German population has included a large number of Catholics. Several archbishops and other leaders in the Catholic hierarchy have been German Americans. Information on the attitudes of the German prelates toward Milwaukee's Italians is not readily accessible, but their presence may have mediated potential animosities between the archdiocese and Italian immigrants. Had the Church leadership been more dominated by the Irish then, perhaps, a sterner attitude, similar to that practiced in some East Coast cities, may have resulted. Also, the comparatively small size of the Irish and Italian populations and the lack of intense Irish-Italian neighborhood conflict differentiate the Milwaukee situation from that of cities such as Boston. It is probable that Milwaukee's Irish Catholic leaders were less threatened by the "Italian problem" than were their counterparts on the East Coast.

11 Joseph Lopreato, *Italian Americans* (New York: Random House, 1970) 88, 90.

12 Vecoli, *op cit*: 26.

13 Silvano Tomasi, "The Ethnic Church and the Integration of Italian Immigrants in the United States," *The Italian Experience in the United States*, eds. Silvano Tomasi and Madeline Engel (New York: Center for Migration Studies, 1970) 173.

14 *Ibid.*, 6 Oct. 1900: 5.

15 *Milwaukee Journal*, 2 Feb. 1900: 53.

16 Neacy and two other individuals each gave $1,000 to the building fund and when manufacturer Robert A. Johnston offered $6,000, the Italians simply couldn't believe it. The chancellor of the Milwaukee Diocese, Rev. Augustin Schinner, held a meeting with a delegation of 40 Italians and "had some difficulty in convincing them that there were no strings attached to the gift or that nothing was expected in return." *Catholic Citizen,*, 6 Oct. 1900: 5; 20 Oct. 1900: 5; 9 Nov. 1901: 3.

17 *Catholic Citizen*, 17 Jan. 1903: 3.

18 *Ibid.*, 17 Oct. 1903: 3.

19 *Milwaukee Sentinel*, 16 Oct. 1903: 3.

20 *Ibid.*, 17 May 1904: 4.

21 *Ibid.*, 15 May 1905: 8.

22 *Evening Wisconsin*, 13 May 1905: 5.

23 *Milwaukee Sentinel*, 27 May 1906, Sec. 4: 7; *Catholic Citizen,*, 7 Sept. 1912: 3.

24 Scrapbook of Katherine Hauerwas, Milwaukee County Historical Society; William Blake, *Cross and Flame in Wisconsin* (Stevens Point: Worzalla Publishing Company, 1973) 154-155.

25 Scrapbook of Katherine Hauerwas.

26 *Ibid.* As a Mason, Giuliani had access to wealthy non-Italian business people who could meet his requests for food and clothing.

27 Dante Germanotta, "From 'Italian Missions' to 'Community Churches'," unpublished paper, Immigration History Research Center: 22.

28 Jacqueline Johannson, personal interview, 30 April 1981; Lucy Ruscitti, personal interview, 2 May 1981; Adriel Chilson, *Trial and Triumph* (Elko, Nevada: Heritage Publications, 1976) 119, 185.

29 Josephine Agrusa, personal interview, 16 July 1977.

30 "Our Work Among the Italians," 1922, unpublished manuscript, 8 pp., provided by Frances LaMantia; John Neuenschwander— *Kenosha County in the 20th Century* (Kenosha County Bicentennial Commission: 1976) 19, 365,

31 "St. Rita's Church 25th Anniversary Jubilee Booklet," 1961; *The*

Fifteenth Census of the United States, 1930, Wisconsin Supplement, gives the figure of 12,444 for first and second generation Italians in Milwaukee that year.

[32] U.S. Immigration Commission, *Reports of the U.S. Immigration Commission,* Vol. 32, Children of Immigrants in Schools, (Washington, D.C., 1911) 83; *Catholic Citizen,* 11 May 1918: 3. Seventeen of the youngsters attending parochial school were northern Italians.

[33] *Catholic Citizen,* 18 Aug. 1923: 14. The CIL was founded in 1912 and became very active in many dioceses and overseas, especially in Chicago, Milwaukee, Detroit, Toledo, Cleveland, St. Louis and Manila, Phillipine Islands, *CIL Messenger* Aug. 1936: 24.

[34] The Bay View Italian colony, which had its beginnings in 1903, was not well-received at nearby Immaculate Conception church, a heavily Irish parish. Father Fagan, its pastor, advised the Italians to build their own church or to journey to Our Lady of Pompeii. Like the southern Italians, most of the northerners possessed no great amount of religious zeal and many had been content to simply avoid church altogether. Fred Boggio, personal interview, 6 July 1973; Mr. and Mrs. Frank Gardetto, personal interview, 2 May 1974; Pete Marino, personal interview, 27 June 1974.

[35] *Catholic Citizen,* 20 Oct. 1917: 3.

[36] *Catholic Citizen,* 7 July 1917: 3; 1 Dec. 1917: 3; 11 Nov. 1922: 3; 7 May 1927: 1.

[37] Scrapbook of Katherine Hauerwas.

[38] *Catholic Herald* (Milwaukee); 11 March 1926: 1; 8 April 1926: 2.

[39] Libby Gagliano-Kotechi, personal interview, 25 April 1981; Julian Turano, personal interview, 11 April 1981; Pat and Bernie Becker, personal interview, 28 March 1981; Tess and Charles Mazzone, personal interview, 31 March 1981; Frances Rossi, personal interview, 14 April 1981.

[40] Ted Mazza, personal interview, 23 June 1973; Rev. John O'Grady—*Directory, Catholic Charities, U.S.* (1922): 354, 360-61. There were sewing classes and other activities for girls, but protective Italian parents would only allow their daughters to attend daytime activities and refused to let them participate in social events.

[41] *The Wisconsin Baptist,* January 1927: 17-19; Scrapbook of

Katherine Hauerwas. Raffone, who like Giuliani was a Mason, was well aware of the Evangelical missions in Kenosha, Racine and Milwaukee and did not do aggressive proselytizing in Milwaukee, which he perhaps viewed as Giuliani's turf. See "Our Work Among the Italians."

[42] Other Milwaukee Italians were active in Protestant denominations. From 1936 to 1969 Rev. John Congelliere was the pastor of the Community Gospel Church and Ignazio Castagna, a leader among Cream City Italians, became a lay minister in the Christ Bible Church. Sam Aria, telephone interview, 28 May 1987; Virginia Knapp, telephone interview, 9 April 1981; *Milwaukee Journal*, 9 March 1936; *Milwaukee City Directory*, 1936-1969.

[43] Various interviews.

[44] Vecoli, *op cit*: 34.

[45] In 1898 the *Catholic Citizen* reported: "The fervid devotion of the Italians to Our Lady, which some find difficult to comprehend, is nowhere better shown that (sic) in the quaint and curious ceremonies with which the Madonna is honored on Aug. 15...It was an odd and picturesque sight." *Catholic Citizen*, 20 Aug. 1898: 4.

[46] *Milwaukee Sentinel*, 17 Sept. 1906: 5.

[47] *Catholic Citizen*, 19 Sept. 1908: 3.

[48] *Ibid.*, 4 June 1910: 3.

[49] *Ibid.*, 19 Sept. 1908: 3; 30 Aug. 1924: 3; 24 Aug. 1930: 3.

[50] Vecoli, *op. cit.*; p. 27.

[51] Ted Mazza, personal interview, 23 June 1973.

[52] *Milwaukee Journal*, 2 Dec. 1955: 1-2.

[53] *Milwaukee Leader*, 16 Aug. 1927: 4; *Milwaukee Sentinel*, 11 Sept. 1927: 7.

[54] Similar episodes characterized Italian-Protestant clergy. Rev. Giuliani, a native of Rome, occasionally "lost" some of his Sicilian converts because of unpopular actions—for instance, his remarriage to one of the non-Italian missionaries of his church after his first wife died in 1916. Some of the church members resigned in protest because they felt Giuliani should have selected his mate from the eligible Italian women in the congregation. Joe Famularo, personal interview, 28 Dec. 1973.

[55] Dominic Gardetto, personal interview, 5 Nov. 1976. In 1917 Rev. Giuliani held several street meetings in Bay View that stressed support of the American war effort. He was confronted by a group of northern Italian anarchists, two of whom were killed in the ensuing confrontation with police. Two months later, in an apparent act of revenge, a bomb was planted at Giuliani's church in the Third Ward. The bomb was discovered and carried to Milwaukee Police headquarters, where it exploded and killed ten people. See John Andreozzi, *"Contadini* and *Pescatori* in Milwaukee: Assimilation and Voluntary Associations,"* unpublished master's thesis (University of Wisconsin-Milwaukee, 1974) 46-47.

[56] Memo to the officers and members of the Mount Carmel Society from Archbishop Stritch, 29 June 1929; in "Our Lady of Mt. Carmel File," Archdiocese of Milwaukee Administrative Office.

[57] Rev. Alfred Valentino, personal interview, 8 April 1976.

[58] Rev. Alfred Valentino, personal interview, 8 April 1976.

[59] "Blessed Virgin of Pompeii" (1968); James Groppi, also from the Immaculate Conception neighborhood in Bay View, entered the seminary a few years later.

[60] Ted Mazza, personal interview, 23 June 1973; Frank Gardetto, personal interview, 2 May 1974.

[61] The ten percent increase was computed by comparing the list of church members in 1931 with that of 1934; "Resoconto Finanaiario Dell Chiesa Madonna Di Pompeii: 1931 and 1934." Frank Gardetto, a Piedmontese from Bay View, was brought in by the Archbishop because he was the only Italian in Milwaukee who had previous experience as a member of St. Vincent De Paul. The purpose of a St. Vincent De Paul conference is to provide food, clothing, furniture and referral services to needy members of a parish.

[62] "Resoconto Finanziario Della Chiesa Madonna Di Pompeii Per L'Anno 1931.": 6.

[63] Ted Mazza, personal interview, 23 June 1973.

[64] "St. Rita's Church 25th Anniversary Jubilee Booklet," (1961).

[65] *La Vita Parrocchiale,* July 1937, as quoted in "St. Rita's Church 25th Anniversary Jubilee Booklet," (1961).

[66] *Ibid.*

[67] "Solemn Dedication of St. Rita's Church and School," (June 11, 1939).

[68] "25th Anniversary, Sisters of Charity of St. Joan Antida," (1957) 22, 35.

[69] Rev. Corradin, personal interview, 7 March 1985.

[70] Bureau of the Census, *Census of Population and Housing: Milwaukee, Wisconsin, 1980* (Washington, D.C., U.S. Department of Commerce, 1983) 84-94, reported 29,996 persons of Italian ancestry in the Milwaukee metropolitan statistical area, 21,454 of whom resided in the City of Milwaukee.

[71] This paper does not consider other behaviors such as participation in confesion, reception of Holy Communion, etc. See Vecoli, *op cit*, for an overview of studies that have examined these areas.

A View of Two Major Centers of Italian Anarchism in the United States: Spring Valley and Chicago, Illinois

Gianna S. Panofsky

A history of the Italian anarchist movement in the United States has yet to be written. (Bettini,a.) However, the profusion of the Italian anarchist press provides ample information and firsthand sources for the study of the theoretical framework as well as the issues, personalities and activities which inspired the Italian-speaking anarchists.[1]

The geographical dimension of the movement spans the whole continent, with major centers emerging in the East (Paterson, NJ and Barre, VT)[2], the Midwest (Chicago, Spring Valley and the Illinois mining centers), and the West Coast (San Francisco and Los Angeles).

The Italian anarchist movement in the United States originated with recurring waves of exiled leaders who fled Italy in the wake of severe repressions which began in 1890.[3] Great fugitive leaders like Malatesta, Galleani and Ciancabilla became active propagandists and were especially successful in communities where there were concentrations of workers who had migrated from regions where anarchism was strong. Thus the early anarchist character of the Italian labor movement was strengthened abroad at a time when it was greatly weakening in Italy. The activities of Italian radicalized immigrants are therefore of great historical interest because they intersect with the histories of Italian emigration and U.S. unionism, and also insofar as they affected the behavior of other immigrant workers.

Based upon an examination of the anarchist press and other sources,[4] this study focuses upon the activities of Italian-born anarchists in the two major centers of the Midwest: Spring Valley, Illinois, and Chicago.

The city of Spring Valley is located in North-central Illinois about a hundred miles west of Chicago in the Illinois River valley. It used to be the center of the Northern Illinois coal mining industry. Founded in 1884, Spring Valley fell into decline when the mines closed in the mid-nineteen-twenties. (Lloyd, a.) It was in this city that a few dozen anarchist activists within an Italian community of about one thousand succeeded in playing a dominant role from the early eighteennineties up until the repression of 1917. With the possible exception of Paterson, N.J. (Carey) and the Carrara region of Italy, no Italian anarchist grouping was ever able to claim as much.

To this day a brief enquiring trip to Spring Valley reveals a keen sense of local history and a sharp collective memory. It is true that memories of labor strife pervade all the Illinois mining communities, but in Spring Valley these memories are immediately connected with "the" anarchists. It is not so much the ideology of anarchism which is remembered as the larger-than-life individuals whose names are still remembered three or four generations later: Antonio Andrà, Joe Corna, Joseph Casazza, Antonio Canarina, Giacomo Rossetto, Giovanni Bottino, Luigi Ronchietto[5], Alfredo Bagaglino[6] and scores of others.

As a simple matter of correct procedure these men regularly reported to their official press organs. One can read of their plans, dreams, and proselitizing in the nearby communities, as well as more humble tasks such as subscription drives and fund raising. They also wrote about issues that united or divided them, their relationship to other groups and to Italy, and of their efforts to rid their communities of the "prejudices" of religiosity, patriotism, militarism, bossism, ignorance, alcoholism, and extremely dangerous working conditions.

Locally they are remembered as a colorful bunch. In a 1982 article (Sweeney,a) local historian Bernice Sweeney,[7] mentions the memoirs of A. Butterwick, who told the story of having come into town on Columbus Day, 1899, and witnessing a parade. The marshall of the parade was anarchist Joe Gariglietti. He was wearing a Napoleon-style hat and rode a beautiful white horse. Butterwick observed that the anarchists fought to have their red flags at the heads of all parades, but Mayor Del Magro, owner of one of the 45 Spring

Valley taverns, denied them this right. On Labor Day that very same year, the Internationalists, as the anarchists called themselves, led by Emma Goldman, pre-empted the official parade by taking to the streets in great numbers with their flags and their songs, fully occupying the official viewing stand (*La Questione Sociale*, a.).

Anarchists led the Spring Valley miners who participated in the protracted strike of 1894. One of them, an Italian by the name of William Troy, was singled out by the Chicago papers as the pistol-firing leader of a band of anarchists who marched to Toluca, Illinois, on April 27 to persuade the miners there to join the strike. Troy, however, denied his role in that episode and minimized its consequences. (M. Fitton, a.)

The papers also talked of race riots when, later in the strike, miners led by anarchists attacked the camps of black scabs who had been brought in by the mine owners to break the strike. The anarchists pointed out that there had been no deaths on that occasion but that three innocent Italian bystanders had been killed during the strike by overzealous U.S. troops called in to free a blockaded train convoy. (Donley).

How did the anarchists come to Spring Valley? Where did they come from? First of all one must note that they were not only Italians, but also French and Belgians. Most had been recruited in Europe directly.

Local sources (Lloyd b., Johnston a.) tell of the care with which the miners were recruited. Companies such as the Superior Coal Company sent recruiters to strike-torn northern France[8] to select literate and intelligent miners. It is therefore ironic that this selection would work to the disadvantage of the owners as so many of the literate miners were militant and experienced in labor struggles. Local residents (Sweeney) recall that the anarchists were also eloquent and could speak of Darwin and Spencer.

An anti-anarchist resolution issued by the city fathers in 1901, the climactic year of the movement, states that there were about five hundred anarchists in Spring Valley; one hundred of these were said to be French and Belgians, and four hundred were Italian. In fact, the Italian figure in all probability refers to the membership of the Cristoforo Colombo Mutual Aid Society, which was heavily influenced by its anarchist members and which shared the premises of the Prosperity Club, the anarchists' headquarters.

A report by Antonio Andrà, one of the society's anarchist members, describes the anarchist influence on the mutual aid society and on the Italian community in general. (*La Questione Sociale, b.*) He states that the character of the Cristoforo Colombo society was drastically changed since a great number of anarchists had joined and worked hard to eliminate the "prejudices" of religion and patriotism. The former, he says, "... was easy to overcome.... now nine out of ten people who die have a civil funeral. If they choose to have a religious one, the society will attend the service up to the church entrance only." "As for patriotism," he adds, "the most recent victory and sign that the exploited workers have no country was the elimination of the national flags, parade clowning and para-military trappings."

The actual findings from *La Questione Sociale* show that a core of about 40 activists can be identified over a long period of time. In the early eighteen-nineties they founded the Germinal Club, allied to the French and Belgian Club Les Affamés, and hard at work when their first reports reached *La Questione Sociale* founded in Paterson, N.J., in 1895 with the help of Pietro Gori.

Contributions from Spring Valley Italian anarchists had reached *Il Grido degli Oppressi* as early as 1892. Ten names of Spring Valley contributors appear in the November 1893 issue.

The Spring Valley Italians, many of them recruited in France[9] (Stanley) were from the northern regions of Italy, but there was also an outspoken number of miners from Abruzzi in south-central Italy. The regions most represented were Piedmont, Emilia-Romagna (particularly the province of Modena), the Veneto and the Abruzzi.

It would appear, as would be expected from the Italian historical pattern, that in places like Ladd, Illinois, just North of Spring Valley, which had a majority of Modenesi or Emiliani, there was an early preference for socialism and electoral politics. In 1899, J. Rolando became mayor of Ladd in spite of anarchist opposition to electoral politics. For the same reason Toluca became an early socialist center.

In 1907, a group from Staunton, Illinois, calling themselves the Abruzzesi (*La Questione Sociale*, c.), complained that northeners who considered themselves radicals were not intransigent enough and even went to church. On the whole, southern Italian immigrant radicals clung to anarchism longer and promoted direct action rather than delegated offices.

What is so special about Spring Valley is that within its small boundaries the whole spectrum of anarchist tendencies came to full flowering. The Germinal group was and remained to the end thoroughly "organizationalist" in its attempts to act upon the directions issued by E. Malatesta following the Capolago convention in 1890. In 1896 the group worked for the establishment of a Federazione Socialista Anarchica dei Lavoratori Italiani in Nordamerica [Anarco-Socialist Federation of Italian Workers in North America] (*La Questione Sociale, d.*). In 1899 the Germinal group forcefully supported a Federazione Socialista Anarchica (*La Questione Sociale, e.*) and again in 1908 (*La Questione Sociale, f.*), which marked the last attempt to form an Italian Anarchist Federation in North America.[10]

The Germinal group remained the catalyst for the majority of anarchist miners who believed in organization and union participation. However, the anti-union libertarian individualist group which existed inside and outside the Germinal group split in the year 1900 and formed the group "I Nuovi Viventi" ["New Life"]. This group identified with Giuseppe Ciancabilla's fiery opposition to the organizational principle espoused by the newspaper *La Questione Sociale* and embodied in Malatesta. Spearheaded by Giacomo Rossetto[11] and aided by the French group, "I Nuovi Viventi" became strong enough to oust, in an election, the Germinal group from the management of the Prosperity Club, and invited Ciancabilla with his newspaper *L'Aurora*.

It is difficult to say what success the new arrangement in Spring Valley would have met with had Ciancabilla's efforts been allowed to continue undisturbed. From *L'Aurora* one learns that a host of activities was taking place: a "Gruppo Giovanile" was formed; the women's group "Luisa Michel" planned the publication of their translation of a French anar-

chist educational text, "Le Avventure di Nono"; Angela Mari-
etti,[12] the group's correspondent, announced strategies to
fight for women's emancipation (*L'Aurora, b.*); a library and
reading room were set up in the Aurora headquarters; a new
printing press was purchased in Chicago; E. Travaglio from
San Francisco came to Spring Valley to publish his newspaper
La Protesta Umana as the literary supplement of *L'Aurora*
(Bettini, b.); Ciancabilla launched an anti-union campaign de-
nouncing them as inevitably tyrannical, denying that anarchists could change unions.

All the activities which stemmed from *L'Aurora's* supporters suddenly collapsed after a series of debilitating blows.
First Ciancabilla himself acknowledged that his paper was
failing to take hold among the miners (*L'Aurora, c.*). Then the
newspaper failed to obtain second class postal privileges
(*L'Aurora, d.*), and finally the Prosperity Club was forced to
apply for a costly city licence. Moreover, Ciancabilla was sued
by the Italian Consul for slander after he accused the Italian
Consulate of sending spies to anarchist centers (*L'Aurora, e.*)

All these reversals took place in the wake of the assassination in July 1900 of the Italian king Umberto I at the hand of
Antonio Bresci, an anarchist who had reached Italy from Paterson, NJ The event marked the beginning of the U.S. repression of anarchists and dangerously exposed the organized
tendency of the movement.

With the assassination of President McKinley in September
of the following year, the repression intensified. On October 2,
Ciancabilla was arrested on charges of postal fraud, brought
to Ottawa, Illinois, and finally was obliged to move to Chicago
for the trial. There he started the publication of *La Protesta
Umana*. *L'Aurora*, temporarily supported by the workers but
with debts piling up, had to fold. Rocco Montesano, Ciancabilla's assistant, finally brought the equipment to New York.
(Bettini, c.).

In the meantime the Spring Valley city fathers called a
town meeting and issued a proclamation vowing to drive all
the anarchists away.[13] The declaration stated that loyalty
oaths would be requested on pain of deportation, the distribution of anarchist propaganda in the schools would be prohibited, and *L'Aurora* would have to suspend publication

(*L'Aurora, f.*) At the same time *L'Aurora* subscribers were intimidated (*L'Aurora, g.*) This spelled doom for *L'Aurora* and a deep crisis rocked the movement nationwide---the anarchist resources in Paterson, for example, were wrecked---but it was too late to stop anarchism in Spring Valley. It had become embedded in unions and civic life and there was a quick revival. Italians had been and would continue to be affected by the anarchists, especially in their resistance to church authority, a priority on their agenda.[14]

In a community of seven hundred Italians, priests as well as protestant pastors consistently had to give up their efforts, allegedly "because people preferred to go to anarchist meetings rather than to church" (*La Questione Sociale, g.*). In 1903 Andrà reported (*La Questione Sociale, h.*) that the union had decided to collect money to give a set of miner's tools to a priest who had been sent to Spring Valley to build a church. Upon delivery of these tools, he promptly disappeared.

In 1904 (*La Questione Sociale, i.*) one Sclarini reported from nearby Dalzell that the Reverend Sbrocco did not meet with better luck there. In the same issue Joe Corna stated, "Before coming he should have informed himself of the kind of spirit he would have found in Spring Valley." Corna concluded sarcastically, "The village is now lit by electric light which is not favorable to 'bats nesting.'"[15]

On December 31, 1904, the Spring Valley anarchists reporting to *La Questione Sociale* told of one more attempt to build a church there. This time the tide was more difficult to stop and many more people contributed to the priest's efforts. But by February 1906 the anarchists had redoubled their resistance and established a Lega di Resistenza Anticlericale (Anticlerical Resistance League), no doubt to allow other radicals to join them on this issue. Among other forms of propaganda they printed a poster of "Il Popolo Lavoratore," and soon after, A. Andra could announce that Don Rosciotti had left the city with the $500 he had collected.

The anarchists' anticlerical successes in Spring Valley and elsewhere in Illinois did not go unnoticed in the English-language press. The *La Salle Daily Tribune* of June 1906 reported that Father Jachini had had to give up his efforts there and was going to Spring Valley. The reporter noted: "...it is due to the lack of religious sentiment on the part of the Italians in this city together with other circumstances and not to any fault of the hard working priest that the Italians cannot or will not support a church in this city and that his labors after nearly two years have been in vain."

In June 1905 the Spring Valley anarchists launched a motto: "Not Churches but Libraries." Joe Corna, who had founded the UMWA Italian local in 1898 and went on to found the IWW local in 1906, had also accepted the management of the union library inherited from the Knights of Labor. Corna was among those who spoke out against a Carnegie-endowed library because, it was claimed, it would become a collection alien to the miners' interests. In time the radical library merged with the Carnegie-endowed library built in 1912 and the miners were allowed to place one of their representatives on the board. Corna was selected for the job.[16]

Judging from the number of anarchist circles successfully established in the area surrounding Spring Valley after the crisis of 1901, the Germinal group reasserted itself in a series of organizational efforts.[17] The Spring Valley miners continued to host the propaganda tours of anarchist organizers like Pietro Raveggi, Pedro Esteve, and Lodovico Caminita. Writing on their visits, they spoke with awe and wonder of the "Spring Valley spirit." This was all the more astonishing considering the appalling conditions of the miners' lives. Working in "the grave of the living" in darkness, dampness, and bad air for long hours and in grave danger, with no sick benefits, the miners emerged to find themselves overwhelmed by the problems of existence, including scarce food, water, and bad housing utterly controlled by the companies. Child labor, an economic necessity, presented the most ghastly sight of brutalized humanity.

An early report on these conditions came in 1896 from Gesualdo Gentiletti of nearby Toluca (*La Questione Sociale, j.*) Gentiletti and Andra denounced the apathy and ignorance that came as a result of brutalization. "Duvicu" (Lodovico Caminita) wrote a portrait of the Italian miner (*La Questione Sociale, k.*): "...ignorant, tired, hopeless, he works in dreadful surroundings, digs about five tons of coal a day, equivalent to $2.75--$3.00. He works about three days a week. After a poor dinner he usually gets into the tavern where he drinks and gambles. He does not want to read, learn, discuss. He is semi-wild. The exceptions are heroes."

One Airola from Livingston, Illinois, wrote about frauds perpetrated against ignorant and disunited miners. In Benld, he states, there were three mines. The Superior Mine Company exploited them by buying the whole camp for $60.00 a lot. No one was allowed to work unless they paid $75.00 for the same lot. So the company made money just from the land. "Why do people accept this?" asked Airola.

If workers paid $75.00 a lot just to work, why did they not put together the money and buy the mines themselves? Their stupidity, according to Airola, was topped by that of the UMWA, which approved and encouraged this type of prevarication. (*La Questione Sociale, l.*)

The anarchists among Italian miners in Spring Valley saw themselves as the direct heirs of the First International (*La Questione Sociale, m.*) and fought for the economic, social, and moral redemption of the miners. They joined unions, founded union locals, became the unions' official speakers (especially Joe Corna and Antonio Andrà), participated in conventions and strikes, and issued calls for a nation-wide General Strike on the occasion of a four-thousand-strong rally in Spring Valley to protest the Ludlow massacre in Colorado.

The untiring efforts of these self-taught activists created an unusual social climate in Spring Valley. P. Esteve, reporting on a visit there, wrote that it seemed to him like "an oasis in the desert" even though the work in the mines was as frightening as anywhere. (*La Questione Sociale, n.*) S. Rigotti and some friends from Lathrobe, Pennsylvania, visited Spring Valley in 1906 and sang its praises as "one of the links in the International movement...a center of progress and civilization."[18] (*La Questione Sociale, o.*) They mentioned Andrà of Spring Valley and Signori of La Salle as the outstanding leaders.[19]

Another occasion when the Spring Valley spirit triumphed was the Radical Italian Convention called in September 1915 by the Germinal Club. In a unique show of unity (which had failed elsewhere),[20] Italian radicals of all persuasions met in Spring Valley to protest militarism and the war in Europe. A proclamation was issued in which it was resolved to refuse to collaborate with any war efforts in the United States or in Italy. The conveners also agreed to launch a unified anti-war propaganda campaign sharing a common pool of carefully selected speakers.[21] Until late 1917 the Germinal group flourished and its Filodrammatica Moderna [modern drama club] successfully performed anti-war plays.

It would take the 1917 repression, and the raids and suppression of all anarchist papers, to dim the records of the final years of anarchism in Spring Valley. Also working against anarchism in Spring Valley were the economic decline of the city[22] and defections to syndicalism, socialism and communism.

The twenty-year ascendancy of Italian anarchism in Spring Valley presents a stark contrast with the persistent but highly rarified Italian anarchist presence in the Chicago metropolitan area. The gravitational impulses of the two Illinois groupings were different. The Germinal club of Spring Valley favored organization and union participation. It was exemplary of the kind of movement Malatesta worked so hard to achieve. When contacts were established with Chicago they were part of the anarcho-syndicalist thrust that took place around *La Propaganda,* organ of the Chicago Avenue Italian socialist-syndicalist section.[23]

The reports sent to this newspaper by Joe Corna show how important it was for the Spring Valley group to show solidarity with syndicalist unionism. Not so for the Chicago anarchists. Unlike the miners of Spring Valley the anarchist activists of the Chicago area, especially those of the West Side, were a heterogeneous crowd with greatly differing work experience. This, and the vast distances separating the group members caused an inevitable dispersion of energies and favored the individualist, anti-organizational tendencies.

The Chicago groups identified with the ideology of Galleani, brilliantly reflected in the pages of *Cronaca Sovversiva*. Since its inception in 1903, *Cronaca Sovversiva* became the paper of choice of the Italian anarchists and their sympathizers in Chicago.

The early beginnings of Italian anarchist activities in Chicago can be traced back to the 1880s to an anarchist publication in Italy. (*Il Paria, a.*). (Bettini, b.) By 1892 the group had gathered enough strength to attract to Chicago *Il Grido degli Oppressi,* the anarchist organ founded by Francesco Saverio Merlino in New York. *Il Grido* was published in Chicago during 1893 but was brought back to New York by the editor, Luigi Raffuzzi, whose negative editorials stated that the Chicago group could not or would not sustain it. Raffuzzi and his co-editor, Vito Solieri, (Bettini, c.), solidly in the libertarian camp, were eager to save the paper from the influence of "i falsi fratelli" [false brothers].

What the actual inclination of the Chicago group was can only be guessed. Reports on the trips of Merlino and Gori in the early nineties do not help. In their visits the Italian leaders seem to have addressed themselves more to the cosmopolitan anarchist groups of the city than to the Italian one in particular.

The Chicago Italian group at that time was called "La Solidarietà." (Bettini, d.) It was probably responsible for a demonstration in front of the Italian consulate observed by the playwright Giuseppe Giacosa in 1892 (Giacosa) to protest the consulate's failure to celebrate the anniversary of Rome's annexation to the Italian state. This historical event was perceived by the Italian radicals as the day of emancipation from clerical oppression.

It is also probable that the members of the Chicago Italian anarchists embraced Merlino's design for an Association of Italian Workers in North America. One can detect from the pages of *Il Grido* a certain animosity toward other language groups. J. Most opposed Merlino accusing him of obscurity and even went so far as to advise the comrades of Pittsburgh and Cincinnati not to receive him. On the other hand, Gori's trip to Chicago in 1895 was a triumph. He spoke at rallies in English, French and Italian and was elected American Trade Union representative at the London Congress later that year.

One also learns from the pages of *Il Grido* of the existence in 1894 of a second Italian anarchist group in Kensington, on the city's far South Side. This is an important date because from then on the activities of two distinct Italian major anarchist circles in Chicago can be followed until the end of the 1940s.

Their reports to *La Questione Sociale*; and then more regularly after 1903 to *Cronaca Sovversiva*; reveal a steady number of supporters of about 30 to 50. They tried mainly to spread anarchist propaganda among Italian immigrants and forever battled the socialists, who, according to their view, seduced the workers into the blind alley of electoral politics.[24] In 1902 the two groups could not gather enough strength to sustain *La Protesta Umana*; which Ciancabilla had started in Chicago after the short-lived attempt to publish *L'Aurora* in Spring Valley.

The repressions in the wake of the Italian king's assassination and then that of President McKinley in the United States had killed *L'Aurora* in Spring Valley and had temporarily dispersed the Chicago groups. In 1903, Ciancabilla had to leave for good "questa impenetrabile, inerte, assopita Chicago" ["this impenetrable, inert, slumbering city"].

Ciancabilla represents the aspect of the movement as it would continue to develop in the Chicago area. With the exception of some organizing fringes in the Kensington group, challenged by a strong syndicalist contingent, the libertarian element eloquently upheld by Ciancabilla became ingrained in the city's Italian anarchist spirit, and found in Umberto Postiglione its most enthusiastic interpreter from 1911 to 1916.

Ciancabilla had preached from *L'Aurora* that "Anarchy is that social order whose political ideal is the absolute freedom of the individual to be found in the absence of any ruling authority." (*L'Aurora, f.*) In the first Chicago issue of *La Protesta Umana* in February 1902, he defined anarchists in his own characteristic negative way: "We are not a party which begs governments for the right to exist. We are the rebellious ranks who do not beg and do not forgive; we are the anarchists intolerant of any controls, any form of coercion, who want to transform the masses into educated individuals."

The movement in Chicago followed this blueprint and its destiny seems to have closely matched that of the movement in Italy, coming full circle in the 1940s, when the Italian leader Armando Borghi, speaking in Chicago soon after World War II, recognized in Ciancabilla's *L'Aurora* the first source of his libertarian ideals. (*L'Adunata dei Refrattari, c.*)

Internal and external pressures on the Chicago groups caused their frequent demise and resurrection, especially in the case of the West Side group.[25] But if the names of the circles and their addresses were subject to vagaries, not so the membership and the leadership, which remained constant over a long period. Annibale Ferrero, for example, a self-taught baker, remained one and sometimes the only speaker for the two Chicago groups from 1904 to the early 1940s, forever mending rifts and patching up divisions. Other solid presences were A. Sistoni and Rigoni for the Kensington group, A. and Ida Rossi, Cimini, V. Vallera, R. De Rango, A. Allegrini, and D. Forte for the West Side group. They created the atmosphere and the supportive network which sustained the formation of an anarchist leader like Umberto Postiglione. Among them Postiglione matured into a leader of national stature, an eager learner as well as teacher, and never forgotten by his comrades, who commemorated his life by staging his plays and publishing his essays.

Postiglione arrived in Chicago in 1910 from his native Raiano, Abruzzi, when barely eighteen, finding accommodation in the very building where his future adversary Giuseppe Bertelli lived, in the heart of the Tuscan neighborhood at 24th and Oakley Streets.[26] Educated, eloquent, and a good writer, he soon became the protegé of Galleani and a contributor to Galleani's *Cronaca Sovversiva*.

Through his frequent and long contributions, one becomes familiar with an ideological and philosophical mindset widely shared by his readers. First and uppermost was the necessity of creating a social order free of the chains of ignorance and oppression; on the basis of rational enquiry and freedom of expression mankind would evolve healthy social relationships. Spreading the ideas of Fourier, Proudhon, Kropotkin, and Darwin, among others, Postiglione wrote articles on private property, usury, mercantilism, primitive accumulation, and political power.

One of the most original of Postiglione's contributions was an essay on Japanese culture, "Banzai," which appeared over two issues of *Cronaca Sovversiva* beginning April 27, 1912. At a time of nascent Japanese activism and apparent strides in modernization, Postiglione observed that the lack of a state religion and of a rooted methaphysical religiosity correlated with a high capability for exploration, innovation and cultural change. Free from religious dogma, societal forces, he said, could focus on progress.

Postiglione was tireless in promoting these ideas among the Italian anarchists in Chicago, where he twice attempted to launch an Italian-language organ of "practical propaganda," once in 1913 with *Germinal* and again in 1915 with *L'Allarme*. He was particularly keen to rally his compatriots from Raiano, whom he spurred in 1913 to help establish a "Casa del Popolo" [proletarian cultural center] in their native village in Italy. The West Side group to which he belonged had already gone through quite a number of metamorphoses when, by 1915, he helped transform it into the "Gruppo I Liberi." It had previously been the "Gruppo XI Novembre," the "Circolo di Studi Sociali" (CSS), the "XI of November Reborn in 1909," and then finally "Il Gruppo Libertario."

The Kensington group had called itself "Circolo di Studi Sociali" (CSS) since 1910. A CSS was also founded in suburban Cicero (1910) and Chicago Heights (1910), as well as a short-lived one on the East Side, mostly in response to strong socialist organizing there.

By 1911 the Chicago groups felt strong enough to issue an invitation to *Cronaca Sovversiva*. The invitation was not accepted. In 1912 regular meetings were held on the first Sunday of the month at the corner of Taylor and Des Plaines Streets on the Near West Side. In July 1913 the West Side group became the "Gruppo di Propaganda Anarchica".

In the meantime the Libyan War (1911), initiated by the Italian state for the possession of that territory, had begun to reveal a potential rift within the anarchist ranks between interventionists who believed in "bold initiatives" and those, by far the great majority, who stuck with the antimilitarist principles of anarchism. As on earlier occasions, the decisive influence of Malatesta (1914), later adopted by Galleani, confirmed and sealed the Italian anarchists' opposition to all wars.

This was not without traumas. Postiglione had hailed war as an opportunity for revolution as late as September 1914. He could easily have gone the way of the syndicalists De Ambris, Rossoni, and self-styled anarchists like Massimo Rocca

(alias Libero Tancredi) and Vico Covi. Yet Postiglione's intimate contacts with Italian anarchists, and the miners in par-
ticular---and no doubt because of his ties to Galleani---brought
him back from the brink, and he became a tireless opponent of
the war, and as such was a favorite speaker of the Italian anarchist communities.

In April 1916, Postiglione took on the editorial duties of
Cronaca Sovversiva when Galleani was arrested. Shortly before that event he had founded the paper *L'Allarme* which he
tried in vain to sustain in Massachusetts. His last public appearance in Chicago was in February 1916 when he held a
public debate with John La Duca, secretary of the Italian Socialist Federation.

February 1916 was also the time of an alleged anarchist
plot in Chicago, which only slightly involved Italian anarchists. The Chicago anarchist John Crones, a cook at the University Club of Chicago, had laced with arsenic the food
served at a banquet in honor of the recently installed Cardi-
nal Mundelein, causing the brief illness of two hundred
guests. (*Cronaca Sovversiva, a.*), (*Chicago Tribune, a.*). It was
only a prank but the rumor of an anarchist plot spread. The
police, cracking down on all anarchists, arrested A. Allegrini;
A. Ferrero was held only briefly. *L'Allarme* translated into
English, was scrutinized and its editors, Postiglione and Di
Biase, singled out as incendiary leaders. Allegrini, who had
shared a room with Crones, was held longer but at the end
was cleared.

In the wake of the 1917 repressions and loyalty demands,
Postiglione fled the country and slowly, via Central America,
made his way back to Italy, where, already a broken man, he
died in 1924. (U. Postiglione, a.)

When the Chicago groups re-formed after the First World
War, both *Era Nuova* and *Cronaca Sovversiva* had ceased
publication. The rising star of the Italian anarchist press was
L'Adunata dei Refrattari, published in New York by a libertarian group opposing all attempts to involve anarchists in a
joint radical struggle against Fascism. Elena Purgatorio,
originally from Farmington, Illinois, was the eloquent correspondent to *L'Adunata* for the Chicago anarchist groups during the 1920s. During the Pittsburgh anarchist meetings of

1925, the Chicago groups showed dissension, exhibiting once
again their historical hostility toward the New York Italian
anarchist establishment. They founded *Germinal,* a periodical
sustained by the authoritative pen of Luigi Fabbri, and the efforts of the Chicago anarchists A. Tiberi, S. Spada, 0. Cesaroni[27] and, not far behind, the anarco-syndicalist Erasmo
Abate (alias Ugo Rolland).

Germinal was published from 1926 to I930. It encouraged a
more cooperative stance with the antifascist groups, including
the communists. Both *L'Adunata* and *Germinal* rallied their
best energies for the defense of Sacco and Vanzetti. On hearing of their execution, Chicago anarchist Aurora D'Angelo led
a vast march through the city in spite of a near state of siege
until she was arrested with thirty other demonstrators.
(*L'Adunata, d.; Germinal, a.*)

The Chicago groups mobilized around these two newspapers until *Germinal* could no longer be sustained. The groups
survived through the thirties under the name of "I Libertari,"
which now included Chicago Heights and Roseland, and the
CSS in Kensington. They were later named "I Refrattari" and
"I Colombiani." Both supported the same causes and their
drama group, La Filodrammatica Novella.

The early thirties saw the attention of the Chicago anarchist groups engaged in the long drawn-out struggle in the
coal fields of Central Illinois and the emergence of the Progressive Miners Union, opposed, like all others, by the
Chicago anarchists on grounds of organizational tyranny.

By 1934 the "Gruppi Riuniti del West Side e di Kensington"
established a common address at 8085 S. Western Avenue,
perhaps suggesting a greater Kensington strength. Close to
60 names appear in the supporters' list. (*L'Adunata dei Refrattari*, June 29, 1935.)

Throughout their metamorphoses the two Chicago groups
never came to severe or irreparable divisions. If the South
Side were inclined toward unionism and organization and the
West Side took a more libertarian line, the two shared the
same scarce resources, leadership, and major goals. In their
long twilight they still looked to Italy for inspiration and
guidance. Their weakness was due to the relatively superior
numbers of the socialists, syndicalists, and later the commu-

nists; and not least, at the end, the pacifying climate of the New Deal.

If any conclusion from these closely documented activities can be drawn, one can perhaps point to two forms of influence for social change exerted by Italian anarchists in their communities. One is the extent to which they established themselves as role models because of their rationality, combativeness, self-reliance, and literacy, once the stereotype of the "incendiary anarchist" had been overcome by the listening public. The other is something one can only glimpse at: the anarchists' cultural impact on the Italian immigrant communities. These must have lived constantly in the presence of an alternative political culture, with its symbols and institutions often paraded in the open during rallies, picnics, counter-holidays, and lectures, as well as in the vast array of newspapers, almanacs, postcards, and flags (Miller). Immigrant families often joined these celebrations in great numbers and many absorbed the ideas and values of the anarchists, as can be gathered from the reminiscences of those whose political consciousness was thereby raised. (La Morticella)

References

L'Adunata dei Refrattari, New York, 1922-71. microfilm, New York Public Library
  a) June 6, 1936
  b) November 3, 1929
  c) May 5, 1945
  d) August 13, 1927

L'Allarme, Chicago, 1915-16, Somerville, Mass., 1917, Umberto Postiglione, ed. Microfilm, University of Minnesota Immigration Archives (UMIA)

L'Aurora, Periodico anarchico, Paterson, N.J.; Johoganny, Pa.; Spring Valley Il., 1899-1901. G. Ciancabilla, ed.
  (a) September. 28, 1901
  (b) December 22, 1900
  (c) February 9, 1901
  (d) March 9, 1901
  (e) March 16, 1901
  (f) September 28, 1901

(g) November 4, 1901
(h) October 21, 1899
Microfilm, UMIA

Bettini, Leonardo, *Bibliografia dell'Anarchismo.* CP Editrice, Firenze, 1976
(a) vol. 1, pp. 289-297.
(b) vol. 1, p. 181.
(c) vol. 1, p. 290.
(d) vol. 1, p. 291.

Carey, George, "The Vessel, the Deed, the Idea: Anarchists in Paterson, 1895-1908, Antipode, Worcester, Mass., 1979, 10/11; pp. 46-58

Chicago Tribune, February 13, 1916.

Cronaca Sovversiva, Ebdomadario anarchico di propaganda, Barre, Vt., 1903-1919, Direttore Luigi Galleani.
(a) February 19, 1916.
Microfilm, UMIA

Donley, Glenda, "The 1894 Coal Strike in Spring Valley, Illinois." Unpublished manuscript, April 21, 1976, Spring Valley Public Library.

L'Era Nuova, Paterson, N.J., 1908-1917. Microfilm, UMIA.

Germinal, periodico di propaganda anarchica, U. Postiglione, direttore, Chicago, Il., September 7, 1913. Microfilm, UMIA.

Germinal, mensile di propaganda anarchica, Chicago 1926-1930, Erasmo Abate, Armando Tiberi, Silvestro Spada, eds. Original Text: Feltrinelli Foundation, Milano (through 1928 only), and microfiche, International Institute for Social History, Amsterdam, the Netherlands.
(a) Aug. 15, 1927.

Giacosa, Giuseppe, "Gli Italiani a New York e Chicago," *Nuova Antologia,* August 1892, vol. XVI, pp. 619-640.

La Gogna, Kensington (Chicago), Il., November 1909. Single issue. Corradino Luciani, former editorialist of Il Proletario, defends himself against alleged attacks by Chicago and Utica, N.Y., socialists.

La Propaganda, Chicago, Il., 1908-1909. At first, the organ of the Italian socialist sections of the Midwest, and then of the Chicago

Avenue section, the last Chicago remnant of the eastern Italian Socialist Federation.

Fitton, Maureen, "The Early Labor Movement in Spring Valley, Illinois." Unpublished manuscript, no date, Spring Valley Public Library.
(a) pp. 6-9.

L'Intesa, Single issue, Convegno Anarchico Nordamericano, Dicembre, 1925. Microfilm, Institute for Social History, Amsterdam.

Johnston, Madeline, "Anarchist Movement in Spring Valley." Unpublished manuscript, no date, Spring Valley Public Library (a) p. 1.

La Morticella, Anthony, La Parola del Popolo, September-October 1980, vol. 154, pp.42-44.

Lloyd, Henry D., The Story of Spring Valley. Chicago, 1890, (Johnson reprint, 1970)
(a) *passim.*
(b) p. 4.

Miller, Eugene, "The Mario Manzardo Papers," paper presented to the Illinois Labor History Society, Chicago, June 6, 1980, p. 4.

Il Paria Ancona.
(a) July 26, 1885

Per la Chiarezza, Chicago, IL, February 1930, single issue.

Microfiche, Institute of Social History, Amsterdam.

Il Piccone, Taylorville, IL, March 1909, single issue, Giosue Imparato, ed., (Personal attacks against most of the Italian anarchist leadership of North America.) Microfilm, UMIA.

Postiglione, Umberto, *Scritti Sociali V,* Vallera, ed., Pistoia, 1972
(a) Introduction by Vallera, pp. 5-13.

La Protesta Umana Chicago, 1902; San Francisco, 1904, G. Ciancabilla, ed. Microfilm, UMIA.

La Rivolta, Madison, Il., 1913, Vico Covi, ed. Microfiche, International Institute for Social History, Amsterdam.

Sweeney, Bernice, "Anarchists in Spring Valley." *Spring Valley Gazette,* January 29, 1980.

Stanley, Otto, "The Involvement of M.J. Casazza in the Labor Movement in Spring Valley." Unpublished manuscript, Spring Valley Public Library

(a) pp. 1,2.

La Questione Sociale, periodico anarchico, Paterson, N.J., 1895- 1908
(followed by *L'Era Nuova*). Circulation in 1899 was 3,500
(a) September 16, 1899
(b) June 13, 1904
(c) August 17, 1907
(d) July 30, 1896
(e) November 4, 1899
(f) February 1, 1908
(g) November 26, 1898
(h) December 19, 1903
(i) January 16, 1904
(j) May 30, 1896
(k) September 22, 1906
(l) August 11, 1906
(m) March 26, 1899
(n) December 5, 1903
(o) March 24, 1906
Microfilm, UMIA.

Footnotes

[1] Paul Avrich talks about Italian anarchist literature as a flood. About anarchist newspapers and journals he states: "...more were issued by the Italians than any other immigrant groups." Paul Avrich, *Anarchist Portraits*, Princeton University Press, 1988.

[2] For the story of the anarchists in Paterson see: George Carey, "The Vessel, the Deed, the Idea: Anarchists in Paterson, 1895-1908," *Antipode*, Worcester, Mass., 1979, 10/11; pp. 46-58.

[3] R. Canosa, A. Santuosso, *Magistrati, anarchici e socialisti alla fine del 1800 in Italia*, Milano, Feltrinelli, 1981. On the Italian American connection see: G. Cerrito, "Sull'emigrazione anarchica Italiana negli Stati Uniti d'America," *Volonta*; August, 1969; L.V. Ferraris, "L'assassinio di Umberto I e gli anarchici di Paterson," *Rassegna Storica del Risorgimento;* Anno LV, N.1 (Gennaio-Marzo 1968); Arrigo Petacco, *L'Anarchico che venne dall'America*; Milano, 1969.

[4] The major Italian anarchist papers published in North America were: *La Questione Sociale*; followed by *L'Era Nuova* (1895-1919),

organs of the organizational wing; *Cronaca Sovversiva* (1903-1917), edited by Galleani, representing the moderate and more enduring libertarian wing opposed to formal organization; *L'Aurora*; Ciancabilla's organ upholding the "anti-authoritarians" and probably the closest in principle to the other U.S. cosmopolitan groups.

5 Ronchietto, not unusually, protested excessive anarchist involvement with unions and other hierarchical organizations. Nevertheless, he belonged to Germinal, the organizational group in Spring Valley, and to the IWW local. In his opinion only popular pressure could bring about fundamental changes. He made his point relentlessly but, in his own words, was hardly given any attention. (*La Questione Sociale*, April 7, 1906.) It was not apparent to him that his intransigent line was perceived as irrelevant by the workers he addressed. He even opposed recently implemented workers' compensation provisions because he thought it was illusory to trust a law made by people who did not obey other laws. (*Era Nuova*, September 21, 1912.)

6 Alfredo Bagaglino, longtime activist of the Germinal group of Spring Valley, had been a member of the organizing committee for the 1915 initiative against the war, sponsored locally by all radical groups. He had previously been active in committees supporting international causes like the Parma strike of 1908 and the Mexican Revolution of 1910. He was deported, probably with other activists, in 1917, and returned to his native Turin, where he was soon hounded and imprisoned by the Fascist authorities. His funeral on May 14, 1936, reported in the United States (*L'Adunata dei Refrattari, a.*), was the occasion for an anarchist rally attended by about 30 people, and was secretly prepared so as to surprise the Fascists, who arrived too late to break it up.

7 Bernice Sweeney took the task of local historian over from her husband, Cyril Sweeney. He had kept a scrapbook in which he recorded the memories he collected about the Spring Valley anarchists. It is ironic that Sweeney, a descendant of one of the signatories of the 1901 anti-anarchist proclamation, became a keeper of anarchist memories, and passed on to his wife and daughter Sarah a sense of the deep significance of the Spring Valley anarchist past. See the paper by Sarah Sweeney Allen, "L'Aurora Comes to Town: Spring Valley, Illinois, 1900." Illinois History Symposium, December

5, 1986, Illinois State University, Bloomington.

[8] Twelve thousand miners struck in Anzin, France, in February 1884.

[9] One of the first Italian immigrants to come to Spring Valley via France was the father of Joseph Casazza. In an interview by Otto Stanley in 1974, Casazza, himself a lifetime union leader, recalled how his father arrived in 1887, three years after the city was founded. He became a member of Local 8617 of the Knights of Labor and went to work in the No. 3 mine. He worked ten hours a day until 1898. His son Joseph dropped out of school and went to work in the mines in 1905. (Stanley)

[10] In *Era Nuova*, September 19, 1908, R. Canarina of the Spring Valley Germinal group wrote about the necessity of reviving the *Federazione Socialista Anarchica*: "only a strong organization can guarantee a positive result." Canarina went on to explain that, after the secession of a group of activists in Spring Valley (the Aurora group), it was a struggle to start work on behalf of the Federation again. He announced that the reconstituted group agreed to be the center of correspondence of those groups which intended to become part of the Federation. For Canarina: "La mancanza di organizzazione e per conseguenza il nessun accordo e affiatamento per un lavoro pratico e fecondo e per noi il caos, la negazione dei nostri principi di lotta, la impossibilita assoluta di una preparazione rivoluzionaria." ["The lack of organization, and consequently the lack of coordination and cooperation for a practical and fruitful activism is, in our opinion, equivalent to chaos and negates the principles of our struggle by precluding all revolutionary preparations."] An editorial comment to Canarina's "oration" praised the initiative of the Spring Valley group: "...che riteniamo come uno dei piu forti ed attivi degli Stati Uniti." ["...which we believe to be one of the strongest and most active in the United States."]

[11] The name of Giacomo Rossetto never appears in the lists of supporters and members of the Germinal Club, published in *La Questione Sociale* on several occasions, leading one to conclude that he never actually was part of it and therefore never actually split from it.

[12] The Mariettis were also principal actors in the anarchists' drama club in Spring Valley.

13 *L'Aurora* published the entire resolution in the September 28, 1901 issue. J. Sweeney signed the proclamation as secretary of the town meeting which issued the resolution.(*L'Aurora, a.*)

14 In 1901 A. Andra wrote: "Gli anarchici hanno qui antiche e immutate simpatie di educazione e redenzione morale." ["As for education and moral redemption, the anarchists here have deep and enduring bonds."] (*La Questione Sociale*, October 5, 1901.) In 1904 he wrote: "L'opera loro si esplica qui da anni in una lenta e penosa fatica." ["Their work has been unfolding here for years with slow and painful efforts."] (*La Questione Sociale*, January 13, 1904.)

15 "Bats" (pipistrelli) was the epithet used by the anarchists to describe priests in a pejorative way.

16 Joe Corna was the UMWA's Italian local delegate and in that capacity he attended union conventions, about which he reported in great detail in the pages of *La Questione Sociale*. He was an enthusiastic union man, unlike many of his fellow anarchists, whom he debated effectively on the necessity of spreading anarchist propaganda within the unions. Feeling betrayed by the UMWA for the abrupt end of the 1905 strike, he devoted himself to the organization of an IWW local. Corna's activities can be followed in the pages of *L'Era Nuova* up to the crisis of 1901. His sudden disappearance from the Spring Valley scene at that time leads one to believe that he was deported along with at least one other anarchist, Alfredo Bagaglino.

17 In Toluca---about twenty miles South of Spring Valley---the first anarchist circle was established in 1898. It was renewed in 1901 with Gentiletti, Buda, and Rolettino reporting and battling the socialists. Fourteen names appear on their contributors' list. In nearby Granville, where the first anarchist group had been founded by the Spring Valley leadership in 1898, a new Gruppo Aurora was activated in 1901 by Luigi Ronchietto, formerly of Spring Valley. In Dalzell an anarchist group was formed in 1903, with one Sclarini reporting. Further to the South a great number of anarchist groups were formed or renewed after 1901: Blue Mound (1906), Taylorville (1907), Staunton (1899), Gruppo Ravachol [Staunton] (1909), Herrin (1909), Roanoke (1910), Benld (1910), Pawnee (1911), Virden (1911), Farmington (1914), and West Frankfort (1915).

18 For the sake of the original text's flavor, the rest of the quote reads: "Nacque allora e non fu illusione, ripetiamo, vivissimo il nos-

tro desiderio di avvicinarci a quell'attivo ambiente che piu esemplare e piu attivo del nostro in Pensilvania seppe conservare intatta o meglio ampliare la sua posizione di propaganda malgrado le prove subite della reazione e il difetto del dissidio originato in noi colle due tendenze nocive di libera organizzazione e antiorganizzazione. In questo lasso di tempo e proprio quando la reazione infieriva contro di noi, ebbimo modo coll'amato compagno Andra... di intuire in lui le proprieta caratteristiche di cui sono evoluti quei buoni compagni per la libera organizzazione sociale, riflessione omogenea e matura da esperienze di studi e di pratica dopo molti anni di lotte."

[19] Signori might have been responsible for Andra's conversion to socialism around 1910, which in practice meant his acceptance of electoral politics. Unlike Joe Corna, who became an IWW organizer, Andra remained in the UMWA.

[20] See the reports from New York in *Cronaca Sovversiva*, October 23, 1915.

[21] Intellectual would-be radicals like Edmondo Rossoni and, more locally, Massimo Rocca (alias Libero Tancredi) and Vico Covi, had embarrassed the anarchist workers when they turned out to be ardent interventionists and proto-fascists.

[22] The Spring Valley mines were closed almost entirely during the 1920s.

[23] This section, located at 108 E. Chicago Avenue on the East Side, was what remained of the socialist formation connected to the IWW-linked Italian Socialist Federation with headquarters in the Eastern States. After the publication of *La Parola dei Socialisti* in Chicago in 1908, and the founding of the Italian Socialist Federation (ISF; linked to the Socialist Party of America) most of the other Chicago Italian socialists joined the newly-formed federation. The Chicago Avenue section in Chicago held on hoping to become a socialist-IWW center in the Midwest.

[24] All Italian anarchist groups opposed and harassed the socialist organizations in their communities. This obligatory obstructionist task was an important aspect of anarchist activism. The anarchists focused on the perceived potential danger of the tyrannical forces they saw as congenital to other radical formations rather than on the fight for the economic and political emancipation of the workers. Individual responsability, they held, should never be surrendered.

Herein lies the difference, and the source of contention, between anarchists and other radicals. The anarchists' attention was riveted on the time after the revolution. The other radicals organized for the power shift leading *to* the revolution.

25 The manner in which anarchists circles disappeared and quickly reappeared in slightly changed location suggests that this was not only a response to frequent raids and police pressure but a methodical response to internal tensions and conflicts which were overcome by the departure and eventual return of the dissenting members, who in turn would attempt to strengthen ther position by forming a new circle. If this interpretation is correct, this institutionalized method to overcome stalemates and stagnation would be a peculiarly, albeit not exclusively, anarchist choice of organizational behavior in the absence of formal cadres and hierarchy.

26 V. Vallera, formerly a Chicago anarchist, published a selection of Postiglione's writings, *Scritti Sociali*, Pistoia 1972. In his introduction he tells how Postiglione, having found lodgings with a relative, discovered that he was living in the same building as Giuseppe Bertelli, the foremost Italian socialist leader in Chicago. This proximity provided numerous debate encounters and clashes, which sharpened Postiglione's abilities in propaganda work.

27 Osvaldo Cesaroni had been a controversial figure within the Italian Local of the Amalgamated Clothing Workers Union in Chicago. He became its president in 1920 but was forced to resign, having almost caused a revolt on account of his dictatorial and abrasive personality. (Guidetti interview by E. Miller, March 23, 1981). From the pages of *Il Lavoro* of November 3, 1923, we learn that he was still president at that date. Cesaroni became a frequent correspondent to *L'Adunata dei Refrattari* after its inception in 1922. He was part of the founding group of the Chicago-sponsored *Germinal* in 1926. When the newspaper failed he gathered the supporting group, now called "gli sbandati" [the scattered], at his house at 711 S. Western Avenue. (*L'Adunata, b.*) In 1932 he was still part of the committee responsible for collecting funds to erase the debts left by the defunct *Germinal*. By 1936 Cesaroni was active raising funds on behalf of the Spanish Civil War fighters. On February 12, 1938, he called a meeting at Hull House to publicize the forthcoming publication of the works of Bakunin, an activity promoted by all the international an-

archist groups in the area.

The Italian Massacre at Walsenburg, Colorado, 1895

Conrad Woodall

References to the lynching or threats of lynching of Italians and the often mute response of Americans are scattered through the literature of the Italian experience in America. One episode took the lives of three Italians in Walsenburg, Colorado in 1895. Another, the 1891 lynching of 11 Italians in New Orleans is well known and provides a nearly perfect example of the crime--the infliction of punishment, usually death, without the form of law. Lynchers have usually succeeded because of inadequate police protection. Tacit acceptance, and even overt approval of community leaders have often played a part. There were other such episodes. A total of six of them, including Walsenburg and New Orleans led to separate diplomatic protests and payment of indemnities by the United States to Italy. Only New Orleans has been accorded thorough historical treatment.

On the night of Tuesday, March 12, 1895, Stanislao Vittone, an Italian coal miner living in Rouse, Colorado was shot and killed at the Bear Creek Bridge about a mile from Walsenburg. The killing was the work of six or seven masked men. Vittone, along with three other Italian miners was being transported six miles by wagon from Rouse to the Walsenburg jail. They were being held in connection with the beating death of a saloon keeper two nights before. One of three deputies, twenty-two year old Joseph Welsby, who drove the wagon, was also killed. Of Vittone's three fellow prisoners, Francesco Ronchietto was wounded, and Pietro Giacobino and Antonio Cobetto escaped into the night. [1]

Ronchietto, who was not badly hurt, was brought to the Walsenburg jail to join Lorenzo Andinino, who had been taken there earlier in the day by Huerfano County Sheriff Walter O'Malley. Sometime around 1 a.m., another half-dozen masked men got into the jail despite two deputies, and shot both Italians. Andinino died immediately and the twice-attacked Ronchietto succumbed in a few minutes.

In less than forty-eight hours, two Americans and three Italians died. One of the escapees from the ambush, Pietro Giacobino, would suffer amputation of his feet from frostbite. He would live to accuse one man of being an attacker. A coroner's inquest found saloon keeper Abner J. Hixon's death to be the result of injuries inflicted by Andinino "and others... with felonious intent." Another inquest would decide that the three Italians and Welsby had been killed with "felonious intent" by "unknown persons." The latter conclusion would be confirmed in February, 1896, by a Grand Jury of the Third District Court of Huerfano County, Colorado.[2]

The failure of armed guards to protect the prisoners and the inability of authorities to find suspects who committed the "Italian Massacre" to the designation of "lynching" almost immediately. Acting Italian Consul at Denver, Dr. Joseph Cuneo, referred to it as such in a protest to Colorado Governor Albert W. McIntire the day after. Secretary of State Walter Q. Gresham used it in a letter to Governor McIntire on 5 April 1895, and six months later, Acting Secretary Edwin F. Uhl referred to the Italians "lynched" in Colorado in a letter to the Italian Ambassador."[3]

In the popular mind, memories of the New Orleans lynching of 1891 were quickly raised, and McIntire, with prompting from Washington, began inquiring into the citizenship of the victims. The stage of naturalization of victims would be a diplomatic consideration as it would be after other incidents over the next sixteen years.[4]

The Walsenburg killings bear on a number of questions. Was it a lynching? Did it have the tacit approval, if not the open participation of community leaders, as had been the case at New Orleans? Were these men victims because of their nationality? Did the victims suffer for political beliefs, as some scholars have suggested, or for involvement in organized labor?

In *Lynch-Law* (1905), James E. Cutler was concerned with the "frequency and impunity" of lynching in the United States. He found it to be somewhat peculiar to this country. The Wellesley economist concluded that the cessation of lynching would be dependent on "strong and uncompromising sentiment against it" and was pessimistic about possible federal anti-lynching law. At the same time, he distinguished between "frontier" lynching, where formative societies act in lieu of established regulations and the actions of older societies. In these older societies, Cutler found several causes of lynching: "contrast in population," instances of disreputable characters who could not be convicted for lack of evidence, or especially heinous crimes that shocked the community. Cutler, whose work became the statistical authority on lynching made no specific judgment on Walsenburg, but the Walsenburg victims are included in his count of 180 lynched in 1895.[5]

Answers to historical questions and assessment in terms of Cutler's observations require detailed examination.

The capture of the Italians

The murder of Abner Hixon was discovered early on Monday, 12 March 1895. He was found unconscious from blows to the head and never regained consciousness. Hixon, who worked in Rouse, had been in Walsenburg on Sunday. He had ridden the six miles back and stabled his horse before joining a group of Italians. The reason for the gathering and the exact location are not clear, but at some point there was an altercation and Hixon was cautioned to leave. Not all of the Italians spoke English and drinking might have aggravated a misunderstanding. Hixon apparently left, but returned to look through a window, which either exacerbated the matter or startled the Italians. The result was two heavy blows to the head. Hixon was carried to a street corner a few hundred yards away.[6]

The newspaper accounts of the apprehension of suspects is the stuff of dime novels. A superintendent at the Rouse coal mines had recently acquired a bloodhound. The dog tracked the scent of Hixon's blood to a cabin and then to a saloon, or to a saloon and then to a cabin, depending on the newspaper. Four Italians were found in this initial roundup. They showed knowledge of the murder and identified several other Italians who had been present, two of whom had already "headed south."[7]

Justice of the peace dockets show that Sheriff O'Malley

charged six men as probable assailants on the same day,
Monday, March 11 and eventually held nine. The coroner's
inquest began at 11 a.m. on Monday and continued until 4
p.m., by which time all suspects had been caught. The nine
were taken safely to the Walsenburg jail and returned to
Rouse the next day for continuation of the inquest.[8] Early on
Tuesday the inquest determined that Andinino had struck the
fatal blow. He was taken, without incident, to Walsenburg by
the sheriff and placed in a cell with a German immigrant being held on a charge of rape.[9]

Ambush at Bear Creek Bridge

Grand jury testimony reveals that at about six on Tuesday
evening, Assistant District Attorney Henry Hunter determined that Vittone, Ronchietto, Cobetto, and Giacobino
should be returned to the jail. An undersheriff with Joe
Welsby on the wagon and a deputy followed on horseback. Sheriff O'Malley stayed to see whether the remaining prisoners
would be held, although Hunter's account suggests O'Malley
would have been free to leave with the wagon. Further grand
jury accounts indicated that seven horseman rode from Rouse
while the wagon was on the road. Four rode together, as did
two others, and one rode alone. None of the groups remembered seeing any others or hearing gun shots.
    The jury was hearing its last witness when word arrived of
the attack on the wagon. Coroner D.W. Mathews told Hunter
privately and suggested he not say anything until the last
witness was heard. Hunter heard the last witness and hurried
five of the six miles toward Walsenburg in time to meet a
crowd at the Bear Creek Bridge.[10]
    The attack itself had been brief, six or seven men rode up
behind the wagon, forced the deputy to dismount and run, and
then overtook the wagon. While halting the wagon, Welsby
had been fatally shot. The Italians jumped and ran. While
Giacobino and Cobetto escaped, some of the several dozen pis-
tol shots fired at the fleeing prisoners wounded Ronchietto
and killed Vittone. The sheriff took Ronchietto to the jail.[11]

The attack at the jail

The strongest contradiction in the eventual grand jury testimony came over the guarding of the jail holding Andinino, Ronchietto, and the German. O'Malley insisted that he was alone on guard until nearly midnight. A deputy had been sent out to get assistance but was unsuccessful. The deputy was sent home. At about 11:45 p.m. Deputy Henry Farr and City Marshall William Smith came to relieve O'Malley stating that "his undersheriff" had told them he needed help. That was according to O'Malley.

Farr, however, testified he had been asked "in town" to help by O'Malley, which he did about 8 p.m. He said he was joined about 10 p.m. by Smith, at which time the sheriff left. Smith's story varied slightly. He said he was summoned by Farr who was soliciting help for O'Malley and had arrived about 9:30. He also had O'Malley leaving at least two hours before O'Malley's claim of 11:45.[12]

The conclusion to the night's tragedy was depressingly like the attack at the bridge. Smith and Farr sat down to a game of "seven-up." In response to a knock on the door at about 1:00 a.m., Smith asked who was there. To the answer of "Walt" he unbarred the door to be greeted not by O'Malley, but by armed masked men. Though Smith reached for his gun at first, they both saw they were outnumbered. Two members of the gang took the keys, went to the darkened cell, shot the Italians, and fled, leaving the cell door unlocked. After the gang had left and slammed the front door, Farr and Smith fired several shots into the door and then went out to give a brief chase.

Dr. T.D. Baird and two or three other townsmen who lived three to four hundred yards from the jail, were first on the scene and saw to the removal of dead Andinino and Ronchietto, who soon died in great pain.

Sheriff O'Malley was apparently not summoned. He testified to having not returned to the jail until the next day after trying to track down the two Italians who had escaped during the bridge attack. In fact, beyond hearing Smith and Farr's testimony at the inquest into Andinino and Ronchietto's death, O'Malley testified to not even discussing the attack on the jail with them![13]

Indemnity

The incident had international implications and brief journalistic notoriety, but the road to the indemnity of $10,000 that Congress granted fifteen months later was not direct.

Immediately, questions came from Washington through Governor McIntire: Is there danger of further violence to Italians? How soon will the lynchers be brought to justice? What was the official citizenship of the victims?[14] Many of the official messages were published by newspapers.

The first news account of the sequence of events appeared in the Tuesday editions of the *Denver Republican* and *The Rocky Mountain News*. The *Republican* carried a brief account of the finding of Hixon, the bloodhound's tracking of four men, the expectation of the capture of two more without reference to the nationality of the suspects. The story noted that in Rouse, "The men are very much excited and say if they were sure of the man who struck the blow he would never hear the result of the inquest."[15] *The News* story, also on page one, listed nine obviously Italian suspects, included a paragraph on the possibility of lynching, and reported that Andinino would be charged with striking the fatal blow. This account described men scattered along the road to Walsenburg, but gave assurances that there was "scarcely a possibility" of violence.[16]

On the following day, with the jail attack coming so late, *The News*, *The Republican*, and now *The Pueblo Chieftain* carried only the story of the attack on the wagon. The accounts were inaccurate concerning the numbers transported or killed. Ironically, *The News* was optimistic about the maintenance of order: "The summary manner [of revenge]... will provoke considerable malice, but as none of the men lynched were men of families or older residents of this camp it is quite possible that open warfare will not occur."

Acting Consul Cuneo had become aware of the bridge attack, and his early Wednesday message to the governor - that two had been lynched and that seven more were in custody and required the governor's protection - was quoted in *The News* and *The Chieftain*.[17]

The "Italian Massacre" was a diplomatic event before its full effects were known. On Wednesday, there were twelve telegrams concerning it between Cuneo and McIntire; Cuneo and Baron Fava, the Italian Ambassador; the State Department and McIntire; and McIntire and Sheriff O'Malley. Fava even bypassed normal channels to wire McIntire directly. They were all reported in several newspapers.[18] By Thursday there were stories and quotations from officials in *The New York Times* and *The New York Tribune*. The front page accounts, with their diplomatic language, inaccuracies about the number of victims, and some imagined Western heroics, also reported visits of concern paid by Fava to Acting Secretary of State Edwin T. Uhl and by Cuneo to McIntire.[19] (While Baron Fava usually addressed Secretary Gresham, most communication from the State Department was from Uhl. On rare occasions, and apparently to add emphasis, Gresham wired McIntire himself. After Gresham's death on May 28th, Secretary Olney took a similar approach.)[20]

In this public fashion, Fava, Cuneo, and Uhl all asked McIntire about Walsenburg. McIntire passed the questions along to Sheriff O'Malley. McIntire's answers concerning the citizenship of the victims were tentative. Eventually, this tentativeness would become frustrating for the State Department. On March 14, McIntire, who had less than full cooperation from the district court clerk, Fred Roof, wired, "It is not yet known" whether the victims were Americans. The clerk of the district court had responded to the governor's question: "Wish you would consult your superintendent of irrigation and not me in matters affecting this county." He went on to state that two of the dead had "first citizen and probably second citizenship" papers, that Andinino's status was not known, and "it is asserted" that the two escapees had first papers. (Unlike most of the early telegrams, Roof's reply was not directly quoted by McIntire in his report to Washington.)[21]

McIntire forwarded the information to Gresham on March 16 and gave assurances that authorities would be speedy with arrest and conviction.[22] Confirmation of citizenship would wait a while. The question of the safety of other Italians waned with time and the absence of new violence.

The governor provided assistance aimed at prosecution. He

announced a $1,000 reward and wrote letters of introduction to Walsenburg for a visit by Consul Cuneo. Cuneo's satisfaction with McIntire's actions and the "course of authorities" at Walsenburg after his visit there were all reported to Baron Fava by the consul within a week. [23]

On March 14, *The Walsenburg World*, a weekly, anticipated Cuneo's visit, "In many particulars, this is a parallel to the case at New Orleans a few years ago." The next week's *World* described the visit of Dr. Cuneo (who was a practicing physician in Denver), finding him very much the gentleman with "very little of the foreign in his appearance and manner save the accent given to some of his words." The next week, Pietro Giacobino, who had wandered without food for four days, was found several miles east of Walsenburg near Cuchara and taken by Sheriff O'Malley to a hospital in Pueblo "as quietly as possible." The other ambush escapee, Antonio Cobetto, was reported seen near Cuchara, also.[24]

The question of citizenship and the search for justice

Cuneo's report to the ambassador told the story of the nine jailed, named the five attacked, recounted Cuneo's having talked to Giacobino at Cuchara and word of Cobetto. It also included verdicts of the Hixon inquest, accusing Andinino "and others," and the Vittone inquest, finding him the victim of "unknown persons." Cuneo also noted Vittone and Ronchietto's first papers. At this time the consul believed that a single horseman had made the bridge attack, and he took pains to point out that the deputies "made no resistance whatsoever." He made no judgment about the circumstance when seven men "penetrated into the county jail, deceiving the guard..." and had "no cause for complaint," with the authorities at his disposal and the governor's reward offer. He did observe that Sheriff O'Malley advised Giacobino "to say that he was a Frenchman" on their trip to Pueblo. Baron Fava, enclosing a translation of Cuneo's report, wrote Gresham that Cuneo's story had "never been contradicted" by any of the governor's telegrams. This "evidently settles the responsibility of the local authorities, and I... call the special attention of your excellency and... of the governor of the state to this responsibility, placing full reliance upon the impartiality of both for an equitable adjustment of this serious question."[25] Whatever Gresham's idea of an "equitable adjustment" might have been, on April 5, he pressured Governor McIntire on the issue of citizenship. Quoting the governor's inconclusive messages of March 15, 16, and 18, the secretary said, "...it will doubtless occur to you that the Department should be placed immediately in possession of any evidence tending to show the exact political status [of the victims]." He also stated concern for eventual justice.[26]

McIntire shared Gresham's concern but seemed to be at the mercy of others. On March 16th, District Attorney R.R. Ross had responded to the governor's urging for a quick investigation saying he was in the midst of an important criminal term in the county south of Huerfano and promising a thorough investigation. On April 11, McIntire wrote to Ross asking him to consult with the judge, Jesse Northcutt, concerning a special term of court. He also asked him to try to "ascertain the nationality... that I may answer [Washington's] questions." The same day he invited Dr. Cuneo to meet with him and bring "the documents you had the other day."[27] Whatever transpired with the consul and what his documents were have not come to light.

On April 12, McIntire, explained to Gresham that he had questioned the district attorney and had no more definitive answer on citizenship. He also reported having raised the question of a special term of the district court. Although he had been informed that schedules "prescribed in law" would not allow that, he felt "reassured" that the district attorney and judge would take appropriate action.[28]

On May 23, McIntire reminded Ross that he still needed citizenship information.[29] Then, on June 3, District Attorney Ross suddenly reported having received McIntire's April 12 request for citizenship information and a special court term. The letter had been addressed to the wrong county and rerouted twice. Ironically, Ross would pass the request for citizenship information to Clerk Fred Roof. On June 15, Roof confirmed from county records that the three dead men had not been United States citizens and the first papers of Ronchietto and Vittone.[30]

On the issue of a special term, Ross wrote in his June 3 response to the misdirected letter: "...when the district court convenes in Huerfano County (in October), or sooner if you desire, we will call a grand jury in order to make a thorough investigation of the lynchings... I will be in Denver some time during the month of June and see you in person."[31] As with the Italian consul, the governor's discussion with Ross is not recorded.

Anticipating some special judicial action, Richard Olney, who had succeeded Gresham as Secretary of State, found it necessary to explain to Baron Fava. Referring to a letter from the governor, the secretary wrote on June 25, "...it is difficult for one accustomed to proceedings in thickly settled communities to understand apparent delays in sparsely settled regions... The district court... embraces a large number of counties, in which the terms... are by law held at certain stated periods, generally with not more than two terms a year."[32]

While diplomatic records and the governor's files contain no reference to Walsenburg in July or August, Judge Northcutt wrote to the governor on September 13 expressing "no little annoyance" at court officers' inability to supply evidence. He then asked the governor for advice. Governor McIntire had been a district court judge before his election in 1894. Recognizing it as a case "peculiarly demanding the attention of a Grand Jury," Northcutt noted: "There is considerable objection on the part of the citizens of that county... on account of the additional expense, but I feel it is the only way to relieve the district attorney of the charge of dereliction of duty. I should be very glad to receive your views... I will probably hold court in Denver this coming week... and while there should be glad to call upon you... [I] thank you for frankly calling my attention to the subject. I feel myself, that on account of the international interest involved, an extra effort should be made."[33]

Whether at the advice of McIntire or not, at the October session of the district court, Northcutt called for a grand jury to convene in February, 1896. This was, he wrote, "contrary to the opinion of the leading citizens of Huerfano County." Two days later, the governor asked the Italian consul to visit about something he had received from Northcutt.[34]

There is no record of Cuneo's reaction to the delay or if he reported it to the ambassador. It appears from correspondence that Baron Fava was still unaware of the grand jury date on November 27th.[35]
While awaiting action in Colorado, the Italian embassy had acquired information from officials in Italy's Piedmont region, the birthplace of all five men attacked. On October 18th, Baron Fava wrote to Secretary Olney enclosing information on the families of all five and left it to "your high and benevolent appreciation to suggest the amount which may be deemed suitable to indemnify the families of the victims." While newspapers had recalled the $25,000 payment and the brief break in diplomatic relations in 1891 over New Orleans the embassy had not yet raised the possibility of indemnity. Of course, such a claim had been the reason for the concern about citizenship status. Acting Secretary Uhl wrote McIntire of Fava's observation and asked his views "as to the probable action of the State of Colorado."[36] Uhl's request of McIntire, a copy of which was sent to Fava, was strange and appears to have gone unanswered.

Witnesses

Perhaps the governor was diverted by the appearance of clues to the identity of the lynchers.
In October, Mary Welsby, whose son was the driver killed at the Bear Creek Bridge, wrote to the governor. She claimed that "deeply interested" officials were afraid to investigate her son's death and that Frank Olk, the German immigrant left alive in the jail attack, could "name every one of the murderers if proper protection is given him." Olk was by then serving a sixteen year sentence in the state penitentiary. After suggesting that the sheriff would not provide protection, she said one of the Italians who had escaped—presumably Pietro Giacobino—had told her, while at the Colorado Fuel and Iron Company Hospital in Pueblo that, "he knew all of the men who did the crime."[37]
Soon, the convict, Olk, addressed the governor directly. In a November 3rd letter, the prisoner, offered "to tell the names of the men who done the shooting as I known and saw them"

in return for his release and reward. He insisted on his inno-
cence of the rape for which he was imprisoned. McIntire took
Olk seriously enough to write to Warden John Cleghorn at
Canon City on November 14. Asking him to look into Olk's
story, he stated some reservations. "It is difficult to believe
that if... he is sure nobody saw the men except himself, it will
be probable to convict." A release would be unusual, he went
on, "and I cannot see justification... however anxious I may be
to bring a conviction."

Cleghorn wrote that Olk refused to give names or details
without a pardon. In a November 22, McIntire wrote Cleghorn
that he could not see his way clear to pursue Olk's testimony
because, "No witness of his standing and character with the
additional disadvantage of giving his testimony for a pardon
and also a reward, alone and uncorroborated, would have any
standing whatever in the mind of a jury."[38] Olk would not be
called before the grand jury.

As the grand jury session approached, the governor, if not
spearheading action, at least reacted to suggestions and information, especially if they came from Washington. In a December 7 letter, Mrs. Welsby had asked the governor for a
change of venue. On December 27, Secretary Olney relayed a
similar suggestion from Baron Fava. McIntire immediately
consulted with Colorado State Attorney General B.L. Carr
and wrote to Judge Northcutt. Northcutt's opinion, and apparently Carr's, was that "the action of a grand jury out of the
county would be null and void."[39]

At the same time, McIntire took initiative on another front.
He offered District Attorney Ross legal assistance from Attorney General Carr which Ross accepted.[40]

One last lead and an accusation

The governor's most surprising action was to provide Judge
Northcutt with the names of two suspects. Responding on
January 15 to Northcutt's opinion on the change of venue, and
assuring the judge that all of their communications were con-
fidential, he explained, "I have received information to the effect that two brothers by the name of Chown, one of whom
bears the Christian name of Bob... were implicated in the

lynching and... left Walsenburg and were, at least recently, in Lake City."

McIntire "supposed" he would give the information to Carr who would be assisting the prosecution. Northcutt wrote back on January 18 to ask if he should submit the names to the district attorney or leave that to the attorney general. Northcutt added that he had secured some information "that seems to be correct" though difficult to prove, but he did not share it with the governor. On January 28, McIntire requested Carr to stop in so they could "fix up the Walsenburg matter."[41]

How the governor was tipped to the Chown brothers is not known. Whether Frank Olk talked or another informant mentioned them did not matter, because, as with Olk, the Chown brothers were not heard before the grand jury when it met on February 11, 12, and 13. A George Chown was mentioned in testimony as having ridden from Rouse to Walsenburg with John Flemming. It was Flemming who had testified to being was one of the riders who had seen and heard nothing unusual on the road from Rouse. It was also Flemming who was accused before the grand jury by the crippled Giacobino of being the first hold-up man at the Bear Creek Bridge. Flemming, who had already testified, was recalled after the accusation and restated that Chown and a William Babbitt had ridden with him all the way from Rouse. Neither Chown nor Babbitt testified. It is apparent from the transcript that two different people questioned witnesses, but which questioner was Attorney General Carr is not indicated. It is possible that neither Carr nor District Attorney Ross had been given the Chown lead. Carr's official report to McIntire of his participation gave a brief and somewhat inaccurate summary of the lynchings, included a copy of the transcript, and made no mention of suspects.[42]

The only actual contradiction in testimony explored before the grand jury was that dealing with the timing and reason for the relief of the sheriff before the jail attack. As has been noted, the grand jury was unable to bring indictments.[43]

Even before the wheels of justice were ground to a halt in Colorado, the Italian embassy pursued indemnity. Neither Olney nor Fava was clear as to whose place it was to recommend, but on November 29th, the ambassador finally wrote asking Secretary Olney to state an amount. No amount appeared in correspondence, and in his January 30, 1896 report, "The Killing of Certain Italian Laborers," Olney only recommended that something be done, at the discretion of Congress, "to whom it can hardly be necessary to cite the statutes of many States of the Union fixing the maximum... in the case of death caused by negligence to be $5,000." President Cleveland's February 3 letter covering the report, urged some pecuniary provision for the injured and the families of the deceased "without discussing the question of the liability of the United States... by reason of treaty obligations or under the general rules of international law." This language would become standard. Congress did act, and on June 12th Secretary Olney presented Baron Fava with $10,000 "To the Italian government for full indemnity" and "without reference to the question of liability."[44]

Walsenburg and the other Italian lynchings

Of the incidents of lynched Italians for which the United States paid indemnities, the first, bloodiest and the one yielding the largest amount—$25,000—was that of New Orleans in 1891. The last indemnity was $6,000 for a 1910 Tampa attack that killed one person. By the time of the aftermath of the Florida lynching, discussion of indemnities had become negotiations. The Italian embassy readily suggested a dollar amount and the State Department debated the citizenship of the victim and his legal status in Italy. Due to this haggling, President Woodrow Wilson's recommendation to Congress concerning Tampa came three years after the event.

Walsenburg was a precedent in these negotiations. In 1897, Secretary John Sherman compared a lynching of three at Hahnville, Louisiana, to both New Orleans and Walsenburg and suggested $6,000 for the death of three Italians. Secretary John Hay, mentioning the Walsenburg "precedent" suggested some provision be made for victims of an 1899 Tallulah, Louisiana attack on five, of whom two were Italian citizens. Four thousand dollars was paid. In 1902, Theodore Roosevelt forwarded Hay's recommendation that some indemnity be provided for the death of two at Erwin, Mississippi. Hay had cited Walsenburg and Hahnville. Five thousand dollars was granted.[45]

Historiography of Walsenburg

The beginning, and perhaps the end, of recent historiography on Walsenburg is found in John Higham's *Strangers in the Land.* Citing a compilation of foreign relations documents and *The New York Tribune* of March 14, 1895, Higham offers: "Time and again, lynching parties struck at Italians charged with murder . . . .. In 1895, when the southern Colorado coal-fields were gripped by violent labor strife, a group of miners and other residents systematically massacred six Italian workers implicated in the death of an American saloon keeper."[46]

Several writers on the Italian experience have accepted and paraphrased Higham's interpretation. With slight variations - the lynchers are simply "miners," a mob, or "settlers" and the crime is sometimes "slaughtering." The theme, however, is still Higham's, with labor overtones and usually with the erroneous counting of six victims. In one account the victims are "six Italian labor agitators." Gaia Servadio in *Mafioso* (1976), correctly numbers three victims and omits reference to labor problems but incorrectly states that the victims had been acquitted of homicide. [47]

There is scant evidence for a labor-related interpretation of Walsenburg. There was barely a labor issue. In the midst of exaggerated headlines and stories about revenge and potential "race warfare" only one newspaper made even the slightest connection to labor. On 14 March 1895, the *Walsenburg World* observed that the motive for Hixon's murder was a mystery because he was so well-liked and in passing noted he had served as a deputy sheriff during the coal strike of the summer of 1894.[48] There had been a strike in mid-1894 that closed the Rouse mine over wages and payment with company scrip, but it was not the cause of reported violence.[49] Serving occasionally as a deputy was not unusual in Huerfano county. Joe Welsby, the driver killed at the bridge had been hired as a deputy for the day and authorized payments for occasional deputies were common in the proceedings of the County

Board of Commissioners.[50]

Lorenzo Andinino, Francesco Ronchietto, and Stanislao Vittone do not appear to have died for a cause. Their deaths seem an unfortunate manifestation of a what James Cutler might have called a "frontier" community in 1905. Some of Cutler's elements explaining lynching in more established societies were present. There was a "contrast in population," but the death of Hixon was not a case where "disreputable characters" would not be convicted for lack of evidence. And Rouse was, after all, a mining town and a tough one. The death of Hixon would not have been one of Cutler's "especially heinous crimes."

It is tempting to assume in Walsenburg the stereotypical nativist reaction to a feared immigrant minority threatening to overpower the community. The facts, however, show that the heavy wave of Italian immigrants would not hit Huerfano County's coal mines until after the turn of the century. By 1900, the Italian population of the county's more than 4,000 inhabitants was 163.[51]

Conclusion

The lynching at Walsenburg was an isolated event. Being part of any ethnic group would have been a handicap in that circumstance. The Italians had a language barrier. Interpreters were required at the Hixon inquest. They may well have admitted to more than they knew. Since they were largely without family and had lived in Rouse only a few years, they were without support in the face of an angry populace.

Beyond the loss of life, failure of prompt investigation may have been caused as much by unfortunate timing and incompetence or inexperience as by the callousness of Walsenburg's citizens and sheriff. Dr. Cuneo, who had no diplomatic training, had just been made acting consul in late January, 1895. McIntire was barely two months into his only term of statewide office. Secretary Gresham died in late May and official prodding from Washington ceased for two months.

Being strangers in the land helped kill Lorenzo Andinino and his countrymen, but there seems to be no evidence to add involvement in labor struggles or politics to their disadvantage. They may have been plagued by the same circumstances that took Italian lives in Louisiana, Mississippi, and Florida, but if generalizations about those episodes are as faulty as the ones about Walsenburg have been, more work needs to be done before conclusions are drawn.

The other Italian lynchings need study. The United States' practice of indemnifying foreign powers for failures to protect their nationals in various states has provided a convenient source of documentation, but that documentation alone is of limited value. It is not only selected publications of the Congress that illustrate the shortcomings of law enforcement in Walsenburg. It is unlikely that similar documents tell the full story of Hahnville, Erwin, and the others.

New work on the number, causes, and demography of lynching victims is needed. Research on pre-1900 events has continued to rely on Cutler's 1905 statistics, and little has been done on lynching since the 1930s. If anything, Cutler's numbers seem understated. Newer techniques might yield significant results and provide better understanding of the Italian circumstance.

---

[1] The spelling of names and places is standardized and based upon the best authority. For names, the form used by officials is used where available, and the Christian name appears before the family name.

[2] U.S. Cong., House, *Killing of Certain Italian Laborers in Colorado,* 54th Cong., 1st sess., H. Doc. 195 (Washington, D.C.: GPO, 1896), pp. 1-20; "A Report of the Grand Jury," of the 'Italian Massacre,'" 5 March, 1896, Correspondence of Governor Albert W. McIntire, Colorado State Archives, Denver, Colorado.

[3] Dr. Joseph Cuneo, Letter to A.W. McIntire, 13 Mar. 1895 Albert W. Correspondence of Governor McIntire, Colorado State Archives, Denver, Colorado; "Five Men Killed," *Rocky Mountain News* (Denver), 13 Mar. 1895, p. 1; *Killing of Certain Italian Laborers* p. 16.

[4] "Italy Inquires," *Rocky Mountain News,* 14 Mar. 1895, p. 1; *Killing of Certain Italians,* p. 4.

5 James E. Cutler, *Lynch-Law* (1905; rpt. New York: Negro Universities Press, 1969), pp. 1-2, 160-192, 259, 279.

6 "Caught by a Hound," *Rocky Mountain News*, 12 Mar. 1895, p.1; "Last Week's Tragedies," *Walsenburg World*, 21 Mar. 1895, p.1.

7 "Caught by a Hound," *Rocky Mountain News*, 12 Mar. 1895, p. 1; "Last Week's Tragedies," *Walsenburg World*. 21 Mar. 1895, p. 1; "Killed by a Mob," *Pueblo Chieftain*, 13 Mar. 1895, p. 1.

8 "Five Men Killed," *Rocky Mountain News*, 13 Mar. 1895, p. 1; "Killed by a Mob," *Pueblo Chieftain*, 13 Mar. 1895, p. 1; *Justice of the Peace Criminal Docket Book*, 11 Mar. 1895, Huerfano County Courthouse, Walsenburg, Colorado, Precinct 15, pp. 238-243.

9 "A Brutal Murder at Rouse," *Denver Republican*, 12 Mar. 1895, p. 1; "Caught by a Hound," *Rocky Mountain News*, 12 Mar., 1895, p. 1. "Grand Jury," pp. 1-66.

10 "Grand Jury," pp. 15-21, 53-62.

11 "Grand Jury," pp. 2-8, 38-51, 60-61; "Five Men Killed," *Rocky Mountain News*, 13 Mar. 1895, p. 1; "Shot from Ambush," *Denver Republican*, 13 Mar. 1895, p. 1; "Killed by a Mob," *Pueblo Chieftain*, 13 Mar. 1895, p. 1; "Cruel Work of a Colorado Mob," *New York Times*, 14 Mar. 1895, p. 1; "Italians Killed by a Mob," *New York Tribune*, 14 Mar. 1895, p. 1; "A Brutal Murder," *Walsenburg World*, 14 Mar. 1895, p. 1.

12 "Grand Jury," pp. 2-21.

13 "Grand Jury," pp. 2-37.

14 *Ibid.*, pp. 2-9.

15 "A Brutal Murder at Rouse," *Denver Republican*, 12 Mar. 1895.

16 "Caught by a Hound," *Rocky Mountain News*, 12 Mar. 1895, p. 1; "A Brutal Murder at Rouse," *Denver Republican*, 12 Mar. 1895, p. 1.

17 "Five Men Killed," *Rocky Mountain News*, 13 Mar. 1895, p. 1; "Killed by a Mob," *Pueblo Chieftain*, 13 Mar. 1895, p. 1; "Shot from Ambush," *Denver Republican*, 13 Mar. 1895, pp. 1, 5.

18 "A Mob of Avengers," *Denver Republican*, 14 Mar. 1895, p. 1, 3.

19 "Cruel Work of a Colorado Mob," *New York Times*; "The President is Pleased," *New York Times*, 14 Mar. 1895, p. 1, 18 Mar. 1895, p. 1; "Italians Killed by a Mob," *New York Tribune*, 14 Mar. 1895, p. 1.

20 *Killing of Certain Italians*, p. 10, 16, 19.

21 Fred Roof, Telegram to A.W. McIntire, 14 Mar. 1895, Correspondence of Governor McIntire; *Killing of Certain Italians*, p. 4.

22 *Killing of Certain Italians*, p. 6.

23 *Ibid.*, pp. 8-9.

24 "A Brutal Murder," *Walsenburg World*, 14 Mar. 1895, p. 1; "Last Week's Tragedies," *Walsenburg World*, 21 Mar. 1895, p. 1; "Escaped in the Dark," *Rocky Mountain News*, 18 Mar. 1895; "One Survivor has been Found," *Pueblo Chieftain*, 18 Mar. 1895; "The Affair at Walsenburg," *Denver Republican*, 19 Mar. 1895.

25 *Killing of Certain Italians*, pp. 8-9.

26 *Ibid.*, pp. 10-11.

27 Governor's Correspondence, Letter Press Book 11, Colorado State Archives, Denver, Colorado, pp. 234, 236.

28 *Killing of Certain Italians*, pp. 11-12.

29 Letter, A.W. McIntire to R.R. Ross, 23 May 1895, Letter Press Book 11, p. 441.

30 *Killing of Certain Italians*, p. 13.

31 *Ibid.*, p. 12.

32 *Ibid.*, p. 14.

33 Letter, J.G. Northcutt to A.W. McIntire, 9 Sept. 1895, Correspondence of Governor McIntire.

34 Letter, J.G. Northcutt to A.W. McIntire, 17 Oct. 1895, Correspndence of Governor McIntire; Letter, A.W. McIntire to J. Cuneo, 19 Oct. 1895. Letter Press Book 11, p. 248.

35 *Killing of Certain Italians*, p. 17.

36 "Italians Killed by a Mob," *New York Tribune*, 14 Mar. 1895; "A Mob of Avengers," *Denver Republican*, 14 Mar. 1895, p. 3; "Two More Killed," *Pueblo Chieftain*, 14 Mar. 1895, p. 1; *Killing of Certain Italians*, pp. 16-17.

37 Letter, Mrs. M.A. Welsby to A.W. McIntire, ? Oct., 1895, Correspondence of Governor McIntire.

38 Letters, F.G. Olk to A.W. McIntire, 3 Nov. 1895 and J. Cleghorn to A.W. McIntire, 16 Nov. 1895, Correspondence of Governor McIntire; A.W. McIntire to J. Cleghorn, 16 Nov. 1895 and 22 Nov. 1895, Letter

Press Book 12, p. 308, 342.

[39] Letter, Mrs. M.A. Welsby to A.W. McIntire, 7 Dec. 1895, J.G. Northcutt, 10 Jan. 1896, Correspondence of Governor McIntire; *Killing of Certain Italians*, p. 19.

[40] Letter, R.R. Ross to A.W. McIntire, 28 Dec. 1895, Correspondence of Governor McIntire.

[41] Letter, A.W. McIntire to J.G. Northcutt, 15 Jan. 1896, to B.L. Carr, 28 Jan. 1896, J.G. Northcutt to A.W. McIntire, 28 Jan. 1896, Leter Press Book 12, pp. 448, 476, 478.

[42] Letter with transcript, B.L. Carr to A.W. McIntire, 3 Mar. 1896, Correspondence to Governor McIntire.

[43] "Grand Jury," pp. 58-62.

[44] U.S. Cong., House, *Papers Relating to the Foreign Relations of the U.S.*, 54th Cong., 1st sess., H. Doc. 1, Pt. 2 (Washington, D.C.: GPO, 1896), p. 426.

[45] Luciano J. Iorizzo, "Italian Immigration and the Impact of the Padrone System," Diss. Syracuse 1966, pp. 212-214; U.S. Cong., House, *Angelo Albano* 63rd Cong., 1st Sess., H. Doc. 105, pp. 1-3; *Heirs of Certain Italians*, 55th Cong. 1st Sess., H. Doc. 37, pp.1-3; *Lynching of Certain Italian Subjects at Tallulah, Louisiana*, 56th Cong., 2nd Sess., S. Doc. 194, pp. 1-5; *Killing of Italian Subjects at Erwin, Mississippi*, 57th Cong., 2nd Sess., pp. 1-2.

[46] John Higham, *Strangers in the Land: Patterns of American Nativism 1860-1925* (New Brunswick, N.J.: Rutgers University Press, 195), p. 91.

[47] Alexander DeConde, *Half-Bitter, Half-Sweet: An Excursion into Italian-American History* (New York: Charles Scribner's Sons, 1971), p. 125; Patrick J. Gallo, *Old Bread, New Wine: A Portrait of the Italian-Americans* (Chicago Nelson-Hall, 1981), p. 126; Luciano J. Iorizzo and Salvatore Mondello, *The Italian-Americans* (Boston: Twayne Publishers, 1980), pp. 82-83; Richard Gambino, *Blood of My Blood: The Dilemma of the Italian-Americans*, (Garden City, Doubleday and Company, 1977) pp. 138-139; Vincent N. Parrillo, *Strangers to These Shores: Race and Ethnic Relations in the United States*, 2nd. ed., (New York: John Wiley and Sons, 1985) pp. 98-99; Gaia Servadio, *Mafioso: A History of the Mafia from its origins to the Present Day* (New York: Stein and Day, 1976), p. 56.

48 "A Brutal Murder," *Walsenburg World*, 14 Mar. 1895, p. 1.

49 Colorado Bureau of Labor Statistics, *Biennial Report 1893-1894* (Denver, Smith-Brooks Printing Co., 1894), p. 245; Scamehorn, *Pioneer Steelmaker*, p. 121.

50 *Proceedings of the Huerfano County Board of County Commissioners*, Book E, Huerfano County Courthouse, Walsenburg, Colorado, April, July, and October sessions, 1895, not. numbered.

51 U.S. Cong., House, *Compendium of the Tenth Decennial Census*, 47th Cong., 1st Ses., H. Misc. Doc. 64, Table XXIII; *Compendium of the Eleventh Census*, 52nd Cong., 1st Sess., H. Misc. Doc. 340, Table XIII; U.S. Census Office *Twelfth Census of the U.S., Census Reports* (Washington: U.S. Census Office, 1901), vol. 1, p. 495. Colorado Commissioner of Census, *Census of Colorado, 1885* (Denver CO, 1885), Table 1.

Drops within the Social River: Many Idioms of the Shopfloor from an Italian Perspective

Ferdinando Fasce
University of Genoa

Dealing with the American working class memory may prove at the same time frustrating and misleading. The frustration stems from the crucial importance this society has traditionally attached to modernity, change, and mobility to the point that it seems as if in some way America is striving to organize amnesia. This appears especially true for minorities and historical experiences which for different reasons of oblivion or censorship could not easily find a place within the mainstream of the legitimated past.[1] On the other hand, this situation can make the historian vulnerable to the very opposite danger, that is to *overemphasize* the significance of those scattered pieces of living memories that oral sources are able to unearth.

New developments in the field of immigration history show how both the problems mentioned above can be overcome when an appropriate use of oral testimonies is skillfully combined with other, more traditional sources.[2] Such studies find an important parallel in a number of recent contributions from European oral historians dealing with their own national working class memories. These stress the need for a more accurate examination of realms such as meaning, subjectivity, and language in the analysis of non-hegemonic classes. In order to do this, an extensive use is made of instruments taken from both the anthropologist's and literary critic's toolbox.[3]

Though framed to some extent in this rich current debate, this paper has much more limited goals. It is based on four life stories, two collected by Jeremy Brecher, and two by myself, of Italian workers who were connected to a brass company, the Scovill Manufacturing Company of Waterbury,

Connecticut, between 1916 and 1925. Scovill employed between 6,000 and 13,000 workers during that period from various nationalities, of whom the largest percentage (about 20%) were Italian. The interviews are part of a more comprehensive project aimed at reconstructing the history of the factory and of its immigrant workers (many of whom were from a handful of villages around Benevento and Potenza) from 1900-1925 by using business, labor, federal and state records.[4] Here, however, I limit myself to investigating a few aspects of their peculiar narrative form (self-presentation strategy, plot, velocity) and of the culture that underlies them. This approach will illustrate dimensions of workers' lives that may elude more structural or aggregate perspectives. It will help us to understand how the Italian-American individual and collective identity has been made and remade over a given period of time.[5]

"The Right Way, in the Halls, Not in the Streets"

Pasquale (Pat) De Cicco, the first informant, worked at Scovill in his youth during World War I.[6] He was interviewed in 1985 in his Waterbury office where, at the age of 85, he still practiced law. When asked about his life, he started his account with a vivid memory of his experience as a student at New York University's Law School, where in the 1920s, he was a classmate of Vito Marcantonio and had a close relationship with Fiorello La Guardia, who had also studied there. Firmly centered on law and ethnic politics, De Cicco's story is pervaded by a strong sense of decision and iron will. This latent *Bildung* scheme, however, never superimposes on facts like a linear evolution or a destiny marked by some sudden sign of inspiration. Instead, gradual steps and discontinuities appear throughout a description that revolves around two fundamental sources of continuity and support, kinship and ethnicity.

It is the family that in February 1916 introduces fifteen year-old Pat into Scovill. As part of the large influx of immigrant workers flooding the Naugatuck Valley during these war boom years, young De Cicco left his mother and younger brother and sisters in New York, where the whole family had settled four years earlier coming from native Casteldono (Benevento), and moved to Waterbury. Here he joined his father and older brother, Gus, who worked both at Scovill and in his spare time as a barber. At the Italian barber shop Gus introduced Pat to a man from the Scovill employment office, a department newly established to coordinate the company's burgeoning payroll (see appendix).

As is evident from the records of Scovill and other firms, this method of hiring was quite common. No less common was the practice of adding a few years onto one's age. Pat claimed he was sixteen instead of fifteen to evade the Connecticut state law on child employment. Before long this was to create his "first difficulty." In the atmosphere of the preparedness mobilization, "when people's ordinary life became more than burdensome for the reason that all males over a certain age had to register for the Army draft [...] it became very difficult to part with so many friends presumably of my own age. Some of them never returned." This is the only sad note of the whole part of the narrative dealing with the almost three years De Cicco spent at Scovill. Underlying this attitude is something more than the usual nostalgia for one's youth. De Cicco "was glad to be employed...and help my family" as part of a reciprocal relationship which brought him not only material but emotional support. In fact,

> [...] at the end of the month, the envelope bearing the weekly pay in cash, included a ten percent cash bonus for the total month. This so-called bonus worked very much to my advantage because my mother, bless her soul, allowed me to keep the ten percent monthly bonus, with which I bought some wonderful volumes from the Every Man's Library [...] [and] lot of books in Italian from the then famous Libraria del Progresso Italo-Americano.

Thanks to a fortunate concurrence of his age, his position in the family life cycle, and his own personal temperament, De Cicco came to see his situation at Scovill as a temporary one. Not only did this help him to endure the long hours and establish good terms with his room foreman, but after some time spent "on a kid's job," on a bench, he felt encouraged to ask the boss "to give me something more, something higher

...become a checker...and get a raise." Apparently, the reason
given for this request proved convincing:

"I said: 'The reason is I bought these books [...] and
besides I wanna be a lawyer,' because I had read a law
correspondence course ad saying 'how to become a
lawyer.'"

In view of these facts, one can understand the mixed feelings De Cicco displays when after these rapid glimpses at war
time in Scovill, he hastened to talk about the post-war period.
On the one hand, concern emerges for the situation he had to
face because of Scovill's tough months: "at the end of the war
the shops closed up. I couldn't find a job anywhere." But immediately other, apparently deeper emotions come to the surface. Shortly after the Armistice was signed, at the end of a
big victory parade which was to earn a long article and a picture in the *Scovill Bulletin*, the company's official publication,[7] the body of a pig dressed in a Kaiser helmet was
brought to the cemetery. Pat helped his brother Gus to transport the body, something no one else would do because of the
Spanish influenza epidemic. Pat caught the influenza "and
laid in bed for three days and read a lot." In a kind of rite of
passage De Cicco "first learned the importance of Italian literature" and became acquainted with what was to become
soon his favorite poet, Giacomo Leopardi. The informant re-
cites Leopardi's *A Silvia* at length and by praising the "Italian
literary ingenuity" for a moment he turns the discourse into
what oral historians call a "bridge." This is a shift from an
anecdote to a more general view. In this case it serves the
function of casting a retrospectively legitimating light on De
Cicco's efforts to climb up. As a descendant of the Italian cultural community, he seems entitled to exploit fully whatever
educational opportunity American society could offer.[8]

Soon, though, the ethnic factor resumes a more prosaic tone
as the informant described how in 1919 he was apprenticed by
his older brother at an Italian barber shop in New York. Work
as a barber first in New York and then again in Waterbury at
his brother's newly established shop and increasing portions
of time devoted to study, thanks to his family's help, form the
core of what follows. From this point on De Cicco's personal
advancement runs parallel to what he calls the "progress of

Italians" in Waterbury. This expression means that during the 1920s and especially in the following decade Italians gradually learned "to do it the right way, in the halls, not in the streets" and acquired an ever increasing reputation within the social and political circles of this "Irish town" ("in the meantime the Irish allowed us to go anywhere").

Now the factory disappears completely from the story. When asked about the spontaneous immigrants' strikes of 1919 and 1920 which hit Scovill after some 20 years of successful open shop, all De Cicco recalls is just one "Dr. Verde...who saved the life of a man who was wounded." Yet what he does recall and give us as a final sign of his deep-seated interest and respect for labor and "people, even the lowest of the low" proves no less illuminating of Waterbury workers' lives in the 1920s. In 1922, while De Cicco was in the fourth year of high school, Carlo Tresca, the renowned radical militant, visited the city and spoke at the Springfield Street Hall. He was introduced by the Di Cicco brothers. Unbeknownst to Pat, one local newspaper said it was the De Cicco brothers who had introduced him. The next day the school's principal singled out Pat and asked him to explain the phrase: "The laborer is worthy of his hire." In our informant's words, "I must have read something about labor, Gompers, Debs, so I said: 'The worker should get respect for his function just as capital does,' for which I was heavily blamed." That afternoon, skimming through the newspaper, De Cicco discovered that the principal had grilled him because he thought Pat had introduced Tresca. And again it was his brother's good connections, in this case at the newspaper, that helped settle the trouble. As we shall see, the other informants would have hardly failed to recognize in the episode a direct bearing on what they had just experienced or were experiencing in those very years behind the factory gates.

"They Would Fire Us"

It would be interesting to know whether Pat De Cicco was ever visited, while staying at his bench, by another Italian immigrant who also spent the years 1916-18 at Scovill "pushing a little truck and bringing the goods and products from one department to another." [9] His name was Mario De Ciampis. He was born in a small Southern Italian village, Morcone, in the province of Benevento, and he had emigrated to New York in 1912 at the age of 18. Like De Cicco, in 1916 he joined his brother, who was already in Waterbury, coming from New York in search of a job. For him too the Scovill experience was a temporary one, but for quite different reasons from those mentioned by his younger fellow worker. The answer lies with those pages of the *Scovill Bulletin* warning workers against "spies and lies" (i.e., labor organizers). The *Bulletin* urged them to "be a detective," by following the example of the company's employment department which informed the local police against any alleged radical. As a secretary of the local branch of the Federazione Socialista Italiana (FSI), De Ciampis did fit the model of the "spy and lie" perfectly. In his own words, in 1918 "before they would arrest me because I was working in the shop, I quit the job and I went to New York because they (company's management) were looking for me."

A sincere, lifelong commitment to social change marks the whole account, that unfortunately is much more fragmented than the other ones because of the informant's very poor health at the time the testimony was collected (De Ciampis died shortly after the interview took place). After a few, cursory references to the native village, what emerges from this testimony is a careful selection of data regarding the informant's gradual self-education as a radical militant. This developed first in Naples, where he was employed as an errand boy at the municipal telephone company, then in New York. Having originally emigrated with an aunt who crossed the Atlantic to join her sons, De Ciampis, before long, came into contact with such leading figures of the FSI as Flavio Venanzi and Angelo Faggi and in 1915 he was elected secretary of the New York section of that organization. Shortly afterwards the attractive labor market of the war industry centers pulled him to Waterbury, where he "was well known... already" in local radical quarters.

Without any further mention of either his family or his private matters (his brother appears briefly only a couple of times and in both cases as a member or sympathizer of the

FSI), De Ciampis' narrative definitely focuses on his efforts to "form our own group" in Waterbury. Any single aspect of the work experience, including the character of the job, is seen as an opportunity to be seized in order to set up a class organization. In fact, De Ciampis notes, by moving "from one department to another...I knew Scovill...I knew every fellow at Scovill." Interestingly enough, no use of such abstract notions as "class" or "proletariat" is made. Instead, ethnicity does come into a picture made up of concrete people within concrete situations. Due to the language barrier, at Scovill and elsewhere, even within the leftist ranks, "every nationality had its own group." But the basic roots of this "circle of recognition" had to be found at that very level, the native province or village, which the most recent ethnic studies have been disclosing as one of the persistent crucial pillars of immigrants' lives in their new country. The members of the De Ciampis group came "mostly from provinces Foggia, Avellino, and Benevento... From provincia di Foggia...all of them more or less they were relatives, close friends, more or less they all knew each other, stuck together."

By taking advantage of whatever source of help, be it "a friendly restaurant or a supportive store," the ethnic network might offer, the small but active radical group looked at the larger Italian colony as one major target for its activities. And here it came to clash with the Catholic church and with the *prominenti* who controlled most of the mutual aid societies organized by the province or town of origin with a heavy nationalistic perspective. At an ideological level the contrast could not be more profound:

> In those days we were not quite in good relations with those people on the right. They hated us... I never belonged to those societies because most of them were in the hands of [...] mutualistic ideas and we never could stay with them because we were socialist. They mostly more or less had nationalistic ideas we couldn't agree on that thing.[10]

However, De Ciampis implicitly acknowledges the powerful role which at least some of these institutions and, more often, some individuals, especially those who had close relationships with the native establishment, played on their fellow countrymen's behalf. Such was the case with one Mrs. Besozzi, who headed the Italian branch of the conservative National Civic League for Immigrants, "a private enterprise on behalf of the Italians that requested their help."[11] Mrs. Besozzi "was an honest, a very honest person and she treated everybody well. She was never on the side of the bosses. She treated good in a nationalist way." Likewise, Luigi Scalmana, the Catholic editor of the Italian conservative weekly, *Il Progresso del New England*: "really he was a spy for the companies, but we (De Ciampis' group) were his best friends, he respected us, we respected him." Moreover, during the 1920 strike Scalmana, who was well acquainted with Scovill's owners and with some prominent political figures of the city, performed a controversial but significant role as a community leader, a fact that De Ciampis grasps with great subtlety: "They [nationalists like Scalmana] had to take part in the strike because they were nationalists, not in the sense that they believed it politically, but that they tried to help everybody that needed to be helped."

At the head of a strike he had tried to avoid in every way, conservative Scalmana endeavored to give a moderate interpretation of a vicarial function, filling a void left by the physical absence from the scene of labor and radical organizers like De Ciampis. Behind that absence there lay the constant threat of being fired and arrested, which forms one of the central, recurrent themes of this life story: "As soon as they spotted us, we were thrown out, they would fire us." "If I had come back [in 1919] they would arrest me right away." "If you were well known as a radical agitator, you would never get a job to be reemployed." All such claims find substantial confirmation in the long list of arrests and deportations that marked the two strikes. And yet, if we are to give credit to both the files of the Federal Department of Justice and the records of the Scovill employment office, at least a few members of the De Ciampis' group were still active, largely at an underground level, among the "radical persuasion" in Waterbury until the end of the second strike.[12] This may explain part of what our next informant is going to tell us about that fight.

"I Lose the Case, I Lose My Brother"

James Tiso, the third informant, did not work at Scovill.[13] In fact, he spent some 35 years as a tube mill laborer at Chase, another major brass company in the Naugatuck Valley. Yet, during the 1920 strike Scovill was to play a crucial role in his life. At its gates, during a dramatic clash between the strikers and the mounted squad of the company's private police, his younger brother Libero (19 years old) was shot dead. It comes as no surprise, then, that the strike emerges as a landmark, a climactic moment around which seven years of hardships and difficulties ("we all [our family] came in 1913... and that's what America it is, if you were a working man you couldn't make that money") crystallize and precipitate.

The narrative of this event opens with the description of the strikers' meeting which took place the very day before the demonstration that was to end so tragically. Here Luigi Scalmana, the editor of *Il Progresso del New England* whom De Ciampis had depicted as a "spy for the companies" occupies the center of the stage. But in Tiso's words the qualifications used by the radical militant ("he's never done us any harm") give way to a vehement tirade against Scalmana the traitor who "finished the meeting...go to the police station...go rapport [sic] what is gonna be happening tomorrow to the police...gonna be happening a big strike, we're gonna shut down at Scovill."

Adequate evidence regarding the specific claim made by Tiso is lacking in any available published or unpublished record. Nonetheless, the episode is quite revealing on two grounds. First, it contributes to set the kind of epic and religious tone which characterizes the whole narrative and which is consistent with the informant's avowed strong religious sentiments and sense of transcendent destiny ("[one] figured that way, but the devil figured another way"). This is clearly revealed by the scene which follows immediately. It shows the Scovill police fired on the crowd and then "put my brother [...] on the truck, hanging him on like a pig [...] hung up like a dog." In this context one can hardly miss how Scalmana-Judas serves as an appropriate contrasting character to young Tiso-Christ.

Even more importantly, the violent attack against the ethnic "big wheel" echoes the reshuffling of allegiances and loyalties which the strike brought about within the Italian colony. Despite its tremendous material and psychological costs, the struggle, far from representing a mere source of disruption, is perceived and recalled as a crucible which contributed to redefine the bonds of identification and social belonging along new lines first through the parades and strike meetings ("they joined at Scovill, they joined at American Brass, they joined at Chase"), then through the extraordinary solidarity expressed by "all Polish people, all Italian people, French, Germans, all mixed." Before and after the impressive funeral given his brother, James Tiso and his family could grasp a sense of oneness ("we had all combination of people") that went well beyond the traditional limited scope of one's neighborhood or mutual aid society.

This proved all the more striking when contrasted with the refusal of the local Italian Catholic church to bury the young striker on consecrated ground because he had been involved in an armed clash. Backed by their Lithuanian and Russian fellow workers, Italian strikers joined James Tiso in his appeal to the archbishop ("I'm a Catholic... What kind of a law is this?"), which ultimately won him permission to give his brother a consecrated grave.

The impulse that led Tiso to go against his religious mentor, Father Felix Scoglio, the local assistant pastor, is but one example of the many, unpredictable (and sometimes contradictory) relationships between professed values and behavior that the unusual openness of the strike situation and the wide circulation of novel catchwords and practices created. So, for example, Tiso repeatedly rejects any specific political label that might have been attached either to him or to his brother ("We don't say we're anarchists, Fascists, or Communists ... Was [my brother] an anarchist? Was he a Bolshevik?"). Rather, he reemphasizes their common Catholic faith that, thanks to its universality, was supposed to earn them respect and legitimation within American society ("I am a Catholic... He [his brother] was a Catholic like the rest of the people in America"). But when it comes to recalling the strike meetings his most appreciative remarks are devoted to an avowed Italian anarchist who, through his inflammatory speech to an audience of "green" immigrants, "opened the eyes of the people in the state of Connecticut" and for that reason was immediately arrested and expelled from the city. By the same token, the powerful and dramatic image of Libero Tiso's funeral is dominated by "one German fellow, big guy, he wouldn't cave in to nobody. He wasn't scared to talk. He picked on the city, on the police, on the shop, on how they treated the people, how they really are in this America." Then, suddenly this stunning exhibition of workers' solidarity which struck any local observer fades into a hopeless admission of impotence:

> Now I passed lot of troubles ... because I had to watch my family, I had my kids, I had my wife. What had I got to do with my family? ... We've got no credit and that's what America is; you look by yourself.

Incidentally, it is of some interest to contrast this statement with what another Scovill employee, an English skilled toolmaker who served as a strike breaker in the State Guard during the 1919 strike, would say while trying to explain why he preferred his new country to the old world: "You were more on your own here." More to the point in our case, however, Tiso's words, seemingly so "private," do overshadow, without any mention of the further development of the strike, what happened early in July 1920, only a few days after Libero Tiso's funeral. Almost starved by a three-month strike carried out with no support on the part of the native skilled workers, the immigrant workers had to give up. Hence the isolation of the immigrant family which is portrayed while experiencing the impact of the strike in all its traumatic consequences ("you look by yourself").

Any horizontal source of identity having been shattered in the pacified factories of the "lean years," Tiso turned back to the ethnic colony and resorted to Judge Mascolo, a prominent member of the Italian community, to bring the case against Scovill to court. But lack of money and the fact that Mascolo "the big wheel in Waterbury he did not wanna hit the other people in Waterbury" frustrated such efforts.

Going back to his job "in Chase smoke" 30-year-old Tiso was never to forget the mixed lesson of sorrow ("I lose the case, I lose my brother"), independence ("the company did not want to give it to you. What you do? You call a strike") and submission ("[Scovill] shut off all your ways") learned in 1920. In his own concluding remarks, "[when you organize], you just keep your mouth well shut ... that's why the union go little by little."

"La Fattoria Era Grande"

Nel 1924 ero a Scovill nel buff room. Mi hanno dato certi lavoretti nel cosmetics on piece work, a stajo...ogni tante dozzine che fai, o migliaia se sono pezzi piccoli... The boss and the time setters already in 1924 fissavano, davano i tempi... Il boss era Irish... La fattoria era grande, se io era in una room, non potevo andare nelle altre. Se ti pessavano, ti dicevano; you don't belong over here. Ma non erano persona che ti mandavano via... Erano i bossi, ma c'erano pure i bossi bravi che comprendevano. Se facevi il tuo lavoro, facevi lo time, col boss non ho avuto mai problemi. A me mi volevano bene perche il lavoro lo facevo sempre bene, non era mai rigettato ... Ci potevi ragionare. Non dovevi parlare di unioni, ma ci potevi ragionare. Se eri nell'unione, ti mandavano via.[14]

This is how Scovill appeared four years after the big strike to John Zampino, our last informant. When he was first hired, in 1924, he was not a "green horn." He had crossed the Atlantic three years earlier, at 17, from his native Montagano (Campobasso) to join an uncle of his who lived in Waterbury. Through the usual channel of kinship ("c'era il marito di mia cugina che era l'operatore, io facevo l'aiutante") just one week after his arrival he was able to secure a job at the local clock shop. Then, three years later "un provinciale," that is a person from the same province of origin, told him about an opening at Scovill. Here Zampino worked for some time, was put on layoff, and then returned on a steady basis in 1927. He was to spend over forty years within that buff department.

A typical blue collar worker, the informant opens his account with an accurate description of the job ladder at Scovill, which places his room at a middle level in the overall skill hierarchy within the plant. Work is the keyword and the fulcrum around which the whole narrative is organized. After a few, quick memories of his "transatlantic passage" and of the arrival at Waterbury, Zampino dwells upon the multifaceted reality of the shopfloor in the 1920s, with its ambiguous interplay of both cooperation and conflict: "erano i bossi, ma c'erano pure i bossi bravi che comprendevano"; "non dovevi parlare di unioni, ma ci potevi ragionare."

Special attention is given to how a particular productive problem was solved or to the different degrees of complexity and variety one job required of the operator. So, for example, Zampino explains how much more varied and challenging the work at Scovill was than that at the clock shop: "Nel clock shop era sempre lo stesso lavoro, a Scovill c'erano tanti lavoretti, cosmetics, carri, lampade, un lavoro vario, più esperienza e piu moneta." This emphasis may appear surprising, given the unskilled or semiskilled nature of the job content, which the informant repeatedly stresses ("nel buff room la maggioranza erano Italiani e Polacchi e pure Irish perche tutti lavori pesanti, sprochi"). However, it is consistent with other oral historians' findings on the importance which people ascribe to any kind of "tacit skills," that is know-how or "instinct of workmanship," which one job requires, even in the case of seemingly marginal operations.[15] From this perspective the above mentioned passages on piece-work and productivity receive noticeable qualifications. To be able to meet a time or a quality requirement, to learn the tricks of a trade or to appreciate its most minute aspects, all these were fundamental assets for giving coherence and meaning to one's work experience, as well as forging those "invisible handshakes"[16] with the foreman which might serve as a barrier against the latter's all too common arbitrary practices. Nor was this attitude devoid of any commitment to a "sting," probably defined on a collective informal basis by the work group:

"Ho sempre pensato: I don't believe che devi lavorare come una bestia. Su otto ore ho sempre pensato che se lavori sei e mezza li basta... I've always believed a fair day's work for a fair day's pay."

Working at Scovill in the 1920s for someone who could neither nurture aspirations for climbing the occupational ladder to professional respectability nor leaned on any sort of "radical persuasion" was a complex exercise in physical and emotional investment, as well as in self-restraint, partial overlapping of interests with the boss, but an unfailing search for small portions of autonomy. Shifting his attention beyond the factory gates for a moment, Zampino proudly recalls how he became a citizen in an absolutely autonomous manner from the company, its English classes, its Americanization campaigns. When he first applied for a job at Scovill he had already gotten his first papers and before long at the local municipal night schools he learned the constitutional notions that would enable him to take his second papers. With that came a formal right that he hastened to exercise: "And right away I started to vote, in 1928. I didn't vote for Hoover, but I don't recall for whom I did vote." This right was completely severed from the workplace, as its treatment in the informant's memory reflects. It would have taken some time before the aegis of citizenship and the law, on one hand, and the "tacit skills" of the job, on the other, would come to mutually reinforce each other, laying the foundations for a collective expression of workers' identity. This happened in 1933, at the time the unionizing drive sweeping the country also reached Scovill. On that occasion Zampino urged his fellow workers to organize:

> "Io l'ho detto: c'è la legge [NRA], siamo tutti compagni, eravamo tanti di Campobasso, Italiani, non possono mandarci via tutti e mettere qui gli studenti, non sanno farlo, il lavoro."[17]

Conclusions

Given the distinctive self-presentation strategy and structure that any single testimony has shown, it is tempting to put each of them into a specific sociological pigeon-hole: self-advancement (De Cicco), class consciousness (De Ciampis), "primitive rebelliousness" (Tiso), and permanent integration into a blue collar condition (Zampino). However easy generalizations strain hard against a closer look at the materials presented here. Through their articulated mixture of facts and emotions encompassing "what...[people] wanted to do, what they believed they were doing, what they think now that they did,"[18] the historian gains access to many different layers of memory, human experience, and language coexisting, over-lapping and mutually reinforcing or opposing each other. These, in turn, reflect the several competing values and cultures immigrant workers had been exposed to daily in their interaction with separate realms of reality (the factory, the ethnic community, etc.) and the ways they would manipulate such values to interpret this many-fold reality.

Thus, behind the success story one can easily single out the decisive contribution of kinship and ethnicity that first made possible and then smoothed the transition of the social actor from Scovill to the New York University Law School. Along-side these two factors a persistent sense of "peoplehood" sur-faces, both a deeply felt commitment to one's roots and a com-pensation for the adjustments and psychological costs which the not easy path of moving up required. In De Ciampis' ac-count, far from embodying any monolithic or static notion of solidarity, class consciousness emerges as a process, firmly rooted in ethnicity, and thus open to the ambivalent potential for both horizontal and vertical relationships which ethnic in-stitutions possess. On the other hand, Tiso's case shows how, under given circumstances, kinship and collective mobiliza-tion shaped on the shopfloor may converge and trigger class sentiments, neutralizing and bypassing the vertical aspects of the ethnic enclave. It also demonstrates how such sentiments may find expression through an "unorthodox" religious idiom that helps to reconcile them with more traditional and proba-bly deeper convictions. Nor do hard work and discipline nec-essarily mean subalternity and consensus. Rather, as is clear from Zampino's testimony, the tacit skills one is able to de-velop on a terrain where class lines do overlap and blur, forges a sense of self-esteem that does not exclude some form of commitment to one's fellow workers and ultimately forms the difference between an employee and a worker.

Appreciation of the flexible use which people make of any kind of cultural fragments in order to give coherence to their lives, in the continuous tension between present and past selves, has three consequences for the continuation of our re-search. The first is the need for a critical reassessment of our assumptions about social action. Can we still take more or less explicitly the notion of "working class" for granted or are we to stretch the point made so forcefully by E.P. Thompson and other historians further and dig into the molecular components of a collective identity, in search of how the web of material conditions and human agency leads individual trajectories to intersect and diverge? Next, and consequently, comes the impulse to extend the inquiry into those struggles over meaning[19] that cut across individuals and social groups and that are best typified here by the different interpretations of the word "citizen" Zampino and his employer would give or by the distinctive uses of the term "law" that each informant makes.

Finally, there is the problem of contextualization. The examination of the formal aspects of these life stories as put forth here calls for further textual analysis, including, for example, comparisons with the structure of written autobiographies.[20] Yet, at this point what is especially needed is a more accurate exploration of an aspect, which in our case, has been deliberately reduced to a minimum, that is the larger social setting within which our testimonies should be properly placed by combining them with other qualitative and quantitative sources. Once again the discipline of context claims its rights, and justly so.[21]

---

[1] M. H. Frisch, "The Memory of History," *Radical History Review* (25, 1981); M. Debouzy, "In Search of Working-Class Memory," *History and Anthropology* 2 (March 1986); J. Bodnar, "Symbols and Servants," *Journal of American History* 73 (March 1986).

[2] Bodnar, *Immigration and Industrialization*, (Pittsburgh, University of Pittsburgh Press, 1977); E. Morawska, *For Bread With Butter*, (Cambridge, Cambridge University Press, 1985); G. R. Mormino, *Immigrants on the Hill* (Urbana, Ill., University of Illinois Press, 1986); G. R. Mormino & G.E. Pozzetta, *The Immigrant World of Ybor City* (Urbana, University of Illinois Press, 1987).

[3] E. Thompson, *The Voice of the Past* (Oxford, Oxford University Press, 1978); L. Passerini, *Torino operaia e fascismo* (Bari, Laterza, 1984); A. Portelli, *Biografia di una citta* (Turin, Einaudi, 1985); M. Gribaudi, *Mondo operaio e mito operaio*, (Turin, Einaudi, 1987); De-

bouzy, *op. cit.*

4 The years covered by our testimonies form a crucial period in the process of modernization of Scovill. On this point see F. Fasce, "Bureaucracy, Ethnicity, and Class," *Rivista di Studi Angloamericani* 3 (September 1985).

5 R. J. Vecoli, "The Search for an Italian American Identity," *Ibid.*

6 Pasquale De Cicco, interview by Jeremy Brecher and Ferdinando Fasce Waterbury, Ct., October 7, 1985.

7 Scovill Collection II (hereafter cited as SC II), vol. 313a, Baker Library, Harvard Business School, Boston, Mass.

8 R. Gribaudi, "Storia orale e struttura del racconto autobiografico," *Quaderni storici* 13 (Sept. Dec. 1978); W. Boelhower, *Immigrant Autobiography in the United States* (Venezia, Essedue, 1982); 74-75.

9 Mario De Ciampis, interview by Jeremy Brecher, Waterbury, Nov. 24, 1984, courtesy Jeremy Brecher. On De Ciampis also E. Vezzosi, "La Federazione Socialista Italiana del Nordamerica tra autonomia e scioglimento nel sindacato industriale," *Studi emigrazione*, 21 (March 1984).

10 A. Pizzorno, "Sul confronto intertemporale delle utilita," *Stato e mercato*, 5 (April 1986).

11 On the League see B. Fraser, "Yankees at War," Ph.D. Dissertation, Columbia University, 1976.

12 SCII, box 33a; Dept. of Justice File, RG 65, Roll 799, M-1085, National Archives, Washington, D.C.

13 James Tiso, interview by Jeremy Brecher, Waterbury, December 2, 1980, Brass Workers' History Project, Mattatuck Museum, Waterbury. Some passages of this interview are contained in J. Brecher, J. Lombardi & J. Stackhouse, *Brass Valley* (Philadelphia, Temple University Press, 1982). On immigrants' struggles in this period see D. Montgomery, "Nationalism, American Patriotism, and Class Consciousness among Immigrant Workers in the U.S. in the Epoch of WWI" in D. Hoerder (Ed.); *"Struggle a Hard Battle,"* (DeKalb, Ill., Northern Illinois University Press, 1986); R. J. Vecoli, "Anthony Capraro and the Lawrence Strike of 1919" in G. E. Pozzetta (ed.), *Pane e Lavoro* (Toronto, Multicultural History Society of Ontario, 1980); L. Schneider, "American Nationality and Workers' Consciousness in Industrial Conflict: 1870-1920," Ph.D. Dissertation, Columbia

University, 1975; D. Brody, *Steelworkers in America: The Non-Union Era*, (New York, Harper and Row, 1969) 180-198.

[14] John Zampino, interview by Ferdinando Fasce, Waterbury, October 8, 1985.

[15] L. Cetti, "Work Experience among Italian Women in New York," *Rivista di Studi Angloamericani, cit.*; T. Manwaring & S. Wood, "The Ghost in the Machine: Tacit Skills in the Labor Process," *Socialist Review* 14 (March-April 1984); P. Atzeni, "Lavoro e tempo in miniera," *La Ricerca Folclorica* 4 (April 1984).

[16] M. Huberman, "The Economic Origins of Paternalism," *Social History*, 12 (January 1987).

[17] For a broad examination of this point see D. Montgomery, "Liberty and Union: Workers and Government in America, 1900-1940" in R. Weible, O. Ford & P. Marion (eds.), *Essays from the Lowell Conference on Industrial History*, (Lowell, Mass, 1981).

[18] A. Portelli, "The Peculiarities of Oral History," *History Workshop Journal* (Autumn 1981), 100.

[19] J. T. Lears, "The Concept of Cultural Hegemony," *American Historical Review* 90 (June 1985); L. Fink, "Looking Backward: Reflections on Workers' Culture and the Conceptual Dilemmas of the New Labor History," unpublished paper, 1984.

[20] Boelhower, *op. cit.*; Passerini, *op. cit.*

[21] E. P. Thompson, "Anthropology and the Discipline of Historical Context," *Midland History* 1 (Autumn 1972).

Appendix
Scovill Workforce by Nationality, 1914-21

Year	Total	Amer.	French	Ger.	Rus.	Irish	Ital.	Lith.	Polish	Alban.	Portug.
1914	3,509	—	—	—	—	—	—	—	—	—	—
1915	6,379	38.2%	5.0%	1.8%	1.1%	11.6%	18.8%	7.0%	4.7%	—	—
1916	11,000	36.0%	3.8%	1.1%	8.9%	9.7%	19.5%	6.3%	9.6%	—	—
1917	12,808	40.0%	3.4%	.93%	9.0%	8.5%	19.3%	5.8%	8.3%	—	—
1918	12,900	45.0%	1.41%	.50%	9.8%	5.9%	18.4%	3.6%	12.7%	—	—
1919	7,242	45.9%	—	—	7.5%	6.6%	18.8%	4.0%	3.1%	1.9%	3.1%
1920	6,816	50.2%	—	—	5.2%	7.3%	17.8%	3.4%	2.8%	0.9%	2.5%
1921	4,704	57.3%	—	—	2.5%	7.6%	17.1%	2.8%	1.5%	0.8%	0.9%

Source: SCII, cases 34-35-36.

Italian Emigration to the United States of America: The Case of Sicily (1880-1914)*

Luigi Di Comite and Michele De Candia
Università di Bari

Foreword

In the period 1880-1914, a considerable rate of Italian migratory flow took origin from Sicily: on a total amount of 13.5 million emigrants, 1,333 millions, that is almost 10%, came from Sicily. As already mentioned on a previous occasion (Di Comite, Glazier and De Candia, 1987), in that period, behavioral patterns in international migrations were subjected to radical changes both in Italy and in the United States. As a matter of fact:

a) in Italy, the migratory flows going abroad, which were continuously expanding and overcame 870,000 units in 1913 were mainly directed to three American countries (United States, Brazil and Argentina) and mainly came from the Mezzogiorno;

b) in the United States, the immigration taking origin from the European countries of the Mediterranean basin and from the Slavic countries, which had always been irrelevant, greatly increased and became the majority of the migratory movement,to the detriment to the Anglosaxon, Scandinavian and German immigration (Livi Bacci, 1961).

On this occasion, continuing on a subject we have been dealing with since the beginning of 1980, we intend to study the migratory flows to America concentrating our attention upon the case of Sicily, that is the Italian region which supplied the largest number of emigrants to the United States of America. We have found our sources both in the rich official documentation existing in Italy (Commissariato Generale dell'Emigrazione, 1926) and in the documentation available by the National Immigra-

* Work developed in the context of the research program on "L'emigrazione italiana verso le Americhe" granted by M.P.I. (Quota 60%).

tion Archives of the Balch Institute in Philadelphia (Glazier, 1981).

The Southern emigration, 1880-1914.

The contribution of the Mezzogiorno regions to the migratory flows from 1880 to 1914 continued in increasing. Concerning the total emigration (see Table 1) from the first to the last period of five years, the weight of Southern emigration nearly doubled, passing from 21.82% (1880-1884) to 43.02% (1910-1914). This behavior was surely determined by the progressive expansion of the transoceanic emigration, which Southern populations were more inclined to than Northern ones. According to the data shown in Table 2, the weight of Southern emigration, increased from 48.67% (1880-84) to 69.36% (1910-14), that is from a total of 123 thousand units of the first five years to 1282 thousand units of the last one.

Moreover, the data shown in Table 3 point out the lack of balance existing between the contribution to the migratory flow to the United States given by the Southern regions; in some periods this percentage also overcame 90%.

The case of Sicily

The different weight of the Sicilian emigration, according to the different destinations, and even compared to the national migratory flow, is very well shown both in Figure 1 and in Table 4.

In particular, Figure 1 points out that the weight of Sicilian migration is heavy when we consider the United States (23.5%), medium when we consider the whole American continent (16.5%) and light when we do not consider a specific destination.

The data of Table 4 show that the migratory flows coming from Sicily went more and more increasing, passing from 12 thousand units of emigrants of the first five years (1880-84) to 475 thousand units of the five years 1905-09 and reaching its maximum value in 1913 with 146 thousand units (see Table 1).

Considering that the European continent has always had a very little attraction on the Sicilian population (in fact in the period we are examining, only 26 emigrants in 1,000 went to the

Table 1—Total emigrants, 1880-1914

Years	Italy (A)	Mezzogiorno (B)	Sicily (C)	B/A 100	C/A 100	C/B 100
1880	119901	21138	884	17.6	0.7	4.2
1881	135832	24983	1143	18.4	0.8	4.6
1882	161562	41360	3215	25.6	2.0	7.8
1883	169101	46759	4040	27.7	2.4	8.6
1884	147017	25800	2420	17.5	1.6	9.4
1885	157193	43533	2186	27.7	1.4	5.0
1886	167829	54627	4270	32.5	2.5	7.8
1887	215665	66976	4653	31.1	2.2	6.9
1888	290736	68900	7015	23.7	2.4	10.2
1889	218412	59404	11308	27.2	5.2	19.0
1890	215854	71861	10705	33.3	5.0	14.9
1891	293631	74213	10130	25.3	3.4	13.6
1892	223667	62297	11912	27.9	5.3	19.1
1893	246751	92498	14626	37.5	5.9	15.8
1894	225323	61892	9125	27.5	4.0	14.7
1895	293181	95635	11307	32.6	3.9	11.8
1896	307482	115471	15432	37.6	5.0	13.4
1897	299855	94420	19109	31.5	6.4	20.2
1898	283715	99437	25579	35.0	9.0	25.7
1899	308339	106885	24604	34.7	8.0	23.0
1900	352782	141495	28838	40.1	8.2	20.4
1901	533245	240198	36718	45.0	6.9	15.3
1902	531509	257722	54466	48.5	10.2	21.1
1903	507976	241312	58820	47.5	11.6	24.4
1904	471191	199442	50662	42.3	10.8	25.4
1905	726331	352903	106208	48.6	14.6	30.1
1906	787977	391020	127603	49.6	16.2	32.6
1907	704675	327950	97620	46.5	13.9	29.8
1908	486674	180274	50453	37.0	10.4	28.0
1909	625637	315863	94833	50.5	15.2	30.0
1910	651475	309627	96713	47.5	14.8	31.2
1911	533844	203448	50789	38.1	9.5	25.0
1912	711446	306740	92788	43.1	13.0	30.2
1913	872598	412906	146061	47.3	16.7	35.4
1914	479152	164833	46610	34.4	9.7	28.3
TOTAL	13457558	5373822	1332845	39.9	9.9	24.8

Table 2—Emigrants arriving in America, 1880-1914

Years	Italy (A)	Mezzogiorno (B)	Sicily (C)	B/A 100	C/A 100	C/B 100
1880	33080	16363	430	49.5	1.3	2.6
1881	40871	20330	692	49.7	1.7	3.4
1882	59695	31398	1664	52.6	2.8	5.3
1883	63388	34060	2660	55.3	4.2	7.6
1884	55467	19743	1866	35.6	3.4	9.5
1885	72490	33787	1325	46.6	1.8	3.9
1886	82166	46771	2966	56.9	3.6	6.3
1887	129463	60696	4087	46.9	3.2	6.7
1888	204264	62126	5819	30.4	2.8	9.4
1889	123181	52975	10163	43.0	8.3	19.2
1890	113027	65529	9957	58.0	8.8	15.2
1891	186472	66225	9285	35.5	5.0	14.0
1892	113807	54920	11022	48.3	9.7	20.1
1893	138299	83475	13829	60.4	10.0	16.6
1894	111459	53617	8399	48.1	7.5	15.7
1895	183919	87070	10475	47.3	5.7	12.0
1896	192998	106185	14605	55.0	7.6	13.8
1897	171294	87166	18295	50.9	10.7	21.0
1898	135193	90075	24041	66.6	17.8	26.7
1899	139934	98165	22558	70.2	16.1	23.0
1900	165627	127488	26643	77.0	16.1	20.9
1901	278166	208874	31188	75.1	11.2	14.9
1902	282586	223992	48584	79.3	17.2	21.7
1903	280413	211499	52800	75.4	18.8	25.0
1904	249574	168278	41703	67.4	16.7	24.8
1905	444724	323072	97427	72.6	21.9	30.2
1906	509348	363502	121066	71.4	23.8	33.3
1907	414303	295195	91659	71.3	22.1	31.1
1908	237405	157833	45689	66.5	19.2	28.9
1909	397666	292190	89968	73.5	22.6	30.8
1910	400852	285779	92038	71.3	23.0	32.2
1911	260372	181347	46321	69.6	17.8	25.5
1912	399713	276827	86018	69.3	21.5	31.1
1913	556325	387351	141224	69.6	25.4	36.5
1914	230765	150562	44423	65.2	19.3	29.5
TOTAL	7458306	4825465	1230889	64.7	16.5	25.5

Table 3—Emigrants arriving in the U.S.A., 1880-1914

Years	Italy (A)	Mezzogiorno (B)	Sicily (C)	B/A 100	C/A 100	C/B 100
1880	5711	3869	246	67.7	4.3	6.4
1881	11842	9800	479	82.8	4.0	4.9
1882	18593	16187	1208	87.1	6.5	7.5
1883	21256	18078	1943	85.0	9.1	10.7
1884	10582	8319	1552	78.6	14.7	18.7
1885	12485	9986	1192	80.0	9.5	11.9
1886	26920	24147	2628	89.7	9.8	10.9
1887	37221	34127	3085	91.7	8.3	9.0
1888	32945	29534	4323	89.6	13.1	14.6
1889	25434	21103	5589	83.0	22.0	26.5
1890	47952	42927	8427	89.5	17.6	19.6
1891	44359	39687	7549	89.5	17.0	19.0
1892	42953	35933	10015	83.7	23.3	27.9
1893	49765	42344	9146	85.1	18.4	21.6
1894	31668	27579	6219	87.1	19.6	22.5
1895	37851	33166	6700	87.6	17.7	20.2
1896	53486	47528	9918	88.9	18.5	20.9
1897	47000	41197	12407	87.7	26.4	30.1
1898	56375	50284	18693	89.2	33.2	37.2
1899	63156	55231	18181	87.5	28.8	32.9
1900	87714	78769	21042	89.8	24.0	26.7
1901	121139	104082	23119	85.9	19.1	22.2
1902	193772	164945	42160	85.1	21.8	25.6
1903	197855	163581	46682	82.7	23.6	28.5
1904	168789	132345	36220	78.4	21.5	27.4
1905	316797	256621	77630	81.0	24.5	30.3
1906	358569	281439	90351	78.5	25.2	32.1
1907	298124	227346	75594	76.3	25.4	33.3
1908	131501	99290	31215	75.5	23.7	31.4
1909	280351	223756	72429	79.8	25.8	32.4
1910	262554	205110	68993	78.1	26.3	33.6
1911	191087	142699	38011	74.7	19.9	26.6
1912	267637	202324	64243	75.6	24.0	31.8
1913	376776	283052	109502	75.1	29.1	38.7
1914	167481	116914	37283	69.8	22.3	31.9
TOTAL	4097700	3273299	963974	79.9	23.5	29.4

**Figure 1—Emigration by origin and destination
(A: Total; B: America; C: U.S.A.), 1880-1914**

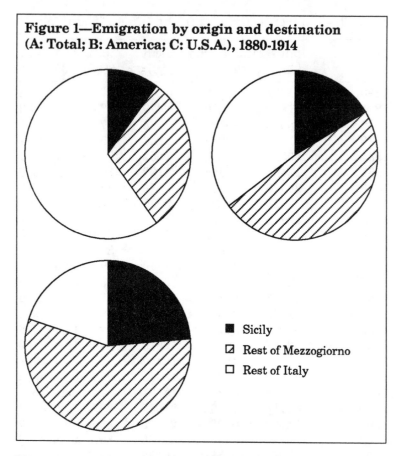

- ■ Sicily
- ☑ Rest of Mezzogiorno
- ☐ Rest of Italy

European continent), the favorite destination was the American continent, where the 92% of the Sicilian emigration was directed, with the United States at first place (72.3% of the total), followed by Argentina (13.8%) and Brazil (3.3%).

Ship passenger lists and emigration to the United States

We have already mentioned, on other occasions, the importance of the analysis of ship passenger lists to study the Italian emigration to the United States.

We mention here what has been recently written (Di Comite,

Table 4—Emigration from Sicily to different destinations, 1880-1914

Years	World	Europe	America	U.S.A.	Argentina	Brazil	Rest of America	Rest of the World
1880-1884	11702	1061	7312	5428	218	8	1658	3329
1885-1889	29432	1814	24360	16817	5419	669	1455	3258
1890-1894	56498	1627	52492	41356	1825	3817	5494	2379
1895-1899	96031	1923	89974	65899	9236	10755	4084	4134
1900-1904	229504	8052	200918	169223	13137	7268	11290	20534
1905-1909	476717	11620	445809	347219	81622	11660	5308	19288
1910-1914	432961	8782	410024	318032	72255	9396	10341	14155
Total	1332845	34879	1230889	963974	183712	43573	39630	67077

Glazier, De Candia, 1987) for the "I Congrès Hispano Luso Italia de Demografia Historica" held in Barcelona:

In the period we are considering, the emigration to America was exclusively by sea: the ship passenger lists, written by the captain when the passengers were disembarking, allows us to analyze the immigration in America, both in the United States and in other countries of Latin America, thanks to the various information we can get from these lists.

These lists, particularly those concerning the United States, which are collected by the National Immigration Archives of the Balch Institute in Philadelphia, show a detailed picture of the socio-demographic characteristics of nearly 25 millions of Europeans disembarked in the U.S. ports between 1820 and the beginning of the first World War (Glazier 1981).

For each immigrant the following characteristics are generally described: name and surname, degree of relationship with other members of the family, sex, age, nationality, town of origin, occupation, literacy, kind of immigration (temporary or definitive), class of journey, port of embarkation and disembarkation, date of disembarkation.

Examining all the information, it is possible to reconstruct the migratory flows between the countries of origin and the United States and to identify the territorial units (towns, provinces, regions) mostly interested in this phenomenon both for origin and destination places.

The data currently available concerning Sicily, obviously taken from these lists, deal with 6,588 persons—on a total of 56,268 (see Table 5)—disembarked in U.S. ports until 1897, that is in the first half period (1880-1914), a period in which the Sicilian emigration was quite restrained and never exceeded 20 thousand units per year (see Table 1).

If we consider that in the period 1880-1897, the Sicilians registered in the ship passengers lists were 6,557 units on a total of 92,626 Sicilians emigrated to the United States, we can say that they represent a sample equal to 7% of the origin universe. The counting of the ship passengers lists did not follow any

Table 5
Emigrants arriving in the United States by sex and years of arrival (data of the 'fragment')

Years	Italy		Mezzogiorno		Sicily	
	Total	Known origin	MF	M	MF	M
1848	58	48	48	34	-	-
1850	11	11	11	11	11	11
1866	250	226	214	117	20	12
1869	4	-	-	-	-	-
1871	55	-	-	-	-	-
1874	110	-	-	-	-	-
1875	108	-	-	-	-	-
1880	786	49	48	26	29	13
1881	843	341	277	222	32	26
1882	2520	1388	1185	1003	285	200
1883	1947	1805	1599	1519	73	72
1884	456	404	329	257	37	25
1885	431	354	319	246	51	44
1886	1639	1550	1413	1044	264	188
1887	1546	1383	1250	947	212	174
1888	1457	1041	966	732	381	249
1889	1533	746	693	434	52	36
1890	8654	5473	4990	4072	324	264
1891	4259	3468	3039	2378	715	491
1892	6480	4706	2831	2074	912	619
1893	10650	9933	7731	6262	1582	1167
1894	3427	3159	2878	2212	590	415
1895	2909	2515	2210	1407	403	238
1896	4393	4004	3641	2848	456	294
1897	1717	1632	1518	1166	159	105
Unknown	25	6	7	3	-	-
Total	56268	44242	37197	29014	6588	4643

statistical method concerning samples, therefore we would like
to call them"fragmentary" from now on instead of samples, both
for the data on Sicily and for the whole country.

Having said that, looking at the data reported in Table 5, you
can deduce the temporal distribution of the phenomenon both in
Sicily and compared with the South of Italy and the whole
country. It is also easy to realize that, even for the fragment, the
amount of emigrants gets more and more elevated as we approach the XIX century and there are more men than women.

Structure by sex and age of the Sicilian emigration

The data of Table 6 give the chance to analyze the structure by
sex and age of the Sicilian emigration to the States and to
compare them with the situation of the South of Italy and the
whole country.

In particular, the chart in Figure 2 points out the following:
a) whatever the age, there are more men than women;
b) the classes going from 0 to 9 years are well represented;
c) there are nearly no old persons (more than 60 years).

Referring to Table 6 we can observe that:
a) the difference between men and women is particularly
evident for the age 20-59, even if this gap is more elevated in the
South and in the whole country rather than in Sicily;
b) the children (0-9 years) are more prevalent among the
Sicilian emigrants than the Southern and the Italian ones;
c) the old persons are very few in Sicily and in the other two
terms of the comparison.

From these observations, we can deduce that:
a) even for the migratory flows coming from Sicily and going
to the States, men in a working age have a considerable weight;
this is an evidence, even if indirect, of the economic nature of the
reasons of these migratory flows;
b) compared with the rest of the country,the elevated number
of women— 29.5% of the total amount of Sicilian emigrants
compared with 22% of Mezzogiorno and 22.5% of Italy—and the
huge presence of children point out the important contribution
of the families.

The information obtained by reading the data of structure by
sex and age are quite significant and, in a certain way, peculiar

Table 6—Structure by sex and age of emigrants arriving in the United States (data of the 'fragment')

Age Group	Absolute Values						Percentage					
	Italy		Mezzogiorno		Sicily		Italy		Mezzogiorno		Sicily	
	M	F	M	F	M	F	M	F	M	F	M	F
0-4	1852	1513	1258	990	388	285	3.29	2.69	3.38	2.66	5.89	4.33
5-9	1622	1173	1081	796	273	205	2.88	2.08	2.91	2.14	4.14	3.11
10-14	2013	887	1387	576	313	144	3.58	1.58	3.73	1.55	4.75	2.19
15-19	3026	1234	1966	797	357	199	5.38	2.19	5.29	2.14	5.42	3.02
20-24	7721	1884	4903	1184	682	272	13.72	3.35	13.18	3.18	10.35	4.13
25-29	7243	1734	4716	1076	701	248	12.87	3.08	12.68	2.89	10.64	3.76
30-34	6538	1350	4398	891	628	194	11.62	2.40	11.82	2.40	9.53	2.94
35-39	5224	872	3572	567	453	114	9.28	1.55	9.60	1.52	6.88	1.73
40-44	3802	663	2592	424	383	97	6.76	1.18	6.97	1.14	5.81	1.47
45-49	2154	419	1526	277	222	75	3.83	0.74	4.10	0.74	3.37	1.14
50-54	1209	333	829	215	125	51	2.15	0.59	2.23	0.58	1.90	0.77
55-59	537	229	351	153	59	24	0.95	0.41	0.94	0.41	0.90	0.36
60-64	213	139	144	98	17	14	0.38	0.25	0.39	0.26	0.26	0.21
65-69	104	62	63	40	11	5	0.18	0.11	0.17	0.11	0.17	0.08
over 70	61	33	37	23	5	5	0.11	0.06	0.10	0.06	0.08	0.08
Unknown	309	115	191	76	26	13	0.55	0.20	0.51	0.20	0.39	0.20
Total	43628	12640	29014	8183	4643	1945	77.54	22.46	78.00	22.00	70.48	29.52

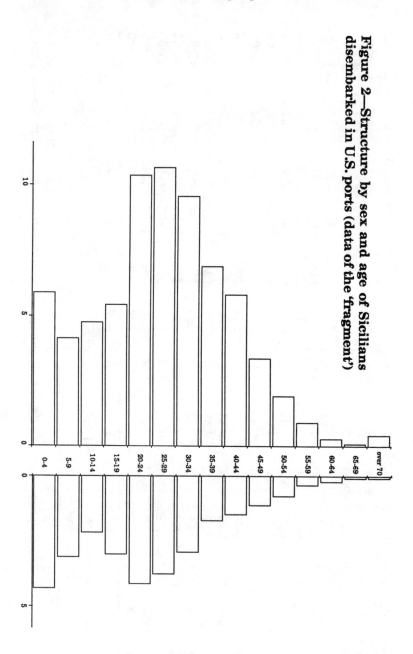

Figure 2—Structure by sex and age of Sicilians disembarked in U.S. ports (data of the 'fragment')

if we consider that all migratory flows whose origins are mainly economic maintain the same characteristics of the "fragment."

Territorial origin

The elementary territorial units which we refer to in this study are the provinces as they are nowadays. At the beginning of the First World War the provinces of Enna and Ragusa, both settled in 1927, did not exist.

The data in Table 7 point out the different contribution given to the migratory flow to the States by the various Sicilian provinces: nearly 60% came from the province of Palermo, 17% from Messina. If we consider the province of Trapani, too, we can observe that 4 emigrants of 5 came from 3 Northern provinces, located on the Tirrenean Sea, in which lived nearly 50% of the island population at the beginning of this century.

The most important role was played by the province of Palermo that represented 22.5% of the demographic size of the island, supplied 60% of the migratory flow to the United States.

The lowest contribution to this migratory flow was given by the three provinces (Catania, Siracusa and Ragusa) which were more distant from the Tirrenean Sea—28.7% of the island population lived there at the beginning of the century and only 5.8% of the migratory flow (see Table 7). These data confirm the importance of territorial distribution of the population referring to the migration propension.

The port of embarkation

The important role played by the port of Naples in the emigration to America is very well known (Glazier, 1981). Together with the ports of Marseilles and Genoa, it was the most involved one in the Mediterranean Sea.

The information taken from the ship passenger list (Di Comite, Glazier, 1984; Di Comite, 1985) showed that the port of Naples was the main one, followed by Genoa, for persons embarking from Sicily. A small amount of Italian emigrants embarked from the ports of Marseilles, Bordeaux, Le Havre and Glasgow.

The data reported in Table 8 concerning Sicily point out the following:

Table 7
Emigrants arriving in the United States by sex and province of origin (data of the 'fragment')

Province	Sex		
	M	F	MF
Palermo	2732	1267	3999
Messina	821	297	1118
Trapani	96	31	127
Agrigento	328	150	478
Caltanissetta	185	41	226
Enna	184	77	261
Catania	131	48	179
Siracusa	21	1	22
Ragusa	145	33	178
Sicily	4643	1945	6588

a) the important role of the port of Naples where 66.7% of Sicilians embarked to emigrate to the States;

b) the second important port was Palermo which absorbed 15.6% of this emigration;

c) the port of Glasgow was the most important one among the non-Italian ports because of cheaper fees.

Occupational groups

Humble professions are more represented than high-skilled ones, as regards the socio-occupational picture of the emigrants who generally showed a low cultural level. Let us analyze Table 9.

The most represented occupational groups were "laborer and mason" 28.7% of the emigrants with a professional qualification, followed by "peasant and day-laborer" with 22.9%.

The third qualification was "engraver" followed by "housewife." The other groups (domestic, shoe-maker, sailor and fisherman) represented less than 5% each. A few emigrants were

Table 8
Emigrants arriving in the United States according to port of embarkation (data of the 'fragment')

Port of Embarkation	Italy		Mezzogiorno		Sicily	
	MF	M	MF	M	MF	M
Italian ports						
Genoa	4352	3153	906	662	159	113
Naples	39882	30967	30663	23895	4399	3113
Palermo	3132	2359	2090	1531	1029	661
Other	4936	4022	2131	1800	406	325
Total	52302	40501	35790	27888	5993	4212
Non Italian ports						
Marsailles	142	102	103	74	6	5
Bordeaux	113	92	2	2	2	2
LeHavre	1299	1077	95	87	20	20
Glasgow	398	303	260	181	260	181
Other	2014	1553	947	782	307	223
Total	3966	3127	1407	1126	595	431
General Total	56268	43628	37197	29014	6588	4643

bakers and carpenters.

If we calculate the total of the groups "without occupation" and "occupation unknown", we get a value (1167 units) nearly equal to the amount of the first two classes per age of Table 5 (0-9 years) that is 1151 units. This consideration shows the inclination in attributing a professional qualification in any case.

Conclusions

Examining the statistical documentation in our country (Commissariato Generale dell'Emigrazione, 1926) and the one existing by the National Immigration Archives of the Balch

Table 9—Emigrants arriving in the United States by occupational group (data of the 'fragment')

Occupational group	Italy		Mezzogiorno		Sicily	
	MF	M	MF	M	MF	M
Laborer, mason	19513	18042	12264	11231	1557	1409
Peasant, day-laborer	16809	14978	12054	10987	1242	1125
Engraver	4235	2458	2855	1672	743	417
Housewife	1760	0	999	0	290	0
Domestic, servant	1014	85	658	39	244	16
Shoe-maker	919	902	654	650	213	212
Tailor	806	586	539	378	108	66
Sailor	454	448	300	295	190	187
Barber	441	436	309	305	118	117
Carpenter	273	269	176	175	34	33
Merchant	214	210	84	83	44	44
Fisherman	176	174	168	166	154	152
Baker	153	151	100	98	41	39
Other occupation	2593	1957	1413	973	443	273
Total	49360	40696	32573	27052	5421	4090
Without occupation	4345	1386	2987	980	705	278
Occupation unknown	2563	1546	1637	982	462	275
General total	56268	43628	37197	29014	6588	4643

Institute in Philadelphia, we tried to deal with some characteristics of the emigration coming from Sicily and going to the
United States of America. We essentially referred to the period
1880-1914 for what concerns the data available in Italy and
1880-1897 for the data available by the Balch Institute.
The main results of our analysis consist in:
a) nearly 964,000 people emigrated from Sicily to the States in
the period 1880-1914, on a total population of little more than 3.5
million, according to the census in 1901;
b) the two provinces which gave more contribution to this flow
were Palermo and Messina, during the XIX century;
c) the professional qualification of the emigrants, among
whom men were more than women, was very low.

Works cited

Bellettini A. "Il quadro demografico dell'Italia nei primi decenni
dell'Unita' Nazionale," *Atti del I Congresso di Storia del Risorgimento Italiano*, Bologna, 5-9 novembre 1980.

Bellettini A. "Aspetti della transizione demografica in Italia nel primo
periodo post-unitario," *Studi in onore di Luigi Dal Pane*, CLUEB,
Bologna, 1981.

Commissariato Generale Dell'Immigrazione (a cura). *Annuario statistico dell'emigrazione italiana dal 1876 al 1925, con notizie sulla emigrazione negli anni 1869-1875*, Roma, 1926.

De Rosa L. *Emigranti, capitali e banche(1896-1906)*, Edizioni del Banco
di Napoli, Napoli, 1980.

Di Comite L. "The Demografic Transition Process in Italy," *Economic
Notes*, 1980, n.2.

Di Comite L. "Problemi statistici delle migrazioni,"*Annali di Statistica*,
Serie IX, Vol. I, 1981.

Di Comite L. "L'emigrazione italiana nella prima fase del processo
transizionale," *Giornale degli Economisti*, 1983, n. 7-8.

Di Comite L. "Aspetti dell'emigrazione italiana verso gli Stati Uniti,
1880-1897," *Analisi storica*, 1985, n. 5.

Di Comite L. "Aspects of Italian Emigration, 1881-1915,"in I. A. Glazier
& L.Derosa (Eds.), *Migration Across Time and Nations*, Holmes &
Meier, New York, 1986.

Di Comite L. and Glazier I.A. "Socio-Demographic Characteristics of Italian Emigration to the United States from Ship Passengers Lists: 1880-1914," *Ethnic Forum*, 1984, n. 1-2.

Di Comite L., Glazier I.A., De Candia M. "Aspetti differenziali dell'emigrazione italiana verso gli Stati Uniti d'America: i casi del Piemonte e della Sicilia," *Atti del I Congre's Hispano Luso Italia de Demografia Histo'rica*, Barcelona, 22-25 abril 1987.

Glazier I.A. "Ships and Passengers in Emigration from Italy to the U.S. 1880-1900," in R. Ragosta (a cura), *Le genti del mare mediterraneo*, Vol. II, L. Pironti Ed., Napoli, 1981.

Livi Bacci M. *L'immigrazione e l'assimilazione degli italiani negli Stati Uniti*, Giuffre', Milano, 1961.

Livi Bacci M. *La trasformazione demografica delle societa' europee*, Loescher, Torino, 1977.

Mac Donald J.S. "L'economia politica delle migrazioni italiane alle Americhe: aspetti amministrativi e sociologici," *Atti del I Congre's Hispano Luso Italia de Demografia Histo'rica*, Barcelona, 22-25 abril 1987.

Nelli H. S. *From Immigrants to Ethnics: The Italian Americans*, Oxford University Press, New York, 1983.

Reginato M., Cuccureddu A. "Alcuni aspetti dell'emigrazione in America dalle valli valdesi," *Atti del I Congres Hispano Luso Italia de Demografia Histo'rica*, Barcelona, 22-25 abril 1987.

Rosoli G. (a cura) *Un secolo di emigrazione italiana 1876-1976*, Centro Studi Emigrazione, Roma, 1978.

Sori E. *L'emigrazione italiana dall'Unita' alla seconda guerra mondiale*, Il Mulino, Bologna, 1979.

La Grande Emigrazione Italiana negli Stati Uniti. Il caso della Calabria.

Giuseppe De Bartolo
Università della Calabria

1.

La società calabrese al momento della unificazione del Regno d'Italia si caratterizzava per la sua staticità: da una parte vi erano i "galantuomini" (cioè i discendenti delle nobili famiglie medioevali) e dall'altra i "villani" cioè i braccianti, i coloni, i piccoli proprietari, gli artigiani. In modo estremamente efficace così il Seminara[1].descrive la società calabrese di quel tempo: "immobile, dominata da una classe che viveva su una rendita parassitaria, priva di stimoli per promuovere una trasformazione e un qualsiasi progresso, anzi interessata e tenacemente aggrappata alla conservazione dei suoi privilegi. Nel latifondo il pascolo si alternava alle colture estensive, nelle quali veniva impiegata numerosa manodopera a basso salario."

In questa collettività verso la fine del secolo scorso si verificò un evento di grande portata, l'emigrazione, che diede uno scossone al suo immobilismo e che come spesso diceva il Nitti fu l'unica grande causa modificatrice della realtà calabrese. Essa fu il mezzo con cui le classi subalterne calabresi manifestarono il loro disagio e la loro protesta. A questo proposito così si esprimeva il De Nobili: "L'elemento lavoratore dopo una resistenza dolorosa contro chi soleva 'sfruttarlo e dissanguarlo,' percorso da tutti i flagelli, finalmente ha ceduto... (ed) è fuggito traverso l'Oceano."[2] L'emigrazione, benchè fosse iniziata in Calabria subito dopo l'Unità, qui assunse proporzioni veramente notevoli solo nel ventennio a cavallo fra i due secoli. Fino agli anni '20 essa si svolse al di fuori del controllo reale dei pubblici poteri; tratto che invece non ebbe successivamente, fino al suo esaurimento completo che possiamo collocare agli inizi degli anni '70, epoca in cui l'Italia ha perduto, forse in maniera definitiva, la caratteristica che l'ha contraddistinta per un secolo: cioè fornitrice a basso costo di forza lavoro del mercato internazionale. Oggi, di fronte ad una realtà interna marcata da una forte disoccupazione strutturale, l'Italia è diventata ormai importatrice di mano d'opera anch'essa a basso costo in provenienza per lo più dal Terzo Mondo [3]

Noi ci limiteremo in questa nota ad un sommario esame della emigrazione calabrese verso l'America dall'Unità alla prima guerra mondiale. In particolare considereremo quel periodo comunemente chiamato del "grande esodo", che per la Calabria può essere collocato nell'intervallo 1881-1911, cercando di mettere in particolare rilievo quella parte dei flussi diretti verso gli Stati Uniti. Con ciò oltre ad adempiere al compito che ci è stato assegnato in questo Convegno, si vuole dare anche un contributo diretto a stimolare l'interesse- che in verità fino ad ora è stato piuttosto scarso, come fa rilevare il Rosoli[4] -verso l'emigrazione dei lavoratori italiani negli Stati Uniti. L'esame sarà effettuato—e qui il compito diverrà senza dubbio più arduo- non dimenticando l'apporto di altre discipline, al fine di tentare una storia, per quanto possile "totale", di cui si sente vieppiù l'esigenza, particolarmente nel campo dell'emigrazione [5]

2.

Com'è noto l'emigrazione calabrese interessò prevalentemente le classi rurali—infatti nel periodo 1876-1905 su una media di 100 emigrati dalla regione 60 furono agricoltori, seguono poi i braccianti, gli artigiani, i muratori, i domestici, le nutrici e le professioni liberali[6]—e fu causata dal peggioramento dopo l'Unità d'Italia della situazione economica generale e nelle campagne in particolare. Infatti, con la nuova situazione politica e con i nuovi rapporti di classe che si vennero a stabilire, dopo l'Unità fu più integrale l'appropriazione delle risorse da parte dei proprietari (usurpazione dei demani e dei beni comunali, accaparramento dei beni ecclesiastici alienati e delle quotizzazioni, gestione di classe dei patrimoni delle opere pie e dei beni frumentari). Inoltre, proprio nel momento di maggiore necessità, venne a mancare l'apparato assistenziale pre-unitario—che aveva svolto fino a quel momento la funzione di contenitore della povertà, in una situazione di aumentata pressione demografica e di espulsione dal processo produttivo—il cui smantellamento si era reso necessario a causa delle difficoltà di bilancio del nuovo Stato.[7] La presa di coscienza da parte delle classi subalterne della loro condizione era maturata dopo diverse vicende. I tentativi miranti alla conquista di un pezzo di terra—antica aspirazione del contadino calabrese—si erano infranti puntualmente per la debolezza del movimento contadino causata dall'inesistenza di una loro organizzazione di classe. Ed infatti erano sempre falliti i loro tentativi di occupazione delle terre, dei demani e dei latifondi. Tentativi, non riusciti, di occupazione si ebbero in particolare nel 1848 in provincia di Cosenza, i quali si estesero ben presto al crotonese dove era più esteso il latifondo. Stessa sorte ebbero i tentativi degli anni '50. Nè ebbe alcun effetto pratico il decreto con cui Garibaldi nel 1860 autorizzava l'uso gratuito dei pascoli della Sila ai contadini di Cosenza e casali.[8] Il deputato Leopoldo Franchetti nel 1883 denunciava le condizioni di vita insostenibili dei contadini del Mezzogiorno; in particolare, egli attribuiva le loro forme di protesta—brigantaggio, tentativi di divisione dei beni comunali—a motivi di pura sopravvivenza, denunciando la totale mancanza di interesse verso le classi agricole anche da parte delle sinistre.[9]

Subito dopo l'Unità l'abolizione delle dogane interne non solo mise in crisi il settore agricolo per la concorrenza delle più moderne aziende agrarie lombarde e anche pugliesi, ma mise in grave crisi anche la fragile struttura industriale della regione, che appunto le protezioni doganali e le forniture statali avevano fatto sopravvivere.[10]

La situazione divenne ancora più difficile con la crisi agraria degli anni '80 la quale si manifestò con il crollo dei prezzi del grano causato dalla diminuzione della domanda internazionale e dall' afflusso di prodotti cerealicoli provenienti dai mercati d'oltre oceano e dalla Russia.[11] D'altra parte le tariffe doganali protezionistiche del 1887, specie sui cereali, avevano aggravato la miseria dei contadini—quasi tutti braccianti, fittavoli e mezzadri—e avevano avvantaggiato solo i proprietari. Per es. in Provincia di Cosenza i contadini continuavano a percepire da L. 0,85 a L. 1. 26 al giorno. Questi valori in media erano più bassi in quanto un contadino lavorava appena due terzi in un anno.[12] La rottura commerciale con la Francia del 1888 poi fece peggiorare una situazione già critica, perchè venne a mancare un mercato, appunto quello francese, verso cui era diretta nel passato la maggior parte della produzione vinicola, olivicola ed agrumaria calabrese. Che la miseria dei contadini calabresi fosse aumentata si trae anche dai rapporti degli organi periferici dello Stato. Per esempio, in un rapporto il Prefetto di Cosenza la qualificava come "durissima."[13]

Che a quell'epoca i salari agricoli fossero estremamente bassi si può desumere per esempio da alcune citazioni della"Statistica dell'emigrazione italiana" degli anni 1884-85 fatte dallo Scalise. Egli riferisce che nella risposta alla circolare Berti del 1884 il Sindaco di Belvedere Marittimo attribuiva le cause della emigrazione dal suo Comune alla mancanza di lavoro, alla miseria provocata dai cattivi raccolti, al gravoso carico fiscale ed all' irrisorio salario giornaliero di 60 centesimi.[14] Nel Crotonese i salari erano scesi alla cifra infima di 50 centesimi a l'ora, ed ancora peggiore era la situazione nel distretto di Gerace, distretto che aveva il triste primato dell'analfabetismo in Italia.[15] A rafforzamento delle sue affermazioni sul peggioramento delle condizione in agricoltura, lo Scalise osservava che nel 1895 il salario agricolo reale in Calabria era più basso rispetto ad un secolo prima.[16] Un'indicazione indiretta del livello di vita dei contadini calabresi prima della grande stagione migratoria si può trarre dal loro regime alimentare molto scarso, basato su pochi elementi nutritivi; tra questi il pane era il costituente basilare; esso però era di scadente qualità: molto diffuso era il pane di farina di castagna; utilizzato era anche il miglio ed il sorgo; il lupino veniva spesso impiegato con la segala.[17] L'alimentazione del contadino calabrese non subì sostanziali modifiche per tutto l'800: la carne era un lusso raro, i legumi non venivano utilizzati in maniera regolare e costante, anche scarso era l'impiego degli ortaggi, mentre con la frutta spesso ci si sfamava; il sorgo veniva regolarmente usato sia come alimento umano sia come foraggio "La soglia che separava—afferma il Bevilacqua—l'alimentazione animale da quella contadina, era quanto mai sottile."[18]

Queste a grandi linee le condizioni dei contadini calabresi
nella seconda metà del secolo scorso, i quali erano le vittime
di continue crisi ed erano sottoposti ad un sistema fiscale
molto pesante: addirittura alcune manifestazioni avevano
avuto come obiettivo il conseguimento di sgravi fiscali; ne è un
esempio la manifestazione del maggio del 1897 in cui circa
200 contadini di Belmonte Calabro, in provincia di Cosenza,
manifestarono per ottenere la riduzione dell'imposta di
famiglia.[19] Nè il sistema creditizio veniva loro incontro, per
cui essi erano costretti a ricorrere sovente all'usura che prati-
cava tassi del 120%.[20] Ma a parte queste forme di protesta in
verità per tutto il secolo XIX non vengono segnalati in Calabria veri e propri scioperi.[21]

3.
   Statistiche attendibili dell'emigrazione italiana si hanno
solo a decorrere dal 1876—anno di inizio delle rilevazioni ufficiali del fenomeno migratorio con l'estero da parte della Direzione Generale della Statistica. Prima di questa data le informazioni sulla emigrazione italiana sono abbastanza incerte
e di dubbia attendibilità[22] e sono dovute a singoli studiosi
come il Correnti, il quale nel suo Annuario Statistico Italiano
del 1858 dà le prime notizie statistiche del fenomeno. Statistiche sull'emigrazione italiana furono elaborate successivamente dal Carpi sulla base delle informazioni ricavate da un
questionario che l'Autore aveva inviato alle Prefetture tramite
il Ministero dell'Interno. Dal 1901 il Commissariato
dell'Emigrazione basa le sue rilevazioni sul termine di emigrante, cioè su "colui che viaggiando in terza classe si reca al
di là dello stretto di Gilbilterra..." Questa definizione viene
adottata dal 1914 anche dalla Direzione Generale di Statistica.[23] L' emigrazione italiana nel corso dell' ultimo secolo può
essere sintetizzata in queste cifre: 25 milioni di espatri nel periodo 1876-1976; però più della metà di questo flusso, precisamente 14 milioni di espatri, era già avvenuto nel 1915. Il
tasso d'emigrazione con l'estero che nel 1876 era del 3,8 x
1000 sale al 24 x 1000 nel 1913 [24]. Nella tabella che segue
abbiamo riportato il numero degli espatriati dal 1876 al 1915.

Tav. 1.
Espatriati dall'Italia dal 1876 al 1915.

PERIODO	ESPATRI
1876-1885	1314670
1886-1895	2391030
1886-1905	4322400
1906-1915	5999450

Fonte: L.Favero, G.Tassello, *Cent'anni di emigrazione...*
op.cit., p.21.

Nel periodo 1876-1915 il 44% degli espatri era diretto verso l'Europa mentre il 56% verso i Paesi extra-europei;[25] la direttrice transoceanica prevaleva di già dal 1881 (Tav.2).

Tav. 2.
Espatri per aree di destinazione (dati relativi a 100 del totale di ogni periodo). Italia 1876-1910.

	PERIODI			
AREE	1876-1880	1881-1890	1891-1900	1901-1910
Europa	73.5	47.3	44.3	40.0
America	24.2	50.2	54.3	58.8
Africa	2.2	2.3	1.2	1.8
Asia-Oceania		0.1	0.1	0.2

Fonte: A.Bellettini, *La popolazione italiana* op.cit., p.204.

Naturalmente la perdita migratoria fu più contenuta rispetto alle cifre degli espatri. Per es. su un flusso di espatri di 17 milioni durante il periodo 1861-1920, la perdita migratoria netta fu invece di soli 5 milioni (Tav. 3).

Tav. 3.
Espatri ed emigrazione netta in Italia nel periodo 1861-1920. Confini dell'epoca. Dati x 1000 di popolazione residente.

PERIODO	MIGRAZ. NETTA	ESPATRI
1861-1870	227	1210
1871-1880	334	1180
1881-1890	1041	1880
1891-1900	1433	2830
1901-1910	1021	6030
1911-1920	992	3830
1861-1920	5048	16960

Fonte: E.Sori, *L'emigraz. Italiana*, op.cit., p.20.

La Calabria partecipa in maniera sempre più importante all'emigrazione del periodo: sul totale dell'emigrazione italiana il suo peso, che nel 1876-80 era del 2%, sale al 7,3% nel 1901-10 [26] e si passa da 5 mila emigrati all'anno del periodo 1876-1885 a quasi 30 mila nel periodo 1896-1905 ed a ben 40 mila espatri annui tra il 1906 ed il 1915 (Tav.4).

Tav. 4.
Espatriati dalla Calabria dal 1876 al 1925.

PERIODO	ESPATRI
1876-1885	51290
1886-1895	133920
1896-1905	292840
1906-1915	400970
1916-1925	167040

Fonte: G.Rosoli (a cura di), *Un secolo di emigrazione*, op.cit., Tab. 4, p.356.

Se si esaminano gli espatri x 1000 abitanti si può vedere come il fenomeno in Calabria interessi via via nel tempo sempre strati piu vasti di popolazione. Per questa caratteristica la regione raggiunge già a partire dal 1880 i primi posti nella graduatoria delle regioni italiane (Tav 5).

Tav. 5.
Espatri medi annui x 1000 abitanti in Calabria e posto

364   *Italian Ethnics: Their Languages, Literature and Lives*

occupato nella graduatoria delle regioni italiane.

PERIODO	TASSOx1000	POSTO IN GRADUATORIA
1876-1880	1.8	9
1881-1890	7.9	4
1891-1900	12.1	3
1901-1910	31.7	2
1911-1913	31.8	2
1914-1920	10.3	2
1921-1930	10.7	2

Fonte: E.Sori, *L'emigrazione italiana*, op.cit., p.25.

La Calabria, come d'altra parte tutto il Meridione d'Italia, si è subito distinta per la prevalenza della direzione transoceanica dei flussi migratori. Infatti nel periodo 1876-1900 su 276 mila emigrati appena 27 mila si diressero in Europa e nel bacino mediterraneo, mentre 249 mila verso i paesi transoceanici, in gran parte verso le Americhe; nel periodo 1901-1913 su un totale di 572 mila emigrati ben 551 mila varcarono gli oceani.[27]

Numerosi furono gli elementi che indirizzarono questi flussi. Tra questi giocò un ruolo fondamentale il calcolo tra costi e ricavi.[28] Se afferma lo Scalise riferendosi alla nuova direzione che le correnti migratorie andavano assumendo— tale emigrazione (quella europea) conviene ai Veneti..., per la posizione naturale dei loro paesi, non conviene agli emigrati della Calabria perchè il viaggio per le lontanissime Americhe costa meno che non per quello degli Stati vicini".[29] Altro fattore importante che influì ad orientare le scelte fu la "catena migratoria" che si venne a costituire sia attraverso gli atti di richiamo di amici o parenti, sia attraverso i biglietti di viaggio prepagati, i "prepaids." Queste forme di richiamo però predisponevano spesso l'emigrato a odiose forme di sfruttamento da parte di "padroni" o privati banchieri.[30]

I paesi d'oltre oceano preferiti dai calabresi furono Brasile, Argentina e Stati Uniti. Dall'inizio del secolo alla vigilia della prima guerra mondiale negli Stati Uniti si diresse una massa veramente imponente di calabresi, oltre 300 mila. (Tav 6).

Tav. 6.
Emigrati calabresi per Paese di destinazione.

PERIODI	STATI UNITI	ARGENTINA	BRASILE	TOTALE
1876-1900	81230	90681	61514	275926
1901-1913	326752	130933	61388	572420
1914-1918	25794	5639	3927	39285
1919-1927	76672	84259	16694	202291

Fonte: Svimez, *Statistiche sul Mezzogiorno*, op.cit., p117.

Fino al 1861 l'emigrazione dalla Calabria era stata di entità trascurabile ed aveva interessato poche migliaia di unità dirette prevalentemente nelle regioni vicine.[31] Dopo il 1861 e fino al 1876 essa si mantenne su valori ancora molto modesti (Tav. 7).

Tav. 7.
Emigrati dalla Calabria dal 1869 al 1875

ANNI	EMIGRATI
1869	1174
1870	679
1871	1126
1872	3038
1873	1809
1874	1301
1875	675

Fonte: L. Izzo, *La popolazione calabrese*, op.cit., p.174.

Dopo il 1876 (Tav. 4 e 5) il flusso crebbe via via fino a raggiungere il massimo nel decennio 1906-15 con 40,097 emigrati annui. All'interno del territorio calabro l'emigrazione si sviluppò dapprima nella provincia di Cosenza; il fenomeno si estese poi alla provincia di Catanzaro, ed infine a quella di Reggio Calabria (Tav.8).

Tav. 8.
Emigrazione dalle provincie calabre per 10000 abitanti.

PERIODI	PROVINCIE		
	CZ	CS	RC
1881-1885	30	145	3
1886-1890	90	185	12
1891-1895	138	168	27
1896-1900	165	165	97
1901-1905	330	270	286

Fonte: D. Taruffi, L. De Nobili, C. Lori, *La questione agraria* op.cit. p.107.

Il rapido sviluppo dell'emigrazione reggina all'inizio del secolo è da mettere in relazione alla crisi finanziaria ed agricola che culminò nel 1894-95 e che causò una forte riduzione dei salari. Altra causa che contribuì ad incrementare l'emigrazione dal reggino fu il terremoto del 1894. Il circondario più interessato al fenomeno migratorio fu quello di Gerace, arido, poco produttivo e con l'indice di analfabetismo più alto d'Italia.[32] Fino al 1900 i circondari in cui il flusso emigratorio era stato più intenso furono Paola, Castrovillari,Cosenza Nicastro, mentre in quelli più poveri, come Crotone, Gerace e Palmi, il fenomeno si era manifestato in forma importante con ritardo e cioè solo verso la fine del secolo (Tav.9).

Tav. 9.
Quozienti emigratori medi annui x 10000 abitanti nei circondari della Calabria dal 1881 al 1905.

CIRCONDARI E PROVINCIE	1881-1885	1886 1890	1891 1895	1896 1900	1901 1905
CATANZARO	14.6	55.6	119.6	144.0	299.2
CROTONE	6.0	67.0	104.9	118.7	305.4
MONTELEONE	7.1	69.9	152.4	199.0	279.0
NICASTRO	94.3	175.5	171.1	192.9	430.5
PROVINCIA DI CATANZARO	30.0	90.0	138.0	165.0	330.0
CASTROVILLARI	168.3	216.8	173.2	197.6	264.7
COSENZA	147.6	152.7	127.4	94.9	219.5

PAOLA	180.4	195.1	219.8	216.1	328.1
ROSSANO	62.1	156.2	177.0	195.3	354.7
PROVINCIA DI					
COSENZA	145.0	185.0	168.0	165.0	270.0
GERACE	0.6	17.0	40.0	130.0	336.3
PALMI	0.4	2.0	13.8	76.7	240.4
REGGIO	8.0	17.0	27.2	85.6	277.2
PROVINCIA DI					
REGGIO	3.0	12.0	27.0	97.0	286.0

Fonte: D. Taruffi et ali, *La questione agraria* op.cit., p.708.

Questa apparente contraddizione—ritardo del fenomeno emigratorio proprio nelle zone più povere—è stata analizzata dall'Arlacchi[33] per quanto concerne in modo più specifico l'esodo dal cosentino e dal crotonese, zona quest'ultima che all'epoca era tra le più povere della Calabria e dove più esteso era il latifondo. Il ritardo della emigrazione dal crotonese viene attribuito dall'Arlacchi proprio al sistema del latifondo, mentre la più alta emigrazione dal cosentino è da collegare al particolare sistema contadino ivi diffuso. Sarebbero stati presenti nel crotonese certi fattori—che invece erano più temperati nel cosentino—che avevano per lungo tempo ostacolato l'emigrazione; essi erano la miseria elevata, la debolezza dei rapporti familiari, lo scarso individualismo imprenditoriale che nella emigrazione trovava una sua manifestazione, la intensa socialità, intesa non come coesione sociale ma piuttosto fatto fisico di vita collettiva. Il fattore che avrebbe però agito con più forza nel ritardare l'emigrazione sarebbe stata la miseria: una miseria paralizzante, stabilmente al di sotto del limite biologico di sopravvivenza, che avrebbe determinato appunto l'esclusione di certe categorie, mentre sarebbero stati favoriti tutti coloro che possedevano qualche cosa da vendere o impegnare, come i piccoli proprietari, i piccoli fittuari, i piccoli commercianti rurali, presenti in maggior numero nel cosentino. A parte gli altri elementi specifici del crotonese presi in considerazione dall' autore ci sembra di poter affermare che la diffusione di una miseria stabilmente al di sotto del limite biologico della sopravvivenza fosse l'elemento esplicativo più significativo delle differenze dei tassi emigratori delle diverse zone della regione.

4.

Com'è stato già accennato l'emigrazione italiana negli Stati Uniti divenne imponente tra la fine del secolo scorso e la prima guerra mondiale. Secondo una statistica tedesca riportata dal Florenzano dal 1856 al 1868 sbarcarono negli Stati Uniti appena 11691 italiani su 2578982 sbarchi.[34] Lo stesso autore, che riporta alcune cifre della immigrazione negli Stati Uniti tratte da fonte ufficiale americana, indica in 8620452 il flusso degli immigrati negli Stati Uniti fino al 1872, di cui 37163 provenienti dall'Italia. Però, sempre secondo il Florenzano, quest'ultimo valore sarebbe errato per difetto ed egli, inoltre, basandosi su informazioni consolari valuta in 70000 il numero dei residenti italiani negli Stati Uniti al 31 dicembre 1871, di cui 15 mila residenti nella giurisdizione di S. Francisco;[35] nel 1910 invece il numero dei residenti italiani viene stimato in 1779059 persone.[36] In precedenza abbiamo constatato come l'emigrazione calabrese diretta negli Stati Uniti fosse notevolmente aumentata nel primo decennio del XX secolo (Tav.6); ma un'idea più precisa di questo incremento può trarsi dalla Tav. 10: notare come la proporzione di emigrati che sceglievano gli Usa fosse in Calabria superiore ai valori del Regno già a partire dal 1876.

Tav. 10.
Emigrazione calabrese e italiana verso gli Stati Uniti dal 1876 al 1909.

ANNI	CALABRIA		REGNO	
	val. ass.	x 100 emigranti	val. ass.	x 100 emigranti
1876-1878	34	2.3	1470	1.4
1884-1886	1575	18.7	16662	10.6
1894-1896	3726	22.0	41002	14.9
1904-1906	33180	64.3	281385	41.8
1907	27510	58.2	298124	42.3
1908	13752	45.0	131501	27.0
1909	32247	61.4	280351	44.8

Fonte: M.D.D'Ambrosio, *Il Mezzogiorno d'Italia e l'emigrazione negli Stati Uniti,* **Athenaeum, Roma, 1924 p. 58**

Le singole provincie presentavano però caratteristiche diverse fra loro: all'inizio della grande emigrazione i flussi verso l'America provenivano nella quasi totalità dalla provincia di Cosenza ed erano diretti principalmente verso il Brasile; solo successivamente essi deviarono verso Argentina e Stati Uniti[37]. Più precisamente all'inizio del secolo su 100 emigrati verso le Americhe 54 emigravano negli Usa, 25 in Argentina e solo 13 in Brasile. Gli emigrati negli Usa provenivano in maggioranza dalla provincia di Catanzaro e dalla provincia di Reggio Calabria, mentre l'Argentina era la meta principale dei cosentini (Tav.11).

Tav. 11.
Percentuale di emigrati nei singoli paesi delll'America per 100 emigrati verso le Americhe nel quinquennio 1901-1905

PAESI DI DESTINAZIONE	CZ	CS	RC	CALABRIA
Argentina	13.1	50.7	11.8	25.2
Brasile	13.9	21.5	4.7	13.4
Stati Uniti	70.5	25.2	67.9	54.2
Altri Stati	2.5	3.6	15.6	7.2

Fonte: D.Taruffi et ali, *La questione agraria...* **op.cit., p.735**

Questo cambiamento di direzione dei flussi transoceanici verso gli Stati Uniti venne visto da molti con favore specialmente dopo le notizie sulle vicende degli emigrati italiani in Brasile ed Argentina.[38]

Invero questa immigrazione fu inizialmente incoraggiata da parte statunitense, oltre che nel tentativo di far fallire le rivendicazioni della classe operaia nativa, anche per bloccare i flussi asiatici non graditi che stavano diventando piuttosto consistenti.[39]

Gli immigrati italiani nella stragrande maggioranza si stabilirono nelle grandi metropoli, a dispetto dei tentativi da parte americana di dirottarli verso le regioni agricole degli States—tentativi peraltro assecondati dai gruppi italiani favorevoli ad una emigrazione colonizzatrice, i quali, consapevoli della forza che veniva acquistando il movimento anti immigratorio d'oltre oceano, cercavano di rinviarne in questo modo gli effetti.[40] Altre informazioni sulla emigrazione calabrese verso gli Stati Uniti ce li fornisce il D'Ambrosio per alcuni anni finanziari successivi al 1915 (Tav.12). Come si può notare dopo il periodo bellico, periodo in cui prevalsero i ritorni sugli espatri, l'esodo riprese immediatamente.

Tav. 12.
Espatriati e rimpatriati per anni finanziari in Calabria verso gli Usa e verso le Americhe.

ANNI FINANZIARI	STATI UNITI		AMERICA	
	Esp.	Rimp.	Esp.	Rimp.
1916-1917	2059	1724	2451	3662
1917-1918	158	1195	226	2159
1918-1919	104	3877	360	4701
1919-1920	9625	8416	15295	10479

Fonte: M.A.D'Ambrosio, *Il Mezzogiorno d'Italia...* op.cit., p. 101-104.

L'emigrazione mise in evidenza con una eco che travalicava i confini nazionali i mali che affliggevano la società italiana. Tra questi sottolineò per esempio il basso livello di istruzione degli emigranti, specialmente del Mezzogiorno, come è possibile constatare dalle cifre di una statistica americana del 1902-1907, riportata dal D'Ambrosio,[41] da cui si vede come gli italiani del Nord fossero più ricchi e meno analfabeti degli italiani del Sud, e come il tasso di analfabetismo degli italiani del Sud fosse paragonabile a quello dei Turchi e dei Portoghesi. Com'è noto, il problema dell'analfabetismo assunse nel dibattito sull'emigrazione italiana nei primi anni del secolo un ruolo molto importante quando negli Stati Uniti il movimento restrizionista fu sul punto di rendere effettivo il Literacy Test approvato nel 1897. In realtà alcune punte elevate della emigrazione italiana verso gli Usa trovano la loro spiegazione con la paura da parte degli aspiranti all'emigrazione di non poter più partire: ne è un esempio la "corsa" del 1895-96 [42] Certamente la minaccia rapprentata dal Literacy Test fu un forte stimolo per migliorare la scolarità ed infatti in Calabria tra il 1901-02 e 1907-08-periodo di intensa emigrazione- il tasso di scolarità aumento'di ben 7 punti. Tale miglioramento non si ebbe per esempio in un' altra regione meridionale con scarsa vocazione migratoria come la Puglia.[43] Per migliorare il livello di istruzione degli emigranti vennero istituiti corsi speciali e questo tipo di politica si protrasse fino al 1921 anno in cui la stretta antimmigratoria messa in atto dagli Stati Uniti divenne questa volta effettiva.

5.
L'emigrazione ebbe conseguenze non trascurabili su molti aspetti della vita regionale. Certamente fu una delle cause dello spopolamento che si verificò in molti comuni della regione nel periodo del"grande esodo".[44] Questo particolare fenomeno ebbe inizio nel cosentino, tra il 1861 ed il 1881, e successivamente si diffuse anche nelle altre tre provincie. Tra il 1881 ed il 1911 risultava "spopolato" il 67.1% dei comuni cosentini; il 55.4% dei comuni del catanzarese ed infine il 37.5% di quelli del reggino.[45] Altre conseguenze dell'emigrazione furono l'aumento dei salari agricoli ed il miglioramento dei patti agrari. Alla mancanza di braccia si sopperì con l'aumento dei giorni lavorativi: in media in un anno si passò da 120-150 giorni lavorativi a 200.[46] I vuoti dell'emigrazione portarono anche un accrescimento dei salari, i quali—rimasti invariati per più di un secolo[47]—si andavano man mano adeguando alle nuove esigenze di vita che si venivano instaurando nei paesi con il ritorno degli "americani."
Legati al fenomeno del rialzo delle mercedi in agricoltura furono la diminuzione dei terreni messi a coltura e l'impiego dei salariati solo per le colture più redditizie.[48] Un'ulteriore conferma della esistenza di una relazione fra aumento dei salari ed emigrazione ce la fornisce lo Scalise, il quale mise in evidenza come l'aumento dei salari si fosse verificato per primo in provincia di Cosenza, che fu tra le provincie calabre

quella in cui l'esodo si manifestò per primo, come è stato più volte osservato.[49] Gli aumenti salariali furono all'inizio del secolo dell'ordine del 30-35% in tempi normali e del 40-50% in tempo di raccolta.[50] Migliorarono anche i patti agrari ed il costo della terra salì nei luoghi dove per il ritorno degli"americani" erano cresciute le richieste.[51] `E fuor di dubbio che le rimesse degli emigrati contribuirono in qualche modo a migliorare le condizioni economiche delle zone di esodo, anche se questa massa monetaria non riuscì—come sottolinea il Sori[52]—a modificare i rapporti estremamente sfavorevoli alle classi subalterne. L'invio del denaro avveniva generalmente attraverso "banchieri" privati, categoria molto diffusa, che com'è noto dietro compenso forniva i più disparati servizi all'emigrato italiano, il quale, a causa della scarsa conoscenza della lingua, utilizzava poco i servizi bancari e postali. Il Caputo all'epoca constatava che ve ne erano 5 o 6 operanti tra New York, Pittsburgh, Denver e Montreal.[53] L'aumentato benessere si riflesse anche sul miglioramento dello standard nutrizionale: minor uso del granone, aumento del consumo di carne, della patata e del vino.[54] In genere le rimesse venivano affidate alle casse postali, i cui depositi dal 1887 al 1901 erano quadruplicati. L' aumento dei depositi aveva seguito lo sviluppo della emigrazione: prima Cosenza, poi Catanzaro, quindi Reggio Calabria. Infine, non trascurabile fu anche l'ammontare delle rimesse che venivano affidate dai contadini direttamente ai "galantuomini" dei paesi.[55]

6.
Com' è stato già osservato i rimpatri furono sempre consistenti (Tav.12). Essi inoltre furono strettamente legati alle vicende economiche e politiche dei paesi di immigrazione. Per esempio, nel 1903 e nel 1904 nei paesi della Calabria si potevano osservare molti "americani" rimpatriati in seguito alla stasi dei lavori pubblici determinata dalle elezioni presidenziali.[56]

Gli emigrati rimanevano in America complessivamente dai 10 ai 15 anni e ritornavano in patria 4-5 volte. Il Caputo attraverso le sue osservazioni dirette aveva stimato che il periodo di dimora era in media di 6 anni per l'America del Sud, invece di 3 anni per l'America del Nord, con ritorno ogni 3-5 anni.[57] Questi valori non si discostano da quelli calcolati dal Livi Bacci su tutta la massa degli emigrati italiani negli USA.[58] I ritornati restavano in patria da pochi mesi ad un anno, poi ripartivano. La nota distintiva dell'emigrazione calabrese, come anche dell'emigrazione meridionale in genere, fu dunque la temporaneità. Per questa caratteristica l'emigrazione meridionale veniva indicata con l'appellativo "Birds of passage." Questi "uccelli di passaggio" erano individui che per il 75% emigravano soli—generalmente nei mesi di marzo e aprile, dopo aver espletato i lavori dei campi necessari ad assicurare di che vivere alla famiglia per tutto l'anno[59]—si fermavano oltre oceano per pochi anni, il tempo necessario per risparmiare una certa somma, poi ritornavano e quindi ricominciavano un'altra esperienza migratoria. Questo modello, che aveva come presupposto la libertà di movimento, venne sconvolto però dalle restrizioni sempre piu rigide che gli Stati Uniti imposero all'immigrazione a partire dalla fine della prima guerra mondiale: entrata in vigore del Literacy Act nel 1917, introduzione del sistema delle "quote" nel 1921.

---

[1] F. Seminara, *Emigrazione in Calabria*, in P. Borzomati (a cura di), *L'emigrazione calabrese dall' Unità ad oggi*, CSE, Roma,1982, p. 306.

[2] L. De Nobili, *Appunti sull'emigrazione dalla Calabria, La Riforma Sociale*,Vol. XVII, 1906, p. 403 .

[3] Su questa recente realtà, oltre ai contributi contenuti nel volume "La presenza straniera in Italia: nuovi contributi conoscitivi, Studi Emigrazione, n. 82-83, 1986", si vedano anche le comunicazioni presentate al Seminario su: Les migrations internationales: problèmes de mesure, évolutions récentes et efficacité des politiques, Seminario che si è svolto all'Università della Calabria dall'8 al 10 settembre 1986.

[4] G. Rosoli, *"L'emigrazione italiana negli Stati Uniti: Un bilancio storiografico,"* in R. De Felice (a cura di), Cenni storici sulla emigrazione italiana nelle Americhe e in Australia, Milano, F. Angeli, 1979.

[5] Questo bisogno è stato avanzato per esempio dal Sori: cfr. E. Sori, Indicazioni di storiografia e di ricerca sull'emigrazione, in *L'emigrazione calabrese dall'Unità ad oggi*... op. cit. , pp. 295-298.

[6] D. Taruffi, L. De Nobili, C. Lori, *La questione agraria e*

l'emigrazione in Calabria, G. Barbera, Firenze, 1908, pp. 731-732.
Per quanto riguarda in particolare l'emigrazione delle nutrici gli autori fanno osservare come il movimento migratorio calabrese abbia avuto inizio con la partenza di balie dal catanzarese verso l'Egitto presso le famiglie dei residenti inglesi.

[7] E. Sori, *L'emigrazione Italiana dall"Untia"* alla seconda guerra *mondiale, Il Mulino*, Bologna, 1979, pp. 70-72.

[8] L. Izzo, *Agricoltura e classi rurali in Calabria dall'Unità al Fascismo*, Librairie Droz, Ginevra, 1974, p. 109-110.

[9] L. Izzo, *Agricoltura e classi rurali in Calabria*, op. cit., p. 111.

[10] Si vedano L. Luzzatto, "L'economia Italiana dal 1861 al 1894," Torino, Einaudi, 1968 e F. Milone, "Le industrie del Mezzogiorno all'Unificazione d'Italia," in *Studi in onore di G. Luzzatto*, vol. III, Milano, 1950.

[11] E. Sori, *L'emigrazione Italiana*.., op. cit., p. 115.

[12] L. A. Caputo, "Di alcune quistioni economiche della Calabria," *Giornale degli Economisti*, 1907, p. 1173.

[13] L. A. Caputo, 1907, *Ibid.*, p. 1173. L' A. richiama nel suo lavoro le citazioni contenute nei rapporti ufficiali riportati nei volumi della "Statistica dell'emigrazione italiana all'estero" che vanno dal 1880 al 1890.

[14] G. Scalise, *L'emigrazione dalla Calabria*, Pierro Editore, Napoli, 1905, p. 44.

[15] G. Scalise, *Ibid.*, p. 44.

[16] G. Scalise, *Ibid.*, p. 47.

[17]P. Bevilacqua, "Emigrazione calabrese transoceanica e mutamenti dell'alimentazione contadina fra Otto e Novecento," in *L'emigrazione calabrese*, op. cit., pp. 65-71.

[18] P. Bevilacqua, *Ibid.*, p. 67 e p. 69.

[19] L. Izzo, *Agricoltura e classi...* op. cit., p. 113.

[20] L.A. Caputo, *Di alcune questioni* op. cit. 1907, p.1174.

[21] L. Izzo, *Agricoltura e classi...* op. cit., p. 113.

[22] A.Bellettini, *La popolazione Italiana*, Einaudi, 1987, p.202

[23] Per quanto riguarda i problemi definitori, oltre alla sintesi riportata in L.Favero, G. Tassello, "Cent'anni di emigrazione italiana"

(1876-1976), in *Un secolo di emigrazione italiana (1876-1976)* (a cura di G.Rosoli), CSE, Roma, 1978, p.9-111, si veda anche il volume: Commissariato Generale dell'Emigrazione, *Annuario Statistico dell'emigrazione italiana 1876-1925*, Roma, 1926.

24 I dati precedenti sono stati tratti da L.Favero, G.Tassello, *Cent'anni di emigrazione Italiana (1876-1976)*,op. cit.

25 L. Favero, G.Tassello, *Ibid.*, p.21.

26 cfr.: A.Bellettini, *La Popolazione italiana*, op.cit., tav. 21, p.206.

27 Svimez, *Statistiche sul Mezzogiorno d'Italia 1861-1953*, Roma, 1954.

28 E.Sori, *L'emigrazione italiana*..op. cit., p.29.

29 G.Scalise, *L'emigrazione dalla Calabria*, op. cit., p.10.

30 Cfr.:E.Sori, *L'emigrazione italiana*...op. cit., pp. 296-297.

31 L.Izzo, *La popolazione calabrese nel secolo XIX*, ESI, Napoli, 1965, p.171.

32 D.Taruffi et al. *La questione agraria*...op.cit., p.707.

33 P. Arlacchi, *Mafia contadini e latifondo,nella Calabria tradizionale*, Il Mulino, Bologna, 1980; ed anche dello stesso autore: Perchè si emigrava dalla società contadina e non dal latifondo, in "L'emigrazione calabrese dall'Unità ad oggi" (a cura di P. Borzomati), op.cit., pp. 157-169.

34 G.Florenzano, *Della emigrazione italiana in America comparata alle altre emigrazioni europee*, Napoli, F. Giannini, 1874, p.63.

35 G.Florenzano, *Ibid.*, p.112.

36 *Bollettino dell'Emigrazione*, n.1,1912.

37 D.Taruffi et ali., *La questione agraria*..op.cit. p.734.

38 D.Taruffi et ali., *Ibid*, p.736.

39 E. Sori, *L'emigrazione italiana*.. op.cit., p.383.

40 Nella ricerca qui più volte citata, Taruffi, Nobili e Lori per esempio a sostegno della necessità di dirottare nelle zone agricole degli Stati Uniti descrivono con enfasi le violenze e le angherie cui erano sottoposti gli italiani una volta approdati nelle metropoli americane, le insidie dei ricettatori e degli usurai,le angherie di bosses, la brutalità dei formen, la costituzione nelle grandi metropoli di"piccole Italie meridionali" in cui vengono riprodotte le misere condizioni di

vita dei luoghi di partenza, l'importazione da parte dei numerosi rimpatriati di malattie infettive come la tubercolosi.Cfr.: D.Taruffi et ali, *La questione agraria* op.cit., p.735-737 .

[41] M.A. D'Ambrosio, *Il Mezzogiorno d' Italia e l'emigrazione negli Stati Uniti*, Athenaeum, Roma,1924, p. 148.

[42] E.Sori, *L'emigrazione italiana*..op.cit., p.207.

[43] *Ibid.*

[44] Com'è noto si considera spopolato un comune che nell'intervallo tra due censimenti presenta una diminuzione di popolazione. Per un'analisi degli aspetti di metodo riguardanti questo fenomeno si rinvia a E. Sonnino, "Problemi di metodo e primi risultati di una ricerca sullo spopolamento dei comuni italiani dopo l'Unita", in E. Sori (a cura di), *Demografia storica*, Bologna, 1975, pp. 359-387.

[45] A.Nobile, "Gli anni del 'Grande esodo': emigrazione e spopolamento in Calabria (1881-1911)," in *Atti del I Convegno di Studi della Deputazione di Storia patria per la Calabria*, Editori Meridionali Riuniti, Reggio Calabria, 1977, pp. 197-220.

[46] L.A.Caputo, "Di alcune questioni economiche della Calabria," *Giornale degli Economisti*, 1908, p. 137.

[47] G.Scalise, *L'emigrazione dalla Calabria*,op.cit., p.46.

[48] L.A.Caputo, *Di alcune questioni*..op. cit., 1908, p.149.

[49] G.Scalise, *L'emigrazione dalla Calabria*, op.cit., p.43.

[50] G.Scalise, *Ibid.*, p.48.

[51] G.Scalise, *Ibid.*, p.49-50.

[52] E.Sori, *L'emigrazione italiana*..op. cit., p. 160.

[53] L.A.Caputo, *Di alcune questioni*...op. cit., 1907, p.1185.

[54] *Ibid.*, p. 1186.

[55] *Ibid.*, p. 1192.

[56] *Ibid.*, p. 1165.

[57] *Ibid.*, p. 1172.

[58] M.Livi-Bacci, *L'immigrazione e l'assimilazione degli italiani negli Stati Uniti secondo le statistiche demografiche americane*, Giuffrè, Milano, 1961.

[59] G.Scalise, *L'emigrazione dalla Calabria*, op. cit., p. 14.

Memoirs

Oral History: Our Ethnic Past is a Foreign Country

Michael La Sorte
SUNY at Brockport

In relation to written materials, oral history has two major functions in the development of a body of historical knowledge: To create a record of the past through verbal testimony where documentary evidence is too fragmentary or missing; and to develop perspectives on group and individual dynamics within the framework of recorded historical events.[1]

Even when substantial written and visual records exist in the form of census manuscripts, papers, artifacts, and the like, the full story of an event cannot be told because of the many gaps that will remain in the historical record. The available material is necessary but not sufficient to the task of a definitive history. The information we have on immigrants, for example, is more about such items as the process of assimilation as a collective phenomenon, and its consequences, than about the immigrants as individual actors in this complex process. The statistical (aggregate) view, the social, structural, and the cultural profit from objective documentation. Data for the intrapsychic, personal, and interpersonal (particularly in regard to small groups like family and peers) levels—that is, those levels of inquiry not amenable to the macro approach—can only be gathered from the primary person(s) or those once- or twice-removed from the person(s) or event. Ideally, to fill in all of these levels with definitive data would be to present the actors and the phenomenon in full 3-D depth perspective.

An example of a field developing in this direction is Italian American studies. Samuel L. Bailey has made a case for micro-level data to avoid obscuring notable variations at the Italian American individual and sub-ethnic levels and the causes for the variation.[2] And, in fact, the literature has revealed a growing consensus on multi-causal explanations.

Simplistic views of the migration process as unilinear and closed, and the migrant as either the product of change or continuity (but never both), which has standardized our approach to the immigrant generations as well as our approach to successive generations, have given way to much more subtle, open-ended, and interactive models. By simplistic views we mean those heavy-handed, large-scale analyses that lack the actualities of the immigrant dimension. Everybody when reduced to a statistical norm—the aim of the large-scale study—seems the same. Abstract statements of boundaryless scope are generated from such data, invariably producing a facile and hard-to-penetrate stereotype (e.g., Italian immigrants preferred outside labor to factory work; the immigrants were poor, miserable wretches from a "medieval" society who were presumably paralyzed by the experience and could not react to opportunity when it knocked). This interpretation leaves no room for variability or exceptions or any humanness to peek through. If these individuals had any wills of their own, it is rarely evident from the record. It is through the subjective perspective that we can develop material on the individual as initiator in the historical process, not as a mere observer or reactor, pushed hither and yon by forces beyond his comprehension and control. One has to look to a philosopher like Jean-Paul Sartre for an encapsulation of this point of view. He wrote, "The essential is not what 'one' has done to man, but what man does with what 'one' had done to him." We can understand the human condition, he continued, by noting the choices men and women made and the consequences of that behavior on important historical processes.[3]

Oral history can overthrow long-held assumptions about ethnic personality and motives, and open the way for microinterpretations of such phenomena as family dynamics, relationships among job-home-community and the realities interior to persons and primary groups. We read, for example, that the Italian family has been husband-governed and wife-centered, and that the husband-wife relationship has been, from a modern perspective, rather perfunctory. Cherished myths or fact or normative expectations? What variations have existed? Is the normative statement related to the actualities at all? Might it be possible that the reality better fits a multidimensional model rather than a single flat statement? Was coital pleasure actually the prerogative of the husband and thus the act for the woman was of necessity nasty, brutish, and short? Was the typical marriage really prearranged without consultation with the principles? Was such consultation significant in rendering the final decision? Once we open up to examination the groups in which the ethnic has participated such questions proliferate.[4]

Although the American Oral History Association was established as recently as 1948, the general notion of oral history has had a previous heritage. The use of interviews to tap primary wellsprings by scholars is old and perfectly compatible with professional standards. In one sense, oral history was the first kind of history and represents the method of collection and preservation of folk impressions in non-literate societies. More than once in the past, oral testimony was transcribed by anthropologists to preserve on paper the last gasps of a dying non-literate culture. The present-day configurations of oral history technique stem largely from developments since the 1930s in methods of field research in American social anthropology and sociology. This methodology has been tested, refined, and perfected in a multiplicity of research settings ranging from market research to community studies to psychological profiles.

The impulse in the late 1940s by historians to follow the lead of the Columbia University Oral Project, initiated by Allan Nevins, to tape the thoughts of famous persons, as basic raw data for future scholarly efforts, has been broadened considerably to include profiling the lives of common persons, people marginal to traditional history, especially those for whom only a scanty written record exists. These are the undocumented, but not necessarily inarticulate masses, those who dwell in the different American ethnic/economic groups, who have been participants (with millions of others) in one or another major historical process but have often as a group been ignored as legitimate subjects of direct inquiry. The oral histories of the Federal Writers' Project in the 1930s and the earlier community inquiries such as the Middletown series were forerunners of an array of studies employing oral history, both popular and academic, during the present era.

Mention can be made of the studies on the urban and rural ethnic minorities by Oscar Lewis and Robert Coles, the talking journalism of Studs Terkel, and an impressive list of works on ethnic and immigrant history.[5]

The ethnic woman is an excellent candidate for oral history. This segment of the population, especially the immigrant woman, has been silent, not only because the judgment on what and who was important in the society has chosen to ignore her contributions, but also because being outside the business and intellectual mainstreams, she has left few written expressions of her life and personality for posterity. These women appear only as statistics in the records compiled by authorities.[6]

More work is being done on the ethnic woman, but it is not a priority. Hasia R. Diner suggests that the answer is to be found in the preferences of historians. "That immigrant women have not been studied is not because the material was not there. ...Historians, with their own biases of gender, class, and culture, have been basically deaf to the voices of such women and have assumed that they cannot be studied."[7] Francesco Cordasco argues that the problem goes beyond academia, that modern American feminism has championed the successful, single, professional woman to the exclusion of the other types. "The leaders of the contemporary American feminist movement have...ignored their immigrant sisters...preoccupied...with creating a hagiology of female illuminati they have quite naturally turned their attention to early American women reformers (their own middle-class predecessors)...."[8]

The deficiencies in oral data—some immediately obvious, some not—weigh heavily on the questions of reliability and validity—those two major guidelines by which social scientists judge the authenticity of data.

Some of the major drawbacks of oral data are that they are most likely to be less detailed than written accounts, not as carefully thought out, not as meticulous in the recalling of events. The time gap between the incident and its report is sometimes so great as to make detailed recall improbable. Critics of oral data are particularly skeptical of descriptions of the elderly of events significant in their lives. A.J.P. Taylor dismisses such oral reports because they degenerate into "old men drooling over their youth."[9] His cutting observations on those "professional" recollectors who forget the truth and manufacture myth are serious comments that deserve attention. However, they are not sufficient for condemning oral history in toto. There is nothing sacrosanct about the written record; it can be fabricated as well and it can be as incomplete as any oral account. If subjective motives shape oral presentations, they certainly will be found shaping official documents. The British politician Richard Crossman noted, for example, that he discovered, "having read all the Cabinet papers about the meetings I attended, that the documents often bear virtually no relation to what actually happened. I know now that the Cabinet minutes are written by Burke Trend, not to say what did happen in the Cabinet, but what the civil service wishes it to believe happened, so that a clear directive can be given."[10] Robert Coles has mounted a vigorous defense of oral history against those who contend that it cannot compare to the reliability of written sources. Coles concedes that not everything is said, and what is said is uttered through a personal prism that distorts. "But what of those written sources, those diaries, the various correspondence, and even the official or semiofficial records—do they not present the same challenges to the scholar, the reader? People lie in courthouses and hospitals and schools. People even lie when under oath."[11] The danger, then, is found not in the naive acceptance of oral evidence, but of an uncritical acceptance of evidence from any source. Unfortunately, in the social sciences, rigid tradition and snobbery render some data sources as "better" than others. Sociologists swear by the closed-structured questionnaire while the historian directs his nose upward at all but that precious piece of "objective" parchment. The class-biased elitist attitude that a report by an educated professional is honest and above board and that of the man on the street is immediately suspect, for the latter does not have the sophistication to render objective judgment or was not properly placed relative to the event, permeates the social sciences. All evidence needs to be evaluated and assessed in exactly the same way, although all evidence may not serve the same purpose. To the extent that documentary records are insufficient and thereby misleading, oral evidence can act as a corrective and supplement to existing sources and can open up new avenues for analysis and interpretation. Depending on circumstances and sources, oral evidence collected soon after the event can be far fresher, more detailed, and more revealing than a compiled account by nonparticipants. Some of the earlier government reports on immigrant work exploitation, for example, relied heavily on oral testimony from the victims.

The content and intent of oral data can be difficult to evaluate. Documents, in many respects, are easier to work with for they focus on issues that have been clearly delineated before their production.

There are three types of oral history: the topical (which focuses upon a specific event); the biographical (which focuses upon a specific individual); and the autobiographical (the total history of the interviewee). The autobiography presents the most problems. The demands placed on the person are great for it purports to cover a lifespan and is most likely to produce a hodgepodge of superficial observations. Without a structured approach the result can be a mass of material representing personal narrative (some fairly comprehensive, others snippets), subjective accounts of specific events, opinion, attitude, supposition, and contradiction. The intermingling of fact, fancy, and interpretation have to be expected when such demands are placed on the respondent. Where there is too little the effort will be a failure; where there is too much the problem is artistic—what to use and where. There is often desire to give undue stress to the unusual and vivid (indeed to seek them out during the interview) at the expense of the mundane and banal. But then who wants to read about the mundane and banal when the fascinating is available? Humans can be obsessed with their own illusions—some will insist that what is obviously false must be true for it has been confirmed by others time and again. Those who press their life stories on you are those whose remarks need to be most carefully checked. The autobiographical technique also assumes cohort representation, which is never the case. Only a fraction of a cohort survives to old age, and what that fraction is in regard to the representativeness of the oral testimony sought can never be known. Oral histories of the elderly, then, must come from the survivors, most of whom will be women. The number available for interview is further reduced by those who are uncooperative, who disarticulate, suffer from memory loss or are being protected by relatives. The Amoskeag oral histories serve as convenient examples. This project, which is an oral history of the textile industry in Manchester, New Hampshire, as viewed through the eyes of retirees who had labored in the shops, produced thousands of pages of protocols. Most of the material was from women (who did constitute about 50 percent of the work force) and, in the words of the authors, was "much too fragmented to provide a coherent narrative."[12] The salvageable material was reduced further to those who were the most articulate observers to both their lives and jobs and the general community environment, and even more to those precious few whose powers were such that they made model informants. By necessity, greater weight in an analysis is given to the most observant and articulate. The average space allotted in the book to each interview was two to four pages, while the best respondent, as admitted by the authors, was given no less than 12 pages. And rightly so, because his statements were more detailed, more perceptive, less banal and, presumably, more reflective of past realities.

The unintentional distortion is more difficult to uncover and correct than the deliberate lie. Oral history suffers from what Oscar Handlin once referred to as "deceptive retrospect." Since memory plays tricks, those who uncritically accept everything told to them by informants may find themselves woefully misled. While this caution is obvious and elementary, it should be applied automatically to certain types of respondents and to certain categories of events. One is the "personalized" story, which seems to be tailored to create a certain image or impression. Suspicion should surround the "total recall" of an event, since an intense episode in one's life—one that served as a milestone—can be carried down to the present day in rationalized, mythical or neurotic form. The fact of "total recall" may indicate that the episode has been reviewed several times over the years and told and retold, that it has been filtered through several screens of contemporary experience and in the presence of varied audiences.

The ultimate judgment regarding reliability has to be a judgment regarding the person. Is he sufficiently intelligent? Does he have an axe to grind? Is he able to look at the total picture? Can he respond to questions he himself has never entertained previously? Most people are not so clever at prevaricating that they can keep it up for very long without detection. The best defense against deception is a thorough knowledge of the ethnic experience, and peripheral subject areas. In the Amoskeag study the authors uncovered several errors of fact in the oral reports. One woman, for instance, claimed to have voted in 1912 for Teddy Roosevelt, before women had the franchise. More than one person has assured me that his surname was changed at Ellis Island. (The reason is always prejudice or the foreignness of the surname.) Immediately suspecting such information, on close examination I have always found that it is a convenient tale that many uninformed persons will accept in order to cover up a deliberate name change. One woman told me that a judge had "forced" her father to change his surname. "What was he doing before the judge?" I asked her. "To get our last name changed," she replied. Then she went on to confess the true story, not the culturally-approved version: Her father sought a name change because as a businessman he felt it would be to his benefit. Because all types of communication have intended audiences, it is not surprising that the woman had to tell me the truth when she realized that I was not to be duped as she had duped others. Sherna Gluck was able to tap deeper layers of the immigrant experience when her Jewish respondents realized she was one of them. "They were much more willing to talk without pretense," she writes, and much less likely to lead her down the garden path.[13]

The thin line between fiction and nonfiction is crossed many times, and with benefit to both. This interplay serves to enrich narrative data and to give such data a substance and immediacy not found in objective histories. Gaps will always appear in an historical record. Most information about the past is never recorded at all, and most of the rest was evanescent. The problems of total recovery and authentication are simply too immense. As David Lowenthal has indicated, ..."it is impossible to recover or recount more than a tiny fraction of what has taken place, and no historical account ever corresponds precisely with any actual past." Objective historical narrative is more a hope than an achievable goal. "No account can recover the past as it was, because the past was not an account; it was a set of events and situations. As the past no longer exists, no account can be checked against it; we judge its veracity by its correspondence with other reports, not with the events themselves. Historical narrative is not a portrait of what happened but a story about what happened." If history, then, is "retrospective reconstruction," to use Levi-Strauss's term, why not add to oral narrative constructed scenarios and conversations based on what probably occurred or was said. Fact is too thin, too dry, too small and above all, too passionless. Woven together with reliable historical fact, creative oral history can capture the richness and diversity of the ethnic experience in a way that traditional narrative history cannot. This approach is no more sheer invention or less scientific than the imposition of subjective inference (the most likely fitting together of the facts) or filling in with interpolations, as is customarily done in social science research. The best method of verification remains public scrutiny and consensus—the dialectic process. "The weight of evidence ultimately corrects many errors and exposes mendacities."[14]

All too often published ethnic oral histories are dull and unidimensional. Why? Because these histories generally interview persons who review their lives without revealing any amount of information that is truly noteworthy. Taken together, these oral histories do not form a mosaic, a perspective, a pattern that bring into focus a set of interrelationships, which in the process produces a panoramic view of a slice of the ethnic experience. Put differently, the personal material taken together does not form a story: there are too many strands that remain dangling and too many dimensions that remain untapped. These kinds of oral histories cannot stand on their own. By themselves they are nothing more than individual case studies—undigested raw material.[15] To reconstruct the story of which these individual case histories are a part requires, as June Namias has stated, "a novelist's willingness to select, emphasize, to give shape to words uttered, to use a spoken narrative in such a way that a particular person's character emerges and, not least, the drama of a given life history gets told."[16] The imagination can be aided and abetted by recourse to several sources: a chance remark, a phrase from an interview or conversation, an observation in an official document or history, census material, a written quote, a journal, an autobiography, a memory, a piece of a letter. This approach differs from the writing of fiction in that factual material from oral and written sources would serve to delimit and determine the reconstruction and to prevent flights of fancy.

Good oral history is a product of thorough preparation and an ability to create the proper interview atmosphere. Besides the all-important establishment of rapport, the interviewer must be able to probe in such a manner as to jog the memory of the respondent by commanding names, dates, and events. By nudging the respondent to go beyond the normative statement, the respondent can gain insight into his own life and produce information from it that in a sense is even new to him. Most props will stand in the way of full disclosure. Structured interviews and tape recorders inhibit and intimidate.[17] Too much structure also produces standard responses, particularly the "official" versions that are limited to a very narrow perspective and reduce down to a set of generalized cliches. The result is not so much interview as recitation. Essential detail and self-critical analysis are missing. The sharp edges of life are smoothed away. These types of individual life stories, where all the pieces fit together into a seamless pattern and all the ragged corners are tucked in, remind one of Max Beerbohm's sage comment about the study of history: "The past is a work of art, free of irrelevancies and loose ends."

In America where the obsession is with success, a great favorite as one's "official" life story has the same plot as the tried-and-true rags-to-riches Hollywood script: I came, I struggled, I conquered. Or the story will dwell on an issue from the family closet but related in the form of a rigid stereotype. Women who are still getting their revenge on their deceased husbands are reluctant to tell you anything positive about them or give them credit for ever manifesting more "acceptable" behavior during the course of the marriage. If the wedding night was a catastrophe that is what she remembers. The fact that her sex life afterwards was uneventful or downright enjoyable will not be volunteered. And there are just as many who on the death of the spouse will recall no conflicts at all. Everything was easy, everything was fine, you will be told, without being told anything. A man will insist that his father was an authoritarian bully. But on probing it turns out that in reality over the course of the family cycle the authority structure was never that linear and underwent a number of changes.

The best kind of oral history, where depth is achieved and intimacies revealed, comes with the establishment of a solid and enduring rapport with carefully-selected persons who understand what you are about and willingly become co-partners in a detailed exploration of the ethnic experience. It is apparent that the successful in-depth oral history is contingent on an equation that includes both the respondent and the collector. "The narrator's perspective and predilections shape his choice and use of historical materials; our own determine what we make of them."[18] What results is an achievement that both interviewer and respondent help produce, a joint activity organized and informed by the historical cadences of both participants. The exploration brings a critical focus to the respondent's recollections and enriches his memory. The more attuned to these recollections the researcher is, the more he will get and the more he will contribute. The retired person, with time to kill, is most likely to be the best candidate for this time-consuming endeavor, particularly if he is at the stage of "life review".[19] Without the contributions that oral history can make to ethnic literature, the shape of our past will remain a foreign country—a dim outline, not accessible from within—where they do things differently.

---

1 Franc Sturino suggests a four-part typology: Oral history as technique; as a type of historical source subject to the rules governing historical data; eyewitness reports or oral testimony; to denote oral tradition -- that which is transmitted verbally from one generation to the next. "Oral History in Ethnic Studies and Implication for Education," *Canadian Oral History Association Journal* 4 (1979): 15. In this paper we discuss oral history in the context of the first three

types.

2 Samuel L. Bailey, "The Future of Italian American Studies: An Historian's Approach to Research in the Coming Decade," Lydio F. Tomasi (ed.), *Italian Americans: New Perspectives in Italian Immigration and Ethnicity* (N.Y.: Center for Migration Studies, 1985), pp. 193-201.

3 Quoted in Alan M. Kraut, *The Huddled Masses* (Arlington, Ill.: Davidson, 1982), p. 179.

4 For an analysis of the relationship between norms and behavior, see A.L. Maraspini, *The Study of an Italian Village* (Paris: Mouton, 1968).

5 See, e.g., Salvatore La Gumina, *The Immigrants Speak: Italian Americans Tell Their Story* (N.Y.: Center for Migration Studies, 1979); June Namias, *First Generation: In the Words of Twentieth-Century American Immigrants* (Boston: Beacon, 1978); Ailoh Shiloh, *By Myself I'm a Book! An Oral History of the Immigrant Jewish Experience in Pittsburgh* (Waltham, Mass.: American Jewish Historical Society, 1972); Joan Morrison, Charlotte Fox Zabusky, *American Mosaic: The Immigrant Experience in the Words of Those Who Lived It* (N.Y.: Dutton, 1980); John Bodnar, *Workers' World: Kinship, Community, and Protest in an Industrial Society*, 1900-1940 (Baltimore: Johns Hopkins Univ., 1982); Donald S. Pitkin, The House that Giacomo Built: *History of an Italian Family*, 1898-1978 (N.Y.: Cambridge Univ., 1985); Elizabeth Ewen, *Immigrant Women in the Land of Dollars: Life and Culture on the Lower East Side* (N.Y.: Monthly Review, 1985).

6 Examples of Italian female oral histories include Marie Hall Ets, *Rosa: The Life of an Italian Immigrant* (Minneapolis: Univ. of Minn., 1970); Judith E. Smith, *A History of Italian and Jewish Lives in Providence*, R.I., 1900-40 (Albany: SUNY, 1985); Collean L. Johnson, Growing Up and Growing Old in *Italian American Families* (New Brunswick: Rutgers, 1984).

7 Hasia R. Diner, *Erin's Daughters in America: Irish Immigrant Women in the Nineteenth Century* (Baltimore: Johns Hopkins, 1983), p. 12.

8 Francesco Cordasco, *The Immigrant Woman in North America: An Annotated Bibliography of Selected References* (N.J.: Scarecrow,

1985); see, also, Helen Barolini, Dream Book (N.Y.: Schocken, 1985).

9 Quoted in Richard Holmes, *War: The Behavior of Men in Battle* (N.Y.: The Free Press, 1985), p. 10.

1010. Quoted in ibid., p. 51.

11 Quoted in Namias, op.cit., p. xii.

12 Tamara K. Hareven, Randolph Langenbach, *Amoskeag: Life and Work in an American Factory-City* (N.Y.: Pantheon Books, 1978), p. 32. See, also, T.K. Hareven, "The Search for Generation Memory: Tribal Rites in Industrial Society," *Daedalus* 107 (Fall 1978): 137-149.

13 Sherna Gluck, "Women's Oral History," David K. Dunway, Willa K. Baum (eds.), *Oral History: An Interdisciplinary Anthology* (Nashville: The American Association of State and Local History, 1984), p. 226.

14David Lowenthal, *The Past is a Foreign Country* (N.Y.: Cambridge Univ., pp. 214-15. For a discussion of the "dialectic process" as a verification technique in social research, see Gideon Sjoberg, Roger Nett, *A Methodology for Social Research* (N.Y.: Harper & Row, 1968), pp. 223-46.

15 George E. Evans calls this type of oral history "instant history," where there is "little attempt being made to relate these facts to the historical context of informants, to their place...in time and its continuity with a long past. "I am a Tape Recorder: Oral History," *Encounter* 47 (Nov. 1975): 72.

16 Namias, op.cit., p. xi 17.

17 See Sturino's comments, op.cit., p. 18.

18 Lowenthal, op.cit., p. 26.

19 A method for collecting the "life story" is suggested in R.A. Rizzo, "Interviewing Italian Americans about Their Life Histories," *Italian Americana 3* (Autumn 1976): 99-109.

The Burden of a Name

Adria Bernardi

Always, as long as I can recall, there was the explaining of names.

The names of three grandparents did not translate into English. Giovanni may become John; Maria, Mary; but Massima, Mariuccia and Nello are names forever formed in Italianate letters.

For a child in a subdivision of colonial homes it was hard work answering when playmates winced and said, "What are their names again?"

My other grandfather, Antonio, was called Tony, an easy name but one that sometimes became the topic of conversation. You see, my grandfather's first and last names rhymed: Tony Vanoni.

When you are claimed by different worlds, it is hard to find a name that will fit into both. My Nonna Massima worked in a shop alongside American seamstresses. I remember sitting on the floor in my grandmother's kitchen while my aunt, then nineteen or twenty, tried out different names on my grandmother—as if she were suggesting a new hairstyle: "We'll call you Masie." This adaptation offended me. "Massima" may have been difficult, but "Masie" was ugly. The names of my grandparents' world were confusing. They were part of the past, and I was a new guest at a dinner table where the conversation had originated before electricity altered night and day. They were names spoken frequently yet I was not acquainted with them. They were people, I was told as I listened, my feet not yet touching the floor, who were mine, who were me. They appeared to me only as a vague veil that surrounded me lightly but stretched to the very edges of my perception. How could I possibly be bonded to these people I knew only so loosely, their names a mystery?

The names were ancient names. They were not the names given by American movie directors to Italian characters. They were old names, given by old mountain people to children who favored the modern world and faced it saddled with unfashionable names: my uncle Bernardi, named Virgilio; his friend Massinelli, named Attilio. The husband of my grandmother's cousin, Zagnoli, named Valerio. On my father's side of the family, there was a great-great-aunt named Lucrezia, and another named Estere. There was a great-great-uncle named Giacinto. And on my mother's side, a great- great-aunt named Ravinia. I had a great-great-grandmother named Prudenza, and a great-grandmother named Cherubina.

Often, at the table, I had heard the name of Adelmo Bertucci. He was part of my grandfather Nello's clan. Adelmo, who was called Delmo, lived in the yellow house and was married to Menga and played the accordion. And, then, there was Elmer Bertucci, who was golf superintendent at Old Elm Country Club and gave people jobs. I had been a guest at the table for twenty years before I realized that Delmo and Elmer were the same person.

These are the tricks the ear plays when you are not fluent in the language.

There was my grandmother's cousin, Delcisa, whose name to me sounded as pungent and foreign as the peccorino cheese she oiled and hung. She had a prominent, angular chin, and in my mind, her name, "Delcisa," was derived from the words "chin" and "cheese." It was only when I saw the remembrance card printed at her death that I realized "Delcisa" was a shortened version of her given name, Maria Adalgisa, a name free of harsh consonants.

Names may seem simple, as they were in the case of my grandfather Nello's twin brothers. The babies, born first and second in the family, were called Primo and Secondo. I have known of men named Terzo, Quarto, Quinto and Sesto—third, fourth, fifth, and sixth. Most names are not so straightforward. Like all immigrants, the Italians of Highwood straddled different worlds, and their names signified a complicated identity.

Domenico Linari quickly changed his name to Domenick, adding a *k*—a graphic resolution of ambiguity. He said, "Domenico, seemed like at the time, especially in the coal mine, nobody could spell it, nobody knew what I was talking about. So I put Domenick with a *k*, and it seemed like it worked."

Fanny Cassidy's husband was among the first Italians to join the Highwood police force. A friend of her husband, an American who was a lawyer and in the real estate business, had suggested the family change the name: "He used to say, 'Oh, Cas - si - ta- ri, that's too long. Change your name. Change your name. Make it Cassidy.' Then we decided. Stupid. We decided to change and make it legal. Nobody was never call him Cassitari. Even the Italians." Perhaps it better suited a policeman in Highwood, still largely an Irish town, to be named Cassidy.

Mary Baldi, born in a small town in the Piemonte, came to the coal town of Dalzell, Illinois. She was used to hearing American and she didn't like her husband's name: "Oreste sounded like such a funny name. Oreste. So I started calling him Rusty."

Italian names became Americanized. If the translation was not satisfactory, there was aural adaptation: Sante became "Sam," Domenico became "Donald." And when the names were too difficult, they were changed. In the Lake Forest home where she worked as a laundress, Eritrea Pasquesi was called "Dorothy."

The names of the past, of the language of birth, are not always so easily shed. I have known women named Menga, which is the word in the Modenese dialect for Domenica. This same word means Sunday. Both the woman and the sabbath are called Mengha. And if the woman is tiny, she is called Menghina.

Insults and inside jokes could sometimes be transported more easily than trunks, and the nicknames of the dialect stuck. Strappaneicci was named after "nicce" pancakes made out of the flour of chestnuts. *Strappa* means "snatch". So this man, who liked his chestnut flour pancakes, earned the name pancake-snatcher. And there was a family in Italy who used to eat their gruel of chestnut flour plain, without milk. When asked why she didn't give the children milk with the porridge, the mother said, "Then the cats will die." So this :family became known as 'I *Gatti*', "the cats," a name that followed them to Highwood.

There was Faggiolo (string bean). Cavrin', (the little goat). Il Gallo (the rooster). There was Il Mulo, the mule, who was a great, strong man. And *Perla*, the little pearl, a name of irony assigned by a father weary of his son's trouble-making: "La mia Perlin'."

Biases, tastes, hopes, religious and political sentiments are conferred upon children through names. And in a new generation, if those sentiments are not shared, the names become archaic. Some children of the immigrants, who saw their first operas in this country, were given the names of opera's most popular characters: Violetta, Enzo, Gilda. My Zia Teresa's sister-in-law named her boys Ferruccio, Osvaldo and Turrido. They shed these names and became Bill, Tom and Bob.

Eritrea Pasquesi tells of the names her father chose for his daughters. He was a coal miner in Thurber, Texas, an anticleric and a free-thinker:

"We had very peculiar names. Svezia, which means Sweden. Then, my name, of course, Eritrea, which is in Abbysinia, and then my sister Veneranda, which means 'venerated'—I guess for once that comes from the church. Because my father was an atheist. He named us all very funny names. And then my sister, Ribella, was the oldest." (*Ribelle* means rebel.)

Did he name his daughter Eritrea out of a fierce nationalism, in support of Italy's belated attempt to become a colonial power? Or was it a joke, naming her after the disastrous Eritrea military campaign of 1886? What would this man, who purposefully shunned the names of the saints, have said upon learning that two of his mightily named daughters had become known as "Dorothy" and "Swannie"?

My surname, itself, is a long story. Bernardi, contrary to the rules of progeny naming, was not my paternal grandfather's name. His was Piacentini.

My father, starting out in business in Chicago in the late 1950s, was given a piece of advice by a mentor, just as Fanny Cassidy's husband had been: Change your name.

And so, my father, an only child and only son, took up the difficult task of trading his father's name for another. The name Piacentini was so foreign, so intricate, that it would have been an insufficient gesture to merely drop the final vowel, following the immigrant's custom, a custom by which Lombardi became Lombard and di Filippo became Phillips. Nor did he, as I have seen done, warble out a new name from the old, a phonetic rendering with no meaning. (If he had, would we have become the Pace family?)

No, my father did not acquiesce entirely to the brisk demands of the Chicago business world. He opted for a compromise. He renounced neither family, ethnic heritage, nor provincial origin. He took the name of his maternal grandmother.

The havoc wreaked by a son renouncing a man's name for the name of his wife's family must be a terrible thing to witness. The rage and confusion created in his parents' household I cannot imagine.

But in choosing the name of an uncle he admired, Bernardi, a man with an accessible name, my father believed he had found an acceptable answer for a condition in which harmony was impossible. He chose a name he felt would allow him to carve an identity as an American businessman without sacrificing the link to his first community. Had he chosen the name Pace, however, I wonder if it would have been easier for my grandfather to accept.

A name is a mighty load we carry on backs. For those born with a good name, there is the responsibility of protecting it. Those born into a family with a name besmirched by an untidy event carry the burden of restoring—or denying—the name.

There is another meaning for the word "burden," however. In olden times, in England, a burden was a melody accompanying in the bass voice. A burden was a refrain, the chorus. Not that we need, necessarily, trumpets announcing our every consonant and vowel, it is good nonetheless to see that each component is laden with meaning that ties us to places and people, going backwards and forward. If our names are a burden, perhaps it is best to see them as a repeating constant that will carry us through.

And if it is not the name we would choose for ourselves, if the burden is a dissonant refrain or somehow tangential to the chorus, so much the better.

"The Burden of a Name" is an excerpt from *Houses with Names: The Italian Immigrants of Highwood, Illinois,* published by the University of Illinois Press, 1990.

First Encounter with Molise: Land of My Father

Richard N. Juliani
Villanova University

A number of American scholars were invited to participate in a conference on immigration from Molise to other parts of the world that was held in the city of Campobasso in June, 1987. It was a distinct privilege for me to have been included among this group of Americans and to have been asked to present a paper on this program of distinguished scholars before an international audience. So it was with great enthusiasm and energy that I plunged into the preparation of a paper on the immigration and resettlement of Molisani in Philadelphia.

The same occasion, however, contained a deeply personal dimension of experience for me. It afforded not only a long-awaited opportunity to make my first trip to Italy, but also to go to the particular area from which my father had emigrated 65 years earlier. The conference site in Campobasso would enable me to visit the *paese* of my father, about 80 kilometers away; to renew my acquaintance with fondly remembered cousins whom I had last seen as a child some 35 years ago when they left their American home in Yonkers, New York to return with their parents to Italy; and to meet for the first time two aunts, several cousins, their spouses and children, and other relatives who had been until this time only vaguely known as names in many letters and holiday cards that I had read at my parents' house. Consequently, I anticipated the truly exciting opportunity at the conclusion of the conference to visit the town of Guglionesi, near the Adriatic Coast, and to discover my roots in that community as a member of *la famiglia Iuliani*. But it also provided the possibility to establish a foundation for some new research and writing that would focus upon village life in Italy which had not been previously a part of my own scholarly agenda. The subject of the present paper is the confrontation of the expectations of one Italian American in search of his personal past as well as of research possibilities and the actual experiences that unfolded in one phase of this quest.

Several different sources of information and imagery, greatly varying in amount, accuracy and usefulness, formed the foundation for my first expectations about what Molise as a physical place and as a personal experience would be. One potentially excellent source, the immigrant father who had spent the first 22 years of his life in the region, could only provide a limited picture recalled from a distant time. Hours of conversation provided impressions of Molise in the early 20th century, but not very much from more recent periods. It was, in fact, this frozen vision of life in the remote towns of the region before World War I that had already once led the father, 25 years ago, to discourage the son from planning a previous visit. As with so many immigrants, the struggle to survive and to succeed in the United States had produced another pragmatist who feared that his son would not endure even the temporary loss of the personal conveniences found in a middle-class American home.

Another source of information, the mail from relatives over the years, did little to alter this picture of the region as the messages reported news of family events, but not much about the broader conditions of life in Molise. The one contrast to the older images came from an occasional postcard which contained a scene or two, along with a few lines of clarification, of Petacciato or Termoli as modern beach resorts. But there was no great need to resolve the apparent contradiction between memories and postcards.

More scholarly sources could be sought in some of the better known treatments of village life in Southern Italy that have been published for American readers. But these works, whether by professional writers such as Carlo Levi[1] and Anne Cornelisen[2] or by social scientists such as Edward Banfield[3] and Joseph Lopreato[4] tended also to be of limited value. First, these works were originally published from nearly 20 to 40 years ago, and are by now, like the immigrant father, not only of considerable age, but also projecting images of a time past. Second, these works were not concerned with Molise, but with other areas of the Mezzogiorno, largely concentrating on towns and villages in Basilicata (what was previously Lucania) and in Calabria. Similarly, Rudolph M. Bell's more recent study of 180 years of demographic and cultural change in rural Italy includes communities in Campania and Calabria but no other regions of the South.[5] The one major exception is the recent research by William A. Douglass on Agnone in the province of Isernia in Alto Molise.[6] In this important study, the author presents a thorough examination of the implications of local demographic and political conditions for migration overseas and, conversely, of the consequences of migration upon the social, economic and political structure of the town. Although primarily focused upon a particular community, Douglass provides invaluable information and ideas on the historical background, the emigration process, and the contemporary character of life for anyone interested in other specific communities in Molise or in the region in general.

Despite the scholarly nature of the Douglass study, or perhaps because of it, what was still missing was some graphic sense of what everyday life in a town in Molise today would be like. In the absence of any available ethnography of the immediate and ordinary, the prospective visitor can turn to the standard publications of the tourist industry. The result of this alternative, however, is not only even much more lacking than what can be derived from reading scholarly sources, but a bleak, perhaps chilling picture. The latest edition of a very popular guide for tourists to Italy, *Frommer's Dollarwise Guide to Italy*, provides nearly 600 pages of information and advice.[7] In Chapter XXI, entitled "Southern Italy-Apulia," an introduction focuses entirely on Apulia and unmistakably gives the otherwise uninformed reader the impression that the Abruzzi is a section of the larger district of Apulia. Devoting all of slightly more than one page to the entire Abruzzi, this guide describes two basilicas, one fountain, one hotel and one restaurant, all in Aquila, and does not mention Molise even once.

In contrast to this work, a competitive volume, with a pleasantly irreverent style, published by presumably more erudite students from Harvard and Radcliffe, at least recognizes that Molise has been an autonomous region since 1963.[8] Moreover, this guidebook not only acknowledges the existence, but also the attractions of the larger towns of Termoli, Campobasso, and Isernia as well as the smaller ones such as Capracotta, Pietrabbondante, Carpinone and Agnone. Despite some rather positive observations, it devotes no more than one page to the entire region. Unfortunately, this brief section still presents some darker impressions to its readers such as when in describing Campobasso, the largest town and capital of the region, it declares "if, by some misadventure, you must spend the night here...", then proceeds to recommend an inexpensive hotel. In general, however, the treatment of Molise is not disparaging and certainly should not discourage the more adventuresome traveler.

A final attempt to supplement these sources was made by a request for descriptive materials to the Italian Government Travel Office. Considering the great number of Molisani who immigrated to North America in past years, it would seem reasonable that an official state agency would be prepared to anticipate a new era of tourism and to accommodate those travelers who would today prefer to leave the beaten paths of packaged tours and seek out instead the towns and villages of their ancestors. It was a great disappointment, therefore, to be informed by the New York City office of this agency that no materials on Molise were currently available to the prospective visitor. This result, along with the inadequacies of the published guides for the traveler in Italy, contributes evidence to the rising suspicion that the region may be the least known and least visited by Americans.

In short, the American visitor to Molise must undertake a trip with very limited and often obsolete information that is likely to generate quite inaccurate expectations of what actually awaits him. In our case, the initial entry occurred on a beautiful day in late June, 1987. First traveling by bus from Rome on the autostrada toward Naples, then shortly after passing below the monastery at Monte Cassino, we turned east on secondary roads winding toward *i monti del Matese*. Our guide, Giose Rimanelli, took the microphone of the public address system of the bus to begin some remarks. As the bus plunged into yet another mountain tunnel, Rimanelli advised the passengers that our trip was nearly over. As we left the tunnel for the bright glow of a soft evening sun setting at our backs, Rimanelli informed us that we had entered, as he so lovingly put it, the happy land of Molise. For the student of Italian immigration, a first reaction had to include some attempt to imagine this area a century ago and to wonder how anyone could have managed to leave this difficult, mountainous terrain. For the more subjective person lying beneath that professional exterior, a first reaction might also include a more tragic feeling of why anyone would have wanted to leave this beautiful land. For the American visitor, a first reaction is the discovery of a spectacular landscape, as dramatic and overwhelming in its physical character as almost any other area of the Italian peninsula, and the realization that no previous information could really provide an adequate sense of the actual experience. As I looked at this beautiful land for the first time, I tried to imagine what my father might be doing at that very moment at his present home back in New Jersey. I closed my eyes for a moment to say to him " I hope you are well." A few days later, when I sent him a postcard from his home town, I would also be able to tell him, " Il vostro Molise adesso è il nostro Molise."

But the principal reason for going to Molise had not been to admire the landscape. It was to participate in the conference which focused, as its title indicated, on "Il Sud e L'America: Molise ed Emigrazione." But a similar sense of surprise at experiences for which one could hardly have been prepared and which would clash with ill-conceived expectations would repeat itself during the course of the next few days. On the first morning of the conference, my initial encounter with relatives in the region occurred. Knowing that they were coming, I waited outside of the hotel. About nine a.m., after watching many people enter the lobby for the conference, I saw a man and three women approaching. One of the women wore my face. We looked at each other and simultaneously as she said "Riccardo," I found myself calling out "Pierina." Two cousins, one from Molise and the other from Philadelphia, who had never met before, had found each other. The instant recognition between two people who had never seen each other before, but who shared the same family face was immediately

surpassed by the mutually felt conviction that we had always
known each other.

At the conclusion of the formal sessions on that first day,
during dinner, another stranger approached to introduce himself, and I made my first friend, outside of relatives, from
Guglionesi. My expectations had prepared me to extend my
warmest friendships to the simple peasant folk that I knew I
was to meet, and the first one was Filippo Salvatore. Mildly
surprised to learn that Filippo was on the program, I found
myself staring in greater shock at his Harvard University
necktie, which reflected the institution of his Ph.D. Now a
university professor in Montreal, who would later serve as a
delightful guide to Guglionesi itself, Filippo Salvatore was the
first step in the shattering of my stereotypes of the town and
its people. On the final day of the conference, a young lawyer
introduced himself by asking if I were "Iuliani" and declaring
that I was also Guglionesano. While I protested that I was
only to reach the town for the first time tomorrow, with even
greater insistence, Serafino continued to tell me that I was
truly Guglionesano. To come from a society in which all of us
are strangers to one another to a place where one finds instant acceptance and immersion into family and community is
not only a remarkable discovery for the academic sociologist,
but a profoundly humbling personal experience as well.

My own presentation at the conference was mainly a historical study of Molisani immigration to Philadelphia. In its final
section, a more sociological question was raised of what was
happening to later generations of descendants of the Molisani
who had settled in that city. In contrast to the interpretation
that cultural assimilation and social mobility had nearly
completely erased the final traces of ethnic identity, another
view was offered as a conceivable alternative. Proposing a new
twist to Marcus Lee Hansen's well known "Law of the 3rd
Generation Return," my conclusion raised the possibility that
the greater material wealth and psychological security of
Italian Americans as Americans afforded them the opportunity to renew interest in their ethnic heritage. In particular, it was suggested that Italian Americans were more
likely than ever before to visit Italy as tourists. But it is also
possible that Italian Americans might no longer be content

with the sights of Rome, Florence, and Venice, but already turning toward a search for more personal origins. The conclusion was that if that is happening, we would also find increasing numbers of Italian Americans discovering their actual roots in the villages of Molise along with their origins as Molisani and perhaps even their present identities as Molisani Americans.[9]

But this conclusion as well as the entire paper and the trip in general had simultaneously been shaped by academic analysis and by intensely personal emotions. The tension between these two levels of thought and feeling was still being internally resolved as the conference began. Here so close to the first home of my father, I was being haunted by some recent words that he had spoken to me. While listening to earlier presentations, I had decided to extend my paper with one further paragraph. My now revised paper would end with the following remarks.

One final issue that perhaps should be discussed before concluding this paper is that of the attitudes toward their experiences of the many Molisani who had to leave their native region to migrate to places such as Philadelphia. It is of course, no longer possible to interview immigrants from the last century or even from the earliest years of the present one. But the remarks of one individual of a more recent time who is still living might provide some clues to the thoughts and feelings of these immigrants. When I first planned to make this trip, I asked my father, who had left his town of Guglionesi in 1922 and has never been back, if he would come with me at this time. But at the age of 86, he does not travel very well any more. Before I left for Italy, when I visited him for the last time, he said that he had two messages for me to carry on this trip. The first was for me. He said simply, "In my heart, I am going with you." Then he gave me a second message that I was to deliver to his people in his town. "When you see them," he said, "tell them that I think of them every day." Perhaps by these words, he was speaking not only for himself but for the many other Molisani who had to suffer this separation.[10]

In counterpoint to the poignant words of this emigrant from the region, we were about to learn that Molise was also thinking of its people overseas. With the presentation of my paper, my own role shifted to being primarily a relaxed observer as the conference proceeded to unfold much to the apparent satisfaction of its participants. For three days, speakers continued to deliver papers of consistently high quality. The organization of the conference was flawless; and the hospitality offered to all of us by the organizers and officials of the region was wonderful. We can only look forward to a continuation of such programming with great enthusiasm and willingness to cooperate. But the conference concluded with a final session in which Molise spoke to us. Various leaders, including the President of the regional government, the commissioners of the offices of tourism, culture, and emigration, and representatives of seven political parties joined in a roundtable discussion on the problems and prospects of Molise and its emigrants overseas. This provocative exchange of ideas on trade, tourism, transportation, technology and tradition suggested that the region is ready to embark upon a bold program to develop a new relationship with the rest of Italy and the world.

The formal closing of the conference also meant re-entering a more personal phase of our time in Italy, but subsequent experiences would serve only to reinforce the themes introduced by this final session. In particular, a sense that Molise is at a watershed moment in its modern history would become increasingly apparent. Ironically, this phase began with a tour by the conference group of some centers of very early human civilization in the region, first the Paleolithic Museum at Isernia and then the ancient Samnite sites at Sepino and Pietrabbondante. It became immediately apparent that this beautiful land has always demanded much from its inhabitants as the price for their survival. As E. T. Salmon declared, "Samnium was a rugged nurse of rugged men." [11] These rugged men also provided ancient Rome with the greatest challenge for domination of the Italian peninsula which they nearly won during more than 50 years of bitter warfare. Never actually conquered, but instead co-opted by the granting of citizenship, the people of this region, again in Salmon's eloquent words, "...more than any other put Rome on her mettle and bludgeoned her into greatness." [12] In these places today, one sees spectacular ruins that may have even greater archeological significance than Pompeii, but which remain almost entirely unknown, unreached and unappreciated by the outside world, perhaps also serving as a metaphor for the situation of Molise in modern times.

After final farewells to our academic colleagues, we left Campobasso early that evening in the warm company of local cousins for the 80 kilometer drive to the ancestral *paese*. Located about three kilometers north of the Biferno River and 15 kilometers inland from the Adriatic coastal town of Termoli, Guglionesi rests more than 1200 feet above sea level. Since ancient times, the primarily agricultural and pastoral economy of the Biferno Valley has depended upon its river to provide irrigation. But to approach Guglionesi from the west today, it is necessary to drive the final few kilometers on the Bifernina, the superhighway that crosses over *il lago di Guardialfiera*, the second largest artificial lake in all of Europe, formed about 10 years ago by the construction of a new dam.

Human settlement in the area of Guglionesi can be traced back as far as the final period of the Paleolithic Age, and it has often been marked by violence and war.[13] In ancient times, this territory was occupied by the Frentani, described by Strabo, perhaps the most eminent Greek geographer and historian of the period, as a "beastly" people.[14] Following Roman expansion into the vicinity of Guglionesi, a long succession of later invaders, beginning with the Visigoths in the early 5th century, also left their mark. About the 10th century, however, a less violent band of newcomers, Benedictine missionaries, arrived not only to convert the population to Christianity, but also to introduce the cultivation of olives and grapevines. Over the years, Longobards, Normans, Turkish Saracens, Spanish Bourbons and the French attempted to subdue the land and its people. With the unification of Italy in 1860, foreign domination was succeeded by internal sources of conflict. Hostility toward the new state and class oppression encouraged peasant resistance and uprisings, often in the form of brigandage.[15] In World War II, during the brief struggle for Termoli in the first week of October, 1943, Guglionesi and its surroundings were struck by aerial bombings before *la prima linea* of land combat swept the Germans from their entrenchments on the high ground north of the Biferno.[16]

Although traces of physical damage as well as personal memories can easily recall the war years, the past nearly half-century has been much kinder to Guglionesi and its inhabitants. The most recent years have been a time of dramatic change and perhaps, as for the region of Molise as a whole, the beginnings of very significant growth and development. In 1901, the population of Guglionesi was 7,171.[17] In the late 1950's, it reached about 9,000. Declining greatly in the next two decades, by 1971 it had fallen to 5,821. But during the last 20 years, it now appears to have stabilized itself, and today stands at just under 5,800. In 1986, Guglionesi consisted of 1,979 families. The official report of the local government does not indicate any individuals without families. During the same year, the number of births, 66, was slightly greater than the number of deaths, 61, but not significantly so. A more encouraging sign can be found in the fact that 83 individuals returned to the town, while only 62 departed from it.[18]

As one approaches Guglionesi even for the first time, another significant feature of its population becomes immediately apparent.Guglionesi is spreading down the side of its slopes. Since the 1960s, despite the decline in its population Guglionesi has, somewhat ironically, witnessed a tremendous development of new housing. In fact, Guglionesi *nuovo* appears to be larger than Guglionesi *vecchio*. Although the exterior of the new buildings is mainly in the drab architectural style of high-rise *casa popolare* apartments that have sprouted all over Italy, it has provided improved housing for the population. Therefore, with this formidable change in the ecology of the town, there has also been a sharp reduction in the density of household units. The interiors of these newer buildings, moreover, contain the most modern and fashionable styles of design and decoration. The renovation of older housing has occurred to some degree in the older section of the town as well. On the fringes of Guglionesi, where the most recent building has been done, construction has managed to introduce more innovative and imaginative designs.

The physical transformation of Guglionesi has been paralleled by economic and cultural changes over the same period. The construction of the spectacular dam and lake has profoundly altered the agriculture of the area. For the first time in its long history, Guglionesi and a vast part of the region has a guaranteed system of regular and controllable irrigation. The rolling land which for so long was covered by olive trees has undergone a massive shift to *i girasoli*, sunflowers, as its principal crop. Raised partly for its seeds, but more for its safflower oil, this crop represents a far more intensive use of the land and a more profitable commodity for the market. But the traditional olive oil, tomatoes, grains, and wine continue to come from these fields as well. Within a few kilometers of Guglionesi, several major food processing establishments can be found, including tomato packing, sugar refining and a wine cooperative. Local residents claim that many products of Molise, particularly pasta, tomatoes, olive oil and wine, are now the best in all of Italy, but that they are marketed and sold under false labels that identify these products as having originated in other regions.

Beyond agriculture, however, a more industrial economy has been emerging in and around Guglionesi. In recent years, there has been established a steel products factory which makes machine parts; a gravel factory which produces materials for building foundations; an electronics equipment plant which provides filaments for television sets and high tension wires; and a massive new FIAT assembly plant employing about 4,000 workers. Within Guglionesi itself, in addition to the long familiar shops of the butchers, tailors, barbers, cobblers, and florists, the businesses catering to more modern life styles can be found—the auto mechanic, the camera shop, the dry cleaner and the electronic appliance store.

But these changes are not entirely positive. While the dam and the lake have helped to transform the economy of Guglionesi, they may also contribute to *la foschia*, the haze that constantly hovers over the area, as well as to the oppressive humidity problem of the area that local residents claim did not exist previously. While some inhabitants insist that the effects of the Chernobyl accident in the Soviet Union in the previous year are still being felt, it is probable that industrialization throughout Italy as well as long term weather and climate cycles are altering the physical environment.

For many Guglionesani, however, the most important and distressing changes are occurring in the patterns of local culture. For the few Guglionesani who have been to the United States, it is apparent that everyday life is becoming more like that in America. Adults believe that younger members of the community are adopting American music, sports, and clothing styles, but also drugs. Similarly, it is believed now that young people are too freely allowed to follow their own tastes in such matters. Language differences between generations provide particular source of concern. While older Guglionesani continue to use their traditional dialect which remains for them an important device of personal identity and social solidarity, the young tend to use standard Italian. But one resident, who had lived in New York for twenty years, expresses an even greater fear. Noting the growing influence of television, she lists some American words that are now commonly used by the young—disc jockey, boss, show, speaker and popcorn. She is convinced that in another ten years the young may all be speaking English.

Although members of the older generation strongly voice their concerns over such matters, it is the young who are really caught at the center of these changes. Traditional customs, not long ago so highly sacred to this community, are being widely abandoned by the young. Marital engagements, for example, can now be broken. When the young dissolve themselves from such bonds, it may become a matter of grave distress and embarassment to their parents. Consequently, some adults believe that the young do not care about their families any longer. In support of the older generation, the Church apparently has embarked on a program to preserve traditional values and folkways. For young children, summer camps under religious auspices reflect such efforts by the Church. But even in Guglionesi, young adults soon enough find themselves caught in the struggles between lay movements such as *Azione Cattolica* and *Comunione e Liberazione*. The presence of non-Catholic alternatives such as the Jehovah's Witnesses further complicate the choices of young adults.

We arrived at Guglionesi on the evening of June 30, a very significant date for our relatives in the town. As my father had pointed out before we left the United States and we were now again being reminded by a cousin, the other son in the Iuliani family would have been my uncle Nicola, from whom I received my middle name, and it was on this date that he had drowned in the Biferno River some 66 years ago. It was the death of his younger brother that had brought my father back to his family on an early discharge from the Italian army. It was apparent that everyone in the family today was still very much aware of this anniversary. It also provides some sense of how profoundly important family events remain for these people as well as how time is measured in these towns and villages. When this subject was introduced to our conversation, we could only offer the relatively immodest response that we hoped that our arrival could give this date a somewhat happier meaning for the family from now on.

Shortly after our arrival, we walked to the apartment building where my two aunts lived and where we would meet them for the first time. But this grand occasion began with a ritual of recognition. I soon realized that the two aunts and several cousins were inspecting and discussing my facial features. It was obviously necessary, just in case an imposter had been sent from America. As I listened to the evaluation of my forehead, eyes, nose, chin and so on, the family committee soon concluded that a sufficient number of Iuliani physical characteristics were present. It was comforting to receive their vote of authenticity. The subject of physical characteristics would remain an important topic of conversation throughout our days in Guglionesi. Sometimes such conversation revealed interesting layers of meaning. At one point, with her constant playfulness, *zia* Tanina remarked that I was very tall just as she believed her brother to be. When I protested that my father was really not very tall, but rather short in fact, she replied that he certainly was tall at the time he first left home and, therefore, it was America that must have made him short.

This reunion with all the members of the family in Guglionesi was unquestionably the most joyful and meaningful experience of the entire trip to Italy. Sitting between my two elderly aunts, *zia* Diamante and *zia* Tanina provided an overwhelming sense that for me, at least, a long broken circle had been finally reconnected. Because they are so emotional, these two women had been warned by their children not to cry at this moment. But since no one had made the same demand on me, as I held tightly to their hands and stared at their marvelous faces, I did cry. The returning family member becomes acutely aware of the devastating effects of the separations that once took place when earlier emigrants were forced to depart from family and native land. The years in America have sadly deprived most of their descendants of any real fluency in the ancestral language. Consequently, like so many others, we struggled to speak with cousins in our best classroom Italian while they so playfully labored to teach us a little bit of the local dialect that might truly have enabled us to enter their world. All the while we painfully regarded each other—first cousins who could not easily speak in words, but had so much to ask and to tell one another.

I asked my cousin Lucy one day to tell me what our grandmother, Concetta Rocchia Iuliani, was like. From my father, I had known that she was a very strong person, tall for these people, and a dominant figure in family matters. But Lucy provided a somewhat different view. Lucy remembered *nonna* Concetta saying her daily rosary for one intention alone—that her emigrant children would someday return to her in Guglionesi. When she finally died, of her seven children who had left the town for the Americas, only one had ever returned to her. When we visited the family crypt in the cemetery, I wanted to tell her that one grandson now sought her embrace.

From its beginnings, the founding fathers of social science were concerned with the transformation of traditional societies to more modern forms of culture and social organization. Guglionesi represents a very recent example of a community that is today experiencing this type of transition. It is also typical of the kind of villages and towns in Southern Italy that once had to lose so many of its inhabitants as emigrants to other parts of the world. The necessity of many individuals to pursue the greater opportunities of the market economy once required many Guglionesani to abandon their families in the town. So they left with the belief that the only way they could help their families was to leave them. It is a loss that is still acutely felt. One woman in Guglionesi argues that the Italian government owes, at the least, free trips to Italy to the descendants of immigrants for having forced their forebears to depart in the first place. But the industrialization of the area now finally means that the Guglionesani no longer need to climb aboard *il treno della speranza* that once took them off to Milan, Buenos Aires, Montreal and Philadelphia. Instead that train may have a new destination more nearby at this time. But with the death of the present generation of older Guglionesani, some major remnants of traditional culture and customs will be dramatically reduced, if not almost entirely eliminated. The gap between the generations is far greater than in the case of more industrialized societies such as the United States. The changing values and life styles of younger Guglionesani are living markers of the passing of a very traditional society to the kind of modernity that is found today in Rome or New York. What is overwhelmingly clear in this situation is that the land that my father left and that I sought is in many ways no longer there.

My first encounter with Molise, nevertheless, was a valuable and rewarding experience on several levels at the same time. For the social scientist, it presented an opportunity to begin research on a community in transition that remains largely unexamined and represents a natural laboratory for the study of social change. For the American visitor to Italy, the same occasion offered places where one may still be able to forsake the illusions of packaged and sanitized tourism and to recover what little is left of what historian Daniel J. Boorstin had in mind 25 years ago when he referred to the lost art of travel.[19] Finally, for the individual for whom the immigration of parents or grandparents has meant permanent separation from family and community and an almost atomistic existence in a New World, the region of Molise and towns like Guglionesi provide a previously missing vital link in the search for one's own "usable past." For all of these dimensions of this experience, whether as scholar, traveler, or son of an immigrant, when I think now of Molise and of Guglionesi, I also think of the words of my father in the message that I carried to his people—for now I too think of them everyday.

---

[1] Carlo Levi, *Christ Stopped at Eboli.* New York: Farrar, Straus and Company, 1947.

[2] Anne Cornelisen, *Torregreca: Life, Death, Miracles.* Boston: Little, Brown and Company, 1969.

[3] Edward C. Banfield, *The Moral Basis of a Backward Society.* New York: The Free Press, 1958.

[4] Joseph Lopreato, *Peasants No More.* San Francisco: Chandler Publishing Company, 1967.

[5] Rudolph M. Bell, *Fate and Honor, Family and Village.* Chicago: The University of Chicago Press, 1979.

[6] William A. Douglass, *Emigration in a South Italian Town.* New Brunswick, New Jersey: Rutgers University Press, 1984.

[7] Darwin Porter, *Frommer's Dollarwise Guide to Italy.* New York: Prentice Hall, 1987.

[8] Cristina-Astrid Hansell (editor), *Let's Go: The Budget Guide to Italy.* New York: St. Martin's Press, 1987.

[9] Richard N. Juliani, "Molisani in Philadelphia: Settlement and Demographics," in *Il Sud e L'America: Molise ed Emigrazione,* edited by Giose Rimanelli and Francis X. Femminella (forthcoming)

[10] *Ibid.*

[11] E. T. Salmon, *Samium and the Samnites.* Cambridge, England: Cambridge University Press, 1967. p. 18.

[12] *Ibid.*, p. 13.

[13] *Storia di Guglionesi attraverso Documenti e Reperti Archeologici.* Guglionesi, 1984.

[14] Salmon, p. 53 (fn.6).

[15] *Storia di Guglionesi.*

[16] Wesley Frank Craven and James Lea Cate (eds.) *The Army Air Forces in World War II,* volume II. Chicago: University of Chicago Press, 1949, pp. 548-551; W. G. F. Jackson, *The Battle for Italy.* London: B. T. Betsford, Ltd., 1967, pp. 126-128.

[17] Fossati, *Dizionario dei Comuni,* n.d., p. 65.

18 *Comune di Guglionesi,* 1987.

19 Daniel J. Boorstin, *The Image,* 1961, pp. 77-117.

On Translating My Father's Memoirs:
Portrait of the Italian Immigrant as a Young Man 1897-1920

Teresa Cerasuola

At seventy-nine years of age in 1976, my father, Michele Buccino, completed a two-volume history of his family in which he recorded their origins from the year 1820.

Born in Rionero in *Vulture* in the province of Potenza,[1] his recollections include varied societal aspects of life there: Who married whom and why. The family's businesses. Education and occupational training. Who lived. Who died, why and how. Courtship practices. Accumulation and distribution of property. Who emigrated, why and where. Who returned: why? Family honor. And lastly, civic and moral responsibility.

Aside from chronological events, vivid details of World War I battles in which he fought as an Italian infantryman after being repatriated to Italy from Argentina, are matched only by those of his first emigration to Buenos Aires as a teenaged cabinetmaker's apprentice. My father's depiction of experiences while crossing the Atlantic Ocean three times in eight years during the first quarter of this century are poignant for obvious reasons, but important also because of his attention to such mundane details as cost of living expenses, weather conditions and clothing styles. His chronicle is written in Italian with significant phrases, names, nicknames and passages in village dialect. It also contains some Spanish language as spoken by him during his five years in South America. In 1920 my father emigrated to the U.S. where he lived until he died in 1978, returning only once to his native village, fifty years later.

I have chosen to concentrate on three aspects of my father's memoirs. These deal with marriage and courtship practices, his early life as an apprentice in Italy before his first immigration to Argentina and his years in the Italian infantry during World War I.

Courtship and marriage as described by my father date back to 1876 with the union of his parents. His mother, Felice, not quite 17, was the only child of a master sieve maker. Her mother had inherited considerable wealth from her family's business as stone carvers. When Felice married Angelo Raffaele Giuseppe, he was engaged in his family's business as merchants of fine cloth. Between the years 1876 and 1901, a total of 25 years of childbearing, Felice was pregnant 19 times, resulting in 5 miscarriages, 5 children who died in early childhood and nine who grew to adulthood. Michele, my father, was the sixth of seven sons. There were two daughters. Throughout this history, we find that marriages are arranged according to a caste system determined by a family's wealth, its professions or trades, clan respectability and provincial proximity. Donato, the first born, was married in 1898 to a second cousin as arranged by his grandfather. His wife's family were also business people. Donato, who was master shoemaker at age 22, was given a dowry to match his wife's, consisting of a house of two large rooms. Vincenzo, the fourth son, who had returned in 1910 from America, after working there as a brick maker, married the daughter of builders of transport wagons. With dowries from both families, they established a cafe and grocery store, which was quite successful. Erminia, the elder daughter, at 19 was pressured by her parents and brothers to marry a man who had returned from America with money and, unfortunately, undiagnosed TB, leaving her a widow at 20 with an infant son. The second daughter, Teresa, was also pressured to marry a neighbor whose dowry consisted of insurance money accrued from the death of his brother killed in France during World War I.

In the Italian villages, World War I had created a scarcity of marriageable men, not only through deaths in battle, but because the Italian soldier had either married exogamously or was even more intent on emigrating in search of his fortune. Therefore, on my father's return to Rionero, he was the recipient of many proposals of marriage:

Luisa Nardozza, our neighbor, had a nephew of her dead husband who had married and was living in Barile, 2 km. from Rionero. He came to visit, as he usually did and asked why her son should not be married. He know a good catch; the daughter of the Rabaschi family who had a coal business. Luisa refused, saying she had other plans for her son. This nephew met me in the piazza and offered me the same proposal. I assured him I would see him in Barile on a certain day to meet with this girl in his house and if it were destined, I would agree to the marriage. A few days later, at the Nardozza house, Caterina Rabaschi came to borrow something, speaking her native Albanian to Mrs. Nardozza. Nardozza quickly asked them to speak only Italian, so there would be no misunderstandings. There were few words, but many happy glances over a bottle of very good, old moscato, which encouraged even more happy discourse. The second time, at her older brother's, he told me to send regards to my brothers Francesco and Vincenzo, whom he had known in youth. I remained with Caterina and her sister-in-law and learned that all the property had been willed to her from her parents, her brothers having received their shares at marriage. "As soon as your parents and my brothers meet, I will give you 5,000 lire. My older brothers will go along with my choice, although my younger brother is not so anxious for me to marry,'" she said. I met with my brother Francesco, who remembered the Rabaschi, saying they were well-to-do and well organized. He offered his presence or help. My brother Vincenzo's response, on the other hand, was to ask why I would want to marry an Albanian. I discussed my plans with my mother, but she remained cold. The days passed. Caterina Rabaschi was smitten by me and asked to meet me alone. I went. She asked why I hadn't come around. On hearing my reason, she pressed the 5,000 lire into my hands. "They're yours," she said, "I want to leave my brother's house. Please take me away. Right now. I feel like a slave there." I calmed her down and told her that her brother would never forgive the dishonor of an elopement. "Parents forgive their children," I said, "but not brothers. One day he will vindicate himself. Let's wait." Several other desirable marriage opportunities arose, but my mother always refused them. I didn't know why.

It could be assumed then that this system automatically forbade any freedom of choice concerning one's life partner. Yet, my father related how the third born son, Angelo Mario, who while studying for the priesthood in Calabria, was called home by his grandfather to join with the family in the annual Mt. Carmel feast.

Angelo Mario, now known as Frate Ilario, stayed on in Rionero a few extra days. He had fallen in love with one of the beautiful Libutti daughters, but returned to the seminary anyway to prepare for the examinations leading to taking his final vows. When it was discovered at the seminary that he was writing love letters to la Libutti, he was dismissed, to the great disappointment of grandfather Cerulli, whose biggest pride and joy would have been to have a priest in the family, not to mention the many ducati it had cost him for this pleasure.

Once in America, many of these courtship traditions were abandoned. Witness the marriage of the fifth son, Luigi, who as a child had suffered an infection which left him lame.

As a master tailor he emigrated to Boston. In 1914, he heard there was much work in Canada making uniforms for the English, who were fighting World War I. He began hitchhiking, even though he was crippled; working a day at a time along the way, until he reached Montreal, where he found employment. He married Albertine Michel, a French Canadian. They had eight children and he died there, in 1957.

Refuting also that these customs were unbreakable, I cite my own maternal grandmother, Mariantonia Conte, born 1860, of respectable family. She not only chose her husband-to-be at age 23, but arranged her own wedding feast after her parents opposed her marriage to a widower with two sons. Her dowry was the eventual inheritance of farmable land to match his guaranteed income as timekeeper on the railroad.

Images of our parents as youngsters are difficult to visualize, old photographs, perhaps being the only proof that they indeed started out as children. Yet, those passages dealing with his early life, especially of his experiences as an apprenticed cabinetmaker afford great insight into my father's boyhood.

At six years old, having been a student one year and attending school only until the age of 12, I was already considering which trade was to be my life's work. I started as a barber, but was disgusted by lack of proper hygiene and quickly chose the trade of cabinetmaking, which better suited my artistic wants. I was apprenticed to Master Luigi Cardillo for several years, but left when I felt he wasn't teaching me properly. I presented myself next to Master Carmine Traficante who had a habit of leaving after midday dinner for a stroll and a game of "Tre sette" at a local tavern. All the apprentices awaited his return, knowing by the way he held his pipe clenched between his teeth, whether or not he'd won at cards. If his lips trembled, there was hell to pay, even by those older apprentices who were young, married men. However, he was a skilled craftsman, who knew his trade well and from whom I learned much. I left his laboratory as I was about to become a victim of his wrath after one of his midday losses, barely escaping a sound beating with a huge tube of carpenter's glue. My next master was Carmine Pepe who had recently returned from South America. He had established a shop of carpentry and furniture making and I soon profited by his wealth of knowledge and experience. I earned a measly 5 cents per day, 1.150 lire per week, but I deserved much more. So, I left his employ when Gerardo DiDonato who had heard of my ability, offered me 17 cents per day. A year later Master DiDonato doubled my pay to 34 cents, amounting to 10 lire plus change per week. At this time, I was donating 5 lire a week to my mother and used the other 5 lire for my needs, without disturbing my father's wallet. When DiDonato decided to re-emigrate to Buenos Aires, he asked me if I wanted to accompany him and his wife, as they were childless. Without hesitating a moment, I answered yes. When I announced my intentions at home, there came the end of the earth (il fino mondo). So, I left home, working with my Master and living in an inn. My mother got word to me to return home as she had convinced my father to give his assent. He gave me no funds, but my mother had been accumulating my board money. She outfitted me with two custom-made suits, enough linens for two years and four new pairs of shoes. She also gave me 50 lire on the day of departure. It was 1912 and I was fifteen years old. Two days before leaving I started my goodbyes to friends and relatives who gave me gifts of cigarettes and chocolates. As we left Rionero there were seven of us bound for Argentina. Accompanied by friends, relatives and curious paesani, we resembled a procession on its way to a Catholic sanctuary. On 12 December 1912, we left amid enthusiastic good wishes and many, many tears, stopping at Foggia and Pavia and thence to Genova, where we waited several days to embark the Italian ship called Regina Elena. We arrived in Buenos Aires 5 January 1913.

In the following passage, my father's attempts at establishing himself as a master cabinetmaker after his return to Rionero are reflected rather sadly.

I resumed working with my old master, Carmine Pepe, but the pay was miserable. I had a good reputation and many of the masters sought me out as an employee, but I knew their defect at not paying enough and refused. At our house, the doors and frames were in bad shape and I implored my parents to allow me to reconstruct them. They agreed. I used the working space of the Caggiano brothers to construct the balconies in the South American style. When they were all mounted in place, the masters and cabinetmakers of the village were astonished at my new construction methods. They encouraged me to open my own shop, however, I had no funds. My idea was to open a woodworking and furniture shop leaving behind our methods of construction and using more modern techniques and machinery. I also attempted to form a society of cabinetmakers and woodworkers, but they laughed in my face. Many of my paesani had marriageable daughters who came forward with the usual 10,000 lire dowry. This could very well have been used to start my own business, but I renounced them all. I didn't want to begin married life in this way. All doors were closed to me.

Fifty-one years later, on his return to Rionero, these same wooden balconies were still intact in his ancestral home, as they are today. Despite his frustration at not being able to establish himself in Rionero, my father's reminiscences reflect a lifestyle which included a certain degree of social and cultural amenities.

The feast of Mt. Carmel was a great one in Rionero. My mother requested that I accompany my sister Teresa to Mass. In order to get to the church we had to cross XX Settembre Piazza, where we attracted many glances and greetings. In the evening my father arranged for the family to hear the orchestra in piazza. We all sat in the cafe of our compare Don Gennaro D'Andrea, where my father ordered ice cream, a bottle of vermouth and sweet biscuits. After the music, my father ordered us all to return home. I accompanied my parents home and then requested their leave to go watch the fireworks, which were stupendous.

Sixty-four years had not diminished my father's recollections as a soldier during World War I. Beginning with his repatriation to Italy from Argentina:

The Italian Government had advertised its decision to pay passage back to Italy for whomever was willing to fight for his country. One morning, awaking early, I took the train to the Italian Consulate and filled out the proper application for repatriation. It was June and very cold. They served us coffee, bread and butter. I asked if my class of 1897 had been called to fight. I was so anxious to return to Italy, I took the place of another in order to speed the process. On 7 July, 1916 I left Argentina with 400 other young men of approximately the same age. We were all very happy, no one seemed concerned about the German submarines which infested the waters. Always traveling along the coast, we arrived in Brazil 48 hours later to take on coffee destined for Italy. The ship was also carrying 100 horses. We were docked in Brazil for 5 days of loading. Brazilian boys came hawking their wares. Unfortunately, those of us who were on board had scant money for souvenirs. I bought some bananas for my family in Rionero, not realizing they'd be rotten long before my arrival there. Still traveling along the coast in order to avoid the submarines. we finally arrived in Genoa 16 August 1916, 5 weeks in all. I arrived at home by troop train four days later, during Rionero's annual fair. My eldest brother had already gone to war, even though he was the father of five and had been mistakenly sent into the battle zone. I had not seen my two sisters since my departure four years earlier and they asked in wonderment why I had chosen to come back during the war. I answered that there being a great scarcity of work in Argentina, my only recourse was to return to Italy, a soldier. I was soon inducted into the infantry where I was reunited with all my old childhood friends. For one month, training consisted of coffee at dawn, ten minutes rest per each hour of instruction and the same lunch every day of rice in soup. We marched for five miles with full pack of 35 kilos; sleeping from 8:00 p.m. to dawn. The pay started at two cents per day. After five days we received ten cents or 1/2 lira. During battle the simple soldier was paid 2.50 lire per five days.[2] With basic training completed, our regiment was accompanied to the railroad station by a full marching band. The mess was much better, even to the extent of quite good wine as compared with what we'd eaten during training. Our enemy was not even 50 meters away in the trenches. We fought together with the French against the Bulgarians and Germans for five days and nights, with much loss of life and then had to retreat. We returned from the front in Bulgaria to Salonicco on foot, covering 30 to 35 kms per day, always with full pack in the heat of July. On my return to the front I developed malaria, was hospitalized for several days and then re-entered combat. The malaria persisted through short stays in hospital and returns to the front. I had such a severe case, that I was finally sent to a hospital in Milan which specialized in the treatment of soldiers with malaria. We were medicated with large doses of quinine, whose side effect was temporary deafness, but I continued this cure in order to recover. It was during this period of recuperation that we heard sirens and church bells announcing the Armistice on 11 November 1918. After all the loss of innocent blood, the war was over. Civilian strikes followed; there being shortages of work for returning veterans. In order to bring an end to this unrest, one particular night the Commander gave orders to shoot at a huge mob of women brandishing pitchforks who were followed by their men bearing arms. Again, as in the war, so many innocents lost limbs, or were sent to prison because of their participation in the strikes. My next post was a small town 4 km outside of Vicenza in the Veneto region called Torre di Quarto Soli (Tower of the Four Suns). Grandi ricordi—I have so many great memories. I was stationed in a barracks which included a barber, a shoemaker, a launderer, a cook, a guard who took care of the reading and writing materials of the troops and myself, the carpenter. Nearby was the slaughterhouse where old horses were butchered to feed the Austrian POWs. It was a good post and I spent every night in the local hosteria enjoying good food and happy times. I fell in love with Amabile, the tavern owner's daughter, who went along with all my licit wants, without going any further, as she had brothers who I respected and who also watched her very closely. However, I soon became part of their family. Granted a leave, it took five days via troop train to reach home, where I found my younger brother, Giovanni, in the uniform of a Carabiniere. The whole town was impressed by two brothers in uniform on leave at the same time. The nicest part of my furlough was receiving two letters a day from Amabile, to whom I had become engaged and who was waiting for me in the Veneto. I remained in the army eleven months after the end of WWI, stationed in the North where there was much civil unrest. I was discharged from Pistoia, 20 April 1920.

My father never spoke to us children of his years as a soldier. This following passage expresses his sadness at the great loss of life and the futility of war.

Returning from WWI, my brother Vincenzo resumed proprietorship of his cafe, which had prospered under the management of his wife. They had four sons and one daughter. During WWII, Benito Mussolini, without proper approval of the Italian people, aligned himself with the Germans, who descended upon and trampled them; thereby bringing great pain to our family. Vincenzo's son Emilio, 18 years old, was taken in reprisal by the Germans in 1943.[3] He was shot to death in the piazza in Rionero before the eyes of his parents. All the world should know forever the shame and treachery of these cowards.

In 1970 my father proudly accepted the title of Cavaliere della Republica together with two commemorative medals conferred by the Italian Government to all those men who had fought so valiantly in the battle "Vittorio Veneto."[4]

With re-emigration to the United States inevitable, my father's plans for departure were quickly made. Again, the Italian government was paying passage to anywhere in the world, for those men who had returned to Italy to fight during World War I. His feelings were so sensitively descriptive, that to abridge them here would lessen what must have been one of the most crucial periods of his life, so I have selected only these last few sentences. "The entire family offered to accompany me to the station, but I refused, asking only that my father do so. When the train arrived, I embraced and kissed my father. He told me to take care of myself and I answered, 'Goodbye, Ta (the dialect word for Papa was Tata) let's remember each other and goodbye forever, as we'll never see each other again.' These were our last spoken words. The train started towards Naples. I bid goodbye to Rionero, feeling that I would never return. I departed 13 October 1920 on the Italian ship Giuseppe Verdi, again bidding farewell to Naples, Italy and the Italians."

Epilogue

The last of my father's siblings, Teresa, died at age 86 in March of 1987. Angelo Mario, the brother who left the monastery, went on in the 1920s to become the president of his own bank in Boston, losing everything in the crash of 1929. He became a travel agent in Montreal and was instrumental during the 1940s and '50s in aiding hundreds of Italians to emigrate to Canada. My father never did marry Amabile or Caterina Rabaschi, nor did he pursue any of the several marriage proposals annotated in his memoirs. He met and married my mother, Francesca Lucia Conte, in New York City and sadly, was buried on the very day of their 53rd wedding anniversary.

---

1 Rionero in Vulture is approximately 170 km east of Naples, located in the Appenines. It had a population of 12,000 inhabitants at the time of my father's youth. Its population is now 16,000.

2 Average pay for a U.S. Marine in 1910, according to the *New York Times*, January 3, 1910 started at $19 per month. The pay according to my father's memoirs was 2 1/2 lire every five days, which totaled 15 lire every 30 days or the equivalent of $3 per month U.S. money. The Italian lira was worth .193 U.S. cents according to the *Brooklyn Daily Eagle Almanac* 1909-1914. This is the same figure as quoted in my father's memoirs and by my relatives who lived during that time.

3 The incident of Emilio Buccino being shot in the piazza in Rionero by the Germans in reprisal, was recorded in the *New York Daily News*, in 1943, where my father read it first hand. The photograph of this tragedy remained in the family for many years.

4 In 1968 a special law was passed by the Italian Government conferring the title of Cavaliere della Republica, two medals and a $60 per year pension.

One Hundred Years of Italian Immigration In Vermillion County, Indiana (1856-1956)

Edoardo A. Lebano
Indiana University

For the last twenty years the town of Clinton, Indiana—located north of Terre Haute, near the Indiana-Illinois border—has celebrated an Italian festival on Labor Day weekend. The festival, which is well known throughout the area, is organized by LIFT (Little Italy Festival Town Incorporated). LIFT is a citizen's organization which is responsible for the preservation of local ethnic history.

Two of Clinton's attractions, Immigrant Square and Four Seasons Fountain, reflect the town's pride in its ethnic makeup. Built a few years ago along 9th Street, the Piazza dell'Emigrante is surrounded by many flags representing the various nationalities of the people that call Clinton home. In its center there is a handsome life-size bronze statue, the work of an Italian sculptor from Torino, portraying an immigrant with a suitcase in one hand while the other is raised in a departing salute to his fellow countrymen. The all-white Italianate Four Seasons Fountain, overlooking the Wabash River, is located on Water Street in the eastern section of town.

I first visited Clinton in the summer of 1979 in the company of a friend and colleague, Dr. Herbert Kaplan of Indiana University's History Department, at the time Humanist in Residence of the Indiana Library Association. On that occasion I met an old Italian gentleman, Mr. Joseph Airola, who emigrated to Indiana in 1920 from Torino, where he used to work as a carpenter making airplane propellers. He told me that after the end of World War I a large number of Italians, mostly from the Veneto and Piemonte regions of Italy, settled in Clinton and the surrounding coal mining towns of Vermillion County: Blanford, Centenary and Universal.

According to him even though about thirty nationalities were represented in Clinton, at some time or another, more than half the population of this town was of Italian extraction. Mr. Airola also added that his decision to leave his country of birth was determined by the fear that the political turmoil that troubled Europe and Italy immediately after the war would soon be the cause of another major conflict. To escape this danger and to be free to shape his own destiny, he became a coal miner in Indiana, a job he highly disliked but held until the day he was able to set up his own sausage and salami factory for which there was no lack of customers in Clinton.

Stimulated by Mr. Airola's words and urged by Dr. Kaplan who suggested that I pursue the matter further by checking local immigration records, I eventually went to Newport, the tiny seat of Vermillion County. There, in the dusty basement of the County Library, I found twelve large volumes of naturalization papers dating from the middle of the 19th century to the first half of this century.[1] These documents, which in so far as I know have never been the object of a thorough study, give vital information regarding all those who made their Declaration of Intention to become American citizens between March 23, 1856 and January 17, 1952. The truly remarkable number of Italian names I saw while leafing through some of these volumes confirmed Mr. Airola's claim.

It was only several months later, however, that I was able to secure, thanks to a small grant from Indiana University, microfilm copies of the twelve volumes of documents kept in the County Library at Newport. I then proceeded to make a preliminary random examination of Declarations of Intention (DoI) recorded during a one-year period from October 26, 1912 to November 3, 1913.

Certificates number 899 to 1034 showed that even before 1920 Italians constituted the single largest foreign contingent in Vermillion County and that immigrants from Veneto, Piemonte and Emilia outnumbered those from the other regions of the Italian peninsula. In fact, of the 136 individuals who made their DoI, 52 came from Italy.[2] Of these at least 30 were Northern Italians,[3] while the remaining 22 originated from Lazio, Abruzzi, Umbria and Sicily.[4] The tallest Italian, a native of the province of Vicenza, was 6'3"; the shortest, from the town of Ari, province of Chieti, was 5'. The youngest was 12 years old when he landed in Boston, the oldest was 40. It appears that Central and Southern Italians left at a younger age than their counterpart from the North, yet the most "popular" ages to emigrate were 18 and 22 for all immigrants. Half of these hailed from the same towns and several bore the same family names. The largest group was composed of eight members of the Berto family (seven brothers and a cousin), all born in Gallese, province of Viterbo in the Lazio region, between 1882 and 1892, and who arrived in New York from Naples between 1909 and 1912.[5] It is interesting to note that only 4 of the 52 Italians were unable to write their names.

Once I completed this brief, preliminary examination, I decided to extend it to all other documents in the twelve volumes. I was, however, forced to postpone working on the project until the Fall of 1983, when I dedicated my semester of sabbatical leave to reading, cataloguing, and partially transcribing the data contained in the 3,547 valid Declarations of Intention filed at Newport during the period from 1856-1952. The results of this investigation confirmed again the information provided me by Mr. Airola. Of the 31 nationalities represented in Vermillion County, Italians were the largest ethnic group even before the end of the 19th century! Ninety-three came to Indiana between 1856 and 1899; 305 between 1900 and 1912; 265 between 1913 and 1920; 392 between 1921 and 1936; and only 123 between 1937 and 1952. Of the 3,547 foreign born who settled in the Country, 1,178 or 33 percent were Italians, followed by 675 Austrians, 508 British (mostly from Scotland), 363 Hungarians, 189 Russians, 107 Germans and 72 Yugoslavians. The other 24 countries represented included (in alphabetical order): Australia, Belgium, Brazil, Bulgaria, Canada, Czechoslavakia, Denmark, France, Finland, Greece, Holland, Ireland, Lithuania, Mexico, Montenegro, Poland, Prussia, Romania, Serbia, Spain, Syria, Sweden, Switzerland and Turkey.

The first recorded DoI bears the date March 24, 1856 and it was filed by a Russian immigrant; the first DoI by an Italian—a Stanislao Fanlio, from Torino—is dated May 11, 1878. All these documents show that most of the Italians came from

Northern Italy; to be exact, 907 of the 1,178 immigrants, or 77 percent are Northern Italians. Of all the Italian regions, Piemonte is by far the one with the greatest number of emigrants: 427 or 36 percent, followed by Veneto with 93 or 16.5 percent. The towns most represented are: Asiago, province of Vicenza in the Veneto region with 85; Fanano, province of Modena in Emilia-Romagna, with 72; and Feletto, province of Torino, Piemonte, with 68.

As I already noted, many Italians were related, had the same surnames and hailed from the same provinces and towns. The records allow us to reconstruct the story of entire families, such as that of the Avenattis, whose first member arrived in America from Piedmont in 1890, or that of the Masaracchias, whose first member landed in New York from Palermo in 1898.

While most Italians declared coal mining as their occupation, a considerable number were barbers, carpenters, butchers, bartenders, grocers, blacksmiths, merchants, clerks, teamsters, farmers, policemen and salesmen. There was even a physician, Dr. Annibale Salaroglio, a Piedmontese who emigrated in 1906 and made his DoI three years later, and a "Minister of the Cult," a man by the name of Calogero Benedetto Papa. Born in Messina, Sicily in 1883, he emigrated to America in 1905 and made his DoI in 1910. Probably a Catholic priest in Italy, he joined the Presbyterian Church in America for I was told that for some time he conducted services at Hillcrest Presbyterian Church in Clinton before moving out of the County.

Even though women's names appear in their husbands' DoIs as early as October 5, 1916, the first DoI by a woman—a Mrs. Mary S. Antonini, born in Asiago, Vicenza in 1880 and who emigrated to America in 1906—bears the date September 27, 1922. After this date, women (many by then widows) filed for citizenship in gradually increasing numbers.

Perhaps the most time consuming task I encountered was that of determining the region of origin of individual immigrants, particularly those who were born or who resided in small, unknown villages. If indeed most certificates do provide information regarding the applicant's birthplace and his or her last place of foreign residence, they make no reference, however, as to the province in which these towns are located. The matter is moreover complicated by the orthographical mistakes made by the clerks of Vermillion County Circuit Court. These gentlemen not only misspelled names of people and place (they appear to have problems even with English), but frequently provide different spellings for same localities. For example, the town of Castell'Arquato in the province of Piacenza, becomes Casteloquato, Castellorquato and Casteloquapo. As we all know, some of these errors were due to the immigrants themselves, who, not familiar with the pen or English spellings, could offer little assistance to the clerk, who therefore resorted to phonetic transcriptions. Such is the curious case of Giovan Battista Bonotto, a native of Crosara in the province of Vicenza, who in his attempt to Americanize his first name, signed his DoI as Gohon Battista Bonotto.[6]

Once all statistical data was compiled and analyzed, I began working on the oral history phase of my Clinton project. This was made possible by a 1984 Summer Fellowship from the Indiana Committee on the Humanities.[7] Before going to Clinton to interview the few still living original Italian immigrants, their children and grandchildren, I carefully read the Clinton-Rockville Telephone Book, where I found listed about 100 of the over 1000 Italian names recorded in the Newport naturalization papers.

Mrs. Diane Waugh of the *Daily Clintonian* suggested then that I get in touch with a highly respected member of the local Italian community. Mrs. Waugh's advice, which I promptly followed, proved to be most valuable. Miss Pesavento, a retired school teacher and administrator (she held for over forty years the position of Principal of Glendale Elementary School in Clinton), became not only an important source of information concerning life in her town, but was also of great help to me arranging most of my interviews and opening many doors which otherwise might have remained closed.

I spent two entire months recording on tape viva voce interviews—which I later on transcribed—with the members of at least fifty families. I interviewed first of all Mr. Airola, the recognized "Dean" of the Italian community, who was then 88. My last interview was with Attorney Henry Antonini, one of Clinton's best-known and most distinguished citizens. A

learned and a congenial person, Mr. Antonini spoke eloquently and with great admiration about his immigrant
grandparents and the problems they had to face especially
during the Depression, when the family, unable to pay property taxes, lost most of what it had been able to accumulate in
many years of continuous hard work. He vividly remembered
the day when, after one of the sheriff's frequent visits to his
grandparents', he, then still a child, told his grandfather who
had just turned ownership of one of his properties to the
County: "Nonno, I surely like to see that man, because every
time he comes, I get to see his gun." To which his grandfather
replied: "But, Cristo, every time you see his gun, I lose a
house!" Mr. Antonini also spoke of the role many Italians who
lived in and around Clinton played in the production and the
selling of hard liquor during Prohibition, a subject he researched at length for a graduate paper he wrote several
years ago while working on his Master degree.

With a few exceptions, most of the people I interviewed recognized that members of their families were involved in bootlegging activities in Vermillion County during Prohibition.
While it is true that immigrants of all ethnic groups produced
home-made wine and brew, it is also true that Clinton's Italians, whose ancestors had been making wine in Italy for centuries, not only made wine and beer for personal consumption,
but also produced and sold hard liquor when the mines were
closed and they had no other way of supporting their families.
On such occasions even the children helped out transporting
sugar and other necessary ingredients on their wagons, at
times under the nose of unsuspecting federal agents.

Though an unlawful activity which could draw a prison
term, the immigrants never considered bootlegging to be a
real crime, rather a necessary evil. For this reason going to
jail, which was commonly referred to as "going to college", did
not bring shame on the individual bootlegger or his family.
And how could the immigrants think otherwise when most of
their best customers were lawyers, physicians, businessmen
and even law enforcement people living in the cities as close
as Terre Haute, Indianapolis and Chicago and as far as
Columbus and St. Louis?

The interviews revealed also that Italians who emigrated to

Vermillion County after the turn of the century were not re-cruited in Italy by agents of the mining companies. With the exception of a few who had worked in German coal mines prior to their coming to the States, the majority of the immi-grants had no previous mining experience, most of them being farmers in their native land. Several immigrants also came to Indiana not directly from Italy, but after having lived for sometime in Texas, Louisiana, Pennsylvania and other mid-western states such as Michigan, Ohio and Illinois. They moved to Indiana upon hearing that thirty-two mines, each employing 300 to 600 miners, were operating in and around Clinton and that jobs were available.

Information concerning jobs usually reached the immi-grants through either a relative or a friend. Some arrived from Italy with the assurance that a job was awaiting them; others hoped to eventually find one. Many went directly from the boat to the train that carried them to Clinton, crossing a land whose language they didn't know, fearful of what was be-fore them, and with enough money in their pocket to buy a few loafs of bread. Upon reaching their destination, they were met at the station by relatives or friends in whose homes they were lodged until able to afford a place of their own. Many be-came boarders in the home of another Italian family, where they would remain for several weeks, sometimes even many months, while saving enough money to send for their brothers and sisters, and those already married, for their wives and children. Families were eventually reunited and new families were formed, as the girls left behind soon joined their be-trothed in the new land. In the early days, the immigrants normally married immigrant girls or the American-born daughters of earlier Italian immigrants. A few, particularly the younger ones, married women belonging to other ethnic groups. All things considered, the story of Italian immigration in Vermillion County is basically the same as the story of Italian immigration in other regions of the United States.

In Clinton the foreign-born contingent occupied the north end of town, with the Italians living all along 9th Street. Rela-tionships among people of all nationalities were friendly and close, particularly among the Italians who constituted the largest group. Since many of the Italians, especially those from Veneto, Piemonte and Emilia came from the same towns, interaction among them was constant. The few southern Italian families, instead, interacted mostly among themselves. It appears that a few of them even chose to live outside the limits of "Little Italy" thinking that it would speed up their Americanization process. In difficult times, however, all immigrants helped one another and merchants gave easy credit to their customers, knowing that they would surely pay up as soon as they could. Trust was a necessary ingredient in the struggle for survival when jobs were scarce and the mines were closed due to either weather conditions or to strikes.[8] Knowing little or no English, they spoke among themselves in Italian (I was surprised by the quality of the Italian still spoken in Clinton today, a fact which allowed me to conduct many of the interviews almost totally in Italian) or in their native dialects and I was told that immigrants of all ethnic groups had really no problem in communicating with one another.

Parents learned English—even if broken English—from their children. As soon as the oldest son or daughter was of school age, he or she would become the teacher to his/her brothers and sisters. In the earlier part of the century the boys usually attended school until 12 years old, at which time they had to join their fathers in the mines. When the mines were not in operation, they would help by taking care of the ever-important vegetable garden or doing other chores around the house or the neighborhood. Girls, instead, when they were not needed at home by their mothers, were sent to work as seamstresses in Clinton's overall factory.

Life in Clinton was not "easy" in those days; nevertheless all the people I talked with (many of whom were then young boys and girls) have fond recollections of warm family gatherings, of special celebrations, marriages, religious festivities and other community events. More than a few experienced problems in school, which were often made worse by uninterested or insensitive teachers. Many, and not only the children, were deeply afraid of what the Ku Klux Klan, whose members frequently paraded with hooded heads and guns along 9th Street, and occasionally burned crosses in front of the neighborhood hospital, might do to them. There are recorded cases of bombings, violence and intimidation, some by "imported" as well as by local criminal organizations, such as the Mano Nera and the Horse Thieves. Ignorance, prejudice and race discrimination were clearly expressed in the warning that Italians would not be welcome south of Vine Street. (And yet the immigrants took all of this in stride.) Their big "break" came when their children became Clinton's high school leading athletes. As parents of the local heroes they were no longer thought of as foreigners, but were finally accepted as members of the community.

Education was indeed important to the immigrants who wanted their children to be well educated if at all possible. In families with 5, 6 and even 10, 11 children, it usually happened that while 3 or 4 of the older kids hardly completed primary school, the younger children were instead able to finish high school and some even attended college. As the immigrant family financial situation prospered, the number of children that were allowed to remain in school increased. It is interesting to note that the majority of those who first graduated from college became school teachers. Certainly the fact that Indiana Teachers College in Terre Haute (today Indiana State University) was the institution of higher learning closest to Clinton explains this choice, but only in part. I believe in fact that the choice of a teaching profession was also influenced by the respect and the admiration immigrant parents felt for teachers, whom they saw as the depository and the dispenser of knowledge. The fact that many grandchildren of Italian immigrants are today school teachers gives further support to this thesis.

Immigration scholars have established that of all the Italians who emigrated to the States in the first decades of this century, about 60% eventually returned to Italy to stay.[9] Statistics also show that the highest percentage of these returnees was made up of immigrants from Southern and Central Italy. The information I collected basically concurs with these findings. While a considerable number of the Italians who emigrated to Vermillion County went back to visit their aging parents, to marry or settle family affairs, only a handful decided to remain permanently in their country of birth. Most came to America to stay. This quite low percentage of returnees is to be attributed perhaps to the fact that, as I have previously stated, 70% of Clinton's Italians hailed from Northern Italy.

Once they settled in Clinton, a good number of the immigrants, though all born Catholics, joined a local Protestant Church, Hillcrest Presbyterian, which today has a congregation of only a few families. The main reason I was given for this change in religious affiliation was the unusually warm and helpful reception the immigrants were granted by the pastor of Hillcrest Presbyterian Church, located in the very heart of what was to become Clinton's Little Italy.

Italian women played, as wives and mothers, a pivotal role in Clinton's Little Italy. At times of particular hardships or when the mines were closed, many took in boarders (some even had 11 in a three-four bedroom house), whom they fed and whose clothes they washed and ironed. Their working day usually started well before dawn and ended only late at night. They were often the sole means of support for the family and were the real tower of strength in the Italian community.

In the early twenties many of the original Italian immigrants began to leave Clinton to find better and more permanent employment in large metropolitan areas such as Chicago and Detroit. Their exodus continued in the thirties and forties. But the Italians' love affair with Clinton and Vermillion County—which Irma Pesavento's father called "God's Country"—does not seem to have ended. Many of the immigrants' children have in fact returned and are returning to Clinton to retire.

To conclude, the accounts I collected give a story of hard work, sacrifices, and at times of prejudice. But it is also a story of endurance, dignity, and above all hope in man's ability to succeed and prosper. It is in short the story of America, the reason why so many peoples from so many corners of the earth decided one day to leave their country of birth to seek a better life in the New World, a land that was made known by an Italian from Genoa and bears the name of an Italian from Florence.

---

[1] See Vermillion County, Circuit Court Naturalization Declaration

and Intent Records, Vols. I-XII, March 24, 1856 to January 17, 1952.

2 Of the 82 non-Italians, 37 came from the British Isles; 24 from Austria; 6 from Hungary; 5 from Russia; 3 from Montenegro; 2 each from Bulgaria, Germany and Ireland; and 1 each from Australia, Belgium and Serbia.

3 Veneto (with 14, all from the province of Vicenza); Piemonte (with 10, all from the provinces of Torino, Cuneo, Novara and Aosta); and Emilia/Romagna (with 6, from the city of Bologna and the provinces of Modena and Piacenza).

4 Lazio (with 10, from Rome and its province of Viterbo); Abruzzi (with 2 from the province of Chieti); Umbria (with 3 from Perugia and its province); and Sicily (with 1 from the province of Messina).

5 Alessandro, Angelo, Costantino, Eugenio, Giulio, John, Nazzareno, and Santino (Eugenio and John, born in June and in August of 1890, were probably cousins). They all lived at the same Clinton address.

6 Mr. Giovan Battista Bonotto, born September 1, 1888, landed in New York on August 18, 1910 and made his DoI on October 26, 1912.

7 Only 7 of the proposed 79 projects were funded and mine was one of the few that were selected for support from the Committee. This clearly shows Indiana is interested in programs dealing with ethnic studies.

8 Miners were employed for about 200 working days per year. The peak employment period was 1912-1922.

9 See the excellent study by Dino Cinel, *From Italy to San Francisco. The Immigrant Experience.* Stanford: Stanford UP, 1982 (particularly Chapter 3, "American Money and Italian Land", pp. 35-70).

The Italian Immigrant in the American South 1900-1960

Al J. Montesi
St. Louis University

As we all know very well, indeed, during the last part of the nineteenth century and the first of the twentieth, many thousands of Italians from all over Italy immigrated to the United States. Although many of these were attached to vast estates with their padrones as field workers, others were textile mill workers, and still others common laborers and small farmers. Among this last group I would include both sides of my own family.

On my father's side, my grandfather farmed a small area near Senigallia, a town somewhat north of Ancona on the eastern coast of the peninsula on the Adriatic Sea. Surprisingly enough, my mother's people came from a town very near there called Montemarciano, where my maternal grandfather Boldreghini made his living as a shoemaker and kept a small chicken farm. Although both of my parents came from little towns very close to each other, my father's family left Italy some years before my mother's, and they did not meet until they were adults in Memphis, Tennessee.

Although my mother would often regale us with stories of her life in Montemarciano—accounts of her drawing water and gossiping at the town's well, of her trips to the seashore, of her learning from her father how to wring the necks of chickens, of her brothers becoming apprentice shoe makers with their father—my father had no knowledge of his early life in Italy—since he had come to the States when he was only four. At any rate, as matters worsened in Italy economically—as the population was fast growing and there was not enough industry to accommodate it—each of their families decided to come to America.

How they travelled from Ancona to Genoa, I have never been able to determine; but nonetheless my mother's group left that seaport town in the 1880s or early 1890s from Porto Vecchio. On one occasion I found myself in that very seaport town trying to retrace their footsteps as they prepared to embark for America. Once aboard their ship, as my mother retells this account, they were massed in the bottom hold of the boat, where they experienced crowding and lice and other vermin until they landed in New York. The voyage was not altogether grim as Mother would tell it. She was sixteen or thereabouts when they made the trip, and there was a brief encounter with some ship's stewart or sailor, who brought her little gifts of food whenever she would go above deck to sit and watch the sea or read the novel that she brought with her. For although my mother functioned badly in the English tongue, she loved the Italian. When they became Memphians, she maintained her Italian, and it was she who wrote all the letters home for those " immigrees" that could not write. Moreover, I was named Albert after some character she had encountered in her Italian novel reading.

When they finally arrived in New York Harbor, they greeted with great joy and vast relief the newly erected Statue of Liberty that welcomed them to the new world. But, in spite of their happiness at having arrived, they would encounter great sorrow at Ellis Island. Here after being checked by custom authorities, they discovered to their great dismay that their beloved mother could not enter America because of the weakness of her eyes. So, miserable and with great weeping, they were separated from their dear parent, who sailed back to her homeland. My mom never saw her cherished mother again. On a library table in our front room, there was always present a photograph of my grandmother Boldreghini and, beside it a large wedding picture of my dad and mom. And each time my mother told this tragic episode, she would constantly weep, nodding towards her mother's picture.

The next step in my mother's odyssey was to travel from New York to Helena, Arkansas. In Helena, the entire family worked for a time at a cotton mill in order to repay the mill's owner for their passage fare to America. Once this was done, they went on to the nearest large city, which happened to be Memphis. Here the oldest son, my uncle Earnest, opened a small shoe shop, and by degrees Charlie and Sam, Mother's other two brothers, also became shoe makers with their own little shops.

Yet despite the fact that this little brood had secured an economic toe-hold in this southern city, they were indeed still outsiders to the community at large. While most of the Italians in the South worked as sharecroppers, railroad workers, or factory hands until they were self-supporting, many of those settling in Memphis became truck farmers or textile workers. In time, a good number of these people became successful and returned to their homeland, but more remained in their new country to raise their families. However, since they were doubly alienated from the larger southern community by being not only Italian but also Catholic, those that remained formed little pockets of their own social and cultural activities. It was at one of these closed Italian events, a dance of sorts, that my mother and father met and began a courtship that finally ended in marriage.

My father's family, by some method which was never entirely clear to me, had acquired a little farm in Shelby County, Mississippi, where three of the sons, my uncle Fred, Uncle Joe, and my dad were raised. Since they were needed on the farm, they received no schooling whatsoever. They were self-taught readers and writers of their adopted language. And even though my uncle Fred Montesi eventually became a most successful grocery magnate, owning at one time seventy chain stores, he could barely write his own name. These brothers in time left their Clarksdale, Mississippi, homes, and settled in nearby Memphis.

Despite their ostracism from the larger southern community, the Italian-Americans were not entirely starved for culture. They lived among other Americans, but they seldom saw their lifestyle as something to be obsessively copied. They felt intuitively that art must play an important part in every man's life. They, therefore, played the violin and accordion on their "Italian Hour" during the first days of radio; brought early Caruso recordings on those crude heavy disks and played them by the hour to their children; sang, as did my Aunt Josie, arias from all the operas; and read and told old-world legends and stories to their children in their beloved Italian tongue.

Although the outer world was usually indifferent or hostile to their isolated life-world, it could suddenly turn ugly and brutal to these "foreigners" who inhabited it. I can recall instances in my own boyhood, living as we did in a working class neighborhood, when the Klan would place burning crosses in front of Saint Thomas, our little parish church. And once in an open field near this church and its school, a Black was hanged, lynched obviously, but placed there as a double warning to us and the Blacks not to step out of line.

In an effort to provide a shield between us and the culture at large, the Italians, as I have said, created their own little ghettos. And later we combined with other Catholic minorities, the Irish in particular, to enjoy Irish-American carnivals and other social events. As time went on we created a Catholic Club, housed in a very enormous and opulent building in downtown Memphis.

In time, lawyers, judges, doctors, and scholars began to appear in the community with Italian last names. As the years passed on, the Italians became not only major figures in the world of Memphis, Tennessee, but important civic leaders and personages throughout the whole of the American South. But to tell more concretely how they managed to acquire these roles of importance, I would like to turn now to a battery of poems that I have written of their early struggles and hardships.

Sketch: Daguerreotype of Nonno

Observe
how starkly he sits before the
strange camera. Like those figures from
Madame Tussaud's or in the waxworks in
Barcelona. If you would but touch them,
they would spring out at you . . .
from whatever place in time or death
they've been.

I.

Yepp, a condadino

straight from the rocks and fields of Ancona;
there you sit, old grandioso, mugging and scowling
with those ever-smacking mustachios.
And say, what's on top?
Nonno, wherever did you get that 1890s hat?

        Remember Times Square before autos?
        There
        was a great problem with manure. Take all
        those phaetons and carriages with their
        horses.
        The manure piled up in such stacks that the
        city could not control it

What in the hell were you people like—
striking all those wild poses and grimaces?
Were you simply in a gas most of the time from your vino
Or was leaving that good dago soil and coming straight to
those
gaunt frame houses of America too much for you?

        On April 23, 1896, at Koster and Bial's
        Music Hall, in New York, the first
official showing of a motion picture
took place. The first audience moved away
frightened from
        the trains and waves that came straight
        out at them from the new curious
        screen.

        Tell me, old peasant, what was it like being you?

What is a snapshot anyway, Nonno? I
merely see a man and behind him a
stark screen. But look how afraid you
look. You, that great bull of a wop,
braying and snorting. I have seen your like
among other nationals, but rarely in the ranks of
your amici.

Was it not because you were afraid of the language, the
strange new land
and the people?

> Surely wars, as barbaric as they are,
> and migration to other lands are the most
> that has happened to folk so far. For
> some, there was not even these.

Nor can I balk at the spaghetti-gothic of your clothes and
    houses.
For I am now convinced that you and yours were hardly
    afraid of,
or untouched by, genuine, passionate life.
Surely your lives were far richer than mine.

I have seen your " paesan" thrashing and weeping in the arms
    of their fat wives
I remember Angelo whose capelli turned overnight from black
    to stark grey
when his son was slain by the police.
And Zia Josie who sang arias from all the Verdi operas
and did her little jigs
and whose gay laughter rang through that filthy
    neighborhood
where we lived.
And the gaudy weddings and funerals. Remember, Nonno,
how you drank and danced at the Fruella wedding?
How none, young or old, could keep up with you

> On May 5, 1920, two Italian anarchists
>   Niccola Sacco and Bartolomeo Vanzetti,
> were arrested for two alleged murders
> in South Braintree, Mass. They were
> subsequently electrocuted for being, as
> Judge Webster Thayer called them, "Dagoes,"
> "sons of bitches,"and "anarchistic bastards."

And Billy Sunday sang, "Give 'em the juice.
Burn them. We've had enough of foreign

radicals."

In an effort to know the secrets of your life's vitality,
I have tried to retrace your goings as best I could:
I have walked with you through the turnstiles at Ellis Island,
seen your eyes in emigrees entering Heathrow from India,
felt the lice crawling upon you as you emerged from steerage,
even sought for you the Ponto Vecchio in Genoa, where you
disembarked for Amerika, Amerika.

Bootleg trade in the U.S. in violation
of the Eighteenth Amendment and the
Volstead Act, was estimated in 1926
at $3,600,000,000.

I have searched the faces of those peasant women in Spain
    Greece
and near the Appian way,
garbed in their eternal black, as if in mourning for life, for
    some
key to your fine life-sense.
But it will not come. We have lost it.
They are all dying out, those peasant wops. Their sons and
    daughters
are papier-maché and paste.
What gave you your mountains of life?
Was it because you were fortunate enough to be poor and
challenged by it?
Or that your children, experiencing both ill and good times,
never suffered the glut of plenty?
Or was it that we have wandered too far from the soil, and
    you and yours
were never too far from it?
Or simply does life emerge pure only out of conflict and
    suffering?

In the 1920s burning crosses were
frequently found before the workman's
parish church of St. Thomas in South
Memphis, Tennessee. In an open field

a Negro was once hanged so that the
school children from the parish school
could not neglect to see him in their
passing.

Can you recall, old lover, how stained with sweat
you would crawl down from a scaffolding
and give us all a big hug and kiss in your blue overalls.
And if anyone threatened us, you'd loom over them with a
    great scowl
Of course, all backed away: who would fight a Latin giant?
All feared you...even the cops, for you were a mean olddog, my
    Nonno.

With the arrival of radio, in an effort
to better Anglo-Italian relations, an
Italian Hour appeared on the local station.
The twins played the accordion, and Zia
Sofia sang, "Tre, sienta-tre."

And so
        there you stand before me in this black-and-white
    image;
your eyes reaching out to warn and love me still.
I see the huge fist of my age reaching in to stamp out your
    presence,
but there are some that will not let it.
And quiet after making love, I see them will their
    seed into the cells
    of a child who will be like you.
We will get you again, old fox,
and see your features well up again in our children.
Rest well, the photograph still remains.

Dream Visions of Aleco

Landscape #1

Around, around the only rip of
silence... the frayed air nibbling at
the edge of stillness...the wash of
half and no light...the unbearable
weight of nothingness.   ¹

I.

There was a morning freshness about you, Aleco,
as if you had just come from some rain-swept, green-fresh
    valley,
even when we would meet in the muted light of an early
morning
    one of those mornings that belong to the night
    that winter keeps.
As if we two only existed in time.
I stood in awe a little of your enormous paw-like hand,
ursi-formed almost, as it would shadow-box playfully my
head and chin,
and watched as you mixed your morning toddy of whisky,
    sugar, and water,
offering me, a lad of six, a little of your checato.

II.

Then,
    somewhat older,
        there was something wrong with my legs.
And almost wet with tenderness, you would move with me—
    my small body
wrapped in those great arms—towards your Model T to
    Dr. Rudner's.
    This passes, the legs corrected
themselves.
    But I have yet to forget your holding me;
your massive body geared mightily to pour

its
great strength into my pained legs...
sheltering me with your enormous black
   coat clutching me as if I were the most
   precious
item on the earth.

III.

And then we'd be off to cross the wide Mississippi to steal
watermelons on the Arkansas side,
crossing the river at Memphis over the single span of the old
   Harahan bridge...
and then the rows of rich green watermelons against the
   black loam,
and the admonition to hurry
before a burst of buckshot
close to us would send all scurrying to the little Ford.
Over again the bridge with its drop and water below
frightening your squealing but happy children.

IV.

I remember, Aleco, on a Sunday morning
when we scrambled to get ready for church,
five pairs of brushed and polished shoes
waited for us as we frantically tried to get ourselves
together. And on returning...a whopping hot breakfast,
all prepared by those enormous hands.

V.

How did it come about that you were the adult par excellence
with children? You who could never relate to grown-ups,
growing awkward or silent in their midst.
But you were always first with the young ones—teasing,
   mugging,
and scowling your way into their joys.
I can recall going with you as your sole companion, a six or
   eight-

year old tow-headed boy, during the " dry" twenties to some
   hideaway
Negro bar, buried in Black Town, in pursuit of your morning
shots.
Or standing on the bluff side of the Mississippi, during the
   1927
spring floods, watching swirling angry waters
swallowing up the whole of Arkansas.

VI.

I remember, Aleco, when I or others were sick,
after the operation or crisis, alone in a stark, impersonal
hospital room, where all had been forbidden to enter,
suddenly you were there. First always in your coming:
commanding in your presence,
lighting up the room,
scattering nurse and doctor,
dismissing utterly our loneliness and fears.

VII.

Your death had been final and outrageous
as a cancer ate tirelessly through your side.
You who had been such a bulk of a man, muscularly lean and
   large-boned,
it was all I could do to carry you to the john
without feeling the rub of your bar ribs against
my shoulder...you were 70 pounds when you died.

VIII.

And when you were biered, lying in the stuccoed cheapness
of a commercial mortuary,
and we all sat about, longing for you a chapel of trees
and clean earth,
suddenly, there was a sound from an unused side entrance.
There, outline, a man stood with a woman upgathered in his
   arms.
Once in, their figures made clear, we watched as your

beloved Vi,
determinedly up from a hospital bed,
stood out from her husband's arms,
and struggling towards you,
crying, " Daddy," " Daddy,"
collapsed to the floor at your side.

IX.

And yet to others, to that mass of Italian immigrants
Who came, to of all places, the American South,
you were the ill-favored son of a peasant dago dynasty,
all of whom had climbed to great wealth and power.
They had fired you periodically from the petty jobs they fed
     you,
claiming that your endless bottles of beer
and your morning shots of booze
sullied their lily-pure businesses.
But you were horse racing against a sun-filled horizon,
how could they dampen your spirit or will?

X.

I have sought for you since in a hundred other,
catching glimpses now and then in my lovers and friends.
Scanning each new face carefully with expectation and
     desire:
spending long years with a few, believing from some dim
     promise
that the ideal of you as a person had survived.
But the search was futile,
the face and hand empty:
nothing permanent was retrieved.
          O Aleco, Aleco,
          to me still the finest man in time,
          no rude pistol shot ever
          will shoot down from my dreams
          your fierce ride against the sky.

Pavarotti Sings Naples

Outside the stitched land sighs its ice jacket;
the fox is yoked in his lair; the birds are silent.
The nightmare of the new winter has begun.
Inside the stark room,
the long side-view of a picture window.
And then the pouring into the stark, boxed structure
the incomparable swelling, the lift, the gain, the very
    sweep of that master voice,
come caroling through the small room,
of a tenor that rings out
perhaps once every hundred years.
    (Yes, sah, that's ah him, that's ah him.)
its range so rich and varied
that we are made to believe, if only briefly,
that something special is still available to us.
And the old wops, the old dagos,
those whose wine-stained hands are
still around, calling out:
"It's Enrico comah back, and Lanza comah back."
A voice that momentarily sweeps aside all the doubt,
pain, and rancor of our new cybernetic worlds.

All those metals left now behind
and now only that mighty tenor resonance filling
    utterly the room,
and then comes forth from the cheap whirling disk
a whole melody of Neapolitan folk songs
" O sole mio," " Peche?" " A vucchella" and all the rest
that were the sparse heritage of my immigrant people
who had come a generation ago to this now
    snow-covered South.

And he sings, " Ah, Marie, Ah, Marie," a whole band of
those beloved contadini, settling in the American South,
pass in review before me
—expatriated, frightened, cowering within the alien corn—
    (" Sure, I remember, I remember: finah people,
    finah, people.")

There are Zia Josie and Zia Annie, Nonno, and
all the others; all deceased now, all gone to their rest.
Those beloved, pained folk filing past the officials at
Ellis Island, terrified and awed and yet gutsy
    and determined.
And yet as I unreel that spool of memory, I well up,
not over their early misery and ill treatment,
but blowing kisses as they run past,
as Pavarotti provides them with their
new reincarnation,
for the deep richness and beauty of their lives.

And wondering
if our heirs will act thusly
in the shortness of thought
as we, long dead, will file past in their memories,
awakened by some item or event.
Will we be recalled as having been ennobled
    by suffering
or dignified by want and pain?
Or will we be, for them, as our decade remarks us:
pale, bland, and unimpassioned creatures.

What, then, will we have provided for our
    children's memories
Of what then shall a new Pavarotti sing,
on an earth that's lost its veins to ice?

Amerital Unico and 'Festa Italiana' in Chicago

Anthony Fornelli

I appreciate very much the opportunity to participate in the writing of history—more so, because I was a participant in the creation of it. I promise you that I will attempt to faithfully chronicle the events as they occurred without succumbing to the temptation to editorialize and revise the events to suit later purposes.

The genesis of "Festa Italiana" in Chicago actually took place in 1976 at a Columbus Day weekend celebration at the Hyatt Regency O'Hare in Rosemont, Illinois. The hotel was relatively new then and its management was extremely innovative. It helped that the general manager was of Italian extraction and that three members of the Amerital Unico Club of Chicago spent a lot of time in the hotel. It is from such mundane happenstances that many historic events take place.

Those three fellows, James Esposito, Louis Rago and the writer, made a suggestion to a receptive hotel management team that the hotel lobby could be the scene of a very worthwhile celebration of Italian American life. And that's when "Festa Italiana" was born.

We transformed that hotel lobby into an Italian street scene. Picture a bocce court alongside the swimming pool; a grape stomping event next to the elevators. The sights and sounds of "Mora" players completely astounded hotel guests from around the country who were not familiar with that ancient Italian finger game.

For three years, we continued to expand the participation of artists and sculptors and craftsmen exhibiting and selling unique Italian creations. Books and records, leather goods and ceramics exuded an aura of an Italian fair further enhanced by ladies in costumes and young dancers cavorting on makeshift stages.

That was the beginning of a theme that we would expand

through the years. It was the desire of the promoters to: 1. present a celebration of Italian American life; 2. bring together some of the businessmen in the community and afford them an opportunity to reach heretofore untapped markets; 3. showcase Italian American entertainers; and 4. enhance the purposes of our Unico organization to raise money for charitable purposes.

Emboldened by our successes at the Hyatt Hotel, the group decided to take a momentous leap forward and bring the show that we had been trying out in the suburbs to downtown Chicago and the big time—to take it from an event that would draw from 4,000 to 5,000 to one that would attract 100,000 people for a weekend.

In 1979, "Festa Italiana" moved to Chicago's lakefront and for five years thereafter was held at Navy Pier, the old decaying civic monstrosity that had undergone a number of alterations during its illustrious career. The City's administration at that time had grandiose plans to renovate the Navy Pier and return it to its former grandeur as a recreational spot for millions of Chicagoans. "Festa Italiana" was the only ethnic festival to take advantage of that opportunity, and here I believe is one of the foremost contributions of "Festa Italiana" to the City of Chicago. That we were the pioneers in presenting ethnic festivals and that we persevered through adversity, is what makes our singular and unique contribution to the ethnic history of this city.

With a larger platform, we were able to attract big name entertainers and thousands of visitors to "Festa Italiana" enjoyed the work of Anna Maria Alberghetti, Sergio Franchi, Julius LaRosa, Frankie Valli, Jerry Vale and many others.

Mention of visitors reminds me that "Festa Italiana" attracts visitors from throughout the country. It has affected considerably the hotel and tourism business in Chicago and economically impacted on restaurant and parking facilities adjacent to the festival grounds.

Prominent food vendors and restaurant owners became an integral part of the "Festa," serving popular delicacies such as calamari and zucchini, as well as the more common pizza and sausage sandwiches.

By 1984, with a change of attitude in the Chicago city administration, Navy Pier had fallen into great disrepair and was no longer a proper place to have a festival. It was that year that "Festa Italiana" moved to Olive Park.

Olive Park is a man-made, grassy area created by landfill that fronts the Water Filtration Plant. It sits quite regally in a strategically sound location at the foot of Grand Avenue and Lake Shore Drive. Prior to 1984, it was the best kept secret in the city. A few bicyclists perhaps, and of course, the ever present joggers and dog walkers were the only people to utilize this beautiful setting with its vista on Lake Michigan and its background of tall and majestic skyscrapers lining Lake Shore Drive.

The struggle to gain permission to use this tract of land for an ethnic festival took no little effort. Bureaucratic reluctance to attempt something new and different impeded efforts of the "Festa" organizers, but eventually they prevailed.

"Festa Italiana" had a significance beyond the actual event itself. As I said earlier, the promoters were not looking for another food and fun fest, but sought to promote the Italian community, unite its business and professional people, showcase its talents, and at the same time raise funds for charitable purposes. All of those goals have been accomplished with some degree of success, but the most important result was a totally unexpected one.

The reluctance on the part of the Chicago city administration to make Olive Park available for a site for ethnic fests generated a campaign that demonstrated the political strength of the area's Italian American community. "Festa Italiana" had been the forerunner and progenitor of other ethnic festivals. In 1984, when we moved to Olive Park, we were the only one. Subsequently, we were joined by the Hispanics the following year, and after that, the Irish, Polish and African-American communities sought to emulate our success. I say this with some degree of modesty, but as a statement of fact none-the-less, that all of these other ethnic groups look to the Italian community for leadership and guidance in how to best present a festival of this kind. It was no wonder that when adversity struck and it appeared that we would be unable to obtain the location of our choice, these ethnic groups depended on us for leadership. Thus, it was through the late winter and early spring of 1987 that we instituted a campaign to arouse public opinion, influence political figures and thus reverse the decision.

The Italian community was in the forefront of this aspect of the campaign. Just when it appeared that the city administration was utilizing the old tactic of divide and conquer, and when other ethnic groups were beginning to waver and fall in line for an alternative site, we were able to induce our Italian political leaders to press even harder for Olive Park. It was said later that except for the resistance of the "Festa Italiana" committee, the city would have been able to move the ethnic festivals to a less desirable spot.

The significance here is that a seemingly innocuous event as a summer ethnic festival becomes a vehicle on which to assert ethnic power.

We feel that our goals as set forth earlier have been achieved and that we can continue to support the Unico organization's desires to fund charitable and cultural events, thereby expanding our record of giving over a quarter million dollars to all types of worthy causes.

Appendix:
1987 Conference Program
Chicago, Illinois

Co-sponsored by
The Italian Consulate General of Chicago
Amerital Unico Club of Chicago (Festa Italiana)
The Italian Cultural Institute of Chicago
The Fra Noi
Columbia College
Governors State University
Italian Cultural Center
Joint Civic Committee of Italian/Americans

About the Conference

Founded in 1966, The American Italian Historical Association is an interdisciplinary group of scholars and lay people dedicated to the study of the Italian American experience. The organization has a membership of 500 and sponsors a conference each year to explore a particular aspect of Italian—American history. The association publishes the proceedings of the conference and a quarterly newsletter. The 1987 conference focused on the role of language and literature in the experience of Italian immigrants and subsequent generations of Italian ethnics in North America and the World. More than 100 presenters from all parts of the United States and from Italy are on the program. The highlight of the conference was a gala banquet and entertainment at Villa Scalabrini in Northlake.

PROGRAM

FRIDAY, NOVEMBER 13

9:00 a.m. Plenary Session

Welcome:
Virginio Piucci, Vice President
Governors State University
Leonardo Baroncelli, Italian Consul General
Chicago
Dino Danesi Visconti, Cultural Department
Italian Ministry of Foreign Affairs
Lya Dym Rosenblum, Dean
Columbia College
Dominic Candeloro, President
American Italian Historical Association

Introduction of Keynote Speaker
Paul Giordano, Rosary College

Keynote Address
Joseph Tusiani, Professor Emeritus, Lehman College
"Two Languages, Two Lands, Perhaps Two Souls..."

Comments:
Giose Rimanelli, SUNY-Albany
"A Mesmeric Sculpture: Tusiani, The Humanist"
Rudolph Vecoli, Immigration History Research
Center, University of Minnesota

Session 2

Chair: **Aldo DeAngelis,** Illinois State Senate
Frank Cavaioli, SUNY-Farmingdale
"Group Politics, Ethnicity and Italian Americans"
Judith Bessette, Lowell Art Association
"Senator Frank J. Sgambato"
Ernest Rossi, Western Michigan University
"National Security Council and American Foreign Policy toward Italy"
Salvatore Rotella, Chancellor, Chicago City Colleges
"The Labyrinth of Italian Politics"

Session 3 Representations of Italy and Italians in America

Chair: **John Paul Russo,** University of Miami
Helen Barolini, author
"Milton and Italy"
Robert Casillo, University of Miami
"De Stael, Corrine and Italy"
Ferdinando Fasce, University of Genoa
"Drops within the Social River: Many Idioms of the Shop floor from the Italian Perspective"
Cristina Giorcelli, University of Rome
"Adelaide Ristori on the American Scene"

Session 4 Italian American Social Structure

Chair: **Anthony Sorrentino,** Joint Civic Committee of Italian Americans
Andrew Sanchirico, SUNY—Albany
"Small Business and Social Mobility Among Italian Americans"
Nicholas Esposito, SUNY-Cortland
"American-Italian Family Structure: Some Comparisons"
Louis Broccolo, Illinois School District 146
"Italian Immigrants in Chicago in the Early Part of the 20th Century"
Concetta Maglione, Hamilton Township, Board of Education
"Third and Fourth Generation Families of an Italian American Community"
Peter Venturelli, Valparaiso University
"Sociology of Chicago Toscani"

Session 5 - Italian Americans: Presence and Image

Chair: **Silvio Marchetti,** Italian Cultural Institute, Chicago
Carol Bradley, University of Florence
"Documenting a Viewpoint: Crispi, the Government and Italian Life in America"
Joseph Varacalli, Nassau Community College
"What It Means To Be An Italian-American: Initial Reflections"
Judith Baumel, Poetry Society of America "Some Observations on Italian American Poets in the Mainstream"
Vincent Virgulti, Pennsylvania State University
"Goombas, Goons and Gangsters: Media Images of Italian Americans"

Session 6 - Feste in Italy and America

Chair: **Dennis Starr,** Rider College
Mary Lynn Dietsche, University of Illinois at Chicago "La Festa: The Transmission of Ethnic and Cultural Values"
Dominic Candeloro, Governors State University
"San Lorenzo Festa in Chicago Heights, Illinois"
Anthony Fornelli, UNICO
"The Festa Italiana Movement in Chicago"

Session 7 - Oral History

Chair: **Anthony Scariano,** Illinois Appellate Court
Margot McMahon, Sculptor
"Italian Immigrants of Highwood: A Slide Show of Sculpture"
Teresa Cerasuola, AIHA, Long Island
"Portrait of an Italian Immigrant as a Young Man 1897-1980"
Adria Bernardi, Freelance Writer
"An Immigrant's Conceit: Summer Opera and Highwood's Italians"
Michael La Sorte, SUNY-Brockport
"Oral History: Our Ethnic Past Is a Foreign Country"

Session 8 - Italian-American Radical Journalism

Chair: **Rudolph Vecoli,** IHRC, University of Minnesota
"Italian Radical Journalism: Analysis of Images and Symbols"
Elizabeth Vezzosi, Institute of North American Studies, Florence
Susanna Garroni, SUNY, Buffalo

Session 9 - Contemporary Film and Video I

Chair: **Anthony Labriola,** Governors State University
Angelo Restivo, Chicago Film Maker
"Return Trip Tango"
Tom Palazzolo, Chicago Film Maker
"Pets on Parade"
Joe Scelsa and Emelise Aleandri, Italian American Institute
" 'Italics,' The Italian-American Magazine Show "

Session 10 - Contemporary Film and Video II

Chair: **Anthony Labriola,** Governors State University
Steven Delisi, Chicago Film Maker
"Chicago's Little Italy"
Louis Guida, Co-Media, Inc.
"When You Make a Good Crop: Italians in the Delta"

Session 11 - Italian Americans in the South and West

Chair: **Gary Mormino,** University of South Florida
Valentino Belfiglio, Texas Woman's University
"Early Italian Settlers of Tarrant County, Texas: Their Language & Litera-
ture"
Russell Magnaghi, Northern Michigan University
"The Italians of Idaho"
Luciano Rusich, College of Staten Island
"Giuseppe Avezzana in Mexico"
A.J. Montesi, St. Louis University
"The Italian Immigrant in The American South 1900-1960"
Conrad Woodall, Colorado State University
" 'Italian Massacre' at Walsenburg, Colorado, 1895"

Howard Marshall, University of Missouri-Columbia
"Pic-a-Pierre and Cement Men: Northern Italian Builders in a Frontier American Community"

Session 12 - Molise Studies

Chair: **Giose Rimanelli,** SUNY-Albany
Alfonso Di Benedetto, President, Italian Cultural Center "Autobiographical Remarks of a Molisano Immigrant"
Frank Femminella, SUNY-Albany
"Farazzanesi in Cortland, New York"
Richard Juliani, Villanova University
"First Encounter with the Land of My Father: Molise"
Renato Lalli, Molise Regional Historian
"Reflections and Perspectives: Molise-America"

6:15 p.m. Leave by bus for Italian Cultural Center

7:00 p.m.Reception at Italian Cultural Center, 1631 N. 39th Avenue, Stone Park, IL - Hosted by Father Peter Gandolfi, Director

8:00 p.m Banquet Villa Scalabrini, N. Wolf Road, Northlake, Il hosted by Fra Noi

Greetings
Father Lawrence Cozzi, Villa Scalabrini/Fra Noi
Anthony Fornelli, Chicago UNICO

Robert Viscusi, Director, Humanities Institute, Brooklyn College
"What is Italian American Literature?"

Entertainment: Italian and Calabrese Folk Music Music Performed by Pompeo Stillo

SATURDAY, NOVEMBER 14

Session 14 - Language and Culture Promotion

Bruno Arcudi, SUNY-Buffalo
"The Politics of Italian Language Promotion"
Leonardo Baroncelli, Consul General of Italy
"The New Initiative: Promoting Italian Language and Culture in the U.S."
Salvatore LaGumina, Nassau Community College
"Language Retention and Ethnic Politics: A Case Study of an Italian American"
Paola Sensi-Isolani, St. Mary's College of California
"The Pitfall of Cross-Cultural Misunderstanding"

Session 15 - The Immigration Process

Chair: **Ira Glazier,** Temple University
Giuseppe DeBartolo, University of Calabria
"La Grande Emigrazione Italiana negli Stati Uniti: Il Caso della Calabria"
Gerda Homeyer, University of Calabria
"L'Identita Culturale e Storica del Calabrese a Confronto Con L'Europa"
Luigi DiComite and Michele DiCandia, University of Bari
"Emigration from Sicily"
Pietro Lorenzini, Elgin Community College
"Immigrants from Northwestern Tuscany: The Case of Massa Carrara"

Session 16 - Music and Theater

Chair: **Lionel Bottari,** Director of The Italian- American Theater Company
Joseph Bentivegna, Italian Folk Art Federation, Philadelphia
"Revitalization of Ethnic Pride Among Young Italian-Americans After World
War II and The Songs of Nicola Paone"
Anthony Rauche, University of Hartford
"Music in the Life of the Italian Community in Hartford, Connecticut"
Patrick Casali, Oakton Community College
"The Italo American as Reflected in Menotti's 'Saint of Bleeker Street'"
Emelise Aleandri, Italian-American Institute
"Italian-American Theater in Chicago Prior to World War I"

Session 17 - Literature I

Chair: **Fred Gardaphe,** Columbia College
Carol Bonomo Ahearn, Department of Environmental Management, Rhode
Island "A Tale of Two Cultures: Agricultural
Values in an Industrial Society"
Franco Mulas, University of Sassari
"The Ethnic Language of di Donato's *Christ in Concrete* "
Luigi Reina, University of Salerno
"Napolitanita 'fin de Siecle': Patuti, Scugnizzi, e Camorristi nella Poesia di
Ferdinando Russo"
Sam Patti, University of Pennsylvania
"The Impressionists' View"

Session 18 - Community Histories

Chair: **Paul Green,** Governors State University
Edoardo Lebano, Indiana University
"One Hundred Years of Italian Immigration in Vermillion City"
Jerry Krase, Brooklyn College
"Little Italies Today: They Don't Die, They Gentrify"
John Beunker, University of Wisconsin - Parkside
"Calabrese in Kenosha"

Session 19 - Religion

Chair: **Remigio Pane,** Rutgers University
John Andreozzi, IHRC - University of Minnesota
"Converting the Italians: Protestant and Catholic Proselytizers in Milwaukee"
Sister Margherita Marchione, Religious Teachers Filippini
"Religious Teachers Filippini"
A. Kenneth Ciongoli, M.D., Neurological Association of Vermont
"American-Italian Catholics vs. Rome — Why?"
Edward Stibili, University of Wisconsin - Parkside
"Bishop Scalabrini and the Immigrants"

Session 20 - La Famiglia Italiana I-10:45 a.m.-12:15 p.m.

Chair: **Janice Monti Belkaoui,** Rosary College
Judith DeSena, SUNY -Farmingdale "The Participation of Italian American Women in Community Organizing"
Angela Danzi, New York University
"Old World Traits Obliterated: The Case of the Midwife"
Diane Raptosh, Columbia College
"Italian American Women on the Frontier: Sister Blandina Segale on the Santa Fe Trail"

12:15 p.m. Association Luncheon

Greetings
Carl De Moon, Joint Civic Committee of Italian Americans Greetings

Joseph Velikonja, University of Washington
"The Scholarship of the AIHA: Past Achievements and Future Perspectives"

Session 22 - La Famiglia Italiana II -

Chair: **Lucia Chiavola Birnbaum,** Stanford University
Paola Sensi-Isolani, St. Mary's College
"Women From the Lucchesia: Three Generations"
Mary Pecoraro Cawthon, Retired Educator
"Ethnic Identity and Language: The Case of Italo-Albanians"
Margherita Repetto Alaia, Columbia University
"La Famiglia Italiana— in Italia"
Gloria Eive, President AIHA, West Coast Chapter Commentator

466   *Italian Ethnics: Their Languages, Literature and Lives*

Session 23 - Literature II

Chair: **Anthony Tamburri,** Purdue University
Mona Toscana Paschke, writer
"Saints and Sinners: Women of the Renaissance"
Frank Caldarone, Chicago
"Literature and Cultural Conflict of Southern Italian Emigrants"
Sebastiano Martelli, University of Salerno
"America ed Emigrazione nella Letteratura del Sud d'Italia"

Session 24 - Labor and Radicalism 1:30 p.m. - 3:00 p.m.

Chair: **Victor Greene,** University of Wisconsin - Milwaukee
Lucinda Labella Mays, Glenview, Ill., Author "Arturo Giovannitti"
Gianna Panofsky, Northwestern University
"A View of Italian Anarchism in Two Major U.S. Centers: Spring Valley and Chicago"
John Gaziano, Middlebury College
"The Americanization of the Italian Americans: The Irony of Fascist Propaganda"

Session 25 - Language of Food

Dominick Bufalino, Continental Wines
"Italian-Americans and Wine Customs"
Angelo Ciambrone, Italo American National Union
"Food Customs Among Calabrian American Immigrants"

Session 26 - Linguistics 3:15 p.m. - 5:00 p.m.

Chair: **Fabio Girelli Carasi,** Middlebury College
Maria Morato, University of Illinois at Urbana - Champaign
"Italianita and the Italian Migration in Sao Paolo, Brazil: An Historical Overview"
Jana Vizmuller-Zocco, York University
"Politeness and Languages in Contact: Italians in Toronto"
Michael Rosanova, Intercultura
"Demographics of Learners of Italian"
Rina Unali, University of Rome
"Sardinian Immigrants' Adaptation to the Linguistic Differences in America"

Session 27 - Education

Chair: **Nicholas Spilotro,** New York Public Schools
Rose Greco, Loop College
"A Survey of Italian Educational History"
Nancy Jo Zaffaro, Chicago
"A Preliminary Study of High School Italian Immigrants in Chicago"
Sunda Cornetti, Washington, PA
"Assimilation of Italian Immigrants and Children Through Various Educational Experiences in Rural Areas of Southwest Pennsylvania, 1890-1940"

Session 28 - A Century in Chicago - The Italian Consulate

Chair: **Dominic Candeloro,** Governors State University
Leonardo Baroncelli, Italian Consul General of Chicago "Some Reflections"
Rudolph Vecoli, University of Minnesota - IHRC
"The Contadini and the Consulati: Chicago 1880-1917"
Marisa Percuoco, *Fra Noi* and COEMIT "Italian Consulate in Chicago"

Session 29 - Saturday Night Reading

Chair: **Fred Gardaphe,** Columbia College
Lisa Ruffolo, Edgewood College, Fiction
Kenny Marotta, Fiction
Giose Rimanelli, SUNY-Albany "Poetry of an Ancient Molisan Woman"
Diane Raptosh, Columbia College, Poetry

SUNDAY, NOVEMBER 15

Session 30 - Workshop: Italian American Ethnicity in the Year 2000

Joseph Maselli, National Italian American Foundation

Contributors

John Andreozzi is the former Coordinator of "Sons of Italy" Archives Project at the Immigration History Research Center, St. Paul, Minnesota. He has previously published "The Italian Community in Cumberland, Wisconsin," in *Italian Immigrants in Rural and Small Town America: Proceedings of the 14th Annual Conference of the American Italian Historical Association.*

Leonardo Baroncelli served until recently as the Consul General of Italy in Chicago. A graduate of the Law School of Rome University, he completed his studies at Johns Hopkins University Bologna Center. As Chief of the consultative organ *International Civil Services,* Dr. Baroncelli participated in the planning and execution of the earthquake relief programs for western Sicily.

Adria Bernardi is a Chicago writer and author of *Houses with Names: The Italian Immigrants of Highwood, Illinois,* University of Illinois Press, 1990. Her translations from Italian of the poems of Gregorio Scalise appeared in the Autumn, 1989 issue of *Poetry.*

Lucia Chiavola Birnbaum is an Affiliated Scholar at Stanford University. She has published *liberazione della donna: feminism in Italy* and is completing *goddess, black madonnas and Italian socialism.* She is also at work on a comparative history of Italian and Italian American women.

Frank J. Cavaioli is professor of History and Political Science at SUNY-Farmingdale. He is a former President of AIHA and a frequent contributor to the proceedings.

Mary Pecoraro Cawthon is an independent scholar and writer from Oak Arbor, Washington.

Teresa Cerasuola is President of the Long Island Regional Chapter of AIHA and serves two terms as AIHA National Recording Secretary. She has amassed a collection of oral histories of Italian immigrants and is currently at work on a publication concerning notable Italian American women of Long Island.

Angela D. Danzi, M.A. is a doctoral candidate in the Department of Sociology at New York University. She is an instructor at the State University of New York, College of Technology at Farmingdale.

Giuseppe DeBartolo graduated from the University of Rome in Statistics. He worked at the Continental Assurance Corporation of Chicago before taking an Associate Professorship in Demography at the University of Calabria in 1973. He is a member of the Italian Statistical Association (SIS), PAA, and UISSP.

Judith N. DeSena is a sociologist who teaches at St. John's University in New York. She is editor of *Contemporary Readings in Sociology* and is author or co-author of articles and papers which focus on urban issues.

Michele De Candia is a professor of Demography at the University of Bari and frequently co-authors articles with Luigi Di Comite.

Luigi Di Comite is professor of Demography at the University of Bari. He served as the President of the Association Internationale des Demographes de Langue Francaise and is author of over one hundred articles on Italian and international demography.

Ferdinando Fasce is a Research Fellow and Assistant Professor of American History at the Instituto di Storia Moderna e Contemporanea at the University of Genoa. He has published *Dal mestiere alla catena: Lavoro e controllo sociale in America, 1877-1920*, Genoa, 1983.

Frank Femminella is professor of Education and Sociology at SUNY-Albany. He is a former president of AIHA and editor of the 1983 proceedings *Italians and Irish in America*.

Anthony Fornelli is a Chicago-born attorney, past President of Unico National and the Joint Civic Committee of Italian Americans. He is co-founder of "Festa Italiana" and a patron of the arts.

Richard Juliani is the current president of AIHA and editor of two sets of proceedings: *Family and Community Life of Italian Americans* (1980) and *Italian Americans: In Search of a Usable Past* (1986). Juliani is professor of Sociology at Villanova University.

Jerome Krase is professor of Sociology at Brooklyn College of the City University of New York. There he directed the

Center for Italian-American Studies for ten years and for three years chaired the Department of Sociology. He is currently Vice-President of AIHA. Krase is the author of *Self and Community in the City*, 1982 and, with William Egeleman, co-edited the 1985 AIHA proceedings *The Melting Pot and Beyond: Italian Americans in the Year 2000*.

Salvatore LaGumina is professor of History at Nassau Community College of the State University of New York. He is the author of many books and articles on the Italian experience in the United States, among which are *Vito Marcantonio: the People's Politician* (1969), *The Immigrants Speak: Italian Americans Tell their Story* (1978), *The Peripheral Americans* (1984), and a new book on Long Island Italians.

Michael La Sorte is Professor of Sociology at SUNY Brockport. His publications in Italian American studies include: *La Merica* and *Conversations in Rochester*.

Edoardo A. Lebano, a Cavaliere nell'Ordine al Merito della Repubblica Italiana, is Professor of Italian and Director of the Center for Italian Studies at Indiana University, Bloomington and directs Middlebury College's Italian Summer Program. He is the author of several Italian language and cultural texts, and has published articles on pedagogy and criticism of Italian literature.

Sebastiano Martelli is a professor of the Sociology of Literature at the University of Salerno. He is co-editor of *Su/Per Rimanelli: Studi e Testimonianze*, a special issue of *Misure critiche* (65-67) dedicated to the works of Giose Rimanelli.

Lucinda La Bella Mays has a B.A. in Social Studies and an M.Ed. from Washington University in St. Louis. She has taught at the elementary, high school and university levels. She is author of *The Other Shore* and *The Candle and the Mirror*.

Al Montesi is Professor of American Literature at St. Louis University, where he has taught for several decades. He is the author of nine books which include criticism, poetry and children's stories.

Franco Mulas is professor of English and American Studies at the University of Sassari in Sardinia. He received his Ph. D. at the University of California, Berkeley. He has published many articles on American writers of Italian descent and is a frequent contributor to AIHA proceedings.

Gianna Sommi Panofsky, a native of Parma, resides in Evanston, Illinois. She was a Fulbright exchange teacher at Cornell University in 1957. She has taught Italian language and literature at Roosevelt, Loyola and Northwestern universities. She is working on a history of the Italian workers movements in Chicago and Illinois coal mining regions.

Diane Raptosh teaches in the English Department at the College of Idaho. Her poems have appeared in the *Michigan Quarterly Review*, the *Mid-America Review*; the *Malahat Review*, *Kansas Quarterly*; *La bella figura*; and *From the Margin: Writings in Italian Americana*.

Giose Rimanelli is Professor of Italian Language and Literature at SUNY-Albany. His many books include best-selling fiction (*Day of the Lion* and *Original Sin*, theater, poetry (*Arcano, Moliseide* and *Memoria di Celan* all in 1990), travel, autobiography and literary criticism.

Ernest E. Rossi is a professor of Political Science at Western Michigan University in Kalamazoo where he is chairman of the Political Science Department.

Andrew Sanchirico is a research associate in Sociology at the State University at Albany. He is the co-author of "Fear of Crime and Constrained Behavior: Specifying and Estimating a Reciprocal Effects Model," *Social Forces* (March, 1988).

Paola Sensi-Isolani is associate professor and Chair of the Modern Language Department of St. Mary's College of California. She co-directed the 1989 AIHA Conference in San Francisco and is co-editor of that conference's proceedings.

Joseph Tusiani's major works include *The Complete Poems of Michelangelo*, Tasso's *Jerusalem Delivered*, and *Creation of the World*. Writing in Italian, Latin and English, he is the author of *Rind and All, The Fifth Season*, and *Gente Mia and Other Poems*. The first volume of his autobiography has recently been published in Italy as *La parola difficile*.

Lina Unali is professor of English Language and Literature at the University of Rome (Sapienza). She has taught at the University of Washington, Seattle and in 1971 was a Fulbright Scholar at Harvard University.

Joseph Velikonja is professor of Geography at the University of Washington, Seattle. He has been a member of AIHA since 1967 and has served on the AIHA Executive Committee for three terms. He has published numerous articles on Italian American territorial distribution, community formation and periodical publications. He is the current editor of the Association's *Newsletter*.

Robert Viscusi is the Director of the Humanities Institute at Brooklyn College and author of *Max Beerbohm, the Dandy Dante* and has published many articles on Italian American literature.

Jana Vizmuller-Zocco is Associate Professor of Italian at York University, Downsview. She has co-authored two Italian textbooks published by University of Toronto Press. Her articles on aspects of Italian historical, descriptive and applied linguistics have appeared in major Italian and linguistic journals.

Conrad Woodall has studied history at the University of Chicago and American studies at Macalester College. He is completing graduate work in history at Colorado State University.

Editors

Dominic Candeloro served as president of AIHA from 1985-1989. He is former director of the "Italians in Chicago" project and was a contributor to *Ethnic Chicago*, Melvin Holli and Peter Jones, eds. Candeloro is Coordinator in the Office of Conferences and Workshops at Governors State University. His office was in charge of the 1987 AIHA conference.

Fred L. Gardaphe is Associate Professor of English at Columbia College in Chicago. He is co-contributing editor with Anthony Julian Tamburri and Paul Giordano of *From the Margin: Writings in Italian Americana*; he is also co-founder, with Tamburri and Giordano, and review editor of the journal *VIA, Voices in Italian Americana*. His articles on Italian/American literature have appeared in *MELUS*, *Misure critiche*, and other journals and newspapers.

Paolo A. Giordano is professor of Italian at Loyola University and directs the University's Rome Center. He is co-contributing editor with Anthony Julian Tamburri and Fred L. Gardaphe of *From the Margin: Writings in Italian Ameri-*

cana, Purdue University Press, 1990; he is also co-founder and co-editor with Tamburri and Gardaphe of the journal *VIA, Voices in Italian Americana.*

Index